Home, School and Community Relations

A Guide to Working with Parents

3rd Edition

Delmar Publishers' Online Services
To access Delmar on the World Wide Web, point your browser to:
http://www.delmar.com/delmar.html
To access through Gopher: gopher://gopher.delmar.com
(Delmar Online is part of "thomson.com", an Internet site with information on
more than 30 publishers of the International Thomson Publishing organization.)
For more information on our products and services:
email: info@delmar.com
or call 800-347-7707

Home, School and Community Relations

A Guide to Working with Parents

3rd Edition

Carol Gestwicki

Central Piedmont Community College
Charlotte, North Carolina

Delmar Publishers

I(T)P An International Thomson Publishing Company

Albany • Bonn • Boston • Cincinnati • Detroit • London • Madrid • Melbourne
Mexico City • New York • Pacific Grove • Paris • San Francisco • Singapore • Tokyo
Toronto • Washington

NOTICE TO THE READER

Cover Design: The Drawing Board

DELMAR STAFF

Administrative Editor:	Jay Whitney
Associate Editor:	Erin J. O'Connor Traylor
Production Coordinator:	James Zayicek
Art/Design Coordinator:	Carol Keohane
Project Editor:	Timothy Coleman
Editorial Assistant:	Glenna Stanfield

COPYRIGHT © 1996
By Delmar Publishers
a division of International Thomson Publishing Inc.
The ITP logo is a trademark under license

Printed in the United States of America

For more information, contact:

Delmar Publishers
3 Columbia Circle, Box 15015
Albany, New York 12203-5015

International Thomson Editores
Campos Eliseos 385, Piso 7
Col Polanco
11560 Mexico DF Mexico

International Thomson Publishing Europe
Berkshire House 168-173
High Holborn
London, WC1V7AA
England

International Thomson Publishing GmbH
Königswinterer Strasse 418
53227 Bonn
Germany

Thomas Nelson Australia
102 Dodds Street
South Melbourne, 3205
Victoria, Australia

International Thomson Publishing Asia
221 Henderson Road
#05-10 Henderson Building
Singapore 0315

Nelson Canada
1120 Birchmont Road
Scarborough, Ontario
Canada M1K 5G4

International Thomson Publishing-Japan
Hirakawacho Kyowa Building, 3F
2-2-1 Hirakawacho
Chiyoda-ku, Tokyo 102
Japan

4 5 6 7 8 9 10 XXX 01 00 99 98 97

Library of Congress Cataloging-in-Publication Data

Gestwicki, Carol, 1940-
Home, school, and community relations: a guide to working with parents / Carol Gestwicki. — 3rd ed.
p.   cm.
Includes bibliographical references and index.
ISBN 0-8273-7218-3
1. Home and school—United States.   2. Parent-teacher relationships—United States.   I. Title.
LC225.3.G47   1996
370.19'3 — dc20   95-42596
                                                                          CIP

Contents

Foreword

Once upon a time, not much more than a hundred years ago, the United States was predominantly a rural culture. A book purporting to be a "guide to working with parents" would have been an anachronism. The farm family was then a self-contained economic and social unit, the heart of human groupings. With children numerous and desired, the family often included grandparents, sometimes uncles, aunts, and cousins. It was a communal center with parents at the hub, responsible for vocational training, education both religious and secular, discipline, and recreation.

Teachers were a rarity. Perhaps during a few short winter months one would be hired to teach a roomful of multi-aged children. She, or he, would make his or her home with one of the farm families. When spring and planting time came, school would be out. The relationship between parents and teachers was not a particular concern. Though the physical hardships of those days were considerable, a certain simplicity and security for children existed. Firm boundaries of existence and few choices for the individual led to a kind of tidiness in living. How-to volumes were extraneous.

Today the world, the family, and the community are topsy-turvy different. The changes that have occurred in a century are profound. The family has been turned inside-out: single parent homes; step-children of second and even third marriages often blended together; women working outside the home; children bearing children; isolated urban nuclear families; urban life with its noise, crowded housing developments, traffic. All of this contrasts with the simplicity of the rural era. Now there is a very definite need for guidelines to help us cope with this flux.

Child care is now less the responsibility of the parents and more that of the teacher, the professional child-care worker, the after-school counselor, as ever-increasing numbers of young children and babies are being cared for outside the home. School-age children return to empty homes, and day-care centers are facing the need for establishing "sick care" facilities. Though parents remain the most important persons in a child's life, it is certainly true that a child may easily spend most of his or her time with other adults.

The teacher today, or the student training to be a child-care provider, is preparing for a profession quite unlike that of the rural one-room teacher. It is a complicated, ever-changing world out there for teachers and parents. Their relationship—the positioning of their several turfs, division of responsibility, defining the home ground upon which they both stand—provides a unique human relations challenge.

For this reason the appearance of a third edition of this book by Carol Gestwicki, *Home, School, and Community Relations*, is most welcome. It is a lively text (I have used it several times in teaching a community college course, "Working With Parents") that argues effectively for the value and necessity of a partnership between parents and teachers. It is too often the easy way out for them to assume adversarial roles in this hurried age of pressured parents with too little time, and teachers in low-paying positions responsible for too many children.

This book makes clear that an adversarial relationship between parents and teachers is not in the best interest of the children, the adults, or the community. The text is packed with creative suggestions for working cooperatively that will be satisfying to teachers and parents both, as well as promoting the child's healthy development. Research has shown that a parent's level of involvement in a child's center or school is a major factor in a child's well-being. Though Ms. Gestwicki is aware of the hurdles that contemporary society places in the path of teachers, parents, and children, her outlook maintains a positive stance; with determination and good will the confusions of this uncharted territory may be overcome.

This edition includes a section on the value of political awareness and child advocacy. The author discusses ways parents and teachers can combine forces to make a difference. In a country that appears less concerned about children and families than most other industrialized nations, this chapter is of signal importance.

In keeping with the current emphasis on discovery and age-appropriate learning for children, this book might be called a "hands on" text for teachers. In addition to the very specific descriptions of real schools with photographs of children, teachers, and parents, the book includes a vivid assortment of case studies of families and teachers, juxtaposing a variety of lifestyles and attitudes, a rich view of our heterogeneous culture.

As a teacher I know from experience that it is impossible to isolate "teaching" from families. We cannot—we must not—teach in a vacuum, but we must recognize, relate to, and attempt to understand the child's parents. This book is a great help in doing that.

Sue Spayth Riley
NAEYC Ethics Commission
and author of
How to Generate Values in Young Children

Preface

It is not unusual in my classes for teachers and students preparing to become teachers to hear the statement, "I do just fine with the children; it's the parents who—you could fill in the blank—make me crazy, I can't stand, I could do without, make me think about quitting." As more parents and teachers share the care of young children, it becomes obvious that disruptive tensions are more common than rare. Learning the skills of communicating effectively with parents on matters both routine and emotionally charged becomes an important part of a teacher's preparation.

In addition, attention is increasingly focused in our society today on the stresses of the contemporary family. Television specials and politicians have found it appropriate to speak out on the dilemmas of working parents, caught between choices of unaffordable or inadequate child care, and stretched between home and work responsibilities. Efforts are being made in both public and private sectors to offer some external support to alleviate family stresses, as the understanding dawns that family breakdown is responsible for many of the ills plaguing the community at large. Teachers as part of this larger community must participate in the initiatives of family support that are becoming more numerous.

This third edition continues to stress the specific attitudes, philosophies, and practical techniques that teachers in any setting can find useful in building relationships with parents. The underlying philosophy of the book is that those relationships are crucial in providing appropriate experiences for young children.

Section I is designed to introduce students to the experience of parenting. Chapter 1 considers families in our modern world, and the factors that shape their lives. Chapter 2 describes the various roles of parents in bringing up children and creating families. Chapter 3 takes a closer look at what life is like for two families, and reminds students of the need to prepare to work respectfully with families of very diverse backgrounds.

Section II explores the subject of teacher-parent partnerships in early education. Chapter 4 examines the various models and motivations for parent involvement. Chapter 5 identifies benefits for children, parents, and teachers when parents and teachers work in partnership. Chapter 6 considers potential barriers to teacher-parent relationships. Chapter 7 describes the attitudes and conditions that create the foundations for successful partnerships.

Section III moves the student into a discussion of the various techniques that teachers can use to involve parents in the educational process. Chapter 8 describes the orientation process for children and parent, to begin the process of exchanging information and supporting one another during the separation experience. Chapter 9 introduces a number of informal communication techniques, including newsletters, bulletin boards, and other personal methods. Chapter 10 outlines the planning and conducting of effective parent-teacher conferences. Chapter 11 discusses the process of making home visits to families, as well as the home-based education programs that exist nationwide. Chapter 12 focuses on including parents in their children's classrooms in a variety of ways. Chapter 13 considers parent education and meetings. Chapter 14 describes ways that parents and teachers can collaborate to affect community policy and action on family and children's issues.

Section IV moves to discussion of working with parents with specific needs and issues. Chapter 15 , a new chapter for this edition, examines ways to welcome and include all families, no matter how richly diverse their language, culture, race, religion, or family structure. Chapter 16 considers working with families in particular circumstances; families experiencing separation and divorce, families with infants, families with children who have special needs, families who have experienced abuse and neglect, and adoptive families are discussed in particular. Chapter 17 identifies strategies for teachers who are faced with particularly troublesome attitudes and situations. Chapter 18 describes several different early education programs that have found their own ways to involve and include parents.

Each chapter begins with clearly defined learning objectives. Specific examples and dialogues from teachers and parents, who may be quite like those encountered by students, make ideas and suggestions become real, as in the previous editions. The exercises for students listed at chapter end and in the instructor's guide are designed to help students grapple actively with the concepts. Bibliography of suggested readings can help students examine the issues further.

Included in this third edition is a strong focus on local and national community efforts and organizations, to remind teachers that they have responsibilities to work with, and in support of, families beyond the walls of the schools or centers in which they work with young children. There is an expanded discussion of the many components that constitute parent involvement, and a look at the history of parent involvement in this country. Also expanded are lists of books to use with children, related to particular family situations. Throughout the book students will encounter an expanded understanding of the importance of working respectfully with families of very diverse backgrounds. A chapter new to this edition discusses specific techniques

teachers can use to be sure of conveying an attitude of welcoming acceptance to every family. Discussions on dealing with common problems that arise between teachers and parents, including the current issue of testing young children for "readiness," has been expanded. Additional aspects of various models of parent education are included. Chapter 1 has been updated to include the latest demographic information about modern families. There are updates on current legislative and corporate initiatives focused on the family and its needs, and mandates from professional and community organizations that will increasingly demand that teachers no longer focus on the child and avoid the parent. Updated suggestions for further reading will be helpful to students who wish to go beyond the text.

Working with families will always be one of the more challenging tasks for early educators. Students are encouraged to realize that this is not a separate role, but one that is integrated into the concept of working with the whole child, and one for which they need to prepare fully.

❖ About the Author

Carol Gestwicki has been an instructor in the early childhood education program at Central Piedmont Community College in Charlotte, North Carolina for 23 years. Her teaching responsibilities have included supervising students in classroom situations as they work with parents. Earlier in her career, she worked with children and families in a variety of community agencies and schools in Toronto, New York, New Jersey, and Namibia (South West Africa). She received her M.A. from Drew University. She has been an active member of NAEYC for many years, including making numerous presentations at state and national conferences. Most recently she has been a Fellow in the Early Childhood Leadership Development Project at the University of North Carolina at Chapel Hill, and associated with the T.E.A.C.H. Model/Mentor program. Other publications include more than two dozen articles on child development and family issues, and scripts and design of fourteen audio-visual instructional programs. The author has two other books on topics in early education published by Delmar Publishers: *Developmentally Appropriate Practice: Curriculum and Development in Early Education* (1995) and *Essentials of Early Education* (1996).

❖ Acknowledgments

Students and colleagues in Charlotte and throughout North Carolina have been enormously helpful in the continuing discussion of working to support children and their families. I would especially like to mention members of the North Carolina Community College Childhood Educators who shared with me their own feedback and that of their students; Sue Riley, who has been an inspiration in her classroom interaction with children and their families, as well as adult students. I am grateful to Barbara Pimento of George Brown College in Toronto, Ontario for her insightful comments and helpful materials on the Canadian perspective. I am especially grateful to Connie Glass and Christy Shamel, two fine teachers who also take great photos, and were generous in allowing me to use them. Earlier I had received assistance from: Jane Nye of the Junior League of Charlotte; Kim Sellers of Child Care Resources Inc., Pam Crown of the Council for Children; Tamar Meyers of the University of Buffalo Early Childhood Research Center; Judy Sims of the Chapter 1 program in Charlotte; Holly Neville and Nancy Pierce of Open Door School; Barbara Dellinger and Doug Boyd of Bethlehem Center, Charlotte; Lorraine Lima of Bienvenidos Children's Center; Ellen Galinsky; Barbara Stegall; Suzi Beebe of Lands' End, Inc.; the Lamaze Institute for Family Education; Jo Ellen Wade; Tom Covington and Mike Slade of Central Piedmont Community College Media Productions; and Denise Stephens and Debra Hefner, who allowed me to use family photos. Thank you also to Mike Meyers of CPCC, who found resources to pay for the use of a cartoon. I am grateful to the directors and staff of Open Door School, Fair Meadows School, especially Diane Jurek, the State Employees Child Care Center, and the Auraria Campus Child Care Center. I appreciate the helpful comments of the reviewers:

Marion Fox Barnett
Fredonia State University
Clarence, New York

Jerold P. Bauch
Peabody College-Vanderbilt University
Nashville, Tennessee

Kathy Hamblin
Aims Community College
Greeley, Colorado

Margot Keller
Lima Technical College
Lima, Ohio

Dr. William S. O'Bruba
Bloomsburg University
Bloomsburg, Pennsylvania

Barbara Pimento
George Brown College
Toronto, Canada

Jean Proctor
Alamance Community College
Graham, North Carolina

Dr. Carolyn L. Tyree
Arkansas State University
Jonesboro, Arkansas

And as always, I appreciate the support of Ron, Tim, and Jay, who continue to teach me the importance and complexity of family.

SECTION I

Introduction to Parenting

Unless you have already experienced parenthood, it may be difficult for you to appreciate fully the enormity of the emotions and roles that parents experience, and that affect their ability to function as parents. Even if you are a parent, the diverse cultures, communities, and circumstances that influence parents in modern America make individual lives unique; one parenting experience and one family may be quite unlike another. Effective teachers of young children work to understand empathetically the lives of the families with whom they work. This first section will further this understanding. Chapter 1 examines the social circumstances that affect modern parenting. Chapter 2 looks at the phenomenon of parenting itself, considering the separate roles of a parent, and common emotional responses. Chapter 3 encourages a further attempt to understand families' lives with empathy.

It's a note from my parents, my former parents, my step-grandmother, and my dad's live-in.

CHAPTER 1

Families Today

For a teacher of young children, one very important role is communicating with families. Throughout a teaching career, working with families is an inseparable part of the teacher's life. Although many teachers might prefer to concentrate only on the children who enter the classroom each day, children live in the context of their families, and their families are the most important influence on their development. Teachers must understand those family contexts and respect their individuality while drawing them into the child's educational world. The families with whom a teacher works may not resemble the teacher's own, and may be quite unlike each other in their structure, family life-style and values, and relationships. As America grows increasingly diverse, teachers need to prepare themselves to recognize, appreciate, and work with such diversity. Although the media reports that the family is a fatally wounded institution in today's world, in truth the more traditional forms of the family are diminishing while other forms are rising. In this chapter, we will begin to consider some of the reasons for the diversity and change in family appearance that is apparent today in most early childhood classrooms.

OBJECTIVES

After studying this chapter, the student will be able to

1. define family and consider several characteristics of families.
2. describe seven characteristics of contemporary life that influence the nature of modern families.

❖ What Defines a Family?

The family is the most adaptable of human institutions, able to modify its characteristics to meet those of the society in which it lives. Certainly the family has adapted to much in recent decades: industrialization, urbanization, a consumer-oriented economy, changes in traditional religious and moral codes, changes in all relationships basic to family life, between male and female, young and old. During the latter part of this century, these changes have been occurring in every corner of the world, although our primary concern here is the American family.

In a special edition titled "The Twenty-First Century Family," the weekly magazine Newsweek stated:

> The American family does not exist. Rather, we are creating many American families, of diverse styles and shapes. In unprecedented numbers, our families are unalike: we have fathers working while mothers keep house; fathers and mothers working away from home; single parents; second marriages bringing children together from unrelated backgrounds; childless couples; unmarried couples, with and without children; gay and lesbian parents. We are living through a period of historic change in American family life (Newsweek 1990, 15).

This list can be made even more comprehensive when you consider the families you might meet within any classroom or community: single-father families and single-mother families, both never-married or divorced; adoptive families; grandparents functioning as parents in the absence of the intermediate generation; surrogate-mother families; foster families; families of mixed racial heritage, either biological or adoptive—"all are now recognized, if not fully accepted, as ways to put together a family" (Elkind 1994, 31). True; yet family has always meant many things to many people. What comes to mind when you think of the traditional family? In her book *The Way We Never Were: American Families and the Nostalgia Trap*, Stephanie Coontz reminds us that this answer has changed depending on the era and the particular myths of the era: "'Leave It to Beaver' was not a documentary" (Coontz 1992, 245). Despite the obvious fact that the phrase "the American family" is not descriptive of one reality, it is used sweepingly. What most creators of television commercials seem to think it means is a white, middle class, monogamous, father-at-work, mother-and-children-at-home family, living in a suburban one-family house, nicely filled with an array of appliances, a mini-van in the driveway, and probably a dog in the yard.   Such a description excludes a vast majority of American families, according to the last census (which found only three percent of households conforming to "the classic family headed by a working husband with a dutiful wife and two children at home") (Roberts 1993, 30). If you are a student in Canada, you will note that similar sociological changes impinge on Canadian families. For current data on Canadian families, see *Profiling Canadian Families* by the Vanier Institute of the Family, 1994. It is more accurate to note that this mythical family does not widely exist, and that our image of family may need to be broadened to accept diversity.   As Gloria Steinem reportedly said, "Family is content, not form." (See Figure 1-1).

Figure 1-1 Families come in all shapes and sizes. Courtesy Council for Children, Inc.

"Ideal" Family Images

What image comes to your mind when presented with the word family? People's mental images vary greatly, based in part on their individual life experiences.

Try an experiment now as you think about family. On a piece of paper draw stick figures to represent the members of the family you first knew as a young child; who represented family to you then? Then do the same to represent the family you lived in as a teenager. Had your family changed? Was anyone added or removed? What were the reasons for any changes?

Now draw the family in which you presently live. Who is there? What does this say about the changes in your life? And if, as an adult, you have lived in numerous family structures, represent them as well.

Now one last picture. Imagine that you could design the ideal family for yourself. What would it look like?

Sorting through your pictures may generate some ideas about family. One prediction is that most of the ideal pictures include a father, mother, and two children (probably a boy first and then a girl!). This experiment was carried out with over 300 students, primarily eighteen- to twenty-one-year-old women. The ideal family almost always included these members, no matter what the actual composition of the families in which the students had participated or presently lived. Often there were dissimilarities; reality for some students ranged from growing up with one parent, having two stepfathers, a large number of siblings, being an only child, having grandparents or others in the home. All of these real experiences were passed over in favor of the ideal two-parent, two-child home. Some students, who created more elaborate fantasy families, specified that the mother was a full-time homemaker—this from women themselves preparing for a career. The only women whose ideal family approximated the reality in which they now lived were women who had married and had children before becoming students—unless the marriage had been disrupted by divorce. Then their ideal family included another partner.

For many, the image of an ideal family is influenced less by real experiences than by subtle cultural messages that have bombarded us since childhood. The Vanier Institute reports that 86 percent of high school students surveyed, including 78 percent of the teens whose own parents had not stayed together, expect a life long marriage. From magazine advertisements to children's books, and even more pervasively from television shows, the attractive vision of husband, wife, and children beams at us. What has been called the "Leave It to Beaver" syndrome (Rover and Polifroni 1985) has given several viewing generations, including those who are now our leaders and legislators, a clear yardstick against which to measure desirable family characteristics and measurable amounts of guilt and negative feelings when the reality does not match the ideal.

Interestingly, students surveyed are aware that their ideal image is just that, and are also aware of the societal influences that helped produce it. They may be unaware of how insidiously this subliminal image can influence their encounters with real families. If an ideal, lurking unknowingly in the teacher's value system, is considered the "good," a negative evaluation can be made of any family that does not measure up to this standard. The problem with assessing this nuclear family model as the "good" is that it may prevent us from considering alternative family structures as equally valid.

One way to become aware of one's prejudices is to make a list of the names of the families in your classroom (or neighborhood). Mark a check beside each family you would like to be friends with or those you think are doing a good job. Mark an "X" beside those families you feel most comfortable with and those you have contact with frequently. How many of these families look somewhat like your ideal family or the family you grew up in? In doing this exercise, it is important not to make value judgments about which are the "right kind of families," but to merely examine your initial reactions based on prior experiences. It is all to easy for a teacher to feel more affinity and comfort with a family that approaches her or his ideal than with one that is clearly outside her frame of reference.

It is important for a teacher to consider these ideas actively. Recording thoughts about families in a notebook is a good starting place. Asking questions—"Are there any families I feel particularly uncomfortable with? What do I think is causing this discomfort? What can I do about it? This is not to say that teachers have to give up their ideal images, but that teachers notice when these images become limiting factors in relationships with the variety of parents they will encounter.

Samples of Diverse Family Structures

If personal images of family cannot convey a complex enough picture, perhaps brief descriptions of families one might meet and work with will help. We will meet these families now, in order to begin to consider the diversity in structure that corresponds to the differing values, customs, and life-styles that have evolved in our world. These same families will help us later when we consider different relationships and techniques in teacher-parent communication.

A. Bob and Jane Weaver have been married five years. They married the day after Jane graduated from high school. Sandra, blond and blue-eyed just like her parents, was born before their first anniversary. Bob and Jane live in an apartment down the street from her parents, around the block from her married sister. Jane has not worked outside the home much during their marriage. They are hoping to have another child next year. A second pregnancy ended in stillbirth last year. Bob earns $29,750 on the production line at a furniture factory. Jane started working part-time this year to help save for a down payment for a first home purchase. Her mother cares for Sandra while Jane works.

Her income of $750.00 a month after taxes would not go far if she had to pay for child care.

B. Sylvia Ashley, 29, lives alone with her sons Terrence, nine and Ricky, three. Her marriage to Ricky's father ended in divorce before Ricky's birth; she was not married to Terrence's father, who was in one of her classes in college before she dropped out during the first semester. She has had no contact with her parents since before Terrence's birth. Although she lives in a public housing apartment, she rarely has contact with her neighbors; hers is the only white family living in the project. Before Ricky was born she worked in a department store. Since then her income has been from AFDC and food stamp payments, as well as the subsidized housing. This year she is beginning a job training program, hoping to follow through with her plan to become a nurses' aide. Ricky has been home with Sylvia, but he will enter a child-care program when his mother begins the job training program.

C. Otis and Fannie Lawrence have each been married before. Otis has two sons from his first marriage—fourteen and ten—who visit one weekend each month and for about six weeks each summer. Fannie's seven-year-old daughter Kim and four-year-old son Pete see their own father, who has moved out of state, only once or twice a year, and have called Otis "Daddy" since their mother married him three years ago. Fannie is six months pregnant, and they have recently moved to an attractive new four-bedroom house, knowing that even that will still be too small when the boys visit. Fannie teaches third grade and will take a three-month maternity leave after the baby is born; she is on the waiting list at four centers for infant care. Otis sells new cars and is finishing up a business degree slowly at night. Kim goes to an after-school child-care program that costs $35.00 a week. Pete is in a private child-care center, operated by a national chain, that costs $85.00 each week. The Lawrence family income is $65,000 annually. The Lawrence family is African American.

D. Salvatore and Teresa Rodriquez have lived in this country for six years. Occasionally one of their relatives has come to stay with them, but the rest of the family has stayed in Puerto Rico. Right now Sal's twenty-year-old brother Joseph is here, taking an auto mechanics course; he plans to be married later this year and will probably stay in the same town. Teresa misses her mother, who has not seen their two children since they were babies. Sylvia is seven and has cerebral palsy; she attends a developmental kindergarten that has an excellent staff for the physiotherapy and speech therapy that she needs. Tony is four. Teresa works part-time in a bakery. Her husband works the second shift on the maintenance crew at the bus depot, so he can be home with the children while she is at work. This is necessary because Sylvia needs so much extra care. They rent a six-room house, which they chose for the safe neighborhood and large garden.

E. Mary Howard is sixteen and has always lived with her parents in a middle class black neighborhood. Her grandmother has had a stroke and now lives with them too. When Mary's daughter Cynthia was born last year, her mother cared for the baby so Mary could finish the eleventh grade. Cynthia is now in a church-operated child-care center, as Mary's mother needed to go back to work because of increased family expenses. Mary still hopes she might someday marry Cynthia's father, who is starting college this year. He comes to see her and the baby every week or so. Mary is also wondering if she will go on to train in computer programming after she finishes high school, as she had planned, or if she should just get a job so she can help her mother more with Cynthia and with their support.

F. Susan Henderson celebrated her thirty-ninth birthday in the hospital the day after giving birth to Lucy. Her husband Ed is forty. After thirteen years of marriage, they've found adding a child both joyful and shocking. Lucy was very much a planned child. Susan felt well enough established in her career as an architect to be able to work from her home for a year or so. Ed's career as investment counselor has also demanded a lot of his attention. Some of their friends are still wavering over the decision to begin a family. Ed and Susan are quite definite that this one child will be all they'll have time for. Money is not the issue in their decision; their combined income last year was well over $150,000. Susan's major complaint since being at home with the baby is that the condominium where they live has few families with children, and none of them are preschoolers. She has signed up for a Mothers Morning Out program for infants one day a week, and has a nanny who comes to their home each day so she can be free to work.

G. Sam (two) and Lisa (four) Butler see both of their parents a lot—they just never see them together. Bill and Joan separated almost two years ago, and their divorce is about to become final. One of the provisions calls for joint custody of their two preschoolers. What this means right now is spending three nights one week with one parent and four with the other. The schedule gets complicated sometimes, as Bill travels on business, but so far the adults have been able to work it out. The children seem to enjoy going from Dad's apartment to Mom in the house they've always lived in, but on the days they carry their suitcases to the child-care center for the mid-week switchover, they need lots of reassurance about who's picking them up. Joan worries about how this arrangement will work as the children get older. Both the children attend a child development center run by the local community college. Joan is already concerned about finding good after-school care for Lisa when she starts school in the fall, and she knows that it will further complicate things to have to make two pick-up stops after work. She works as a secretary for the phone company and needs to take some computer courses this fall, but doesn't know how she can fit them in and the kids too—let alone find time to date a new man she's met.

H. Ginny Parker and Sara Leeper adopted a one-year-old Korean girl two years ago. They have been together in a lesbian relationship for six years, and they live a fairly quiet life, visiting with Sara's family who lives in the same town, as well as a few friends, including another family they met at an adoptive parents' support group. Anna is in a 3-year-old classroom in a child-care center at a church in their neighborhood. Sara is a nurse's aide on the second shift at the hospital. Ginny works for a travel agency downtown. When asked if they are worried about their daughter growing up without a relationship with an adult male, Ginny responds that Anna has a grandfather and uncle to whom she is close, and that they are more concerned about helping her come to know something of her native culture.

I. Justin Martin, age five, lives with his grandparents. His grandfather retired this year after working for the city as a horticulturalist for thirty years. His grandmother has never worked, having raised five children of her own. Justin is the child of their youngest daughter. She left high school after his birth and has drifted from one minimum-wage job to another since. On several occasions, she left Justin alone rather than find a child-care arrangement for him, and was reported for neglect by neighbors in her apartment building. His grandparents felt they could provide a better home environment for him, so they petitioned the court for his custody. Neither Justin nor his grandparents have much contact with his mother—she did not come over to the house for his last birthday, and she sent some money for Christmas. Justin has started kindergarten. His grandfather takes him to school. His grandmother is quite homebound with arthritis, and often finds a lively five-year old exhausting.

J. Nguyen Van Son has worked very hard since he came to this country with his uncle twelve years ago. After graduating from high school near the top of his class, he completed a mechanical drafting course at a technical college. He has a good job working for a manufacturing company. His wife Dang Van Binh, an old family friend, came from Vietnam only six years ago, and they were married soon after. Her English is still not good, so she takes evening classes. Their three-year-old son Nguyen Thi Hoang goes to a half-day preschool program, as his father is eager for him to become comfortable speaking English with other children. Their baby daughter Le Thi Tuyet is at home with her mother. On weekends the family spends time with other Vietnamese families, eager for companionship and preserving their memories of Vietnam.

K. Richard Stein, and Roberta Howell have lived together for eighteen months. Richard's five-year-old son Joshua lives with them. Roberta has decided she wants no children; Richard and she have no plans for marriage at this time. Roberta works long hours as a department store buyer. Richard writes for the local newspaper. On the one or two evenings a week that neither of them can get away from work, Joshua is picked up from a (neighborhood) family child-care home by a college student that Richard met at the paper. Several times this arrangement has fallen through, and Joshua has had to stay late with his caregiver, who does not like it because she has the care of Joshua and six other preschoolers from 7:00 A.M. until 6:00 P.M. each day.

In this sample, as in any other you might draw from a cross section in any preschool, the "traditional" family, with a father who works to earn the living and a mother whose work is rearing the children and caring for the home, is a distinct minority in the variety of structures; current statistics suggest that less than 10 percent of American families fit this model. In fact, only one in four families is made up of a married couple with children—"a category that has fallen to third most common among the nations' households, behind people living alone and also trailing married childless couples" (Roberts 1993, 30). In Canada, the figures show that typical families are also changing. In 1986, over one half of all families consisted of married couples with children living at home. Just five years later, the combination of all other family types outnumbered those families.

How do we define family? The Census Bureau definition of "two or more individuals who live together and are related to one another by blood or marriage" seems too narrow to include all the dynamics of these sample families. Websters Ninth New Collegiate Dictionary suggests a broader interpretation and no fewer than twenty-two definitions that seem more applicable when considering these sample families: "A group of people united by certain convictions or common characteristics," or "A group of individuals living under one roof and usually under one head." Perhaps the most inclusive definition of a family is "A small group of intimate, transacting, and interdependent persons who share values, goals, resources, and other responsibilities for decisions; have a commitment to one another over time; and accept the responsibility of bringing up children." Or simply, from the definition of a survey by the Massachusetts Mutual Life Insurance Company, "a group of people who love and care for each other" (Roberts 1993, 32). How do you define family?

The Vanier Institute of the Family points out that families: provide for physical maintenance and care of family members; add new members; socialize children; exercise social control over its members; produce, con-

We may be related by birth or adoption or invitation.
We may belong to the same race or we may be of different races.
We may look like each other or different from each other.
The important thing is, we belong to each other.
We care for each other.
We agree, disagree, love, fight, work together.
We belong to each other.
                    —Boston Children's Museum Exhibit on Family Diversity

Figure 1-2 Family defined as caring. Courtesy Boston Children's Museum Exhibit on Family Diversity.

sume, and distribute goods and services; and provide love and affective nurturance. (Vanier 1994) No matter how we define it, family is important to us. See Figure 1-2.

Families may include more than just parents and children. Mary Howard's family includes her parents, grandmother, and child, and the Rodriquez' have Uncle Joseph. The extension of the nuclear family is more for affection and support than for the self-sufficient economic unit the traditional extended family created.

Families may include people not related by blood and hereditary bonds. The Parker-Leeper and Stein-Howell households include parents and children and others whose relationship is based on choice, not law. New relatives, such as those acquired in a stepfamily like the Lawrences, may be added. Families may omit a generation, such as Justin Martin and his grandparents.

Families may be composed of more people than those present in a household at any one time. The Butler arrangement and the "patchwork" (so referred to by sociologists) Lawrence family are examples of separated family structures.

Families change. Their composition is dynamic, not static. It is assumed that Uncle Joseph will form his own household when he and his fiancée marry; Mary Howard hopes to marry and establish her own household. The Butler family may be added to when the parents remarry, as both say they'd like to. The Weavers hope to add another baby. Change occurs as family members grow and develop. Family members are continually adjusting to shifts within the family dynamics that challenge earlier positions. See Figure 1-3. More recently, some of the changes occur because the "nuclear family is reeling from several decades in an economic and social atomsmasher. Spouses, siblings, and generations were separated at dizzying speeds" (Roberts 1993, 30). It is time to look at some of those changes.

Books for Young Children
Celebrating All Kinds of Families

Adoff, A. (1992). *Black is brown is tan*. Boston, MA: Gryphon House. New York: Harper Collins. A family where members are many shades and colors.

Bauer, C.F. (1982). *My mom travels a lot*. Niles, IL: Albert Whitman Concept Books. There are good and bad things about a mom who travels.

Blomquist, G.M. and P.S. (1992). *Zachary's new home: A story for foster and adopted children*. New York: Magination Press.

Bosche, S. (1983). *Jenny lives with Eric and Martin*. London: Gay Men's Press. A child who lives with two gay fathers.

Brownstone, C. (1969). *All kinds of mothers*. New York: McKay. A multiracial book showing mothers who work both outside and inside the home.

Crews, D. (1991). *Bigmama's*. New York: Greenwillow. Trip to see extended family.

Drescher, J. (1980). *Your family, my family*. New York: Walker and Co. This book shows several kinds of families, in different shapes and sizes, all sharing and caring.

Eichler, M. (1971). *Martin's father*. Chapel Hill: Lollipop Power. The book shows a nurturing father doing household tasks with his son and playing with him.

Eisenberg, P.R. (1992). *You're my Nikki*. New York: Dial Books. A young girl's concerns when her mother starts work.

Girard, L.W. (1986). *Adoption is for always*. Morton Grove, IL: Albert Whitman. Answers children's questions and fears about adoption.

—. (1989). *We adopted you, Benjamin Koo*. Morton Grove, IL: Albert Whitman.

Greenfield, E. *Rosie and Roo. An interracial, intergenerational family, single parent*.

Hines, A.G. (1986). *Daddy makes the best spaghetti*. Boston, MA: Houghton Mifflin. Family life at its best.

Jenness, A. (1990). *Families*. Boston: Houghton Mifflin.

Koehler, P. (1990). *The day we met you*. New York: Bradbury Press. About adoption.

Kuklin, S. (1992). *How my family lives in America*. New York: Bradbury Press. Real-life stories of three children from diverse ethnic and cultural backgrounds.

Lasker, J. (1972). *Mothers can do anything*. Morton Grove, IL: Albert Whitman.

Litchfield, A.B. (1984). *Making room for Uncle Joe*. Morton Grove, IL: Albert Whitman.

Merriam, E. (1961). *Mommies at work*. New York: Knopf. A good book about mothers who work outside the home, combined with homemaking.

Morris, A. (1992). *Houses and homes*. New York: Lothrop, Lee and Shepard. Photographs of different ways people live.

Newman, L. (1991). *Gloria goes to gay pride*. Boston, MA: Gryphon Press. An affectionate look at a nontraditional family.

Pellegrini, N. (1991). *Families are different*. New York: Holiday House.

Quinlan, P. (1987). *My dad takes care of me*. Willowdale, ON: Annick Press. Unemployed father cares for children at home.

Figure 1-3 Good books to read with young children to celebrate family diversity.

Rose, D.L. (1991). *Meredith's mother takes the train*. Morton Grove, IL: Whitman. Story of a mother commuting to work.

Severance, J. (1983). *Lots of mommies*. Living in a lesbian household. Chapel Hill: Lollipop Power.

Simon, N. (1975). *All kinds of families*. Niles, IL: Albert Whitman Concept Books. The full spectrum of families—nuclear, traditional, adoptive, racial and divorced households—represented in a contemporary style.

Sonneborn, R. (1987). *Friday night is papa's night*. New York: Puffin Books. Latino family, father works two jobs and comes home on weekends.

Tax, M. (1981). *Families*. Hampton, NH: Atlantic Publishers. Single mother and fathers, stepmother, extended family.

Willhoite, M. (1990). *Daddy's roommate*. Boston, MA: Gryphon House. A positive story about a child dealing with his parents' divorce and a new relationship.

Williams, V. (1982). NY, NY: Greenwillow Press. *A chair for my mother*. An extended working class family.

(**See also list of books about divorced and stepfamilies in chapter 15.*)

Figure 1-3 (Continued)

Demographics of Modern Families

Is it harder or easier to be a parent today than it was a generation or two ago? There is no question that today's parents are functioning under different conditions than their grandparents or even parents did. Changes in family forms and functions are not necessarily bad or worrisome, unless one insists on clinging to the past, maintaining the exclusive rightness of bygone ways. Almost all of the changes discussed in this chapter have had some positive and negative impacts on today's parents.

Some recent trends in contemporary life influencing the nature of families include marital instability and rising numbers of unmarried mothers, changes in role behavior, mobility and urbanization, decreasing family size, increased rate of social change, development of a child-centered society, and stress in modern living. Each of these will be discussed in this chapter. See Figure 1-4.

Marital Instability and Unmarried Mothers

Statistics tell us part of the story. Since 1900, the divorce rate has increased nearly 700 percent. It is estimated that over 50 percent of marriages begun today will end in divorce. Sixty percent of second marriages will collapse. According to Census Bureau predictions, it is likely that nearly half of all children born in this decade will spend a significant part of their childhood in a single-parent home. "Over the whole post-industrial West, fewer than two-thirds of parents who are legally married when their first child is born remain together until their youngest child leaves school"

"*Our family is very secure, except for the possibility of death, illness, unemployment, separation or divorce.*"

Figure 1-4 Families are vulnerable to many external pressures. Courtesy Johns Hopkins University Press.

(Leach 1994, 9). Between 1970 and 1990 the proportion of children growing up in single-parent families more than doubled, to over one in four. Currently a single parent presides over 3 in 10 families (Roberts 1993). The majority of these single-parent families are created by divorce. But divorced parents—70-80 percent—often remarry. At least seven million children presently live with a stepparent. One prediction is that one-third of all children born in the past decade will be a step-child before age eighteen. In many areas, children living with two biological parents are a distinct minority.

In addition, some of the single-parent families are the result of a rising birth rate among unmarried women. Nearly one in three children today are born to never-married mothers, an increase from 4 percent in 1960 to 31 percent in 1990 (Roberts 1993). In Canada, the increase has been from 1.5 percent in 1951 to 19.5 percent in 1991. Of these, about one-third are born to teenaged mothers. Since 1950 the proportion of births to teenaged mothers born outside of marriage has increased more than four-and-a-half times. In some hospitals in poor urban areas well over half of the women giving birth are single teenagers. These families are particularly at risk for premature births, child abuse, unemployment, and poverty. (See Figure 1-5).

While there is no question that many single parents do a remarkable job of parenting capably, additional difficulties face a single-parent family.

Figure 1-5   The birthrate among unmarried adolescent girls continues to climb.
Courtesy Council for Children, Inc.

There is a growing body of social-scientific data to indicate that children in
families disrupted by divorce and birth outside of marriage do worse than
children in intact families in several respects. They are two to three times as
likely as children in two-parent families to have emotional and behavioral
problems, more likely to drop out of high school, get pregnant as teenagers,
abuse drugs, and get in trouble with the law. They are also at much higher
risk for physical or sexual abuse (Whitehead 1993).

Poverty

The term "single parent" does not fully convey the reality that most of
these families, just under 90 percent, are headed by mothers. Fewer than 13
percent of all children live with their fathers alone. Poverty affects about 1
of 16 husband-wife families, 1 of 9 single fathers, but 1 of 3 single mothers.
"In the years following divorce living standards for ex-wives drop by an
average of 30 percent while those for men rise 8 percent" (Hewlett 1991, 51).
This is true despite the fact that 80 percent of single-parent household heads
are employed full-time, though typically in low-paying jobs, and provide
about 60-70 percent of the total family income, with other resources being
alimony, child support, and government assistance. Even if a mother
receives child-support payments, amounts tend to be small. Many fathers
fail to provide child support, and despite successful efforts in some states to
enforce the legal obligations, about two-thirds of fathers' scheduled payments are still in arrears. Child support accounts for only 15 percent of the
total income of single-parent families. Financial stress is a major complaint
of divorced women. Many single-parent families are not able to provide

adequate support services they need, such as child care while a mother works, or recreation or other social relief for a parent.

Poverty in the United States is increasingly linked to family structure. Children in single-parent families are six times as likely to be poor (Whitehead 1993). This is the first decade in the nation's history in which a majority of all poor families are headed by women. In female-headed families the poverty rate is 34.4 percent. One out of every five children lives in poverty; the rate is twice as high for blacks and Hispanics. Five hundred thousand of those children are homeless. Recently benefits of many programs designed to support poor families were either frozen or sharply cut. Stipends for welfare families dropped to 35 percent below the 1970 level after adjusting for inflation. Nearly half-a-million families lost all welfare payments. A million people were dropped from the food stamp program and millions more from the school lunch program. Poor families were left to struggle without the protection of the government safety net. As this century draws to an end, the mood for federal spending appears grim, and welfare reform makes it seem likely to continue to tear away social safety nets for poor families.

Stress

A family that began with two parents and shifts to single-parent status will undoubtedly experience increased stress for some period of time, if not permanently. Adjustments will have to be made by all family members to the changed living patterns that include the loss of a relationship, regardless of how negative; perhaps a move, new job or school arrangements; or other changes necessitated by the constraints of a more limited budget; less contact with one parent, as well as changed behaviors in both. We'll talk more about this stress in chapter 16.

The majority of single-parent families created by divorce are headed by women; a mother in a single-parent family is under the additional strain of adding the father role to her parental responsibilities. Not only do many divorcing fathers abandon their children financially, they also do so emotionally; half of all divorced fathers do not see their children. In one study of divorce, 42 percent of the children had not seen their fathers at all during the previous year (Hewlett 1991). The mother may easily overload herself while trying to compensate for her concern induced by social attitudes that a single-parent family is a pathological family. The mixed data in this area are scarcely reassuring, and real or feared changes in children's behavior can add appreciably to a parent's burden at this time. Social attitudes towards divorce may have undergone a shift towards acceptance, but attitudes towards a "broken family" still leave many single parents with an additional burden of guilt.

If a single-parent family is recycled to create a new blended family, additional stress may be created. A new family may begin with financial problems created when one income must support more than one family, with emotional burdens created by the multiplicity of possible new relationships, as well as the striving to create an instant family, warm and close, guaranteed to make up for the earlier pain and banish the "ugly stepparent" fears. Unfortunately these burdens may be too heavy to permit survival: up to 60 percent of blended family marriages end in divorce within four years. This means that many children may experience divorce, remarriage, and all of the attendant stresses two or three times before they become adults. Chapter 16 will examine in depth the results of stress on all members of these families.

❖ Changes in Role Behavior

In the reruns of old television series of the 1950s and early 1960s, Beaver Cleaver's mom was home baking cookies, and Aunt Bea raised Opie while Andy worked to support the family, but in the 1990s, most moms, both in television sitcoms and in real life, are working outside their homes. Indeed fewer and fewer mothers today are playing the traditional role of homemaker, and more than ever are also working outside of the home. Current census figures indicate that the majority of women in the work force are mothers of children living at home. To put this in perspective: in 1900, only one wife in twenty was in the labor force, but by 1950 the ratio was one out of five, and now it is about three out of five. In 1940, 8.6 percent of mothers with children under age eighteen worked; now over half of children under age one, 60 percent of preschool children, and 75 percent of six- to thirteen-year-olds have working mothers. Canada also reports that in seven out of ten families, both parents work outside the home.

Women's Roles

Statistics alone cannot describe all that has occurred since the 1960s with the redefinition of women's roles. Since the publication of *The Feminine Mystique* (Friedan 1963), women the world over have urged each other to find equality in their relationships with men and in their place in the community and at work. This has not been an easy change for anyone involved. For women, it has meant adding new roles while often retaining much of the responsibility for household maintenance and child rearing. If a woman tries to combine all the roles she saw her mother play at home with her new work roles, she is in danger of falling into the "Super Woman" syndrome and exhaustion and stress may spill over into all aspects of her life. One estimate is that, adding together paid work, housework, and child care, American women work roughly 15 hours longer than men each week (Hewlett 1991).

One of the difficulties for many adult women is that a change in social thinking about women's rights and roles occurred after their early impressions had been formed by examples set by their own mothers and their youthful fantasies of what life would be like as grownup women. The female role they had learned was to nurture and care for others in their small home world; now the movement urged them to care for themselves, to expand into the world. In confusion, many women attempted to fit into the traditional pattern while expanding chaotically in all directions. Thankfully, now a generation later, many women are working out new patterns that better suit them and their situations. There is hope that children raised by women working outside the home will integrate several facets of female behavior into their sex-role perceptions with less difficulty. (See Figure 1-6).

Work is not the only aspect of women's lives to be reconsidered. The language of the women's movement in the 1960s and 1970s spoke of women as one of society's minorities, without equality at home and outside the home. Issues of sexuality and reproduction, of sex-role stereotypes and limitations were discussed nationwide. Some real changes were affected and consciousness was raised. The increase in marital instability may be partly attributable to this questioning of traditional relationships, and the women's movement may prove to have been a major influence on the nature of families and society in years to come. Whether or not women and men agree with the push towards equality, it is virtually impossible for anyone in the country to remain untouched by the debate and its repercussions on lifestyles. But change comes through turmoil, and this environment of changing relationships and role behaviors has pushed women and men in the family into unknown territory.

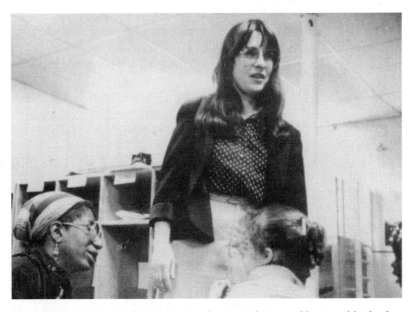

Figure 1-6 Over half of all preschoolers have mothers working outside the home. Courtesy Olga Solomita.

Men's Roles

Men's family roles are on similarly shaky new ground. Not only are they asked to share positions and power in the workplace with women, but at home more is expected of them than was expected of their fathers. They may still not be carrying their equal share of the household chores, but the days of hiding guilt-free behind the newspaper until dinner is on the table are gone. Gone also are the models of paternal behavior they knew as children. But, after all, this is what happened to their fathers before them. Grandfather's role in the family was to exert authoritarian control, but after World War II a father's major role with his children became that of playmate. As fathers received more leisure time due to changing work patterns, and as the expert advice to parents continued to change from stern rigidity to concern with children feeling loved and happy, fathers became someone with whom their children could have fun. Today's father plays with his child, but he also takes his turn sitting in the pediatrician's office, cooking dinner, supervising homework, and carpooling. Frequently he is involved before his child's birth—attending Lamaze classes with his wife to learn how to coach her through prepared childbirth. (See Figure 1-7). But is this involvement as pervasive as some articles in women's magazines portray? In only a very small percentage of families where the mother works do fathers share child-care responsibilities equally, though in a larger percentage fathers assume partial responsibility. According to a recent study, men whose wives are employed are likely to increase slightly the amount of time spent doing housework (and it still averages out to seventeen minutes a day contrasted with the wives' three hours), but the increase in time spent in child care (twelve minutes!) is even less than time spent on cleaning! (Hochschild 1989). In addition, these husbands "watch television an hour longer than their working wives and sleep a half-hour longer each night"

Figure 1-7 Many couples share classes to prepare for childbirth. Courtesy Lamaze Institute for Family Education.

(Hewlett 1991, 97). Some fathers still claim never to have changed a diaper! While some husbands may help out, the primary responsibility for both house and child care remains the wife's, perhaps due to the constraints of role behavior norms for husbands and wives. Certainly there are few models of highly participant fathers, and those few fathers who do participate equally as parents receive little recognition and quite a lot of kidding. But it is probably fair to say that today's father is called upon to share with his wife all aspects of the children's care, to display many of the nurturant behaviors previously associated only with mothers. (See Figure 1-8.) To define what it means to be a man, major shifts in thinking are required. However men may feel about it—and most fathers are pleased with their new roles—the change in women's roles in contemporary society has changed their own

Certainly some shifts in thinking have occurred, though many more may be required. An example of those changes is offered by the doctor who advised so many parents in earlier generations, Dr. Benjamin Spock. In 1946, in his first edition of Baby and Child Care, he was quite definite that it made no sense for mothers to work and hire someone else to care for their children. By 1976, he had changed his position to the idea that both parents had an equal right to a career and an equal obligation to share in the care of their children. Slowly, society has been pushed to alter its expectations regarding the roles of family members, and individuals are caught between trying to balance the external realities and demands and the internal psychological conflict caused by attempting a new social pattern.

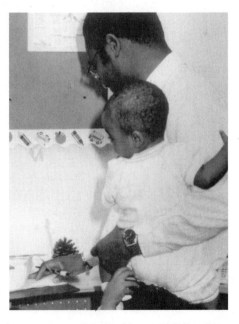

Figure 1-8 Many fathers are more involved in parenting today.

The jury is still out on what impact the different patterns of family roles and parenting have on family members. Certainly there are more opportunities for personal growth with alternatives from which to choose freely. Children have a more democratic family model as an increasing number of fathers take on the loving and nurturing aspects of parenthood, and an increasing number of mothers take on leadership roles outside of the home as well as inside. The women's movement has opened doors for everyone, men and women alike.

Mobility and Urbanization

With increasing industrialization and employment patterns, many workers and their families move frequently in the search for new and better jobs. The average American moves 14 times in his lifetime, and 20 percent of the population moves every year. According to the Census Bureau, over 90 percent of American households relocated between 1960 and 1989, and almost half of all Americans moved from one home to another between 1986 and 1990 (Leach 1994). Canadian families are similarly on the move.

What does this mean to contemporary families? This increased geographical mobility has brought with it less sense of community, more sense of isolation and aloneness. It probably means that the nuclear family, the parents and their children, are far removed from the physical presence of others who may have acted as sources of support in earlier times. A new mother coming home from the hospital with her new baby may know little about how to care physically for the infant, let alone how to deal with the anxiety that arises about 3:00 A.M. Her only support is her husband who may be as ignorant and anxious as she. In a bygone day, she may have been surrounded by her mother, mother-in-law, aunts, cousins, sisters, and neighbors who had known her since she was a baby. As time goes by, the young couple needs baby-sitters to be able to shop in peace or have some recreation time away from the child, someone to care for the sick child when the parents have to be at work, someone to delight along with them with the child's success at school, or commiserate and calm them when the child begins to throw temper tantrums, use bathroom talk, or anything else that may come as a shock to a first-time parent. Increasingly, parents have to turn to others to fill some of the functions that could have been performed by the extended family were they not so far away. (See Figure 1-9.) For example, they might hire the neighbor's teenaged daughter to look after the baby so they can have an evening out, or they might decide they can't afford the expense or the anxiety and just stay home instead. The isolation caused by moving far from traditional sources of support is a cause of stress for today's parents. Parents are totally responsible for everything, creating an ambivalent situation in their home and family. In one sense, the nuclear family so created has a special sense of solidarity that separates this unit from the surrounding community; its members feel more in common with

Figure 1-9 Many nuclear families only see extended family for holiday celebrations.
Courtesy Mark and Denise Stephens family photos; Deborah Triplett, photographer.

one another than with anyone outside the family. While this may produce some warm feelings, a cold feeling of isolation may also be present. "In our nuclear family culture, each new generation searches for its own values, even if it is a lonely search. Without the last generation as a back-up, young families can feel anxious and anchorless" (Brazelton 1989, 41).

Part of this isolation is self-induced. American families, taught to value independence, feel that seeking help beyond the family circle is an admission of failure. Today, without the traditional backup system, this lingering myth further isolates families.

Rearing children in a metropolitan setting offers its own problems for parents in addition to isolation. While the diversity of cultural, religious, and racial backgrounds offers richness and variety, it can also be a potential source of conflict as children are exposed to such a pluralistic society.

Family Size Decreasing

A family unit, according to the Census Bureau,, is two or more persons. Current statistics indicate the average family has decreased in size over the years, from 4.76 in 1900 to 3.67 in 1940, to just over 3 currently, in both Canada and the United States. This decrease is due to fewer children under age eighteen in each household—from 1.34 in 1970 to less than 1 now. There are numerous reasons for this. A major reason is delayed marriage and childbearing with increased standards of education and career expectations. As recently as 1975, 63 percent of women between the ages of 20 and

24 were married; by the 1990 census, this figure had shrunk dramatically to 38 percent (Roberts 1993). Canadian figures also indicate this phenomenon. In 1961, first-marriage ratios for women in their early 20's were 223:1,000. By 1990, this figure had plunged to 88:1,000. (Vanier 1994) In the same period the proportion of never-married women who were childless between ages 20 and 24 rose from 33 to 40 percent; for those between 25 and 30, the proportion without children increased from 20 to 26 percent (Halpern 1987). Other reasons include the economic burden of raising children in times of inflation with no corresponding asset of children's economic contribution to the family unit; changing attitudes about women's roles in the home and workplace; increased expectations for the family living standards and material wants; and the move from rural to urban environments. There are also more single-child families. In practical terms this means that it is possible to become a parent without ever having touched a small baby or having had any share of responsibility for caring for younger brothers and sisters. The earlier form of a larger family offered its members more experience as they grew up with other children. (See Figure 1-10.)

Another factor contributing to the decrease in family size is the increasing absence of adults other than parents living in the home. In the 1920s, more than 50 percent of American households had at least one other adult living in the home—grandparents, aunts, or uncles. It was common for young families to begin married life living with their own parents. By the 1950s, this had decreased to 10 percent; today probably only 3-4 percent (2 percent in Canada) of homes have another adult. The Census Bureau notes the phenomenon of a marked increase in the number of persons living alone, both people older than fifty-five and people in their twenties. In the past, these would have been members of an extended-family household. This implies that the smaller nuclear family is without the additional supportive resources of time, money, and companionship that other adults in the household could offer.

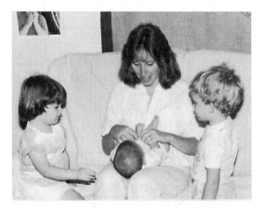

Figure 1-10 This family is an exception; there are many more "only child" families today. Courtesy CPCC Media Productions—Mark Slade.

Increased Rate of Social Change

Parents in a relatively static society encounter less difficulty than those in a society where social change occurs rapidly and drastically, as in America and Canada for the past three decades and more. A generation gap develops when parents play increasingly complex roles in a world their own parents could not prepare them for and to try to help their own children face a world they cannot yet imagine. It is not a comfortable world where parents can just produce children like themselves, but a new world where parents are unsure about their best move—a world of challenge and potential, but also of stress for today's fathers and mothers.

> They themselves grew up in the world of yesterday, a world that is now largely dead, and they internalized that world; they rear their children in the world of today, a world they only partially understand and only partly accept; but they are trying to prepare their children for the world of tomorrow, a world that nobody yet understands (LeMasters and DeFrain 1983, 231).

The rate of change is dizzying as upheaval occurs in every major institution in society.

Major discontinuities in relationships among people develop, as changing values, laws, and norms of behavior result in a different way of life. The civil rights movement, the women's movement, the Vietnam war and turmoil from groups opposing and supporting it, disillusionment with government leaders and with the educational system, the turmoil in the Middle East, concerns about environmental deterioration, fears about drugs invading our lives, about disease without cure becoming epidemic, and about what inflation, debt, and pollution would mean to the future—an endless succession of new ideas and images has bombarded us during recent decades. Closer to home, the structure and appearance of the family, the roles family members play, attitudes towards sexual activity, contraception, abortion—all are different now than they once were.

This makes parents unsure of themselves, and they worry about almost everything that touches their lives and their children's. They worry about whether they're too permissive or expecting too much in a changing world; they worry about television and violence; about the quality of education; and most of all they worry because they are making decisions alone—they are reluctant to seek out advice from others.

The customs of the world make this lack of certainty doubly hard for many parents to deal with.

> All parents worry about making mistakes. . . One reason it can be difficult for successful working parents to adjust to child rearing is that the culture of the workplace is often one of perfectionism and dependable rewards. In raising a family, on the other hand, rewards are rarely dependable. . . (Brazelton 1989, 1)

Parents are not the only ones unsure in a world that has changed so quickly. The society that surrounds them is equally confused. In a recent Gallup poll, Americans supported seemingly contradictory family values. Eighty-seven percent reported they held "old fashioned values about family and marriage," and 68 percent believed that "too many children are being raised in day-care centers today." At the same time, 66 percent rejected the idea that "women should return to their traditional roles in society," and 64 percent also rejected the idea that "it's more important for a wife to help her husband's career than to have one herself." Clearly change has happened too quickly for some of our values and beliefs to catch up to reality. Parents are caught up in the dilemma of rapid change in very real ways. Most jobs are still designed as if there were a homemaker to provide support for a working husband, and many institutional practices assume that all children lived with two biological parents. Social structure has changed rapidly; changes in social and personal values and feelings lag behind.

Child-Centered Society

More than one expert has pointed out how children's role in the family and in society has evolved over the centuries, particularly within the twentieth century in the western world.

In earlier times, a child was measured harshly by the yardstick of the adult world and restricted to fit into it.

> As early as 1820, maternal associations were formed in the larger cities that addressed the Calvinist idea of "breaking children's wills." Editorial space in newspapers and magazines occasionally was devoted to discussions of techniques that would result in children's submission to the authority of the mother (Bigner 1993, 14).

In the late 1920s, parents were still given restrictive advice, as evidenced by this excerpt from the writing of J.B. Watson. "There is a sensible way of treating children. Treat them as though they were young adults. . . . Never hug and kiss them, never let them sit in your lap" (Bigner 1993, 17).

But in modern America, a child is the darling of his world. Whole industries have sprung up to cater to his wishes—toys, children's television, breakfast cereals. The efforts of psychologists and other researchers are more directed towards telling parents what they should and should not be doing to nurture their children. A large part of current research and thinking concerning child development now is available in forms both popular and technical. Bookstores have many shelves of books of advice to parents, often suggesting quite conflicting views of a variety of experts.

Parent education classes are available in almost every community. Anyone who has taught a parent education class knows that there are two frequently heard reactions from the parents involved: one is to marvel that parents in earlier times did an acceptable job of parenting without possessing this knowledge. "My mother raised five kids, and we all turned out pretty well, and she never even heard of Erikson or Piaget!" The other reaction is from the parent who concentrates, with guilt, on what he has already done or missed the chance to do—"If only I'd known this five years ago." Whether the parent decides on his own that he could have done a better job, or whether the society around him does, the result is that the parent comes out the "bad guy" in a culture that centers on the child.

Stress in Modern Living

Twenty years or so ago it seemed that shorter work weeks due to modern technology would make life easier for many families. Unfortunately, that dream was never realized. Today, adults are working harder than ever. According to a recent study, the average work week jumped from under 41 hours in 1973 to nearly 47 hours in 1989, with professional and higher level jobs demanding even more hours. A *Wall Street Journal* study found that almost all top executives were working ten or more hours a day, and nearly one in five were working 12 or more hours (Hewlett 1991). It is no wonder that there seems so much stress on the family and individuals when the adults are spending so much time competing to keep their jobs in a time of employment insecurity. Obviously there is a fallout that affects both parents and children under such conditions. "It seems clear that overload, exhaustion, and strain do not make for good parenting, and yet these qualities are part and parcel of mainstream American life now that there are so many dual-worker and single-parent households" (Hewlett 1991, 106). Hewlett refers to the "parental time deficit" (p. 90), and makes the claim that parents are devoting much more time to earning a living and much less time to their children than they did a generation ago. This is not purely an American phenomenon. The Vanier Institute reports that nearly one half of the respondents in a survey said they felt stressed by the demands of their professional, family, and marital lives (Vanier 1994).

In fact, in recent years modern parents are not only increasing their time at the workplace, but also have greater demands on their nonworking time. There is increased pressure from society for individuals to fulfill self-centered goals. Finding and fulfilling oneself are acceptable and necessary activities which demand time. The highly organized community offers more choices and demands more participation for both adults and children. Someone recently commented that most modern children are being brought up in moving vehicles; this does seem an apt image for the on-the-go style of modern families. Those who point out the extremely busy life of the suburban child, moving from swimming lessons to Boy Scouts to doctors' appointments to activities organized with friends, fail to also mention that behind this busy child are parents who make all the arrangements and drive the child where he has to go! A parent who works full-time at a job has only begun to fill the expected responsibilities at the end of the working day. Chapter 2 looks more carefully at the various roles a parent plays; at this point it is important to realize that a contemporary parent's day is filled with more demands and expectations than there are hours.

The real stress in all this is that parenting, when done properly, takes much more time and energy than almost anything else. "Well-developing children dramatically limit personal freedom and seriously interfere with the pursuit of an ambitious career" (Hewlett 1991, 122). As long as modern parents are pulled in so many directions, stress will accompany the family. Urie Bronfenbrenner stated this well in his statement reporting on the White House Conference on Children:

> In today's world parents find themselves at the mercy of a society which imposes pressures and priorities that allow neither time nor place for meaningful activities and relations between children and adults, which downgrade the role of parents and the functions of parenthood, and which prevent the parent from doing things he wants to do (Bronfenbrenner 1974, 161).

In a more recent statement (1991), he said "The hectic pace of modern life poses a threat to our children second only to poverty and unemployment."

❖ Why Study Sociological Trends?

Beginning teachers may wonder why the conditions in society that currently affect families is a topic that deserves their attention. In fact, it is vital to effective relationships with families to understand the conditions and circumstances in which they grow. It is all too easy for teachers to set up a kind of oppositional stance, an "us against them" mentality, to judge parents as somehow not measuring up to some sort of ideal standard of what parents are "supposed to do." But when the larger picture of changes in our entire society is considered, it becomes clear that all of us are caught up in and affected by the trends that change the face and functioning of families. Rather than judging families against some artificial standard, of perhaps the way we never were, it is vital that teachers be able to recognize the forces that influence the thinking of us all. Empathy and the compassion needed to work with persons very different from oneself are the result of seeing contemporary families against the backdrop of the very real world in which we now live.

Two student teachers were once heard describing their common experience in "both coming from dysfunctional families." When pressed for elaboration, they clarified that they had both been raised by single parents, one as a result of divorce, the other as a result of a parent's death. So influenced were they by the dominant social images of typical families that they confused form with function; because their families did not resemble the usual image, they labeled them dysfunctional. In actual fact, both of their families had functioned well to raise the children with caring, protection, and helpful communication. Studying sociological trends may keep other teachers from making the error of confusing the form of a family with its ability to carry out its important functions.

❖ Summary

The new demographics mean that the American family and the growing-up experiences of many of our nation's children have been drastically altered. It is interesting to note that condensing all aspects of contemporary life, there are benefits as well as disadvantages for parents. The trend towards mobility that has meant enforced isolation for many American families has at the same time brought an increased number of opportunities for employment, prosperity, and personal growth. The trend towards marital instability has brought stress and pain for many adults and children, to be sure; in many cases divorce has also brought the opportunity to find less discordant ways to live. It is not the purpose here to evaluate sociological trends; rather it is important only to stimulate the teachers who will be working closely with modern families to consider the influences in the world that impinge on those families and mold their shape and direction, sometimes without their agreement.

Modern families are beset by difficulties related to new social patterns that have evolved from without and the psychological pressures from within that arise when individuals' life experiences differ from the model they have learned. Parenting is already a complex task, and, within the context of modern American culture, the challenge of parenting is heightened.

❖ Student Activities for Further Study

1. Do your own mini-studies to consider the nature of social influences on contemporary families.

   a. Involve a group of parents of your acquaintance in an informal discussion. What are the differences between theirs and their parents' experiences as parents? Which cultural conditions discussed in the text do you find in their comments?

   b. With parents who are willing to discuss their life-styles, try to learn family patterns of sex-role participation—who shops, cleans, cooks, cares for children, takes them to the doctor, to the barber?

   c. Ask several parents of your acquaintance where they were born and raised, and where their extended families now live. How do your findings agree with the text discussion of mobility?

   d. Note the family structure of children in a preschool classroom. Figure out the percentage of traditional two-parent families, families with two working parents, single parents, stepparents, or other arrangements. What about family size? Are there additional family members in the household?

How do your findings compare with the text discussions of marital instability, changing roles of women, family size?

2. In a journal, reflect on the families described in the chapter. Are there any families with whom you would be uncomfortable? What is causing this discomfort? Which families seem closest to you in values?

3. In class discussion, consider some of the causes of divorce and other changes in family patterns.

4. In small groups, discuss the following questions:

   a. Would you rather be a parent today than in 1950? Why or why not?

   b. Would you plan to stay at home with children, work, or do both, if you were a parent?

   c. What do you consider to be some of the hazards families face today?

❖ Review Questions

1. Define family.

2. Describe two characteristics of a family.

3. List seven characteristics of modern life that influence the nature of modern families.

❖ Suggestions for Further Reading

Brooks, A.A. (1990, April). *Educating the children of fast-track parents. Phi Delta Kappan, 71 (8),* 612-615.

Coleman, M. (1991, May). *Planning for the changing nature of family life in schools for young children. Young Children, 46 (4),* 15-20.

Howard A. (1980). *The American family: myth and reality.* Washington, D.C.: NAEYC.

Loseke, D. (1989). *If only my mother lived down the street: marriage and family in a changing society.* New York: Free Press.

Magid, R.Y. (1987). *When mothers and fathers work.* Amacom.

Procidano, M.E., and Fisher, C. B., Eds. (1992). *Contemporary families: a handbook for school professionals.* New York: Teachers College Press.

Reed, S. and Sautter R.C. (1990, June). *Children of poverty: the status of 12 million young americans. Phi Delta Kappan, Special Report,* K1-K12.

Robinson, B.E. and Barrett, R.L. (1986). *The developing father: emerging roles in contemporary society.* New York: Guilford.

Russell, G. (1983). *The changing role of fathers.* London and New York: University of Queensland Press.

CHAPTER 2

Parenting

In Chapter 1, we considered the cultural context of modern parenting in this country. But parenting has never been a simple task, no matter what the societal conditions. Taking on the responsibilities of parenting involves adjusting to numerous roles and profound emotional responses that are quite often unexpected in the midst of adulthood. No one is ever quite prepared for parenthood and the resultant adjustments in relationships, life-style, and responsibilities that require major reorientations and adaptations. Unfortunately, our society does little initially to assist parents through these changes and as they continue to play complex and often conflicting roles with their developing children. As teachers working with parents who are in the midst of these major adjustments, it is important to understand and recognize the nature of parenting responsibilities in order to support parents optimally. It is also crucial to recognize the deep emotional responses to parenthood, as these will necessarily impact on relationships with others. In this chapter, we will consider both roles and emotional responses of parents.

OBJECTIVES

After studying this chapter, the student will be able to

1. discuss seven roles that parents play and the implications for teachers.
2. describe seven emotional responses of parents and the implications for teachers.

Teachers working with families may become frustrated by the parents' apparent inability to focus their attention fully on matters regarding the children. It is sometimes difficult for teachers to remember that parenting involves many complex behaviors and roles, and that parents may be preoccupied with matters beyond this one particular child in this particular classroom situation. It is important that teachers continually try to remain aware of the complexity of parents' lives to avoid making assumptions that parents are not truly interested in their children's welfare.

Consider the following situation; does the teacher sound at all familiar?

Jane Briscoe is becoming impatient. As she describes it to her director, "These parents, I don't get it. I'm trying to take time to talk with them, and that's tough, believe me, with everything else I've got to do. But some of them just don't seem interested. Mrs. Lawrence, the other day, kept looking at the clock when I was talking. And Mary Howard this morning—she looked as if she wasn't even listening to me. I've tried, but if they don't care about their own kids, what am I supposed to do?"

The director, Mrs. Forbes, is sympathetic. She knows Jane's frustration arises partly from her concern for the children, as well as from the human reaction of wanting response when initiating communication. But she realizes also that Jane is seeing only one perspective and needs to remind herself of how life may seem from the parent's point of view in order to be able to increase both her compassion and effectiveness. A teacher who assumes parents aren't interested decreases her effort; a teacher who recognizes the multiple pulls on the time and attention of a parent keeps trying.

"I know that's frustrating for you, Jane, when you're trying hard. There's no one easy answer, I'm sure. Sometimes I try to imagine what life must be like for some of our parents, all the things that could be on their minds when they walk in here. There's your Mrs. Lawrence—she has all the concerns of twenty-eight third graders on her mind this Monday morning, as well as her own two. And I happen to know her two stepsons visited this past weekend, and that always makes it difficult—both crowded and hectic. And she's been looking tired now that her pregnancy's further along. Must be a lot to think about, trying to get both her children and his children used to the idea of a new baby. Her husband works long hours too—must be hard to find time to relax together, let alone finish up all the chores in that new house."

Jane looked very thoughtful, "You're right, you know. And I guess if I think about it, I can figure out some things that might keep Mary Howard's attention from being completely on me. It's exam time at the high school, and I know she's trying to do well in case she decides to go on to college. And she is still a high school kid, mother or not—I sure remember the million-and-one problems my friends and I had, from figuring out how to get enough money to buy the latest fashions to how to get along with our parents. It must really be hard for her to be living with her parents, still an adolescent, as well as a young mother who needs their help in looking after her own child. There just wouldn't be room for rebellion, would there? I wonder if she gets excluded at school because of her baby. Keeping the baby must have been a big decision for her to make, and she's still so unsure of what's ahead for her."

Jane broke off and smiled ruefully. "I guess I've been spending too much time being annoyed with the parents, and too little trying to get inside their skin to see life from their perspective. Thanks, Mrs. Forbes."

Mrs. Forbes smiled as Jane went out, thinking that the young teacher would be all right; she had made the first big step in working effectively with parents.

She had begun to try to understand the experience of parenting, including the many roles a parent plays and the emotional responses of parenting.

❖ Roles Parents Play

Although the teacher was thinking about two mothers, it should be noted that changes in social attitudes have encouraged people to think of androgynous adult roles—those that are shared by men and women and have similar functions. While recognizing that fathers and mothers may relate and interact differently with their children because of the differences in their natures and their past experiences, many parents no longer separate aspects of parenting and family living into male and female tasks. The text, following that model, will examine these roles and briefly consider the implications for teachers.

The Parent as Nurturer

The nurturing role encompasses all the affectionate care, attention, and protection that young children need to grow and thrive. While this implies caring for the physical needs of children both before and after birth, perhaps the greatest need for healthy development is emotional support and caring. Being a nurturer is the parent's primary role in providing a psychological environment of warm emotional interaction in which the child can thrive. (See Figure 2-1.)

Figure 2-1 An important parental role is to provide warm emotional nurturing.

Researchers have found important correlations between warm and responsive parenting in infancy, including close physical contact between parent and baby and attention to needs, and the development of attachment, defined as the strong, affectional, mutual tie formed in the two years following birth and enduring over time. (See Figure 2-2.) Attachment is felt to be critical to optimum development in every other aspect of development: 1. physical growth and development; 2. interest in and interaction with peers and other adults; 3. cognitive and problem-solving skills, including curiosity and interest in the world; and 4. language development. The basis for differences in behavior and development related to attachment may be that the attachment relationship offers the child a secure base from which to venture forth to explore the world and learn how to interact.

Ainsworth reports that, by toddlerhood, children's responses in observed "strange situations" indicate that attachment is already formed. Indeed, variations in parents' nurturing behaviors determine the kind of attachment the child will have with the parent. Some children show secure attachment behaviors. These include easy separation from mother to explore nearby toys, while periodically touching base with mother; friendly behavior towards a stranger when mother is present; probably crying when mother leaves, but usually resuming play; somewhat friendly to a stranger after the initial distress; warm greeting to returning mother. Babies become securely attached when their parents give them responsive feedback, including attention to the baby's signals, interpreting the signals correctly, and giving appropriate feedback promptly enough so the child feels

Figure 2-2   Warm, responsive parenting in infancy leads to secure attachment. Courtesy Mark and Denise Stephens family photos; Deborah Triplett, photographer.

her communication caused the response. Responsive parents also show sensitivity to the baby's activity, not interfering or intruding.

Anxious attachments in babies may be ether anxious-ambivalent or anxious-avoidant. The anxious-ambivalent baby shows resistance to the mother as well as clinginess. This child usually is wary of leaving mother to explore toys and also wary of new people. When mother leaves, the child becomes very upset, will not be comforted, and completely rejects a stranger's offer to play. But when the mother returns, the child reacts ambivalently, both seeking comfort and rejecting it, sometimes appearing to be angry with the parent. The anxious-avoidant pattern of attachment is evident when the child seems not to particularly care if either mother or stranger is present, leaving both easily to play. No distress or disruption of play is shown when the mother leaves, and the child interacts unemotionally with a stranger. When the mother returns, the child avoids reunion contact with her. Parents of anxiously attached babies respond differently to their babies. They either ignore the baby's cues or respond inappropriately, continuing to play with a tired baby who wants to stop, or holding the baby too tightly and ignoring his efforts to squirm free. Some parents avoid physical contact with their babies, and others express little emotional warmth that radiates to the baby. Other parents show no pattern of consistent responsiveness to their children, either through enforced long periods of separation or through their own emotional difficulties (Ainsworth's work, reported in Karen, 1990).

In recent years, there have been concerns about whether full-time child-care placements in the infant's first year will disturb the attachment relationship between parent and child. The controversy will no doubt continue as each side interprets the evidence in particular situations. It is important for all adults who care for young children to realize the importance of early emotional nurturing and to support parents in whatever life circumstances they do their parenting. (See Figure 2-3.) As caregivers understand the critical importance of parents and children forming attachment bonds, they will recognize that one of their own roles is to support the development of attachment.

Teachers should be aware that children can develop different kinds of attachment to key adults in their lives. For example, two-year-old Enrico might have developed an anxious attachment with his mother, perhaps due

Figure 2-3 Experts disagree on whether full-time child care during infancy may create less secure attachments.

in part to his mother's two lengthy hospitalizations and ill health during much of his infancy. However, when Enrico is observed with his grandmother, a warm woman very sensitive and responsive to his needs and personality, Enrico appears very securely attached.

For years, such nurturance has been equated with "mothering." Little research was done of fathering until the last fifteen years or so. In fact, earlier social scientists felt impelled to explain the necessity for adding the father role to the family, implying that providing physical and economic protection was a less important function and excluding him from the nurturing role. Recent research indicates that earlier myths about the nature of fathering are not presently true, if they ever were.

The consensus of research findings is that fathers do not differ significantly from mothers in being interested in infants and children, they become involved with their offspring if encouraged to do so, they are as nurturant as mothers towards children (see Figure 2-4), and they may engage less frequently in active caregiving but are competent in carrying out those activities that they do perform (Bigner 1993, 77).

And not only competent, but absolutely crucial, according to other findings. "A 26-year study, the first study of empathy that tracked young children into adulthood, shows that paternal involvement was the single, strongest parent-related factor in adult empathy" (Loux 1993, 90).

Figure 2-4 Fathers may be as nurturant as mothers toward children. (A) Courtesy Connie Glass.

There is no question that there are currently two faces of fatherhood: those who come and go, much as busy working fathers often have, and those who have become involved in their children's lives in areas in which their own fathers were excluded or chose not to enter.

Beginning in the late 1960s, practices related to pregnancy and childbirth permitted and encouraged fathers to become more involved from the beginning. This contributed significantly to changing fathers' perceptions of their own role in the family. Several research studies conclude that the father's participation at the time of birth helps the mother assume her role; the birth itself may be a strong stimulus for nurturant behaviors from both fathers and mothers, as well as a time for attitude formation (Bigner 1993). When fathers assist in the delivery room, they go on to change diapers, be involved with toilet learning, and drive car pools. Children may be strongly attached to both fathers and mothers.

Most findings concur that the parenting role most crucial for a child's optimum development is the nurturing role. It is within the context of family that children learn about intimate and personal relationships. This is probably also one of the most demanding roles a parent plays, for this includes the myriad prompt responses to an infant's needs at any hour of the day or night during the long period of infant helplessness and the frequent setting aside of adult needs in favor of the child's requirements and demands.

The need for nurturing in its various forms does not diminish as young children become older. Parents are still the people children look to for comfort, security, and approval. Parents with several children may have differing demands placed on them at the same time—the infant crying to be picked up, the preschooler fearful of being left, the school-aged child needing comfort after an encounter with peers. (See Figure 2-5.) It is no wonder that many parents feel "burned out" from time to time, so depleted by fill-

Figure 2-5 Parents with several children may have differing demands at the same time.

ing the nurturing needs of their children they have little time or energy to
have some of their own needs met.

Implications for the Teacher

- Teachers can help by understanding the importance of the parents' nurturing role and the many demands this places on both mothers and
  fathers. Emotional support from sources outside the family allows parents to devote more energy to nurturing.
- Teachers can supplement the nurturing role without violating the parent-child bond.
- Teachers who are familiar with behaviors in children associated with
  both secure and insecure attachments can be alert to situations that
  indicate trouble and able to help parents learn about the specific nurturing responses that are related to developing secure attachment.
- Caregivers of infants can promote particular classroom practices to
  enhance attachment (see chapter 16).

The Parent in Adult Relationships

Before an individual becomes a parent, there is first a relationship with
another adult. One of the demands on a parent is to foster the continuance
of that relationship, or of another that has replaced the original relationship.

One of the long-standing myths surrounding parenthood is that children give meaning to a marriage, improve the relationship between a couple, help a troubled relationship, and actually prevent divorce.

In fact, the addition of parenthood roles to a marriage relationship
introduces a time of abrupt transition. One researcher reported this as a
time of extensive or severe crisis (LeMasters and DeFrain 1983), though others suggest a crisis of lesser proportions (Rossi 1968; Russell 1974). The
severity of the crisis may depend on the degree of a couple's preparation for
parenthood and marriage, the degree of commitment to the parenthood
role, and patterns of communication. A recent long-term study followed
over 250 couples from the last three months of pregnancy through the third
year with their first child. The study concurred that stress is inevitable, but
the quality of marriage that couples experienced before parenthood is the
determining factor in whether or not the addition of a child disrupted the
relationship between husband and wife. The best marriages stayed the best,
the worst stayed the worst (Harrison 1986). Whether the transition is a time
of severe crisis or not, a couple is unquestionably going to have to reorga-
nize their relationship and interactions; changes will occur in a marriage
with an altered life-style and the addition of new role images and behaviors
associated with parenthood. (See Figure 2-6.)

These changes are linked to a decrease in marital satisfaction. Studies
report a U-shaped pattern in the degree of satisfaction, declining from after

Figure 2-6 The demands of children may interfere with adults being able to pay close attention to adult relationships. Courtesy CPCC Media Productions—Mike Slade.

the birth of a child, as children grow older, then gradually increasing as children are raised and begin to lead independent lives (Rollins and Cannon 1974). Other studies show a decline in satisfaction with no later recovery (Burr 1970). One reason offered for this decline in satisfaction is role strain. This occurs when (1) there are incompatible expectations for a person holding several roles at the same time—recall the earlier discussion of the Super Woman, (2) the demands of one social role are in conflict simultaneously with those of another social role—imagine a candlelit dinner disrupted by the baby's cries, and (3) when strong demands for performance are placed on all social roles—that Super Woman image again! It is difficult for spouses to pay close attention to the needs of their adult relationship while caring for the needs of their developing children.

All of these studies support the idea that using children as a means to improve a marriage is a mistake. The parent as a nurturer of children may discover that the parent as an adult in a relationship may neglect and be neglected. In fact, the probability of divorce is doubled when couples have children during their first year of marriage; evidently many couples are too unsettled to face parenthood before they can work out some of the marital behaviors. However, if children do not improve a marriage, their presence may serve to cement it together a little longer. The median duration of marriages among childless couples before divorce is about four years; couples with several children stay together about fourteen years (Bigner 1993). While there is statistical evidence that children stabilize marriages for at least a while, this is not the same as improving them. Some married couples have their worst disagreements over their actions as parents!

Parents are people first, and there is evidence that those who are fulfilled and contented as individuals are better able to function effectively as parents than those who are disappointed in their personal lives. It is evident that the support one parent gives to the other facilitates the development of the parenting role as well as optimizing conditions for nurturing the child. Although the primary adult relationship may be with a marriage partner, the adult's life may be criss-crossed with a network of adult relationships—parents, friends, former spouses. In fact, many parents of young children are also involved in the concern for arrangements for their own parents' health or living conditions, and must also make complicated arrangements with former spouses to share custody and negotiate financial matters. The relationship with one's child is an extremely important relationship, but it begins out of the context of relationships with other adults.

Implications for the Teacher

- When opportunities arise in conversation, teachers can convey acceptance, approval, and encouragement of parents' efforts to enhance their marriages, to engage in hobbies, to pursue personal and social enrichment.

- It is easy for teachers to be critical when parents do not seem to be devoting all their time and attention to their children, but it is important to remember that a significant gift that parents can give their children is a stable home and the model of caring relationships.

The Parent as an Individual

Americans have come to value the development of the individual person. We are now aware that this personal development is a lifelong process. Parents concerned with nurturing their children's development are also encountering growth in their own lives.

From the turbulent analysis of social values in the 1960s, through the more introspective consideration of personal values and life-styles of recent years, parents expect their lives to continue to develop and change.

It is relevant for teachers to consider how Erikson's theory examines the psychosocial tasks of adulthood that must be resolved.

Many young parents are preoccupied with issues of identity. Erikson speaks of this as the fifth stage, beginning in adolescence. With the prolonging of education and financial dependence on parents, and with the confusing multiplicity of roles, careers, and life-styles to select from, many identity issues are still being actively worked on in young adulthood. One measure of this may be the postponing of marriage, perhaps seen as an entry step into the adult world, a sign that a young person has settled some issues and is ready to embark on adult life. The events of marriage and parenthood cause many young parents to re-examine identity issues as they take on two roles symbolic of adult life. It is not just real-life events that have to be assimilated into an individual's self-concept, but also expectations and attitudes from within the individual and from society that set the standards used to measure the new view of self. There are several problems here. One is that most of today's parents grew up with daily facts of life and social role expectations that are radically different from those of the present. It is difficult to let go of those early perceptions of the way life is supposed to be. When a woman's own mother was always waiting for her in the kitchen after school and had dinner cooked when her father came home from work at six o'clock, it is difficult for her to have to call her daughter daily, knowing her child has gone home to an empty house and will be alone for another two hours, sometimes beginning the supper preparations until her divorced mother comes home from work. Somehow, despite the changed circumstances, perceptions of what should be happening have not changed. Many parents are struggling with feeling less than successful because of their patterns of life.

Many mothers find their self-esteem being attacked, whether they have chosen to fill the traditional role of homemaker or have joined the majority of mothers working outside the home. "Our society has painted mothers into a corner and nobody seems to know what to do about it" (Harrison 1986, 37). Despite the lip-service frequently given in song and verse to the importance of the homemaker and mother's work, the Dictionary of Occupational Titles of the Department of Labor, which ranks 22,000 occupations according to the skills they require, placed homemaker at the lowest possible level! At-home mothers feel they're being dismissed and devalued, but their working counterparts do not fare much better. The media continue to indict working mothers subtly for increasing family stress now that they have added to their traditional roles. Working mothers are themselves caught in conflict and ambivalence. A majority of working mothers and fathers feel that it's bad for the family for mothers to be at work. When mothers return to work, they do so in a climate of subtle societal disapproval. And some of the criticism is directed back and forth between working mothers and stay-at-home mothers, each resenting the other's choice and judging their performance and contribution. [Results of most studies related to maternal employment are inconsistent and conflicting, primarily because of the difficulty of controlling variables (Galinsky 1986). However, it is clear that if a mother is happy at her chosen work, in the home or out, and has satisfactory working conditions and child-care arrangements, she will do a better job of mothering (Gottfried 1988.)] (See Figure 2-7.)

A father's task of assimilating his new role into his identity is no easier. Although more recently he is gaining attention as part of the family, for many years he has been considered nonessential to the functioning of the family.

The Fatherhood Project at the Bank Street College of Education now provides a national guide to services for and about fathers. (For more information, write the Fatherhood Project, 610 West 112th St., New York, New York 10025.) The sad part is that even when men are truly motivated to

Figure 2-7 Many mothers are challenged by combining the roles of mother and career.

share parenting responsibilities in an essential way, society does not make it easy. Most employers find it easier to consider working mothers' family needs rather than working fathers' family needs. (See Figure 2-8.) Men who ask for flexibility or other privileges in their employment conditions to accommodate family needs are often seen as less serious about their careers.

Figure 2-8 Contemporary fathers have new roles to fit into their identity.

Issues of identity are never finally closed. As life circumstances change, a re-examination of roles and relationships and the resulting implications for an individual is necessary. A person's identity as a parent is not fixed either. As children move through successive stages of development, parents are presented with new challenges. Skills and behaviors that served well with an infant, for example, must be abandoned in favor of new strategies to live compatibly with a toddler. Parent's feelings of competence may fluctuate as their ability to adapt with the changing child fluctuates.

Galinsky refers to stages of parenthood in her book, a useful reference for teachers trying to understand the parenting experience (Galinsky 1987). The six stages she describes are: (1) the image-making stage of the prenatal period, (2) the nurturing stage of infancy, (3) the authority stage of toddlerhood and the early childhood years, (4) the interpretative stage of the school years, (5) the interdependent stage of the teen years, and (6) the departure stage of later adolescence.

After identity, Erikson's next task of adulthood coincides with the early stages of establishing of family life until early middle age. The previous attainment of a sense of personal identity and engagement in productive work leads to a new interpersonal dimension of intimacy at one extreme and isolation at the other. By this, Erikson means the ability to share with and care about another person without fear of losing oneself in the process. Family relationships are based on this kind of interdependency. Parents are called upon to share their world freely with their children and each other in caring relationships. It seems obvious from our earlier discussions about identity and nurturing that these tasks actually are occurring simultaneously.

Older parents may have added the dimension of Erikson's seventh stage, in middle age, when the task may be to work from a sense of what Erikson calls "generativity," rather than negative self-absorption and stagnation. Generativity involves the adult's concern with others moving beyond the immediate family to active striving to make the world a better place for future generations. (See Figure 2-9.) Parents with this perspective may become involved beyond the narrower focus on their children and jobs and work for issues that may improve prospects for other families, schools, and communities. (A brief discussion of Erikson's theory is found in Elkind, 1970.)

Implications for the Teacher

- Parents need additional support from teachers as they develop parenting skills to match the changing needs of their developing children.
- Recognition of their skills and positive feedback helps parents develop a positive sense of themselves as parents.
- Teachers will be challenged to work with parents of may different ages and stages of adult development. Parents of all ages are struggling with issues of parental identity. Very young parents may be struggling

Figure 2-9 Many adults are concerned with issues beyond the immediate family. Courtesy Council for Children, Inc.

with issues of personal identity; others are focused on forging relationships of intimacy. Still others can look beyond their own families with concern for society at large. Teachers need to learn as much as they can about adult development, so they can understand and accept individual responses.

5.4 The Parent as Worker

The stage in the life cycle where parenting usually occurs is a time of concern with being productive. Most adults find their means to this goal in one or both of the two channels of parenting and work. However, the two are often in competition with each other, as parents try to balance work and family life, and try to do both well.

Nearly two-thirds of mothers with children under age six are currently employed outside the home; nearly 80 percent of mothers of school-age children are working. This is an increase of more than 10 percent over the previous decade, with the sharpest increase being for married women in two-parent families with children under age six. There are several reasons for this increase in the number of working mothers: increased costs in rearing children and living expenses; an expanded economy with the creation of new job opportunities; earlier completion of families so that women are younger when their children start school; reduced amount of time needed for housework; better education of women; expectations of a better lifestyle; and changes in basic attitudes towards roles, with new social perspectives. Economic reasons are dominant for most women: 35 percent more families would be below the poverty line if both parents did not work.

Despite the fact that a majority of mothers are working outside the home along with fathers, much in our society indicates we are still operating on two related assumptions—that it is the natural role of men to work as providers and that it is equally natural for women to take care of children. One measure of this is that there are no national statistics kept on the number of working fathers, though careful note is made of the number of working mothers. With similar bias, studies are done on how mothers' working affects children; no such research is done when fathers work. While such attitudes may be annoying to many women in the workplace, their effect is more than mere bother; the attitudes frequently translate into equally outmoded working hours and conditions that are neither helpful nor supportive to a parent both working and carrying on home responsibilities.

The majority of these parents have an inflexible working schedule of around 40 hours per week. Only a small but growing percentage of employees have flex-time schedules, according to Department of Labor statistics. The United States government as an employer does set an example here. Over 40 percent of government agencies allow their employees to use flexible scheduling of their hours.

The option of job-sharing, eminently suited to many parents who would like to decrease the demands of their working life, is still only available to a handful. A tiny fraction of adults are able to work from their homes. But many parents are in jobs that require travel away from home. Worse yet, many American workers are asked to change their jobs and move often, disrupting family arrangements. The average maternity leave with pay for American women is six weeks, and only about 40 percent of American working women have paid parental leave; contrast this policy with the more generous six months offered in most European countries. A happier situation also exists in Canada, where women are likely to receive a minimum of 60 percent of their wages during a six-month leave as guaranteed by the government, with some good employers paying up to 90 percent. Only 10 percent of American companies offer fathers an unpaid paternity leave. Some European countries, such as Sweden and Denmark, do offer paternity leave. Since the passage of the Family and Medical Leave Act in 1993—previously vetoed by the president as being too costly for business in 1991—parents working for many employers are eligible to take an unpaid protected leave of up to 12 weeks for circumstances in the family that require their attention, such as the birth or adoption of a baby or illness of a child or parent. Unfortunately, economic realities prohibit many families from being able to take unpaid leave.

What do these employment facts mean to parents? In practical terms, parents as workers spend the majority of their waking hours going to or from work, working or being tired from working. Their young children, who are likely to be awake during these same hours, are of necessity cared for by someone else during the parents' work day. Their older school-age children are probably in school during many of the same hours, but before and after school, the long vacations, and other days off all necessitate making arrangements for child care or leaving the children unsupervised. Numerous special events will be hard for parents to either fit in or miss— the kindergarten field trip, the fifth grade band concert, the mothers' breakfast at the preschool. Employers know that they can expect an increased absentee rate for mothers of preschoolers during the winter months when colds and other infections run rampant. Parents who feel they cannot spare another day off are faced with the dilemma of leaving a sick child at school (pretending the child isn't sick, as most centers will not accept sick children): or facing the employer's wrath. Pulled between the displeasure of the employer and the caregiver, and the needs and schedule of the child, parents may feel resentful, exhausted, guilty, and inadequate to all the tasks.

No matter what changes have occurred in the relationship of men and women and in their child-rearing participation, it is still true that in most families the "psychological" parent—the one who takes primary responsibility for the children's well-being—is the mother. This means that most women never leave for work with a clear sense of division between home and office; the concerns of home and family remain with them through the working day, and when working mothers return home they have less free time than their husbands (Hochstein 1989).

> Only women who have tried to cope with both roles—mother and working woman—can understand the constant sensation of tension and fragmentation, the overwhelming complexity of living in constant uncertainty. And the sense of responsibility is enormous.
>
> Their double roles cause costly divisions for most working women, who find difficulty freeing up energy for the workplace while worrying about adequate child care (Kamerman 1980, 101).

No wonder it is more common to speak of stress in working mothers than in working fathers, though many women keep their stress a private matter, rather than let anyone think they are not equal to these new tasks. Employers who see the worker as more than one-dimensional and provide for family needs in some measure are often rewarded by increased productivity and loyalty from workers relieved of some of their dilemma. Companies that provide on-site child care have found there is less absenteeism, and employees stay longer in their jobs. Generally, American parents find that work frequently conflicts with parenting demands, and they must deal with the life shaped by their work schedule.

Implications for the Teacher

- Community and business attempts to alleviate stress for working parents by providing care for sick children or personnel policies which support families' attempts to care responsibly for their children need teacher support.
- Teachers can try to schedule events for parents at times that may best fit into their working schedules—conferences during after-work hours, programs during lunch hour, etc.

- When teachers and centers keep open visitation policies, parents feel able to come for lunch or story time, or any other time.

⌇.ℱ The Parent as Consumer

With inflation rates that increase every year, the real buying power of modern families continues to decline. Economic survival with the multiple material demands of the late twentieth century has been a major factor in establishing the two-working-parent family structure.

A good deal of the family income is devoted to the rearing of children. Children at one time considered to be an economic asset—more available workers in a rural, self-sufficient family—must now be considered economic liabilities. Recent statistics show it costs $334,000 to raise a child born in 1993—and that's just for basic household expenses from birth through age 17! (Figures from United States Department of Agriculture's Family Economics Research Group, quoted in Newsweek, Oct. 2, 1995) That's more than five times the $66,000 forecast for a baby born twenty years ago. [The estimates include providing for basics of food, shelter, clothing, transportation, and medical care plus an annual inflation rate. College adds many more thousands of dollars for tuition and expenses, with annual increases far outstripping the inflation rate. Note also that these estimates cover only the basics—no piano lessons or summer camp. How much of the family budget goes to raising the children to eighteen? Probably as much as 30 percent for one child, 40-45 percent for two, and 50 percent for three. (Figures from Family Economic Research Group, U.S. Department of Agriculture, reported in U.S. News & World Report, 1990.)

When both parents are working outside the home, a large proportion of income goes to the purchase of child care. Although there are variations by region or city or type of care, the annual cost of care for one child ranges between $2,400.00 and $9,000.00, with the average about $3,400.00 per child; costs for infant care are even higher as the chart in Figure 2-10 indicates. (Figures from National Commission on Working Women.) While the average family spends about 10 percent of its yearly income on child care, low-income families spend nearly 25 percent of their incomes on care. In some cases, mothers find that nearly the total amount of their additional family income is spent on child care plus the purchases necessitated by employment—additional clothing, transportation and food away from home. In this case, continuing employment is probably either for maintaining career continuity or for the mother's feelings about personal fulfillment.

Parents are caught in a child care "trilemma." It is not a question of whether parents should work; they are working, and the income figures quoted above illustrate why they need to work. Nor is it an issue of whether child care is good or bad for children; many studies can support the idea that good care is good and bad care is bad for them. The real trilemma for society is how to balance quality care for children, decent and fair living

Child Care Fees in Various Regions

Average weekly fees charged by licensed child-care centers by age group as of September 15, 1995.

Community	Infants	Preschoolers
Boston, MA	$175-225	$150-220
Dallas, TX	80.50	68.87
Minneapolis, MN	163.00	120.00
Charlotte, NC	100-110	85.00
Boulder, CO	155.00	116.00
Oakland, CA	142.25	122.62
Toronto, Ont.	200-250*	150.00*

* Canadian dollars

Sources: Child Care Resource Center, Cambridge, MA; 4C's for Central Florida, Orlando, FL; Greater Minneapolis Day Care Association, Minneapolis, MN; Child Care Dallas, Dallas, TX; Boulder Child Care Support Center, Boulder, CO; Bananas, Oakland, CA; Barbara Pimento, Toronto, Ont., Child Care Resources Inc., Charlotte, NC

Figure 2-10 Representative child-care fees.

wages for child-care staff, and affordability for parents. Child-care professionals are still providing an unseen consumer subsidy by earning low salaries and few benefits. The result of this involuntary financial assistance to working parents is that child-care workers have high rates of job turnover, more than one-third every year—thereby ironically lowering quality. All sides of the consumer trilemma need urgent attention. It has become obvious that the solution to the problem will have to come from sources beyond the triangle. While a few employers are beginning to see the need to supplement employee payments for quality child care, and government still considers various tax assistance plans, parents are caught paying too much while child-care workers are earning far too little. (See Figure 2-11.).

It is no wonder that many parents feel they are on a financial treadmill. A major concern stated by most parents is money; a leader in the causes of marital friction is "arguing about money." The parent in the role of consumer is stretched thin; when the economic health of the nation is shaky so that many parents lose jobs temporarily or permanently, the family may be thrown into crisis.

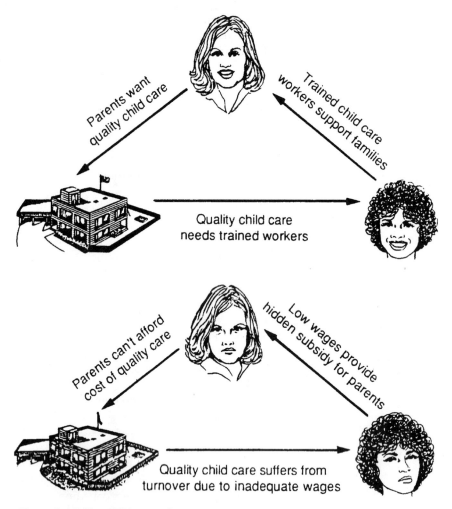

Figure 2-11 The child-care trilemma.

Implications for the Teacher

- Since child care is an expensive item in the average family budget, parents often feel pressed to be sure they are receiving their money's worth. This may help the teacher understand the demands they make for nutritious foods and clean diapers, and the annoyance they express for missing mittens or damaged clothing. Teachers need to be sympathetic to the financial pressures on parents.

- It is in the best interests of parents, teachers, and children for both parents and teachers to support each others' efforts to gain financial relief through support of community or government plans to subsidize the cost of quality child care.

♪♫ The Parent as Community Member

With the increasing complexity of modern life, a growing number of family functions have been taken over by community institutions and organizations: education by the school system; recreation and entertainment by the "Y" and other clubs, as well as the church, which has often expanded its purely religious function. There are as many organizations as there are interests in any given community. The community itself has become more highly structured as groups of people coming together have dictated more rules, legislation, and decision-making, both public and private. But institutions and organizations do not run themselves; there are many demands on community members for their time as volunteers, for their money and other supportive efforts. The parent is asked to support the organizations that benefit his children as well as himself. It would not be unusual to find a week where parents are asked to bake cupcakes for the PTA carnival, spend an hour manning a booth at the carnival, driving children to and from the church junior choir practice, assisting children in magazine sales to aid the efforts of the "Y" to get new uniforms for the basketball team, coaching the team, making a list of telephone calls to remind others of a local environmental group meeting, and soliciting funds door-to-door on behalf of a local branch of a national charity—as well as turning down several requests to participate in similar ways for other organizations. (See Figure 2-12.) The broader the age range of the children, the broader and more fragmenting are the demands on parents. For most parents today, there is constant tension between outside demands on time and energy and the amount available for personal and family needs.

It is also important to note that, as community members, parents may not only give but also receive help from the outside social network of community organizations. As families do not isolate themselves from the larger community, they receive assistance and provide models for children of interacting within a broad base of support. Learning about and utilizing community resources is an important role for parents.

It is also important for parents to realize that their action within the community can help shape opinion and policies on issues of importance to both child-care professionals and families. Parents need communities that care for children and families, and that make children a high priority. As advocates in their own communities, parents speak out on behalf of their children and themselves, and on behalf of all children and families. No one has as much interest in their children as do parents; therefore, they have a right and obligation to stand up for their children. Parents who advocate within their communities for children's and family rights stay informed about children's issues, talk to legislators and vote, speak out in the workplace for family benefits and supports, and support improved working conditions for those who care for their children. By such active advocacy, they can have a powerful influence in the community.

Figure 2-12 Parents may have community responsibilities, such as coaching the Little League team. Courtesy Land's End, Inc.; Archie Lieberman, photographer.

The organization Parent Action was founded by a number of professionals interested in supporting parents, including Dr. T. Berry Brazelton and Bernice Weissbourd. The organization encourages parents to organize in order to educate themselves about issues that affect their families and communities, and to impact issues with action. For more information, contact Parent Action, P.O. Box 1719, Washington, D.C.

Implications for the Teacher

- Any requests for parent participation add another thing to make time for. Teachers must realize this and be very sure the idea is worth what it will cost the parent in time and pressure.

- Teachers must guard against assuming that parents are too busy to become involved and so never make the effort or invitation. Parents have the right to make the decisions about how they spend their time, not to have these decisions made for them arbitrarily.

- It is vital for teachers and parents to build alliances for mutual education on common issues and for support in trying to reach common goals. (See chapter 14 for more on parents and teachers involved in the community.)

The Parent as Educator

Perhaps the role for which parents feel most unprepared is the role of educator, used here to mean guiding and stimulating the child's development and teaching the skills and knowledge that children will need to eventually become effective adults in society. As previously mentioned, other institutions have taken over many of the family's educative functions, so that the primary task of parents is (1) the socialization of their children to the values held by the family, as well as (2) assisting and monitoring children's development as learners and providing preparation for schooling.

Socialization of Children

There are two primary reasons why education towards socialization is such a difficult task for parents. The first was alluded to in chapter 1. In today's rapidly changing world, it is difficult for a parent to be sure what life will be like even in the very near future. Childhood experiences of today's parents were quite different from what they see their children experiencing; their memories of what their own parents did will probably not serve them well in their present situations.

The second reason why parents often find the role of educating their own children overwhelming is that the only on- or off-the-job training most receive is through having been parented themselves. Children learn through living with parents most of the basic information they will ever get for their future role as parents. Adults tend to parent as they were parented, and this pattern will likely be inadequate. (See Figure 2-13.) A high percentage of

Figure 2-13 Adults tend to parent as they were parented. (A) Courtesy Chapter 1 Program, Charlotte, NC (B) Courtesy Mark and Denise Stephens family photos; Deborah Triplett, photographer.

children who were abused by their parents become abusive parents themselves. Studies indicate that the characteristics, values, beliefs, and, most importantly, the practices of one's own parents have the greatest influence on one's child rearing.

It seems ironic that our society has become skillful at imparting technical knowledge and education to prepare workers for a career, but has made little headway in similarly devising methods to prepare young people for the tasks of parenthood. Most parenting skills are learned by trial and error on the job, giving rise to the not-so-funny old joke about parents wanting to trade in their first-born, since that was the one they'd learned on! No wonder many parents find the enormous task of parenthood without preparation overwhelming.

Parents who do seek training (from Lamaze on) often feel pressure to become "textbook" parents, fearing that they will make mistakes or not be able to follow the experts' instructions. This can be overwhelming as well.

It is quite important that teachers become aware of positive parenting models and practices to be able to assist parents in their growth as effective parents. In chapter 13, there is a list of books on parenting issues and effective parenting skills. While these skills cannot necessarily be acquired by reading a book, it can nevertheless be an important starting place. The models of parenting that many parents and teachers have experienced may often be the only sources for learning, unless adults deliberately seek out additional information. While there are as many styles of parenting as there are humans, many psychologists refer to two extremes and a middle ground; most parents likely fall somewhere along a continuum between the descriptions. It is important that teachers realize that parenting style has absolute significance on healthy or unhealthy development for children.

One style that has been defined is the *authoritarian* parent. This parent seems to feel that it is essential to hold very tight reins to control children. This parent retains all the power over children's lives, maintaining rigid rules, and punishing when the rules are broken. This parent tries to retain all the power in the parent-child relationship. Children are not given information or choices that would help them learn how to manage their own behavior. Anger and harshness may color the communication between parent and child. Unfortunately, the results of this extreme in parenting style are often fear of the parent, little development of the ability to control the child's behavior on his/her own, and diminished self-esteem.

At the other extreme is the parent who is overly permissive with the child, failing to provide clear and firm guidance about appropriate behavior. Whether through lack of experience and understanding about children's needs as well as little self-confidence, or through attentions directed elsewhere in their lives, these parents simply allow their children inappropriate amounts of power to regulate their own lives, long before the children are capable of doing so. This creates unhappy situations for children, who give every evidence of craving some limits. They are unable to develop self-control when anything goes, and they suffer diminished self-esteem since no one seems to care enough about them to provide necessary parenting.

Happier situations for children result when parents exercise authoritative and warm relationships, recognizing children's needs for guidance and direction, while understanding and accepting the slow process of children's learning about the world. These parents are more likely to explain reasons for behavior and teach more appropriate behaviors than to punish for the inevitable mistakes growing children make. These parents help children slowly assume more and more control over their lives as they become able, supporting the children with firm but loving evidence that parents are in control but available to help children learn. There is pleasure in such parent-child relationships for everyone, as parents perceive their children's gradual growth, and children see their own expanding abilities. Warm and authoritative parents are usually somewhat knowledgeable about children's development, as well as secure enough in their adult lives to be able to share power as children need their worlds to expand.

Preparation for Schooling

The issue of assisting children's development as learners and providing preparation for schooling has as many facets as there are opinions on appropriate early childhood education. Basically there are two broad viewpoints.

One represents the idea that early childhood is a time for allowing children to learn and develop through play, exploration, and child-initiated discovery. These proponents advocate home and school environments that provide varieties of open-ended materials with opportunities to manipulate, create, and learn with the whole self—body and mind—in direct encounters with materials, activities, and people. The idea is that through play a child learns best to understand the world, others, and her own capacities; this preparation lays the foundation for the more formal academic learning of later childhood. Many teachers and parents strongly believe that young children should be allowed their childhoods and that anything else is "miseducation" (Elkind 1987).

> The "voice of the hurrier" (Gross 1963) has been heard in the land for many years but has now become strident. It is imperative that we listen to our own voices telling us that young children need time to grow, time to learn about the social world, time to explore their own ideas through the use of materials and through play, time to become lovers of books through being read to, time to become productive young members, time to develop self-confidence through success—time (Balaban 1990, 15). (See Figure 2-14.)

Guidelines for developmentally appropriate curricula for children birth through age eight as defined by the National Association for the Education of Young Children (NAEYC 1987) support this viewpoint.

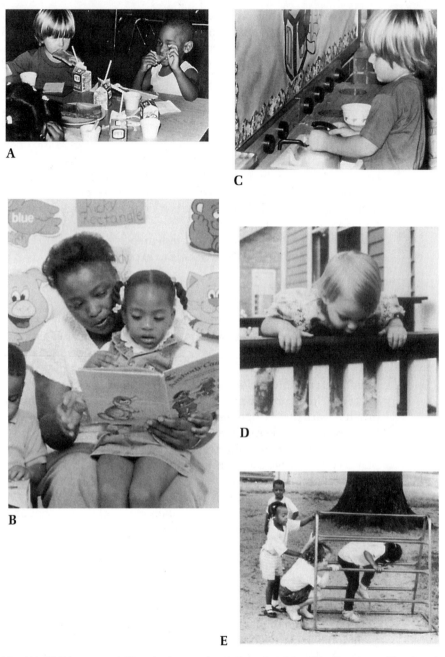

Figure 2-14   (A) Children need time to learn about the social world, Courtesy Chapter 1 Program, Charlotte, NC (B) time to become lovers of books through being read to, Courtesy The Crier, the magazine of the Junior League of Charlotte, Inc. (C) time to explore their own ideas through the use of materials. Courtesy Chapter 1 Program, Charlotte, NC (D, E) and through play, (D) Courtesy Mark and Denise Stephens family photos; Deborah Triplett, photographer (E) Courtesy Bethlehem Center, Charlotte, NC; Peeler Portrait Studio, photographer.

The major alternative viewpoint is that the sooner adults begin to "teach" young children the skills, concepts, and tasks necessary for academic success, the greater the likelihood of achieving that success. Parents and teachers, concerned by reports of declining reading and SAT scores and just about everything else that has been tested in recent years, come to believe that school skills should be taught earlier and more intensely. Proponents of this idea point to the abilities of some young children to learn to read at unprecedented early ages, to play tiny Suzuki violins or speak Japanese. The curriculum from the upper grades has increasingly been pushed down to the lower grades and kindergarten, so that academic expectations have become increasingly higher. But there are those who are concerned about the effects on children and families when developmentally inappropriate demands are made on young children. A major danger is that with the increase in "teaching" young children, there is a need for testing, which is "essentially a method for labeling these sixty-month-old fledglings as failures or passers. The extreme to which this can go was reported in the New York Times (January 5, 1986). The headline read '*On Flunking Kindergarten*'" (Balaban 1990, 15).

The entire assessment process is one that has serious implications for children, parents, and early childhood education professionals. Born from the prevailing trend to evaluate children's progress as a measure of school and program accountability, standardized tests are now frequently being used to test children's readiness to move on or even enter a particular program. Actually, the increased reliance on test scores for school placement points to the bigger problem of schools offering developmentally inappropriate curricula in kindergarten and primary grades, and therefore expecting young children to enter kindergarten "ready" with the skills that once were learned there. Parents become caught in the dilemma of feeling their children are chronologically eligible for school and being told the child has not passed the "readiness test." NAEYC urges parents, teachers, administrators, and others who make decisions to make decisions about children's readiness on "multiple sources of information, including parents' and teachers' observations, and never on the basis of a single test score" (NAEYC 1988). (See Figure 2-15.)

The issue of what is developmentally appropriate in preschool and kindergarten experiences for young children and how children may be considered "ready" for them may well become one of the major issues of concern for both parents and teachers at this century's close. For fuller discussions of the issues and alternatives, see Bredekamp and Shepard, 1989, and Charlesworth, 1989 at chapter end.

Implications for the Teacher

- Parents are often eager to talk with other parents, as well as with child-care experts to share experiences and concerns, to discover they are not

Figure 2-15 Watching children at play may give more accurate information than the standardized tests that are frequently used to assess children's readiness to enter a program. Courtesy Chapter 1 Program, Charlotte, NC

alone in their anxieties, to be supported by others who can identify with their positions.

- Parents need all the information, help, and emotional support they can get as they work towards competence in their parental roles.
- Teachers need to become knowledgeable about the effects of various parenting styles and interaction in order to support parental learning.
- Parents and teachers must engage in active discussion of developmentally appropriate curricula for young children and must support each other in attempts to protect children from the dangers of standardized tests and decisions about readiness made on the basis of these assessments.

❖ Parenthood as an Emotional Experience

People arrive at parenthood via a number of routes. For some, it is a carefully thought out and planned venture, an anticipated and joyful happening. For others, it is the unthought-of consequence in an adult relationship, an event possibly dreaded and resented.

Having children means very different things to different people. Hoffman and Hoffman suggest nine possible motivations at work when people decide to become parents or adjust to the concept after the fact.

1. Validation of adult status and social identity.

2. Expansion of self—a continuance of the family.

3. Achievement of moral value—contributing something or sacrificing in parenthood.

4. Increasing sources of affection and loving ties.

5. Stimulation, novelty, fun.

6. Achievement, competence, creativity.

7. Power and influence over another.

8. Social comparison and competition.

9. Economic utility (Hoffman and Hoffman 1973).

LeMasters points out that some of our cherished beliefs, including some ideas from this list of motivations, are myths that are part of the mystique surrounding parenthood. Raising children is not always fun, nor are all children cute or necessarily appreciative and loving towards their parents at all times (LeMasters and DeFrain 1983). All married couples should not have children nor are all childless married couples unhappy. [Despite the fact that many adults today consider having children to be an option—which increasing numbers are choosing not to exercise—there is still considerable pressure on women particularly to consider that parenthood is an essential experience of adult life. The increasing number of women who give birth to their first child when approaching forty is testimony to the inner pressure of what has been called the "biological clock," as well as cultural attitudes.]

So some of the assumptions people make when deciding to become parents are removed from the reality they will discover.

No matter what their motivation was to have children, there are common realities for all parents.

Irrevocability

There is no turning back. From the time of birth on, parents discover that the responsibility for the care and support of this human being will be entirely theirs for a period of approximately twenty years or longer. Even when other institutions are available to share the task, as in education, the ultimate responsibility rests with the parents. This responsibility may be willingly and joyfully undertaken, but it is always there, twenty-four hours a day, seven days a week, constantly to be reckoned with. As one writer put it, "We can have ex-spouses and ex-jobs, but not ex-children" (Rossi 1968, 32). This is a staggering thought for a parent who, when faced with the reality of the developing child's needs, may feel unequal to the task. However, it's too late—the child is here and the parenting must go on. But the feeling of total responsibility often causes parents to worry considerably about matters both large and small. Yet, paradoxically, whatever mistakes parents make and however burdened they feel, most find it very difficult to hand the job over to anyone else.

Implications for the Teacher

- Teachers can indicate understanding and empathy for the parent's position. Many parents feel greatly burdened by the demands and responsibilities of parenthood and alone in their concerns. They will respond positively to someone who cares about their position, someone with whom they can talk freely.

- Teachers can help by indicating willingness to support them and their children in ways parents decide are helpful for their families.

Restriction, Isolation, and Fatigue

One of the more dramatic changes in becoming a parent is the near total restriction on activity that comes with caring for a totally dependent being. Instead of acting spontaneously, a parent must make elaborate plans to leave the child, even briefly. (There are periods in the child's development when it is difficult to go into the bathroom alone.) And when the child is accompanying the parent, there are myriad preparations to make and paraphernalia to drag along. It is no wonder that many parents restrict their activity, preferring not to bother with it all.

Along with this restriction in activity comes the isolation in which many parents live. Separated from extended family and by the physical housing of the modern city, hampered by the difficulty of finding free time for social arrangements, further restricted by the expenses of the child, and psychologically isolated in coming to grips with the new situation and emotions, many parents feel alone in their parenthood. Preoccupied with the care of a small child and the new experience of parenthood, many parents even become isolated from one another, suffering a loss of the intimacy they knew when they were just a couple. Many parents are reluctant to admit they need help, since becoming a parent is supposed to be a measure of adult status.

Most young parents, especially mothers, complain of fatigue. From early morning until late at night they are responding to the needs of others—children, spouse, employer, and as many more as can be squeezed into the schedule. When mothers are asked what they want most, the common response is "time by myself." For most, it is an impossible dream.

Implications for the Teacher

- Take care not to make it seem as if you are adding still heavier demands on the parent; parents will protect themselves and avoid such teachers.
- Realize that parents do not have excess time to waste. Activities they are involved in need to be both meaningful and streamlined.
- Opportunities for parents to meet other parents for mutual support and socialization help them feel less isolated as they discover common experiences. (See Figure 2-16.)

Non-Instinctual Love

Despite the fantasies promoted by magazine advertisements and movies, many parents do not always feel love for their children. Humans operate beyond the level of instinct and much parenting behavior and

Figure 2-16 Parents are often eager to talk to other parents.

response, including love, comes after time, experience, repeated contact, and learning. Many parents feel ambivalent about their children some of the time, with feelings ranging from exasperation to resentment, with anger occasionally overshadowing feelings of love.

Because parents labor to some extent under the delusions of the "perfect parent," many do not consciously admit these less-than-positive feelings about their children to themselves or anyone else, and are left concerned about their "unnaturalness," and perhaps a little guilty.

Implications for the Teacher

- Become involved in the subtle education of parents to try to remove some of the myths and images under which many parents labor.
- Comment on the positive things you see parents doing with their children.
- Teachers can empathize, displaying understanding and experience that children can be exasperating and frustrating, even for the most caring adult.

Guilt

It is astonishing how frequently today's parents refer to guilt. There are many factors that precipitate this feeling: the ideal parent imaged in the various media; the changes in life-styles and role behaviors, which mean that many parents live quite differently than their parents did; the prevalent feeling that parents should produce children who will do better than they have done; the social attitude that "there are no bad children, only bad parents" (LeMasters and Defrain 1983).

The parent most susceptible to guilt is the mother, probably because she realizes society views her as the most powerful parent. It does not matter whether she has chosen to work outside the home, or not: both employed and stay-at-home mothers are equally susceptible. The working mother may feel guilt because she is breaking a known pattern and is aware of the mixed reviews coming in from researchers and society. "We live with a deep-seated view that a woman's role is in the home. She should be there for her children, so the theory goes, and both she and they will suffer if she's not" (Brazelton 1989, 66). This is a strong message to fight against for most mothers. She may feel bad leaving a crying child with a substitute caregiver, being separated from her child for long hours, and even worse when she is short-tempered with a tired child at the end of her own exhausting day. (See Figure 2-17.) Probably a good portion of the Super Mom phenomenon is fed by this guilt, pushing her to make sure her child misses no right or privilege. The degree of guilt experienced by a working mother is closely related to how hard it was to make the decision to work; to what extent she sees her parenting role as important; how supportive are the attitudes of

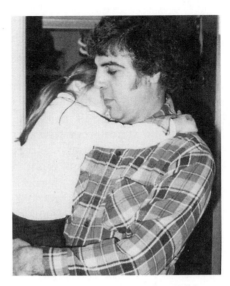

Figure 2-17 It is hard for a parent to leave a crying child.

husband and peers; and the extent to which she feels that her performance as mother is ineffective.

The mother who is at home with her child is not immune from exhaustion or frustration and less-than-perfect maternal behavior. She may feel she is depriving her child of the luxuries an extra income could offer, to say nothing of the worry that her child may become too dependent on her or the feeling that society is pressuring her to be more than "just a housewife." Against the image of the ideal parent, which is impossible to match in reality, the poor parent does not stand a chance, but is left with the guilt that comes from not measuring up.

Implications for the Teacher

- Remember that guilt may lie below the surface in many conversations and encounters with parents. Such an awareness helps the teacher consciously weigh actions and words ensuring that nothing on the teacher's part increases any sense of inadequacy that parents may feel.
- Affirm the child and parent with small appreciative comments as often as possible, since teachers may sometimes have to increase the guilt load by sharing something about the child.

Satisfaction

Despite the obvious negative aspects of total responsibility and restriction, most parents find much to rejoice in. There is great satisfaction in watching children grow and develop, especially when one has played a

large part in the nurturance of that growth. For many parents, the achievements and characteristics of their children give feedback to be incorporated
into the parents' own self-esteem; to some extent, the degree to which the
child does well (or badly) is a reflection of how well the parents feel they are
doing. Most parents feel no one else can know their child as well as they do
and care for him/her quite as well.

Another source of parental satisfaction is the affectionate mutual
attachment that forms between adult and child. It is a very positive feeling
to know you are the most important person in the world to the other.
Because it is so important, many parents fear any event or person which
could be conceived of as disruptive to that relationship. Many parents
experience jealousy or resentment when others become important in the
loved child's life, although frequently these emotions are disguised and not
recognized by the parent.

Implications for the Teacher

- Respect the closeness of the parent-child bond. Ensure classroom attitudes and practices nurture and preserve attachment.
- Be aware that jealousy may lie behind some of your encounters with
  parents so that no actions on your part increase feelings of competition.
- Present comments in ways that avoid personal evaluation and reaction.
  Parents frequently react defensively if they feel their child (and therefore their parenting skills) is criticized.
- Offer tangible and reassuring evidence that the child is cared for ade-
  quately by the supplemental caregiver—and at the same time, reassurance that the child still needs the parent!

Uncertainty

Each child has a unique response to the world; no matter how well-
read a parent is on child development and parenting skills, it is often a different matter putting principles into practice in specific situations with a
specific child! As children change, parents must also, so that parenting techniques that worked well at one point must be discarded and new ones
learned. Often, what worked with one child's personality has no effect on
her sibling. Usually a parent does not feel totally confident that he is performing the task correctly. With the changes within the family and the surrounding culture (discussed earlier in chapter 1), today's parents are doing
the job without role models, clear directions, or firm approval from society.
No wonder most parents often feel unsure of the situation. Societal values
imply that responsible adults know what they are doing. Parents feel they
should not be uncertain.

There is a near-universal bias in our society toward the idea that there is only one right way to do something, while all others are wrong. And if we follow this right way, achieving our goal is a fairly simple process (Bettelheim 1987, 16).

Since every parent feels within that child rearing is not quite so simple, real feelings of uncertainty trigger an unproductive cycle of feeling unsuccessful against this false societal standard.

Implications for the Teacher

- Parents need someone who understands the uncertainties involved in the situation. They do not need someone who believes there is only one right answer in child rearing or who conveys the impression that she is totally certain of her own actions at all times.
- Conveying the impression of looking for answers together is a helpful teacher response.

Real Concern and Caring for Children

However it may appear to an outsider, most parents do learn to love and care for their children. In fact, most parents care passionately with a feeling that is "highly personalized, that comes with a history and a future" (Gonzalez-Mena 1993, 113). Parenting is about these strong connections with their children, a continuity over time. Parents want the best for their children, whether it means physical care, education, or future plans. They care, and they care deeply. Teachers must believe in and value that parental caring.

Implications for the Teacher

- Understand that parents genuinely do care and are concerned for their children. Even when parental behavior strikes you as indifferent or uncaring, believe that caring exists. Many factors may cause behaviors that convey negative impressions. (Some of these will be discussed in chapter 6 and chapter 17.)

❖ Summary

In the area of interpersonal relationships and communications, most breakdowns occur because of insensitivity to the other's position and feelings. There is no question that teachers bring their own needs and emotional responses to the encounter, and these must be reckoned with, but an awareness of the possible roles and emotional responses that accompany parenthood will help teachers to work with parents.

Several distinct roles make up a parent's life. These include

1. the parent as nurturer.
2. the parent in adult relationships.
3. the parent as an individual.
4. the parent as worker.
5. the parent as consumer.
6. the parent as community member.
7. the parent as educator.

Despite the fact that every parenting experience is unique to the individual, there are several common emotions that have implications for the teacher working with parents. Most parents experience

1. irrevocability of parenthood.
2. restrictions, isolation, fatigue.
3. non-instinctual love.
4. guilt.
5. satisfaction related to self-esteem.
6. uncertainty.
7. real concern for child.

❖ Student Activities for Further Study

1. Read a personal account written by a parent. Suggestions:

Birns, B., and Hay, D. (Eds.) (1988). *The different faces of motherhood*. New York: Plenum Press.

Ehrensaft, D. (1987). *Parenting together: men and women sharing the care of their children*. New York: The Free Press.

Friedland, R., and Kent, C. (Eds.) (1981). *The mother's book: shared experiences*. Boston: Houghton Mifflin Co.

Gansberg, J.M., and Mostel, A.P. (1984). *The second nine months*. New York: Tribeca Communications.

Greenberg, M. (1985). *The birth of a father*. New York: Avon.

Greene, B. (1985). *Good morning merry sunshine: a father's journal of his child's first year*. Boston: G.K. Hall.

Harrison, B. (1986). *The shock of motherhood*. New York: Charles Scribner's Sons.

Jackson, M. (1994). *The mother zone: love, sex and laundry in the modern family*. New York: Henry Holt.

Kelly, M., and Parsons, E. (1992). *The mother's almanac*. (rev. ed.) New York: Doubleday.

Kent, C., and Friedlander, R. (Eds.) (1986). *The father's book: shared experiences*. Boston: G.K. Hall.

McBride, A.B. (1973). *The growth and development of mothers*. New York: Harper and Row Pubs.

Schwartz, J.D. (1993). *The mother puzzle: a new generation reckons with motherhood*. New York: Simon and Schuster.

Sullivan, S. (1992). *The father's almanac*. (rev. ed.) New York: Doubleday.

2. Talk with several parents. Choose parents whose children include infants, toddlers, and preschoolers if possible. Talk with at least one father. Discuss their reactions to parenthood: adjustments, negative aspects, positive aspects, changes in adult relationships and life-style. Share your findings with your classmates. Try to identify which of Galinsky's stages of parenthood these parents are in.

3. Talk with a professional in an agency that works to support and/or educate parents. What are some of the major concerns, difficulties, and needs of parents that he/she reports?

4. In small groups, brainstorm additional practical ways for classroom teachers to support parents in the seven different roles of parents as defined in this chapter.

❖ Review Questions

1. List seven roles that parents play.

2. Discuss the implications of these roles for a teacher working with parents.

3. List seven emotional responses of parents.

4. Discuss the implications of these emotional responses for teachers.

❖ Suggestions for Further Reading

Barud, S.L., Collins, R.C. and Divine-Hawkins, P. (1983). Employer supported child care: everybody benefits. *Children Today, 12* (3), 2-3.

Bradshaw, J. (1988). *The family*. Pompano Beach, FL: Health Communications.

Bredekamp, S., and Shepard, L. (1989, March). How best to protect children from inappropriate school expectations, practices and policies. *Young Children, 44* (3), 14-24.

Bronfenbrenner, U. (1984). The parent child relationship and our changing society. In E. L. Arnold (Ed.), *Parents, children and change*. Lexington, MA: Lexington Books.

Brubaker, T. (Ed.) (1993). *Family Relations: challenges for the future*. Newbury Park, CA: Sage.

Cowan, C., and Cowan, P. (1992). *When partners become parents: the big life change for couples*. New York: Basic Books.

Hamburg, D. (1992). *Today's children: creating a future for a generation in crisis*. New York: Random House.

Hanner, T., and Turner, P. (1992). *Parenting in contemporary society*. (2nd ed.) Englewood Cliffs, NJ: Prentice Hall.

Jackson, M. (1994). *The mother zone: love, sex and laundry in the modern family*. New York: Henry Holt.

Kelly, M., and Parsons, E. (1992). *The mother's almanac*. (rev. ed.) New York: Doubleday.

Levine, J.A., (1976). *Who will raise the children? New options for fathers (and mothers)*. Philadelphia: J.B. Lippincott.

Schwartz, J.D. (1993). *The mother puzzle: a new generation reckons with motherhood*. New York: Simon and Schuster.

Sullivan, S.A. (1992). *The father's almanac*. (rev. ed.) New York: Doubleday.

CHAPTER 3

A Day with Two Families: Diversity of Experience

No one is ever likely to find another family that exactly duplicates the family in which they grew up. Families are created by the ideas, emotions, and experiences of unique individuals. Their living places, their foods and family traditions, their styles of communicating and living together are familiar and comfortable to those within the family and to no one else. Even families who share the same cultural, linguistic, or religious traditions will not be alike, because of the unique inner and outer views of the individuals involved. And in contemporary society, with the myriad of cultures and life-styles that live side by side, interacting within the same schools, workplaces, and communities, it is vital that this assumption and celebration of uniqueness be made explicit.

Differences are only divisive when they are seen as frightening, threatening, and mysterious. When they are seen as interesting and enriching to society in general and to the lives they touch in particular, differences are to be valued.

When individuals come together to form relationships and communicate in the spirit of openness that is vital for effective parent-teacher partnerships, a first step is to attempt to understand the other, and to convey an attitude of respect and acceptance. Both understanding and acceptance are products of knowledge. In this chapter, an examination of the hypothetical lives of two of our fictional families introduced in Chapter 1 may help to heighten awareness of the demands and stresses in the lives of parents with young children, and of the individuality of each family's life. The more sensitivity a teacher can develop to the complex lives of different families, the more likely he can approach them with true empathy.

OBJECTIVES

After studying this chapter, the student will be able to

1. list several external factors causing stress in the families portrayed.
2. list several emotional responses evidenced in the parents portrayed.
3. identify types of diversity that may be found in typical communities.

You first met Jane Briscoe as she tried to imagine what life was like for some of the families of her acquaintance, unique in the circumstances of their lives but related by the common roles and experiences of parenthood. No one who is just an onlooker to the living drama of any family can come close to appreciating the thousands of details, interactions, and emotional nuances that compose a family's experience. Researchers (or teachers) frequently do not have the opportunity to record the actions of family members as they live their daily lives, but it is probably only through such methods that the individual threads of the family fabric can be perceived and appreciated. Here is a closer look at two of our fictitious families as they move through a day.

❖ The Lawrence Family

When the alarm went off at 6 A.M., no one moved. Fannie stayed quite still, hoping Otis would remember it was his morning to get the children up and start the dressing and breakfast process. She felt so tired, she couldn't get up yet anyway, she told herself, stifling the guilty reminder that it was eleven the night before when Otis got home from his class and he must be pretty tired too. But this past month she'd seemed to be completely exhausted to start each day. She wondered how she would get through the next three months, and thought again that it might be a mistake to work right up until the birth, but that was the only way she could get three months off afterwards. In her head she reviewed the whole decision, but there appeared to be no other way out. Their income looked fine on paper, but when you subtracted the $500 a month that Otis sent for the boys—more now that Danny had to get braces—there just wasn't any extra for her to take additional unpaid leave.

She groaned, but Otis still didn't move. In a burst of exasperation she maneuvered out of bed and banged the bathroom door louder than was necessary. Otis stretched and turned over, feeling guilty about Fannie, but also telling himself he needed the extra rest after the late night at class, and the late night he would have tonight at work. He'd get up in just a few minutes and help Fannie get the kids ready.

Fannie laid out breakfast things and went back up to wake the children. Pete was tired and hard to get moving, so she practically had to dress him, and Kim was impatient to get her hair done. By the time they were eating breakfast, Fannie looked at the clock and realized she'd have to skip hers and dress quickly, or she'd be late again. In the still-darkened bedroom she fumbled for clothes and shoes, then went into the bathroom to shower quickly and dress. She returned to the kitchen to find the TV blaring and the table a mess of cereal and milk. "Kim, when I leave you in charge, I don't expect you to let Pete watch TV; just look at this mess. Turn that off and at least put the milk in the fridge and get your teeth brushed, and Petey, see if you can't tie your shoes to help Mamma out today."

Kim said, "Mamma, I want a lunch packed. It's that dumb fried chicken for lunch at school today; and I hate it."

"Kim! I told you before, I have to fix lunches at night. I don't have the time. We've got to leave right now, so don't start that." Kim's lip trembled and Fannie turned away abruptly. She did not have time for one of Kim's scenes now; besides, she was getting pretty sick of them, as often as Kim was doing this. Last night she'd spent an hour whining that she didn't have any friends in her class and she hated Miss Johnston. This wasn't like Kim, Fannie thought distractedly. She'd always been a happy child.

Otis appeared in the kitchen just in time to see Kim burst into tears. "Hey, what's the matter here?" he asked cheerily. Fannie glared at him, as Kim sobbed that Mamma wouldn't make a her a lunch and she couldn't eat the lunch at school. "Oh won't she—" Otis began teasingly, but Fannie snapped quickly, "Just be quiet, Otis, I haven't had one second this morning. I haven't even had time for breakfast, so if she wants a lunch, you'd have to make it, but we have to leave right now!"

Otis handed some change to Kim and said, "Well, at least you can eat some ice cream, OK? Now leave your Mamma alone." He patted Fannie's shoulder apologetically. "Slow down, babe. You'll make it. You shouldn't be skipping breakfast. Have a good day. Come on Petey, hurry up, your Mom's in a hurry. Don't forget I work late tonight, Fannie. See you by ten. Try to be awake," he joked, patting her again.

"Fat chance," muttered Fannie and hustled the children to the car, Kim still sniffling loudly. As she drove along, Fannie thought to herself that sometimes she wondered why they'd gotten married. Otis was never home in the evenings, what with work and the college classes. Instantly she stifled the thought and wished she'd at least given him a hug. He did work hard.

She dropped Kim off at her school, with a determined smile. Kim walked off suddenly and Fannie tried not to mind. She noticed that there was no one else entering the door along with Kim. It was early, she knew, but she had to drop Kim off, then Pete, and still arrive at her own school by 7:34 A.M. She just wouldn't have felt right leaving Kim to wait for the bus, but this was one of the things Kim complained about—all the other kids got to ride the bus. She made a mental note to try to see Kim's teacher soon and ask her whether Kim was justified in saying she had no friends. Perhaps she could arrange for a girl to come with Kim after school, on a day when her own schedule allowed Kim to skip going to after-school day care. Anyway, she'd have to ask Miss Johnston if Kim being dropped off early created a problem; she was a little afraid to do that because the teacher was a young, single woman who probably wouldn't understand the morning schedule. Heaven knows it would be worse next year, because Pete's center did not offer care for infants; that would mean three stops before 7:45 A.M. She sighed, then realized they were at Pete's center. Thank goodness he'd been quiet, unusual for him.

"Oh, no," she whispered as they passed the classroom bulletin board with its reminder that the teachers needed toothpaste. "I forgot again." Fannie helped Pete take off his jacket and smiled toward a teacher who approached her.

"Oh, Mrs. Lawrence, I see Pete's got one of his cars again. We really can't let the children bring their own toys; it creates such problems. Please take it with you." Confused, Fannie looked down and realized Pete was clutching a tiny car in his hand. She started to explain to the teacher that she hadn't realized he'd brought it, and fell silent as she realized that made her sound like a pretty careless mother. Pete grabbed his hand away, and Fannie looked for help to the teacher, who looked away. Fannie realized she would have to take the car away. She thought a nasty thought about the teacher and pried the car out of Pete's fingers. Pete burst into tears, and Fannie's stomach tightened. She gave him a quick hug and muttered a few words in his ear, looked appealingly at the teacher—who now seemed even more annoyed—and quickly dashed down the hall. She felt like crying herself as she listened to Pete's wails and thought about what a horrible morning it had been for all of them. She was so preoccupied with thinking about the kids' reactions and making resolutions for a tranquil evening that she walked right past another parent, who called hello after her. Sheepishly, she waved back and then hurried on, her face hot with embarrassment. The trip to her own school was punctuated by stoplights and blocked lanes, and she found herself almost running from her parked car, aware that several bus loads of children had already arrived.

The day went fairly smoothly for Fannie, although with twenty-eight third graders to look after, plus her turn at playground duty, she was very tired by the time the final bell rang. A parent who came to pick up her child wanted to talk about the new reading program, but Fannie had to cut her off to get to the weekly faculty meeting on time. As she hurried down the hall, she reminded herself to make an appointment with Kim's teacher, so she wouldn't start off by annoying the teacher. The faculty meeting dragged on, and Fannie found herself glancing repeatedly at her watch, estimating how long it would take to pick up Kim and get her to her dancing class.

At last the meeting ended, and she rushed out to her car, noticing with longing the group of young women who stayed back, chatting and planning to go out for a drink.

Her heart lifted when she saw Kim playing happily with another girl at the after-school child care where the bus dropped her each afternoon. The college student in charge of the group apologized for not having remembered that it was Kim's dancing class day and having her already changed. Fannie swallowed her irritation, but it became more difficult to control as Kim dawdled in play with her friend to the point where Fannie had to brusquely order her to leave and hurry up and change. Kim began to whine, but stopped when she saw the look on her mother's face.

Fannie tried to relax and make pleasant conversation about Kim's day as they drove to the dancing class. Kim chattered happily about her new friend at child care and asked if she couldn't come to her house to play one afternoon. Fannie promised, thinking uneasily of the logistic problems of rides and permission that might entail. She dropped Kim at the door, promising to try to be back in time to watch the last few minutes of the class. Checking her watch, she tried to organize her errands to fit them into the hour time slot—drop off the cleaning, cash a check at the bank, pick up a few groceries, and get to the post office for stamps before it closed. That would cut it pretty close for picking up Pete, and she hated his day to be so long, but she knew from experience it was worse to drag a tired child with her. Trying to ignore her own fatigue, she hurried on.

Pete looked up hopefully as she walked into his room at the child care center, and she realized with a pang he'd probably been doing that as each parent entered the room for the previous half hour. His teacher said he'd had a good day, after the upsetting beginning. Fannie was annoyed that she'd brought that up again. She just wished this young woman could understand that it was bad enough having to rush Pete in the morning, let alone strip him of all his favorite things for the day.

There was an accident holding up traffic on the road back to Kim's dancing studio, and by the time they'd got there she was waiting in the parking lot with the dancing teacher, who looked in a hurry to leave. Kim's face was stormy as she accused Fannie, "You promised." Fannie tried to explain, but felt both helpless and angry before the eight-year-old's indignation. Impulsively, changing the mood and giving in to her own fatigue, she suggested supper at McDonald's. Amidst the kids' squeals of glee, she thought glumly about the nutritional consequences and decided she wouldn't ask them what they'd eaten for lunch. Some mother, she thought, conjuring up an image of her own mother's plentiful dinner table. And what's more there'd be nothing to keep warm for Otis. Well, maybe she could fix him a nice omelet, if he wasn't too late.

The kids were cheerful and chatty over hamburgers, so Fannie relaxed and enjoyed their stories. "We're doing OK," she told herself. "They're really fine."

It was after seven when they got home. Fannie put Pete in the bathtub and started Kim on her reading homework in the bathroom to watch him so Fannie could unpack the groceries and put a load of laundry in. At least Otis had had the time to clean up the breakfast mess; that was more than she could have stood, twelve hours later!

She read Pete a bedtime story and then tucked him in. He was tired and settled in quickly. Fannie looked back at him tenderly. He was growing so quickly; pretty soon he wouldn't be the baby any more. For the thousandth time she wondered how he'd feel when the new baby arrived.

Kim wanted to watch some television, but Fannie reminded her first to find her clothes for the morning and decide if she wanted a lunch, which she did. Making the sandwiches, Fannie thought, "Maybe tomorrow will be a better day." At bedtime Kim asked her to be sure to give Daddy a kiss for her. Fannie wished again that Otis could be home more at night, so they could feel like a real family. She knew what Otis would say if she brought it up again. "The classes are important, if I'm ever going to be able to stop selling cars at night. It's only a couple more years. And in the meantime selling cars is giving us a good living." He was right, of course, but the kids practically never saw him. Well, for that matter, it was tough on all of them.

Fannie folded the laundry, washed her hair, spread out her clothes for the morning, and lay down on the bed to read the morning paper. Within ten minutes she had fallen asleep. When Otis came in at 10:00 P.M., she was still asleep. He sighed, turned out the light, and went to see if there were any leftovers in the kitchen.

❖ The Ashley Family

Sylvia Ashley got up quickly when the alarm went off at 6:00 A.M. She had washed out Terrence's shirt the night before and wanted to iron it before it was time for him to get up. Anyway, she liked having time in the early morning, when the building was still quiet. The rest of the day there was hardly a moment when someone wasn't yelling or throwing something. She turned on the kitchen light cautiously, knowing the roaches would scurry away from the sink.

She ironed carefully. She felt bad that Terrence had to wear the same clothes over and over, but at least he was always clean and tidy. She hoped the teacher would notice that and not treat him badly. The way some people treated people without money—she hated it for herself, and she didn't want her kids to grow up thinking they weren't as good as everyone else, just because they lived in public housing and didn't have a father to back them up.

She sighed, remembering she had to go back to the social services office today to talk to the social worker. She dreaded that, but because their allowance had been cut two months before, she simply hadn't been able to make it on the reduced amount. Last week she'd had to borrow three dollars from her neighbor across the hall to get some macaroni and milk for the kid's supper, and she knew she couldn't do that again—the woman barely spoke to her anyway. And with trying to get into that job-training program, she knew she'd have to get herself a new pair of shoes. Ricky's sneakers had a hole right through the toe, too.

She unplugged the iron and glanced at the clock. Time to get the boys up. They were cheerful and chattered away, Terrence helping Ricky get dressed. Ricky ate a bowl of cereal, and Sylvia gave Terrence a glass of milk to have something in his stomach until he got to school. He preferred to have breakfast at home, and she'd always let him until things got so tight. Because he was eligible for the free breakfast at school, it made a little place she could save.

She dressed quickly and then cleaned the kitchen up. Terrence was ready at the door, hair neatly combed, when she got there. He grumbled a bit every day about his mother and little brother having to go with him to school, but she didn't like the idea of him walking alone six blocks through this neighborhood. Ricky struggled to keep up. They waved to Terrence from the street as he climbed the school stairs by himself. Sylvia worried about him—he never mentioned a friend, and after school she and Ricky walked him home, and then he played with Ricky. She knew he needed friends his own age, but she kept him in the apartment unless she could go to the playground with them. She'd seen and heard plenty of fights and wildness from some of the kids in their building, and she knew some of them were already in trouble with the police. She was going to keep her boys free of that. Terrence was a good student, a smart boy—he would grow up differently than those other kids.

She and Ricky waited at the bus stop for the bus that would take them downtown to the square where they could transfer to the one that would take them out to the social services building. She barely heard Ricky talking away and pointing out cars and asking questions as they rode along, as she rehearsed what she had to say.

The waiting room was full; she found one chair and held Ricky on her lap for a while, until he got wiggly. Then she let him sit on the floor beside her. She kept listening for the woman to call her name, knowing that Ricky was getting restless. He asked her for something to eat, as he watched a man eating crackers he'd bought from the vending machine. Sylvia didn't want to waste fifty cents on that, and wished she'd thought to bring something for him. Fortunately, they called her name just then, and Ricky was distracted by moving into the small office.

At least this social worker was better than the last one, who'd positively sniffed every time Ricky moved. Sylvia had always been furious underneath, because this woman had to know there was no money for baby-sitters and nobody that could help them out, but it wouldn't have done to let that anger show.

By the end of the discussion, Sylvia felt very depressed. She always hated the questions about whether she'd heard from either of the boys' fathers; she always wanted to say she was thankful she hadn't, and wouldn't take a penny from either of them anyway. It didn't look like there would be any increase in her monthly check because the social worker pointed out that social services would have to pay for Ricky's child care when the job training started in four weeks. Sylvia didn't know how they'd manage, knowing there'd be more expenses with her in the program. But she'd do it. Then maybe she'd be able to make enough to get them into a little apartment somewhere nicer, and she'd have some friends from work, and Terrence could have friends to play with, and things would be better. She had to do it. Her kids deserved more.

Ricky was tired and cranky as they waited for the bus home. He started to cry and she spanked him, not very hard, but she just couldn't stand to listen to that right now or have the bus driver stare at her when she got on with a crying child.

He fell asleep on the bus and she pulled him against her shoulder, knowing he'd wake up when they had to transfer. Poor thing, it had been a long morning for him. Neither of them said much as they rode the last bus and walked home for lunch. Ricky finished his soup and she put him in bed for a nap. She sat, thinking about Ricky starting in child care and about herself starting in the training program. She hoped she could do it. It had been a long time since she'd been in school, and then she didn't have kids and everything else to worry about. She worried about how it would be for Ricky; he'd never been away from her at all. The social worker had told her that the center was a good one, but that didn't reassure her that Ricky would not get upset.

She glanced at the clock. Just a few more minutes until she'd have to wake up Ricky to take him while they got Terrence. Poor thing was so worn out she'd like to leave him asleep, but there was nobody to ask to stay with him. She worried briefly about Terrence, who would have to come home and be by himself for a couple of hours until she finished her class, picked up Ricky, and arrived home. She'd already lost sleep a couple of nights worrying about that, but there was nothing else to be done. She'd warn him about answering the door, not using the stove, and everything else she could think of, and then just hope he'd stay in the apartment, safely, by himself.

Terrence was quiet coming home. In the apartment he unfolded a note and handed it to her. It was a reminder that parents needed to send a dollar the next day to pay for a ticket to a play at the children's theater next week. Sylvia avoided Terrence's eyes as she said that she couldn't send the money, so he could stay home from school the day of the play. Terrence said nothing.

She gathered the laundry and her wallet and keys, and took the boys with her down to the basement laundry room. The children sat, arguing. When another woman came in, Sylvia snapped at the kids to be quiet, and they sat glumly until she asked Terrence to help her match the socks. Back upstairs, the boys watched cartoons while she made hamburgers for supper. After supper, Terrence did his homework at the kitchen table, and Ricky sat beside him and colored in a coloring book she'd bought in the drugstore. She put them in the bath together while she tidied the kitchen. After the children watched some more TV, she put them in bed and sat by herself in the living room, on the couch where she'd sleep. There was nothing she wanted to see on TV, but she left it on to keep her company. After an hour or so, she turned out the light to sleep.

❖ Implications for Teachers

It is a good idea to try to comprehend the lives of the families with whom you will work. Perhaps this has been a useful consciousness-raising exercise for you.

Both of these families have unique living circumstances and experiences, but in both there is a common thread of stress with the roles and responsibilities, the isolation that comes from concentrating on children's care, and the deeply felt concerns for the children's lives. They are alike in that, in common with every other family you will encounter, they have both strengths and needs.

The reader may or may not yet be a parent. If you are, then you have had daily experiences from a parent's perspective and do not need further convincing of the astonishing task of blending and fulfilling these various roles. Separately and on the printed page, they appear demanding; when experienced together, in the context of daily life, they can be staggering.

For those of you who are not yet parents, recollections of your parents' lives during your childhood may be faint and will not do justice to the enormity of life's demands. Even acquaintance with your classroom parents probably does not fully expose you to the extent of the demands on them. An active imagination will help you best here. On a sheet of paper, jot down any facts you know of several of your families' lives—the family members ages, jobs or school, hobbies and interests, special family circumstances.

Now mentally take yourself through a sample of their days—and nights. (Parenting does not have a neatly prescribed limit on working hours!) Remember to include the details of daily life such as doctors' visits, haircuts, trips to the library and bank, as well as the unforseen emergencies that pop up—the car breaking down, the baby-sitter getting sick, the additional assignment at work. Choose a cross section of families to contemplate; remember that the socioeconomic circumstances of any family may add additional strains, whether they be the daily struggles of a poverty-level family or the demands on an upwardly-mobile professional family. If you're doing this right, you will likely soon be shaking your head and tired in your imagination.

This might be a useful exercise to repeat whenever you find yourself making judgments or complaining about families. It is virtually impossible for a teacher to work effectively with classroom families until she is able to empathize with them. Remember, this is only an attempt to mentally understand possible situations; no outsider can fully appreciate what really goes on in any one family. Every family truly stands alone in its uniqueness.

❖ Diversity

In recent years, early childhood teachers have been urged to ensure that the children in their classrooms are supported in developing multicultural understandings and appreciation of the many differences and similarities that exist among people. One of the best ways to do this is to create an environment where children feel comfortable in exploring the differences that occur naturally among themselves and their families, or among families to whom they may be introduced through stories, pictures, dolls, or classroom visitors. A crucial element in such an environment is a teacher who has taken the time to identify personal biases, and has the courage to go beyond bias to reach for real understanding of differences. Biases are mostly the result of fear, ignorance, and misinformation. It is vital that teachers make the effort to become comfortable and informed about the kinds of life experiences, values, and behaviors of diverse cultural groups, and work on developing nonjudgmental dispositions towards working with such diversity.

Culture is a comprehensive term that includes the various understandings, traditions, and guidance of the groups to which we all belong. "Culture influences both behavior and the psychological processes on which it rests. Culture forms the prism through which members of a group see the world and create shared meanings" (Bowman in Burgess 1993). This includes the cultures of: family; ethnic, linguistic, and racial groups; religious groups; gender and sex role identifications; and geographical and community orientations.

In chapter 15, we will explore ways that teachers can incorporate classroom practices that indicate the welcoming of each unique family and the valuing of the contributions their culture can make for rich classroom experiences and positive dialogue. Welcoming each family lays the groundwork for the development of positive identity formation and self-esteem for children, and for respectful communication with their parents. But in the context of this chapter's appreciation of unique family orientations, it is important that teachers see they must take the initiative in attempting to understand the cultural backgrounds of their families. The information to do this may come from published accounts written by members of particular cultural backgrounds. Published accounts, as the earlier imaginary accounts of the daily lives, may be less than perfect sources of understanding, but they can certainly heighten teacher awareness of cultural patterns of behavior and communication styles that might otherwise be misinterpreted or even offensive.

Teachers preparing to work with the diverse cultures represented in America or Canada today should become familiar with literature about working with at least the following cultural groups: African American, Native American, or indigenous people, Hispanic, various Asian cultures, new immigrant families, interracial and biracial families, gay and lesbian families, and homeless and migrant families. In addition, the populations of particular schools or centers may reflect unique characteristics related to their geography, parents' occupations, or class composition. Such reading will at least begin to open the doors of understanding which will increase within relationships with members of the particular cultures; each family will still have their own specific interpretation of their own culture. The extensive list of resources in Suggestions for Further Reading should be a helpful starting place. Teachers are also cautioned that this learning about other cultures is not for the purpose of further separating groups into subjects to be studied, but to bring people closer together through increased understanding and respect. As Janet Gonzalez-Mena warns in *Multicultural Issues in Child Care*, "cultural labels are necessarily generalizations" (p. 6).

❖ Summary

No one can truly understand all the emotional implications of parenthood, for each parent comes to this point with a particular set of needs, experiences, and motivations. Nevertheless, it is important to realize the potential strains of daily life that come with parenthood, so that teachers do not unwittingly ignore or exacerbate strong emotional responses, or add to family stress. Understanding something of the framework within which members of various cultural groups operate is important for teachers.

❖ Student Activities for Further Studies

1. Re-read the summaries of the ten fictional families in chapter 1. Select another family and create an imaginary day in their life. Work with a partner, brainstorming to stimulate your thinking. Share your account with the class.

2. Invite a parent of preschoolers to your class discussion. Ask him to come prepared to present a sample diary of his family's daily life.

3. Read an account of a family or cultural groups that might increase your understanding of various cultures or segments of society. For ideas refer to the Suggestions for Further Reading.

❖ Review Questions

1. List several external factors causing stress in the families portrayed.

2. List several emotional responses evidenced in the parents portrayed.

❖ Suggestions for Further Reading

A selected annotated bibliography on black families. Washington, D.C.: U.S. Government Printing Office, Publ. no. 78-30140.

Barrera, R.M. (1993, March). "Retrato de my familia: a portrait of my hispanic family. *Child Care Information Exchange*, 31–34.

Bozett (1987). *Gay and lesbian parents.* Westport, CT.: Greenwood Publishing Group.

Chavkin, N.F. (Ed.) (1993). *Families and schools in a pluralistic society* (most minority groups). Albany, NY: State University of New York Press.

Clay, J.W. (1990, March). Working with lesbian and gay parents and their children. *Young Children, 45* (3), 31–35.

Corbett, S. (1993). A complicated bias (gay and lesbian families). *Young Children, 48*(3), 29–31.

First, J., and Carrera, J. (1988). *New voices: immigrant students in U.S. public schools.* Boston: National Coalition of Advocates for Students.

Fu, V. (1993, March). Children of Asian cultures. *Child Care Information Exchange*, 49–51.

Hadley, N. (1987, May/June). Reaching migrant pre-schoolers. *Children's Advocate*, 19–20.

Hale, J. (1991, Sept.). The transmission of cultural values to young African American children. *Young Children, 46* (6), 7–15.

Hale-Benson, J. (1986). *Black children: their roots, culture and learning styles.* (Rev. Ed.) Baltimore: John Hopkins University Press.

Hare, J. and Koepke, L.A. (1990, Winter). Susanne and her two mothers. *Day Care and Early Education*, 20–21.

Hidalgo, N. (1992). *I saw Puerto Rico once: a review of the literature on Puerto Rican families in the U.S.* Boston: Center on Families, Communities, Schools, and Children's Learning.

Irujo, S. (1989). Do you know why they all talk at once? Thoughts on cultural differences between Hispanics and Anglos. *Equity and Choice, 5*(3), 14–18.

Klein, H.A. (1995, March). Urban Appalachian children in northern schools: a study in diversity. *Young Children, 50*(3), 10–16.

Kotlowitz, A. (1991). *There are no children here: the story of two boys growing up in the other america.* (inner city) NY: Doubleday.

Kozol, J. (1988). *Rachel and her children* (studies of homeless families). NY: Crown Publishers.

Lee, F.Y. (1995, March). Asian parents as partners. *Young Children, 50*(3), 4–9.

Linehanst, M. (1992). The children who are homeless: educational strategies for school personnel. Ph: *Delta Kappan, 74*(1), 61–66.

Locust, C. (1992). Wounding the spirit: discrimination and traditional American Indian belief systems. *Harvard Educational Review, 58*(3), 315–330.

McCormick, L., and Holden, R. (1992, Sept.). Homeless children: a special challenge. *Young Children, 47*(6), 61–67.

Rubin, L. (1976). *World of pain: life in the working-class family.* NY: Basic Books.

Sample, W. (1993, March). The American Indian child. *Child Care Information Exchange*, 39–40.

Schultz, S.B., and Casper, V. (1992). *Tentative trust: enhancing connections between gay and lesbian parents and the school.* NY: Bank Street College of education.

Sheehan, S. (1994). *Life for me ain't been no crystal stair.* (inner city and foster families). NY: Pantheon.

Siu, S. (1992). *Towards an understanding of Chinese-American educational achievement: a literature review.* Boston: Center on Families, Communities, Schools, and Children's Learning, Report #2.

Taylor, D., and Dorsey-Gaines, E. (1988). *Growing up literati: learning from inner-city families.* Portsmouth, NH: Heinemann Press.

Wardle, F. (1987, Jan.) Are you sensitive to interracial children's special identity needs? *Young Children, 42*(2), 53–59.

Wardle, F. (1993, March) Interracial Families and Biracial Children. *Childcare Information Exchange*, 45–48.

Wellhousen, K. (1993). Children from nontraditional families: a lesson in acceptance. *Childhood Education.* Annual Theme Issue, 287–288.

Whiting, B., and Edwards, C. (1988). *Children of different worlds.* Cambridge, MA; Harvard University Press.

Wickens, E. Penny's question: I will have a child in my class with two moms—what do you know about this? *Young Children, 48*(3), 25–28.

Wilson, W. (1987). *The truly disadvantaged: the inner city, the underclass, and public policy.* Chicago: The University of Chicago Press.

Wright, J. (1989). *Address unknown: the homeless in america.* NY: Aldine de Gryten.

Yao, E. (1988). Working effectively with Asian immigrant parents. *Phi Delta Kappan, 70*(3), 223–225.

SECTION II

Teacher-Parent Partnerships in Early Education

Having completed our initial study of parenting in modern America, it is time to consider the importance of creating teacher-parent partnerships. Because this is a task undertaken with the teacher's initiative, it is crucial that teachers understand why teacher-parent partnerships are a necessary part of the early educator's role. In chapter 4, we consider the various facets of parent involvement teachers may encounter. Chapter 5 discusses the benefits for children, parents, and teachers when parents and teachers work together. Chapter 6 presents the various barriers that may prevent the development of optimum working relationships. Chapter 7 identifies the attitudes and practices that form the foundation for healthy partnerships. You will meet teachers and parents who demonstrate through their dialogue and comments the spectrum of experience that teachers may meet.

"Did Momma's little angel stretch his potential today?"

CHAPTER 4

What Is Parent Involvement?

When the term *parent involvement* is used, different individuals may think of very different activities and characteristics that define the involvement of parents in early education programs. There is no uniform requirement or philosophy that can be applied to working with parents; indeed, many programs seem to feel this is the least important aspect of their function, paying only perfunctory attention to parents, while others work very hard to include parents in as many aspects of their program as they can. In this chapter, we will explore the various motivations that have brought parents into the educational process for their young children, and the models of programs that you might find defined as parent involvement.

OBJECTIVES

After studying this chapter, the student will be able to

1. list three motivations and models for parent involvement, and discuss the ideas that underlie each.

❖ Perspectives on Parent Involvement

Jane Briscoe again. "You know, I'm really confused. At a meeting I went to recently, the subject of parent involvement came up. After several people discussed what they thought about parent involvement, I realized I have been using that term differently than most of them. One of them implied that parent involvement was parents meeting together and making the decisions in a program. Another spoke as if parent involvement meant parents working as aides in the classroom. Somebody else mentioned the early intervention programs in which parents are being taught more about their children so they can expand the ways they help their own children develop. And I've been thinking parent involvement is when I try to let parents know as much as I can about what's going on in their children's classroom lives."

Small wonder that Jane is confused. In program descriptions, research, and in conversational usage among teachers, the term *parent involvement* is used to describe all of these patterns of parent participation in early childhood education.

"Parent involvement" is an all-purpose term used to describe all manner of parent-program interaction: policy-making, parent education, fund raising, volunteering time, and even the simple exchange of information of various sorts with staff. Under a general goal of continuity of care, the desired end involved may be better parenting, better day care, or both. The parent-involvement continuum runs from an expectation of parent control to complete subservience of parents to professionals. Parents may be cast in a variety of roles from experts (on their own children) to students, thus putting staff in positions ranging from servants to savants (Pettygrove and Greenman 1984, 89).

As this statement implies, there is no one model of parent involvement. Preschools have chosen to address the issue of parent involvement in a variety of ways, ranging from a low level to a high level of parent involvement. Centers with a low level of parent involvement allow parents to take part in activities that do not challenge the expertise of a teacher or the decision-making power of the school. Activities such as newsletters, parent meetings, or individual parent conferences tend to keep parents at a distance, learning secondhand about their child's life at school. Schools with a high level of parent involvement provide opportunities for parents to make their presence known, particularly in the educational setting, by parent visits, observations, or visits to volunteer assistance of many kinds; here parents are perceived as a source of help. (See Figure 4-1). The highest levels of parent involvement occur in schools that believe both teachers and parents have expertise, and both parents and the school have decision-making rights. Communicating via many channels, parents have the power to make decisions concerning the education of their children.

❖ Brief History of Parent Involvement

An interest in the involvement of parents in early childhood education is not new. Parents were involved in some of the first nursery education movements in America in the earliest decades of this century. For middle-class parents, parent cooperative nursery schools blossomed throughout the 1920s, 1930s, 1940s, reached a peak around 1960, and continue today to a lesser degree. Often appearing in middle-class enclaves such as university or suburban towns, these schools welcome parents, primarily traditional

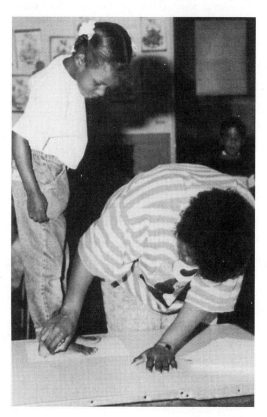

Figure 4-1   Parents may assist teachers with routine tasks in the classroom. Courtesy Bethlehem Center, Charlotte, NC., photographer Peeler Portrait Studio.

stay-at-home mothers, who often undergo some training. The mothers frequently take the position of paraprofessional in the preschool classroom,
assisting a trained, paid, professional teacher. Such a close involvement in
their children's classroom lives offers opportunities for parents to enrich the
lives of their children and themselves. Parent cooperatives usually provide
opportunities to participate in the life of the school, from defining the philosophy and practices to contributing to the care and maintenance of the
facility. The belief is that parents know what they want for themselves and
their children, and therefore should be involved in the school. (The parent
cooperative model has been used more recently even in child care facilities
for parents employed full-time. See Senate Employees' Child Care Center
in chapter 18. The contributions of parents decrease budget costs for such
items as cleaning, accounting, purchasing, and laundry, as well as strengthening the ties between parent and school.)

Parents from lower socioeconomic backgrounds were involved in the
nursery schools and child-care centers set up by the government to supply
children's nutritional and health care needs in families disrupted by the
Depression (Works Progress Administration, or WPA, centers). Later, in
World War II, the Lanham Act Child Care Centers offered child care for parents working in the war effort. Even with the demands of those stressful
times, and coming from backgrounds of cultural and ethnic diversity, these
parent groups were extremely responsive to parent educators associated with
the centers to provide support for parental self-development and learning.

It was another twenty years or so before the field of early childhood
education expanded again, and with this expansion came renewed interest
in efforts to work with parents. Programs for the disadvantaged, including
Head Start and other intervention programs, appeared in the 1960s and
1970s. Parents were involved in most of these programs. (See Figure 4-2).
Shortly after, changes in the structure of American society brought increasing numbers of women into the out-of-home work force. With the growing
need for child care for families with infants and very young children, attention was again focused on finding ways for parents and teachers to negotiate answers to the questions: who has the power, and for what? Currently,
the early childhood field is in the process of trying to clarify its professional responsibilities towards families and define appropriate and helpful
practices. The discussion will surely continue throughout the professional
lives of those who read this text.

> There is no consensus in the field about the operational meaning of
> partnership and similar labels, and hence there is the potential for
> enormous variation in the way similar or identical labels are put into
> operation. (Powell 1989, 19)

Although child care has been around for a fairly long time to help social
workers deal with families in a state of crisis, this new form of child care
used by nearly all American families is puzzling to many adults who did

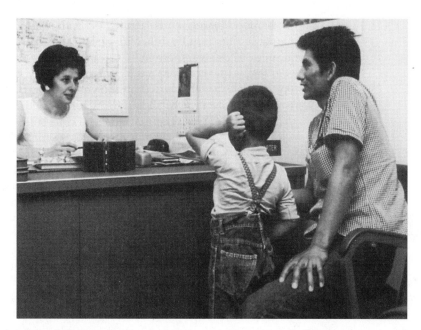

Figure 4-2 Parents are involved in many of the intervention programs. Courtesy Head Start Bureau.

not grow up in such programs and therefore have no clear models of what it is like or how children's experiences should be shared with parents. This creates unresolved tensions about how parental interests and needs should be accommodated in any program. How much weight should be given to parental ideas, based on their commitment to their own children? How much weight should be given to the judgment of the professional staff, based on professional training? Where are the boundaries? The hesitancy is there, along with confusion about what counts as parent involvement.

Just as there is more than one model of parent involvement, there is also more than one set of circumstances that motivate the involvement. At least three separate forces have brought home and school together. One influence on parent involvement has been the research on education and child development that underscores the interdependence of parent, child, and community agencies in providing for optimum development of children. Examples of this include the research on cognitive and social development related to parental interaction and style and involvement with programs, especially the intervention programs. A second set of motives is through force of mandate, enunciated by various laws and funding arrangements, that parents play a part in the education of their children. Examples of mandated parent involvement include Head Start, Title I and Chapter I funding, and the Education for all Handicapped Children Act (PL 94-142) and Amendments (PL 99-451), now reauthorized as Individuals with Disabilities Act (IDEA: PL 101-576). A third influence is community concern and efforts, encouraging parental involvement as a means of both improving the schools and strengthening the family, thus eliminating some problems of concern to the community. Examples here include the collaborative approaches to family support and education that have developed nationwide. All of these motivations suggest larger issues than the get-them-to-bake-cookies-and-go-on-field-trips approach to working with parents.

Today, most American teachers working with young children are not working in programs that have mandates to include parents in a specific way. The rising numbers of private-for-profit child care centers, including child care franchises and family child care homes, and of nonprofit child-care programs, added to the more traditional nursery school programs, place many teachers on the front lines of contact between home and preschool. Some of these teachers are convinced that working with parents may help them find better ways to create a supportive environment for the developing children in their care. Therefore, the text will offer a brief overview of the motives behind the various forms of parent involvement and point in the direction of some of the program patterns and the research done on these, should the students' needs or interests push them to further elaboration.

❖ Research on Child Development as Motivation to Include Parents

A lasting result of the intervention programs of the 1960s and 1970s is a body of research that describes the effects of various kinds of interaction and environmental influences on the development of young children. Such data impels many educators to press for increased parent involvement. Studies suggest that the early years are of utmost importance in setting learning patterns for children and families. It is almost impossible to overemphasize the importance of parenting. Attachment, the strong, mutual, parent-child bond that forms during the first two years of life, is correlated with virtually every aspect of development: physical thriving; the exploration, curiosity, and problem solving that are foundations for cognitive skills; the appearance of language and communication skills; emotional security and social comfort. (See Figure 4-3.) But beyond the overall well-being that comes with that warm parental relationship, studies confirm the assumption that specific factors in the parents' style (particularly mothers) have important and lasting impact on childrens' learning styles, cognitive growth, and educational achievements. For example, it has been noted that many mothers from lower socioeconomic backgrounds, when working with their young children on a particular task, focus most on getting the job done, with little attention to giving verbal directions, helping develop problem-solving skills, or giving positive feedback. It is not surprising, then, that their young children come to the academic environment less prepared for its learning style and interaction with a middle-class teacher who expects children to be able to follow her verbal directions and solve problems independently.

Educational intervention programs are deliberately designed to improve children's first learning opportunities by stimulating changes

Figure 4-3 Attachment is a strong, mutual bond that is crucial for healthy development. Courtesy USM Publications.

within key elements of their early learning environment, including changes in parental behavior. The Head Start program is the longest lasting of all early intervention programs, having started in the mid-1960s as part of President Johnson's War on Poverty. Early studies specific to Head Start suggested an excessive optimism in its evaluation of gains in cognitive development, nevertheless affirming that parental involvement was positively related to children's test scores, academic achievement, and self-concept, as well as to parental feelings of success and involvement in community activities (Midco 1972). Current studies offer more optimistic findings about the long-term effects on school performance, confidence, and self-image, up to fifteen years after children participated in the preschool program (Collins and Deloria 1983). The effectiveness of Head Start is still being questioned, due to inconsistencies in various studies (Schwinhart and Weikart 1986). However, it has been argued that the full impact of a program on children, families, and communities cannot be assessed on the basis of scores alone (Bronfenbrenner 1976).

Other well-known center-based intervention programs include the Perry Preschool Project begun in Ypsilanti, Michigan in the early 1960s. In addition to children attending high-quality early childhood programs for two-and-a-half hours five days a week, parents were visited in their homes by teachers for ninety minutes every week. In this rare long-term study, researchers followed 123 children from the preschool program through their twenty-seventh birthday, as of the latest report (Sweinhart and Weikart, 1993). They did very well in a number of measures of social and educational achievement. They received less remedial education, graduated from high school, and went on to jobs or more education at twice the rate of children without the preschool programs. In addition, they had fewer arrests, fewer teenage pregnancies, and less welfare dependency or other behaviors that create problems for families and the community at large. As adults, they were more likely to be married, own a home, and hold a stable job.

Another well-known intervention program from the early 1960s, the IDS Harlem Project, offered special classes for four-year-olds in neighborhood schools, emphasizing language and cognitive development. The program initiated the first school-based breakfast program. Parents were encouraged to read frequently with their children, and were actively involved through a parent center that worked with them on their own needs and on their relationship to the community and the schools. The program continued working with children and their families until the third grade. Follow-up studies at age twenty-one showed that twice as many were employed as from a control group, one-third more had high school or equivalency diplomas, and 30 percent more had gone on to college or vocational training (Schorr 1988).

As well as center-based programs, Head Start and some intervention efforts also have home-based programs, offering the child and family direct services in their own home. Studies indicate that test scores not only improve over a period of time with this method, but are maintained for several years after the intervention has been discontinued. Effects may be found even in younger children within the family, who had not been directly involved; this indicates that the new skills learned by the parents were having an impact. (See Figure 4-4.) The continuing importance of the Head Start program is indicated by the efforts to expand the program through

Figure 4-4 When parents become involved in their children's programs, there is a correlation with later school success. Courtesy Connie Glass.

Congressional funding so that by 1996 all eligible three-and four-year-olds who want to be enrolled in Head Start can be served.

In Head Start and most other intervention programs, parent participation is considered a necessary component. The Head Start Policy Manual states that involvement of parents is essential:

> Many of the benefits of Head Start are rooted in "change." These changes must take place in the family itself, in the community, and in the attitudes of people and institutions that have an impact on both. (*Head Start Policy Manual* 1970, 3)

In the intervention programs, the emphasis for parent involvement is on (1) parents as learners, increasing parental knowledge about children and their needs, and ways that child development can be nurtured and supported, and (2) parents as teachers, working with professionals in the classroom and/or in the home to enhance and extend the professionals' efforts. The model is for parent education so that families and children can orient themselves successfully toward school. This approach assumes that the educational system is sound, that success in it is desired by a family although they may not know how to achieve it, and that offering chances for new knowledge and attitudes to parents is the key to that success. Some research indicates that the involvement of parents in a program over a period of time is a critical factor in the gains made by children.

Studies also indicate that additional factors related to later school success may be indirectly influenced by parents' involvement in their children's programs. It seems evident that parental interest is positively associated with children's academic achievements. The value the home places on school learning is related to differences in academic performance. In fact, it has been found that home attitudes and factors affect the positive outcome of children's schooling twice as much as do socioeconomic factors, and the single most important factor is the self-esteem of the parent.

There are some obvious ways parental self-esteem is enhanced by involvement in their children's programs. The schools seek parents out to include them as an essential part of their children's education. Improved interaction skills help parents feel more effective with their children and more effective in the parenting role. Parents perceive their own role as important. Experience in leadership skills and decision-making, along with fulfilling social interaction with other adults, all add to parents' positive self-image. (See Figure 4-5.) It is difficult to state that such self-esteem is attributable only to parental involvement in early childhood programs; nevertheless, follow-up studies have shown positive program effects on mothers' financial self-sufficiency and educational levels. Head Start evaluations report that mothers who participated claim fewer psychological problems, greater feelings of mastery, and more satisfaction with their present life situations at the end of the program. Surely spillover effects for children could be anticipated from such positive feelings in parents. (See Figure 4-6.)

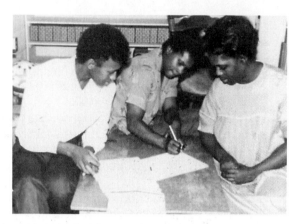

Figure 4-5 Experience in decision-making may help parents' own self-esteem.

Figure 4-6 Parental self-esteem will increase with recognition of involvement in children's programs. Courtesy Bienvenidos Children's Center, Inc.

Research that suggests benefits to the development of children and their parents from parental involvement offers powerful motivation to many programs to work towards parent participation.

❖ Mandated Parent Involvement

When the powers that control funding mandate parent involvement as a requirement of programs, there is no longer any discussion about whether or not to have parent participation! Several legislative efforts have included parent participation as part of the required structure in agencies and actions providing services to children. In addition, recent policies and practice guidelines have proclaimed specific directions for programs to follow in relation to families, sometimes in order to win accreditation or approval of plans. Several examples of mandated parent involvement will be discussed.

Head Start

As a community action program established by the Economic Opportunity Act of 1964, Head Start was required to have "maximum feasible participation" of the families served. In its Policy Manual, Head Start has specified performance standards for four areas of parent involvement:

1. Decision-making about direction and operation of the program, via membership on the Policy Council.
2. Participation in classrooms as volunteers, with the possibility of moving up a career ladder as paid employees.
3. Parent activities planned by the parents themselves.
4. Working with their own children, along with the center staff.

The rationale for parent involvement is stated: "If Head Start children are to reach their fullest potential, there must be an opportunity for Head Start parents to influence the character of programs affecting the development of their children" (*Head Start Policy Manual*, 1). Parents are given a concrete means of doing something for their children. The major role of decision-maker is emphasized to offer parents opportunities to become competent in running the program. Parents set the standards for the hiring of professional staff, often interviewing and selecting staff. They also participate in decisions on budgetary matters.

> The rational for parent participation in decision making is based on the belief that people will not be committed to decisions in which they had no involvement. Furthermore, it is believed that the process of considering information, decision making, and implementation are in themselves educational and aid in developing leadership skills. It also is argued that parents know their own situations best and hence must be involved in planning for their children's education (Hess 1971, 277).

Parent decision-makers influence the agency to become sensitive to the culture and needs of the families served.

> If efforts weren't made to find out who had an interest in this, and efforts weren't made to be patient with that mild interest and fan it, the usual thing would happen. Because poor people were not making decisions, other people *would* be making decisions. We would have missed the essence of the poverty program: to reduce the helplessness people feel about their own fate (Greenburg, quoted in Powell 1989, 5).

In practice, it is obviously not easy for directors and professional staff to share responsibility when decisions must be made. Often conflicting views about what is good for children must be reconciled, potentially a difficult and time-consuming process. Even when they are committed to involving parents, staff must guard against dominating meetings with their greater training and experience in formal meetings and decision-making.

Title I

More recent federal initiatives authorize funds as part of Chapter I of Title I (of PL 100-297). Called Even Start, the family-centered education program funds local efforts to improve the educational opportunities for the nation's children and adults by integrating early childhood education and adult education for parents into a unified family-centered program. (Family-centered is defined as focusing on children and parents as a unit, with the parents becoming active in their children's development, not teaching parents and children in separate and distinct programs.) The mandate calls for plans to build on existing community resources to create new ranges of services that include identification and recruitment of eligible children; screening and preparing parents and children for the program; establishing instructional programs to promote adult literacy; training parents to support the education and growth of their children; preparing children for success in regular schools; providing special training for staff to develop skills to work with parents and children; and integrating instructional services through home-based programs where possible. (See Figure 4-7.)

Figure 4-7 Parents involved in their children's preschool classrooms learn new skills.

Education of Handicapped Children

Parent involvement in plans to provide services for children with special needs was mandated first by PL 94-142, the Education of All Handicapped Children Act of 1975. This law requires parent participation in planning with professionals to develop an individualized education program (IEP) for their children. Parents are enabled to initiate a hearing if they are not in agreement with the child's diagnosis, placement, or IEP. The 1986 Education of the Handicapped Act Amendments require a focus on the family for delivery of services. Parents or guardians are included in a multidisciplinary team that develops an individualized family service plan (IFSP), including a statement of the family's strengths and needs in maximizing the development of the handicapped infant or toddler. These provisions are continued in the reauthorization of the Individuals with Disabilities Act in 1990.

Child Care and Development Block Grants

The Child Care and Development Block Grants, finally funded by the 101st Congress in 1990 and known as the ABC bill during the time of lobbying for its passage, is an historic, free-standing, federal child-care program, the first ever, culminating almost twenty years of efforts following President Nixon's veto of child care legislation in 1971. The legislation lays the foundation for a national system of safe and affordable child care. Many provisions of CCDBG highlight the importance of parental choice and involvement. The bill preserves the rights of parents in the system by stating that nothing in the bill should be applied to "infringe upon or usurp the moral and legal rights and responsibilities of parents." Parents are given the right to help set child-care standards and policies on national, state, and local levels. The legislature sets minimum national standards, including parent involvement, to help parents measure and improve program quality. It is stated that providers of care must ensure unlimited parental access to their children during the day. The bill also funds resource and referral programs to educate parents and the public about child care options and choices, licensing and regulatory requirements, and complaint procedures. Each state must maintain a list of substantiated parental complaints and make it available upon request. These CCDBG provisions recognize the importance of including parents in child care systems.

Goal 2000

In 1990, the first national educational goals were formulated as a result of an Education Summit Conference called by President George Bush. Goal one stated: "By the year 2000, all children in America will start school ready to learn." Parents are specifically mentioned in one of the three objectives to meet this first goal: "Every parent in America will be a child's first teacher and devote time each day helping his or her preschool child learn. Every parent will have access to the training and support they need." The National School Readiness Task Force has made numerous recommendations so that "caring communities" can create vehicles to support the families of young children as they prepare children for later educational success, including parent involvement in development programs for children and family support programs (NASBE, 1991).

Recommendations of Professional Organizations

Beyond these legislative mandates, clear statements issued from several professional organizations point the way towards inclusion of parental involvement in schools for young children as a measure of a quality program.

NAEYC Accreditation

The National Association for the Education of Young Children has developed standards to accredit high-quality programs for young children. Among other things, parent-staff interaction is included as a necessary component. The goal is that parents are to be well-informed about and welcome as observers and contributors to the program.

> *Rationale:* Young children are integrally connected to their families. Programs cannot adequately meet the needs of children unless they also recognize the importance of the child's family and develop strategies to work effectively with families. All communication between centers and families should be based on the concept that parents are and should be the principal influence in children's lives. (NAEYC 1984, 15)

Seven specifics must be incorporated into the accredited program's parent involvement plans:

1. Information about the program is given to new and prospective families, including written descriptions of the program's philosophy and operating procedures.
2. A process exists for orienting children and parents to the center, possibly including a pre-enrollment visit, parent orientation meeting, or gradual introduction of children to the center.
3. Staff and parents communicate about home and center child-rearing practices to minimize potential conflicts and confusion for children.
4. Parents are welcome as visitors at all times; for example, to observe, eat lunch, or volunteer to help in the classroom. Various ways to involve parents and other family members are encouraged, considering special problems of working parents with little time.
5. Verbal and written systems are established for sharing day-to-day information affecting children.

Figure 4-8 NAEYC's Code of Ethics encourages teachers "to respect the dignity of each family and its culture, customs, and beliefs." Courtesy Jakaret Verrswarn, Washington, D.C.

6. Conferences are held at least once a year, and as needed.

7. Other communication methods, such as newsletters, bulletin boards, frequent notes to parents, and telephone calls are used frequently.

The Code of Ethical Conduct and Statement of Commitment, approved by NAEYC's Governing Board in 1989, includes a section of ethical responsibilities to families, articulating seven ideals and eleven specific principles governing actions. (See Figure 4-8.) The ideals include:

1. To develop relationships of mutual trust with the families we serve.

2. To acknowledge and build upon strengths and competencies as we support families in their task of nurturing children.

3. To respect the dignity of each family and its culture, customs, and beliefs.

4. To respect families' child-rearing values and their right to make decisions for their children.

5. To interpret each child's progress to parents within the framework of a developmental perspective and to help families understand and appreciate the value of developmentally appropriate early childhood programs.

6. To help family members improve their understanding of their children and to enhance their skills as parents.

7. To participate in building support networks for families by providing them with opportunities to interact with program staff and families. (Young Children Nov./89 or NAEYC Brochure #503.)

NASBE Report

The report *Right From The Start*, issued in 1988 by the Early Childhood Task Force of the National Association of State Boards of Education, focuses attention on involving parents in the school system from the beginning. One recommendation is for elementary schools to establish early childhood components that will involve parents as essential partners in their children's education, recognizing them as primary influences in children's lives.

> Only through a sincere respect for the parental role can teachers begin to see parents as a source of support for their work and will some parents overcome the suspicion and resistance to approaching educators they may have developed from their own school experiences (NASBE 1988, 19).

National Black Child Development Institute

The National Black Child Development Institute, also concerned about early childhood programs within the public school system, suggests that involving parents is one of ten important "safeguards." Parents should be involved in decision-making related to program policies and curriculum. Specific recommendations include establishing a standing parent committee to work with staff on curriculum issues and making parents active participants in program evaluation.

Some of these mandates and policies result from a growing movement among all citizens, not just ethnic minorities, to press for the community's right to both criticize and support the schools. Parents are learning that their voices can have impact. The existence of "anti-expert" feelings and mistrust of bureaucracy is partially responsible for parents pushing for the right to be involved. (See Figure 4-9.) Most parents have total responsibility for their children, but little control over some of the larger social forces impinging on their children's lives. In the past, when child care was primarily used by families who could not provide for their children, rather than families in the mainstream of American life, it was easier to feel that parents needed no say in what others thought desirable for their children. However, as child care and early education are used increasingly by middle-class parents who choose it as a component of their life-style, parents are increasingly having a say about what they want for their children. This demand for input will continue to increase as the entry age of young children into supplemental care becomes earlier.

Figure 4-9 Parents want to know as much as they can about their child's school life.

It has long been recognized in American society that parents have the primary responsibility for deciding what is in their child's best interest. Public policy now seems concerned with safeguarding family authority in the "education, nurture, and supervision of their children." The increasing official attention to policies involving family matters may lead to more specific mandates regarding parent involvement.

❖ Community Concern for Family Support

The changing demographics of American society that have created changes in the lives of families have focused attention on parents' needs. Parents who today may be more isolated, more stressed, and perhaps poorer, need all the help they can get. As communities count the cost of inadequate parenting and family stress in the numbers of teenage pregnancies, school drop-out rates, drug addictions and other illnesses, crime rates and other antisocial disruptions, there is powerful motivation for schools, social agencies, legislatures, businesses, and other concerned community organizations to mobilize and combine efforts for family support. The family is seen as a complex and dynamic system that sits at the hub of, and is influenced by, other complex systems such as schools, the workplace, the health system, the human services system, and government at every level.

Family resource and support programs have appeared all over the country, offering services to parents that may include parenting education, adult education and job training, emotional support, and varieties of child-care services. The programs are run by teachers, psychologists, social workers, other professionals, or other parents. The difference between the intervention models of the 1960s and 1970s and this more recent family resource movement is that the intervention programs see the child as the unit for intervention, while family resource and support programs see the entire family as the unit for intervention. The focus is not on intervention as a means of solving a deficit problem, but as a developmental service needed by all families, regardless of socio-economic or cultural background, to support them to optimum functioning, particularly at key points in the family life cycle when stresses, crises, and change are the norm. The approach is prevention, not treatment. Not all families need exactly the same kinds of support, so family resource and support programs are individualized, flexible, and adaptive. Collaborative efforts between community agencies offering health, welfare, social services, and education meet the family's comprehensive needs.

State-Funded Family Support Programs

Examples of state-funded family support initiatives include Minnesota's Early Childhood Family Education program, begun in 1975. Operated by local school districts, a variety of approaches is offered to enhance the competence of parents in nurturing the development of their children: child development classes, home visits, parent discussion groups, developmental preschool activities, newsletters, drop-in centers, toy and book lending, and special services for special populations (single parents, Southeast Asian immigrant families).

The Parents as Teachers program in Missouri, also operated through school systems since 1985, offers information and guidance during the third trimester before birth up until the child's third birthday via home visits and individual parent conferences each month, monthly group meetings with other parents, use of a parent resource center at the schools, and periodic screenings for the children.

Kentucky's Parent Child Education program, funded through school districts since 1986, strives to improve the educational future for parents and children by offering GED tutoring for mothers, a preschool program based on the High/Scope developmental model for three- and four-year-olds, joint parent-child activities, and support groups for mothers in self-esteem and competence. Also since 1986, both Connecticut and Maryland have run state-wide systems of Parent Support centers that provide a number of parent education and support services.

Individual Community Efforts

Individual cities and communities have also developed various kinds of programs that offer support and education to parents of young children, including efforts to involve families in early childhood programs. New York City has Giant Step, a program offering health and educational services to four-year-old children, with a family social worker in each classroom. Family Focus, in the Chicago area, operates a number of drop-in centers in a cross section of ethnic and socioeconomic neighborhoods. Parents may choose from various educational and support offerings, while other children are cared for in quality preschool programs. Avance, in San Antonio, Texas, offers a parent support program to Mexican-American families with very young children. The founder of Avance hoped that by teaching parents how to communicate better and motivate their children during the formative years, the high school drop-out rate could be cut, and the cycle of poverty broken.

The Los Angeles Unified School District offers hundreds of parenting and family life education courses. This started as child observation and discussion classes in 1928, attracting primarily middle-class parents. The program has expanded to meet the special needs of many groups of parents—infants and toddlers, adolescents, fathers, working parents, parents who have been ordered by the courts to seek parent education, all socioeconomic classes. Through a multi-disciplinary educational process, parents are given a variety of learning opportunities designed to enhance the parent's competence and the child's growth and development. One typical pattern is for parents and children to come to centers once a week, with some time spent in parent-child activities. A trained teacher models appropriate interaction with children. Later, children are cared for by aides while parents meet for group discussion with professional teachers. Seminars for working parents are offered in the workplace. Since parent education classes are mandated by California state law, there is no registration fee for parent education classes offered through adult and occupational education. Students can earn credit towards high school graduation.

Other similar programs are springing up in communities all over the country. The Family Resource Coalition is a national grassroots organization of 2,000 community programs that offer information, education, advice, and support to families. The purpose of the coalition is to offer information, models of programs, and funding for communities who want to begin their own family resource and support effort. For more information contact Family Resource Coalition, Dept. P, Suite 1625, 230 N. Michigan Ave., Chicago, IL 60601. For sources that describe a number of family resource and support programs in detail, see America's Family Support Programs, Evaluating Programs, Programs to Strengthen Families, Harvard Family Research Project, and Focus on the First 60 Months in the Suggestions for Further Reading section at the end of this chapter.

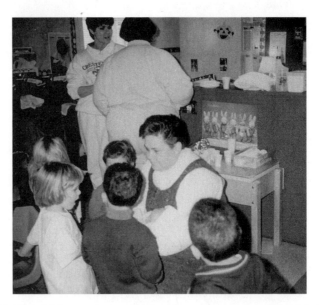

Figure 4-10 The child care center can function as a new form of extended family.

In addition to offering parents psychological support and knowledge necessary to help them understand their children's development and needs, family resource and support programs have set a model for parents and professionals working together as equals: each respecting, valuing, and supporting the contribution of the other. Such a stance makes the preschool become one of the agencies among those offering a constellation of services to the family. The preschool's most important role is to confirm the importance of child rearing and the parent's role in it and not to be a substitute for the family or another source of threat to the unit. The center that shares in child-rearing endeavors with parents may act as a reconstituted form of the extended family, offering parents an escape from the isolation of child rearing. (See Figure 4-10.) The empowering of parents keeps the focus of family power within the family where it needs to be.

As communities focus attention and collaborative efforts to support the family through various programs, the momentum will develop for schools to become increasingly responsive to the needs of families and inclusive of their strengths and resources.

❖ Summary

There are three main reasons to consider ways to involve parents in their children's early care and education:

1. Research on child care and development.

2. Mandates from government and professional associations.

3. Community concern and collaboration for family support programs.

❖ Student Activities for Further Study

1. Find out if your community has a parent cooperative style preschool program. If so, visit and discover in what aspects parents are involved.

2. Interview several preschool teachers. Find out

   a. how they define parent involvement.

   b. what activities and strategies they use to involve parents.

   c. how much time each week or month they would estimate they spend working with parents.

   d. their opinion of the value of parent involvement considering the time involved.

3. Talk to several parents who have children in preschool programs. Find out what they want in terms of their own involvement with the programs and teachers and what they have actually experienced.

4. Find out if there is a Head Start or Title I preschool program in your community. If there is, visit and discover how parents are involved in the program.

5. Call your local United Way office or any information and referral service in your community. Ask what family support and resource organizations exist in your community. Contact those agencies to learn what services they offer for families.

6. Discover if your community has any schools for young children that have received accreditation from NAEYC. If there are, visit to learn how parents have been involved in each of the seven directives listed on pages 98-99. Discuss all findings with classmates.

❖ Review Questions

1. Describe the three motivations for parent involvement.

2. For each of the types of parent involvement, explain the underlying ideas.

❖ Suggestions for Further Reading

Dunst, C., Trivette, C., and Deal, A. (1988). *Enabling and empowering families: principles and guidelines for practice*. Cambridge, MA: Brookline.

Focus on the first 60 months, available from the National Governors Assoc., Hall of the States, 444 North Capital St., Washington, D.C. 20001.

Galinsky, E., and Hooks, W.H. (1977). *The new extended family: day care that works*. Boston: Houghton Mifflin Co.

Gordon, I.J. (1977). Parent education and parent involvement: retrospect and prospect. *Childhood Education, 54*(2), 71–78.

Harvard family research project, available from Harvard Graduate School of Education, Gutman 301, Appian Way, Cambridge, MA 02138.

Kagan, S.L. (1989, October). Early care and education: beyond the school-house doors. *Phi Delta Kappan, 71*(2) 107–112.

Kagan, S.L. (1994, Fall).   Families and children: who is responsible? *Childhood Education, 71*(1), 4–80.

Kagan, S.L., Rowell, D.R., Weissbourd, B.T., and Zigler, E.F. (Eds.) (1987). *America's family support programs: perspectives and prospects.* New Haven: Yale University Press.

Programs to strengthen families. Yale University Bush Center on Child Development and Social Policy.   Available from Family Resource Coalition, 230 N. Michigan Ave., Suite 1625, Chicago, IL 60601.

Schorr, L.B., with Schorr, D. (1988). *Within our reach: breaking the cycle of disadvantage.* New York: Doubleday.

Swick, K., and Graves, S.B. (1993). *Empowering at-risk families during the early childhood years.* Washington, D.C.: NAEYC.

Weiss, H.B., and Jacobs, F. (eds.) (1988). *Evaluating family programs.* Aldine Press.

Zigler, E.F., and Lang, M.E. 1991). *Child care choices: balancing the needs of children, families, and society.* NY: The Free Press.

CHAPTER 5

Benefits of Teacher-Parent Partnerships for Children, Parents, and Teachers

The education and care of a group of young children are serious responsibilities for any teacher in any program or setting, taking enormous amounts of time and energy on any given day. The prospect of adding to this already heavy load by taking time to find ways of communicating and working with parents may be quite daunting. Why would any teacher want to add this role? The answer lies in the profound benefits for children, for parents, and for teachers themselves. Without the establishment of a positive working relationship with parents, much of what teachers would like to do does not get done, or does not get done as well as it could. Everyone in the positive relationship gains and grows. This chapter explores the benefits of establishing a positive working relationship with parents. Teachers have to see for themselves that the effort of working with parents really supports and enhances everything else that they do. Whether you have already had experiences in a classroom or are preparing for them, it is vital for you to become convinced that the work in partnerships with parents will have long-lasting effects.

OBJECTIVES

After studying this chapter, the student will be able to

1. list three benefits for children when parents and teachers work together constructively.

2. list three benefits for parents when parents and teachers work together constructively.

3. list three benefits for teachers when parents and teachers work together constructively.

As the last chapter pointed out, "parent involvement" has a variety of meanings. Variations in the attitudes and emotional responses to these concepts by teachers who are primarily responsible for creating the atmosphere and leading activities may help or hinder such endeavors.

Listen to several teachers in a child development center; we'll see them again later in various activities with parents.

You've already met Jane Briscoe. Jane is twenty-seven years old, single, and has been teaching four-year-olds since she graduated from the child and family development program at State College five years ago. She describes herself as an extrovert, the oldest of a family of four girls. She believes wholeheartedly in working as a partner with parents. She complains that many of her parents seem too busy to spend much time in the classroom, but she keeps on trying.

Anne Morgan is thirty-five, a divorced mother of a ten-year-old daughter and eight-year-old son. She has been working at the center since her divorce four years ago. Before that, her only teaching experience had been student teaching. Anne is often heard to criticize some of the behaviors of parents at the center, who seem to her to be less than conscientious about their parental duties. She does not encourage or invite parents to be involved in her classroom, though she is always polite when she sees them. When a parent with a problem called her at home in the evening, she complained bitterly to her director about the infringement on her private time.

This is John Reynold's first year of teaching preschoolers. He's had to endure a lot of kidding from friends because they feel it's an unusual career choice for an African-American man who played football in college. He's hoping salaries in the field will increase so he can plan to stay in the work that he finds so satisfying. He is deeply involved with the children, conscientious about observing them and making individual plans to fit in with their developmental needs and interests. However, he feels very uncomfortable in his contacts with parents, feeling that they are always watching him. He is unsure how much he should tell them of some of his concerns about the children.

One of the parents asked for a conference next week, and he's afraid this means she wants to criticize. He and his wife expect their first child this year, and he's hoping that may help some of the parents accept him as competent. It's not so much that anyone has questioned his competence with the children, but he's sure that's what they think.

Connie Martinez is enjoying teaching in this center, which she chose because of the good master's program at the university nearby. She is working hard to finish her degree at night, and says that although she believes in parent involvement, she just doesn't have any extra time beyond her planning and preparing activities for the children. She has never told anyone, but she really thinks too many of the parents are letting the center do too much for their young children, and she doesn't believe this taking on of the parents' role should be encouraged. Last week a mother brought in a child who had just come from the doctor's office, and asked if the teacher could give the first dose of the prescribed eardrops, because she had to get right back to work. Connie was very annoyed with this example of parents shifting their own responsibilities to the teacher. When asked if she believes in parent involvement, she says she's too busy to spend much time with parents.

MiLan Ha came to America as a six-year-old. When she graduated from high school, she was second in her class. After a year of college, she took the job in the preschool, and has received some training in workshops. MiLan is a talented artist and encourages creative art with her children. She is a very quiet young woman, with no close friends on the staff. She lives at home with her parents, an uncle, two nieces, and a younger brother. She dreads the conferences and meetings that are scheduled at her preschool, and uses the excuse that her English is not good. In fact, her English is excellent. She is just extremely uncomfortable in social encounters. When parents enter her room, she smiles and quickly turns to the children. The parents feel she is a good teacher, but are also uncomfortable with her.

Dorothy Scott has been teaching for thirteen years. She took five years off when her own son was a preschooler. She has quite definite ideas about child rearing and feels most parents don't handle things with their children as well as they should. She believes it's important to hold conferences and meetings to tell parents what they should be doing, and doesn't mind spending extra time to do these things, though she finds it very discouraging when parents don't attend or disregard her advice. Some of the parents have asked the director privately if it was necessary for their children to be in Mrs. Scott's room, but, unaware of this, she states proudly that she has never had a parent complain.

Jennifer Griffin was hired as an assistant teacher this year after graduating from high school last spring. She is not sure what she wants to do, and felt this would be a job she could do while she was making up her mind. She was rather surprised to have to attend some orientation training and scheduled workshops, as she's always believed her experience in baby-sitting would be enough background for the job. She enjoys the children, but finds herself somewhat puzzled by the guidance policies so she allows her head teacher to handle most of the problems that arise. Because she stays late, it's up to her to respond to parents' questions about their children's day. Because this is a busy time of day, she usually just says that she's just an assistant and wasn't there all day. Her major complaint is the few parents who are frequently late in picking up their children. She's told another teacher that she may really blow up at one particular mother the next time it happens.

Jeannie Sweeney runs a family child care home for six toddlers and preschoolers, including her own three-year-old. She started the business seven years ago when her first child was born so that she could have some income while still caring for her own children. Her earlier job experience has been in retail selling. While she forms close relationships with most of the parents for whose children she cares, she has had several frustrating experiences lately with one family, who have rather different child-rearing values from her own. Despite her request in the parent handbook that children not bring violent toys to school, the child continued to bring action figures that are associated with a television show that Jeannie considers too violent. The parents, when approached, laugh and say Jeannie is taking it too seriously. Jeannie is considering asking them to find other child care, because she feels this is undermining her approach to teaching the children.

Eight different teachers have eight different attitudes that clearly determine the responses and relationships each would offer to parents.

Let's go back and listen to Anne Morgan again. She seems quite definite about her position.

"Look, I'm not their parent, I'm their teacher. There's a lot of difference between the two. All I can do is work with the children for the eight hours or so they're in the classroom at the center. After that they're the parents' responsibility. Goodness knows some of those parents could use some help—some of the things they say and do! I do get annoyed when I work so hard with a child and then see the parent come right in and undo everything I've tried to do. But it's really not my business, I guess. Let them do their job and I'll do mine."

Anne Morgan apparently has decided that there is no purpose in establishing a working partnership between teachers and parents. Chapter 6 looks at her attitudes as barriers to the relationship, but first let's examine the areas Anne is overlooking: the benefits to children, parents, and teachers as the adults learn to communicate and cooperate.

❖ Benefits for Children

Security in a New Environment

In their early years, children are dependent on the key adults in their lives to foster first a sense of security, and then feelings of self-worth. Children develop a sense of trust in the people and world around them as they perceive a predictable and consistent response from their caregivers. Parents are, of course, of primary importance here. An attachment is made to specific people that an infant associates with comfort and warm sensory contact; the attachment is a long-lasting, emotional, learned response. It is this attachment in a parent-child relationship that forms the basis for a child to trust or not trust her environment. Most researchers conclude that this parent-child attachment is crucial for the development of a healthy personality. The presence of the mother or other primary caregiver to whom a child is attached serves as a secure base from which to move out and respond to other aspects of his environment. Preferably, when a child moves into the school world, the first important attachment provides a base of security that can be extended to other adults. (See Figure 5-1.)

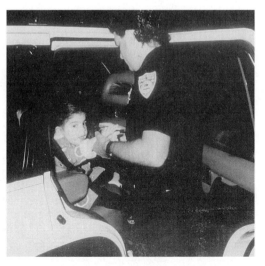 

Figure 5-1 Children can move more easily into new situations from the secure base of that first important attachment.

This task is made easier if familiar, trusted adults are comfortable with the new adults. Contrast the effects, for example, on these two young children.

Susan's mother feels nervous around the new teacher. She feels that the teacher is looking critically at some of the things she does, and does not seem like a friendly person. As a result, she spends little time talking to her, hurrying in and out of the classroom when picking Susan up. She's made some negative comments to Susan's father at home about the classroom situation. Susan's teacher is perturbed by this avoidance behavior, and feels both annoyed and uncomfortable when Susan's mother darts in and out. Susan, puzzled but aware of the strain between the adults, does not allow herself to relax and feel secure in her new classroom world.

Jenny's parents, on the other hand, looked long and hard before they found a preschool that seemed to match their beliefs about child rearing. They took the time to talk with the teacher at length; they discovered that they shared some leisure-time interests. Both parents and teacher now feel comfortable and trusting as they share conversations daily. Jenny seems to feel that her circle of loved and trusted adults has widened; she moves easily back and forth from home to school.

A young child's anxiety in a new school experience may be lessened if there is not an abrupt division between home and school. Children thrive when they feel a continuity between parents and teachers that can be present only when the adults have reached out in an effort to understand and respect each other. (See Figure 5-2.) Just as a teacher's first task in relating to a young child is to build a sense of trust and mutual respect, the same

Figure 5-2 Children feel more secure when their parents appear comfortable with their teachers. Courtesy Olga Solomita.

task is important in working with parents. It is not realistic to expect to like all parents. However, it is essential and possible for teachers to respect all parents for their caring and efforts, and their central position in their children's lives. In most cases, parents do care. This belief is the basis for all teacher interaction.

> Obviously it is not entirely possible to maintain continuity in all areas, nor is it necessarily advantageous to do so. In the case of young children, however, it is believed that such continuity serves to support optimal development by providing the child with a consistent, predictable, social world (Belsky et al. 1982, 101).

Sense of Self-Worth

Children also gain in feelings of self-worth if they perceive that their parents are valued and respected by others. A child's sense of who she is is closely connected with the sense of who her parents are. If her parents receive positive feedback, she also feels worthwhile and valued. On the other hand, if a child observes a teacher ignoring her parents or treating them with obvious distain, her own self-esteem suffers.

> Jenny beams when her teacher comes over to greet her father in the morning and ask how the weekend camping trip went. In her eyes, her teacher and father are friends, and this means her father is somebody special in her teacher's classroom. This makes Jenny herself feel she has been treated in a special way and is therefore valued.

The presence of parents and their welcoming acceptance by a teacher are especially valuable in affirming for children of ethnic and cultural minorities a sense of value for and integration of their own culture in the classroom world. (See Figure 5-3.) The teacher who makes the effort to learn even a greeting word or two in the language of minority families demonstrates such acceptance. We'll talk more in Chapter 15 about classroom practices that convey inclusiveness.

Knowledgeable and Consistent Responses

Another benefit for children in a constructive parent-teacher partnership is the increased ability of all adults to guide and nurture a child's development knowledgeably. Parents and teachers who can comfortably share personal observations and insights, general knowledge and ideas, and specific incidents and reactions expose each other to a wealth of information that may help them provide the most appropriate response for each child. Such an exchange of information surely benefits the child.

Figure 5-3 The welcome and acceptance of her parents are especially valuable for the minority child. Courtesy Olga Solomita.

Last month Jenny missed her daddy very much when he was out of town on a long business trip. At home she became clinging and demanding of her mother. Miss Briscoe noticed lots of crying at school and easy frustration with everyday tasks. At first she was puzzled by the sudden change, but when Jenny's mother shared her description of the behavior at home and the temporary change in the family pattern, she was able to help Jenny talk openly about her concern for her daddy. She read a story book at group time about a daddy who sometimes had to go away; Jenny took it off the shelf almost daily to read it by herself. How lucky for Jenny that her teacher knew, so didn't simply respond to the new crying by seeing it as an undesirable behavior and either ignoring or punishing it.

In some cases, teachers and parents may work together to provide consistent responses, feeling it may help children's learning if all adults respond to specific behaviors in the same way. For example, when Roger's response to frustration is to whine, his parents and teachers have agreed they will ignore the whining and redirect his attention to something else. This approach seems to be helping him decrease the whining.

Some of the gains for children resulting when parents and teachers cooperate, share information, and expand their skills are measurable. (See Figure 5-4.) Research reveals that children gain in academic skills, positive self-concept, and verbal intelligence when extensive parent participation with teachers is required (Honig 1982).

The three benefits to children are

1. increased security in the new school environment,

2. increased feelings of self-worth, and

3. increased number of helpful responses and appropriate experiences due to adults' sharing of knowledge.

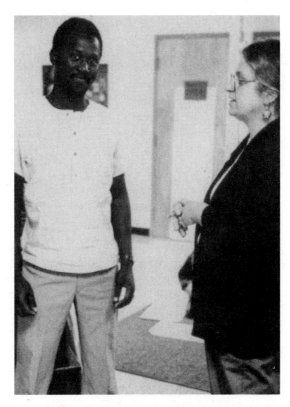

Figure 5-4   When teachers and parents share information, the child benefits. Courtesy Olga Solomita.

❖ Benefits for Parents

What do parents gain from developing a working relationship with their children's teachers?

Feelings of Support for Parenting

An immediate benefit is the feeling of support in carrying out the responsibilities of parenthood. As discussed earlier, the changing nature of American life means that many parents are removed from the natural supports of family and roots, traditions, and models, when they begin the usually unprepared-for task of parenting. The many questions and uncertainties that occur in everyday activities often make parenting lonely, worrisome, and indeed overwhelming. Galinsky writes of the contemporary myth that each modern isolated family feels it should be able to do everything for itself, to be complete on its own (Galinsky and Hooks 1977). In reality, parents can never be totally independent; they need others to watch their child while they work or go to the store, or just to talk to, to make it all less overwhelming. Having an adult who cares about their particular child, to share both the good and the not-so-good times of day-to-day life, is extremely helpful in alleviating anxieties. It has been noted that after mothers have a chance to express their feelings and concerns to others willing to listen with an empathetic ear, they often exhibit more patience with their children, listen more carefully to them, and are more responsive to their needs than before the opportunity to unburden themselves. A parent-teacher relationship can offer much needed support to parents. (See Figure 5-5.) In this way, it has been suggested that the child care center and its personnel can function as a new kind of extended family, part of the constellation of community support that each family needs.

Knowledge and Skills

In addition, teachers provide a background of information and skill from their expertise and experience in dealing with a variety of children, as well as a model for positive guidance techniques. There is no question that parents possess firsthand knowledge about their children, but frequently the experience of living with their children is their only opportunity to learn about child development. Many parents never have the opportunity to learn relevant developmental information and often misunderstand the nature of developing children. They may be unaware of appropriate nurturance at each phase, as evidenced by the current tendency of many parents to push their "hurried children" into early academics, assuming that

Figure 5-5 A parent-teacher relationship can give parents the feeling of being not quite alone in their responsibilities. Courtesy Head Start Bureau.

"sooner is better," rather than understanding that young children are not ready for such learning. When teachers share their knowledge of child development, they help parents respond more appropriately to their children's developmental needs.

Teachers have specific education in the principles of child development and are trained in effective guidance techniques. When parents converse with teachers, and watch and listen to teachers working with children, they can expand their knowledge and ideas and become more effective as parents. (See Figure 5-6.)

"You know," says Jenny's mother, "I sure am glad to have you tell me most four-year-olds tend to get a little out of bounds; when she began to spit last month, I was horrified. Jenny's the first four-year-old I've ever known. My sister's family lives in California, so I never had a chance to see much of her children at that age. It makes it a little easier to live with Jenny to know that it's not just her, or to think we've done something wrong. And it's also been helpful to watch you dealing with some of that behavior in the classroom. It would never have occurred to me to be so calm and suggest she go into the bathroom to spit."

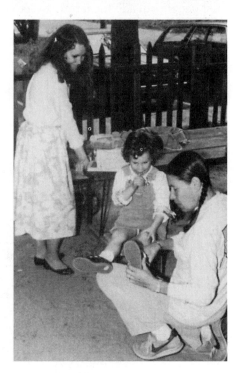

Figure 5-6 Parents learn new skills by watching and listening to teachers working with children. Courtesy CPCC Media Productions—Mike Slade.

Enhancing Parental Self-Esteem

It is essential that parental self-esteem develops in a positive way. Parents who believe in themselves are far better able to develop and use appropriate parenting skills; parents who feel self-confident are far better able to provide their children with a secure environment and foster positive feelings of self in their children. The most important predictor of children's school success is related to positive parental self-esteem. Studies indicate that there is a definite impact on the development of feelings of competence and self-esteem in parents involved in their children's programs. (See Figure 5-7.)

Perhaps one reason for the increase in parental self-esteem is that parents can get specific positive feedback on their functioning as a parent, feedback that is especially meaningful because it comes from an "expert" in child development.

> "You know," says Miss Briscoe, "I admire the way you talked with Jenny this morning. You were sensitive to her feelings, but also quite definite that you had to go. That approach helped her see where the limit was."

Preschool teachers are powerful people, because in many cases they are the first people outside the family to see children and their parents on an ongoing basis; their approval is important to parents.

A positive feeling of parental self-esteem is also nurtured when parents feel they are a vital part of their child's school world as well as home

Figure 5-7   All parents enjoy the feeling that they are part of their child's school world.

world. Teachers who hep parents feel included in the education process contribute to feelings of competency in parents. Parents feel they are in control, sure that their children are getting the kind of care they want, rather than feeling that control is elsewhere, and they are powerless to provide what their child needs. This feeling of being necessary and included is helpful for all parents, especially fathers, who often feel cut off by our culture, unimportant to the overall needs of the child.

> "You know, Miss Peters," Jenny's father said at a recent conference, "I'm very glad you suggested I'd be welcome to come and spend some time any afternoon I can get off work a little early. I really like knowing who the kids are that Jenny talks about at home—just to see what part of her day here is like. It's important to me not to feel as though I have nothing to do with part of her life."

The three ways parents benefit from positive teacher-parent relationships are

1. feelings of support in the difficult task of parenting,
2. knowledge and skills gained by parents to help them in child rearing, and
3. enhanced parental self-esteem from receiving positive feedback on their parenting actions and feeling included in their child's life away from home

❖ Benefits for Teachers

What about teachers, whose efforts to develop a positive working relationship may be the greatest? Are there benefits to justify such efforts? Again, the answer must be yes.

Anyone who has worked in a preschool classroom is aware of the uniqueness of each child's personality and needs. Teachers have learned much that is appreciable about the general characteristics of children at particular ages and stages, but in order to be effective with each child, additional information is needed. Each child comes to the classroom with a past history—years of reactions, experiences, and characteristic styles of behaving that are unique. Each family has its own dreams and expectations for its children, its own patterns of behavior and mores related to the specific cultural or ethnic ethos from which it comes, its own structure, relationships, and needs. Teachers need to know all this and learn it early in their associations with children and families. With this specialized knowledge, parents are in a position to assist teachers in working with their children. One way of describing the difference in the kinds of knowledge that parents and teachers have of children is that parents' knowledge is vertical, having developed longitudinally through the child's life; teachers' knowledge is horizontal, encompassing much about a particular age-group. At the point

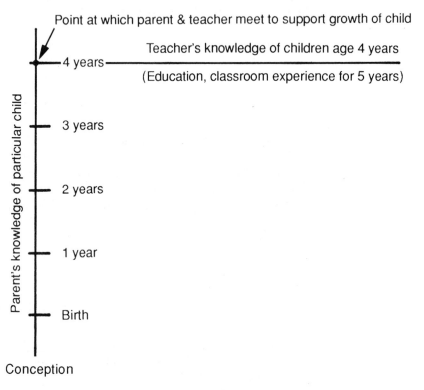

Figure 5-8 Teachers' knowledge is horizontal; parents' is vertical. Where these two points intersect, parents and teachers can strengthen the other's effects.

where these two lines intersect, teachers and parents can support each other in a partnership of knowledge. (See Figure 5-8.) To leave untapped such a resource would reduce teachers' abilities to work to optimum capacity with each child. Teachers who build an effective communication with parents are less likely to be frustrated while working with the many unknowns in children and are more likely to meet realistic goals for each child and support each family in reaching their own particular goals.

At the same conference Miss Peters commented how helpful it has been for her to know, before Jenny's entrance to the classroom, that she was a quiet child who normally took a long time to warm up in a new situation—"Otherwise I'd have been concerned. But that helped me give her lots of time and support and not to expect too much talking until she was comfortable. I was also glad to know she especially liked puzzles—that way I could plan something special for her during those first days."

Positive Feedback Increases Confidence

In addition, when teachers are open to learning from parents, there is much knowledge about the practical aspects of bringing up children that can be learned. Not only can this help a teacher who has not had the first-hand experience of parenthood, but it may increase the teacher's store of ideas to pass along to other parents.

> "You know, I got some really good mealtime tips from one of my parents. Let me share them with you. In fact, the ideas would likely be helpful to everyone—I'll include them in my next newsletter."

Teachers' self-confidence will grow as positive feedback is received from others regarding their job performance. To have their efforts valued and respected, as demonstrated by parents' positive response and desire to cooperate, is an important contribution to teachers' sense of professional well-being. (See Figure 5-9.) There is no question that teachers have frustrating and negative experiences as they work with parents; there is no such thing as one hundred percent success in such complex endeavors involving human personalities, needs, and other foibles. But for teachers who honestly and warmly try to reach out to parents, there is enough success for them to realize that their efforts are effective and appreciated.

The reaching out may be difficult, especially for teachers who are not very comfortable in social situations. In fact, one effect of enhanced teacher self-confidence is that their own social skills may develop and expand. Teachers' personal growth is often a by-product of their experiences with parents that garner positive feedback for them.

Figure 5-9 Teachers benefit when they see their efforts are valued and respected. Courtesy CPCC Media Production—Mike Slade.

Parents involved in schools and centers learn so much about the functioning of preschool teachers that they often become advocates for teachers, urging communities and centers to establish working policies and personnel conditions that benefit teachers and allow them to do their best for children.

"For all you do, that's what they pay you? I think that should be brought up with the board. I'm writing a letter to the editor. This community needs to get behind the efforts to make good preschool education available to all who need it. It's too important."

It is evident that the advocacy efforts of teachers to support quality for children's programs can be greatly strengthened when parents recognize the benefits of good early education and join in supporting teachers' efforts.

It is interesting to note that, through partnership, both teachers and parents may have some of their personal emotional needs satisfied on the subject of competence. "Education is a very human partnership. It depends for its strength, to a great degree, on how teachers and parents feel about each other and what they do to meet each other's needs" (Rich, in Preece and Cowden 1993).

Parental Resources for Enriched Learning Experiences

Teachers have only the resources of one person, with their own limitations on time, energy, knowledge, creativity, experiences, and other resources. Parents may offer additional resources in all these commodities, as well as others. (See Figure 5-10.) The learning experiences teachers can offer children in the classroom are multiplied and enhanced by parents who

Figure 5-10 More one-to-one attention to children can be available when parents spend time in the classroom.

feel invited and included in the educational process. Parents learn a good deal about interacting with their own children and often "teach" very well. Parents as a classroom resource will be discussed further in chapter 12.

A review of research on the importance of involving parents in the education of their young children strongly suggests that the effectiveness of teachers and their programs is reinforced and increased by an active involvement of the families of preschool children. (See chapter 4 and Powell 1989.) One of the reasons for this is that parents can reinforce the teachers' learning activities by conversations and activities in the home if they are fully aware of what is happening in the school.

The three benefits for teachers are

1. increased knowledge, which enables teachers to be more effective with each child.

2. positive feedback, which increases their own feelings of competence in their profession, and advocacy of their interests, and

3. parental resources to supplement and reinforce their own efforts in providing an enlarged world of learning.

The best way for teachers to have an impact, especially a long-lasting impact, on the children in their care is to work to strengthen and meet the needs of the whole family. The partnership between teachers and parents benefits them both, but most of all it benefits the children for whom they both care.

> Beyond any question, when you work closely with parents you pay a price. You adjust to the other fellow's ideas, sometimes going faster and sometimes going at a slower pace than you desire. But there are rewards in working together that isolation could never bring. Teachers do gain. Parents gain. And children are the real winners (Hymes 1975).

❖ Summary

Because there are benefits for all—teachers, parents, and children—it should also be stated that it is difficult to discover any disadvantages to forming a healthy sense of working together. Why, then, are not more teachers and parents involved in constructive partnerships? The answer may lie in examining attitudes and behaviors on both sides that act as barriers to effective teacher-parent relationships.

❖ Student Activities for Further Study

1. Choose one of the teachers described in this chapter. How are you like this teacher? Is there anything you want to change in yourself regarding your attitudes about parent involvement?

2. Talk with a preschool teacher about what he feels he has gained and/or learned from his working relationships with parents. Compare your findings with the benefits to teachers discussed in the chapter.

3. Ask a preschool teacher to think of one specific child in her class. What are some of the things she has learned about that child that could only have been learned through the parents?

4. Talk with a parent whose child has been in a preschool classroom this year. What are some of the things the parent feels he has gained from the teacher?

5. Ask both teachers and parents for examples of situations regarding children where adults have been able to work as partners, coordinating plans and information.

6. Do a study of a group of parents in your school. Compile a list of potential resources those parents offer the school and/or your teaching efforts.

❖ Review Questions

1. List three benefits for children when parents and teachers work together as partners.

2. List three benefits for parents when parents and teachers work together as partners.

3. List three benefits for teachers when parents and teachers work together as partners.

❖ Suggestions for Further Reading

Baskill, J. (1989). *Parents and teachers—partners in learning*. Richmond Hill, Ontario: Scholastic Texts Publications.

Greenberg, P. (1989). Parents as partners in young children's development and education: a new American fad? Why does it matter. *Young Children, 44*(4), 61–75.

James, D. (1989, Fall). Parent involvement. *Research Forum, 5.*

Stone, J.G. (1987). *Teacher parent relationships*. Washington D.C.: NAEYC.

CHAPTER 6

Potential Barriers to Teacher-Parent Partnerships

Although we can agree on the benefits for children, parents, and teachers discussed in the last chapter, we can also agree that some of the attitudes conveyed by the teachers you met in that chapter are not uncommon among teachers working with young children. The complexity of human relationships brings particular attitudes and behaviors existing in teachers and parents that may act as obstacles to communicating openly and comfortably and establishing working relationships. This does not mean that these negative responses are valid reasons for abandoning attempts to create partnerships; rather, these potential barriers must be recognized, examined, and understood by teachers on whom rests the full burden for trying to remove as many barriers as possible. As teachers consider the attitudes and emotions that act to distance psychologically, and some of the program's practices that create physical separateness, they can also discover new awareness of ways they can bridge those gaps. There will always be some barriers and some failures to topple those barriers. This chapter is intended to raise teacher awareness, in order to continue to erase some of the barriers.

OBJECTIVES

After studying this chapter, the student will be able to

1. discuss several attitudes of parents and teachers that may create communication barriers.
2. discuss several emotional responses of parents and teachers that may cause communication barriers.
3. discuss several external factors in the lives of parents and teachers that may create communication barriers.

❖ Why Are There Barriers?

Chapter 5 explored the potential for parents and teachers to offer each other strength, support, and knowledge as they work together for children's benefit. But why is it that sometimes the relationship never gets off the ground?

Some of the parents and teachers introduced earlier may help demonstrate the reasons.

John Reynolds is quite ready to admit it: He's frankly terrified of the prospect of his contacts with parents in his first year of preschool teaching.

"Look, I'm just feeling my way with the kids this year. I'm sure those parents are wondering what's going on, and I'm not comfortable with them asking many questions. And I don't even have any kids of my own, to draw on that experience. I'm sure they wouldn't even listen to me. What's more, some of these parents are well-established in their own professions—I'm not even sure how to talk to them."

Connie Martinez shares his negative feelings about the parent involvement philosophy at the center, but for different reasons.

"Enough time goes into running a good classroom for young children without asking teachers to spend even more time on trying to do things for parents. And if you ask me, the whole idea is wrong, anyway. Parents today are pushing their responsibilities off on someone else, always asking the government or somebody to do more for them. Many of my parents live in public housing and get their child care subsidized already. It's just wrong; the more you do for them, the more they'll let you do. How will they learn to do a good job with their own kids that way, if we're helping them every step of the way? My parents raised six children without any preschool teacher working along with them."

Dorothy Scott shares her pessimism.

"I've been working with young children for thirteen years now and, believe me, the majority of parents just don't seem to care. I've knocked myself out planning meetings to teach them the things they ought to know and most of them never show up. You tell them what they should do, and they keep on doing the same old ways. It can be pretty frustrating, let me tell you."

MiLan Ha won't say much about her feelings.

"I really wish I could just work with my children without anyone suggesting I should also be working with the parents. When parents begin to talk to me, I just freeze up and can't think of a thing to say. With the children I'm fine."

These teachers are expressing strong attitudes that clearly will influence any interactions they have with parents. But some of the parents have equally potent viewpoints.

Sara Leeper says: "That teacher can hardly stand to talk to me. You can see her disapproval written all over her face. I'd like to know who she thinks she is, sitting in judgment over me. I'm a good mother.

Jane Weaver is very uncomfortable around the teacher, but for different reasons.

"She just knows so much. I never went to college and sometimes I don't quite understand some of the words she uses when she talks about what she's trying to accomplish with the children. I'm afraid I'd show my ignorance if I said anything. And she's so very expert—she always knows what to do with those children. She makes me feel—dumb."

Mary Howard explains her biggest problem with the teacher: "I feel like a nuisance. I mean, she's always so busy I hate to bother her to ask her anything. I feel just like I'm butting in, and that makes me feel kind of bad. Cynthia's with her all day long and sometimes I just feel left out."

These comments exemplify some of the attitudes that will be explored. Consider these ideas and emotions in light of your experiences; think of parents and teachers you have observed. Have you heard comments or seen behaviors that convey discomfort or negative attitudes about working with one another? Many of the reactions are very natural human reactions that constitute a problem only when they are unrecognized interferences between parent and teacher. Simply becoming aware of some of these will help.

When considering parent-teacher communication, remember that the initiative must come, in most cases, from a teacher. Since this communication takes place in school, a teacher's home territory, it gives her the advantage of her own environment, and with this advantage comes the burden of responsibility. A teacher is responsible for creating an atmosphere open to dialogue. She must recognize not only those experiences and feelings of parents that might stand between them, but also analyze her own attitudes and behaviors so that she does nothing to exacerbate parents' discomfort.

In one sense, parents and teachers can be described as natural adversaries, not because of the dynamics of any individual relationship, but because of the nature of the relationship that emerges from the roles defined by the social structure of society. Parents and teachers generally have different perspectives in how to approach and view a child, a difference that evolves from the definitions of their social and cultural roles. Our culture defines parents as ultimately responsible for their children's well-being. Because of their attachment, parents tend to be protective and highly emotionally invested in their child. Their perspective is quite focused on the individual, having particular expectations, goals, and intense feelings for their children. Teachers are given the cultural role of rational guide; their perspective can be described as more universal, concerned about children in the context of broad goals of socialization and education (Lightfoot 1975). A teacher can be affectionate and still able to regard a child with an objectivity not possible for a parent, what Katz calls a "detached concern" (Katz 1980). Katz distinguishes between mothering and teaching in several dimensions.

To amplify on these distinctions:

Role Dimension 1: Scope of Functions. Parents must play every role related to the care and development of their children, from trips to the dentist and barbershop to making decisions about dance lessons or vacation plans. It is their responsibility to make sure that the child is healthy, well nourished, emotionally secure, socially happy, stimulated, and responded to cognitively, and that tomorrow's laundry has been prepared! Teachers are concerned about the child's more limited classroom life.

Role Dimension 2: Intensity of Affect. Parents are highly emotional regarding everything that concerns their children, both positive and negative. Teachers are only mildly emotional about the same children, because they are less dependent on children in the classroom meeting their emotional needs.

Distinctions Between Mothering and Teaching in Their Central Tendencies in Seven Dimensions.

ROLE DIMENSION	MOTHERING	TEACHING
1. Scope of Functions	Diffuse and Limitless	Specific and Limited
2. Intensity of Affect	High	Low
3. Attachment	Optimum Attachment	Optimum Detachment
4. Rationality	Optimum Irrationality	Optimum Rationality
5. Spontaneity	Optimum Spontaneity	Optimum Intentionality
6. Partiality	Partial	Impartial
7. Scope of Responsibility	Individual	Whole Group

Source: Lilian Katz, *Current Topics of Early Childhood Education*, v. 3 (Ablex Publishing Corp., 1980), figure 1, p. 49.

Role Dimension 3: Attachment.   Parents are deeply involved in the mutual attachment that endures over time and is essential to the child's development. Teachers care sincerely about children, but do not form deep attachments since they know their relationship is temporary.

Role Dimension 4: Rationality. Parents are supposed to be quite "crazy" about their children; children thrive when they bask in unconditional love. Because of their emotional distance, teachers are able to be quite deliberate and objective in their analysis of a child's strengths and needs.

Role Dimension 5: Spontaneity. Because of attachment and related emotions, parents will often act by emotional reaction, in quite unpremeditated ways. Teachers are more likely to be able to keep cooler heads and can plan and speak with more objectivity.

Role Dimension 6: Partiality. Parents are most likely quite biased on their child's behalf. When teachers complain that some parents seem to believe there is only one child in the classroom, this is a reflection of the parent's partiality. Teachers, however, are expected to show no favoritism or partial treatment of any particular child.

Role Dimension 7: Scope of Responsibility. Parents are responsible for and responsive to the needs and lives of their individual children. Teachers are responsible for the needs of a whole group of children.

Looked at this way, it is not surprising that parents and teachers do frequently approach the same issue from very different perspectives.

Today, more than ever, parents and teachers run into difficulty because so many very young children are being cared for by other adults, causing an overlapping of parents' and teachers' spheres of influence. Much of what caregivers of children in the first three years or so do for them are things also done by parents when they are present. The culture has not yet moved to clearly define roles within this new context, nor can they be easily defined or separated.

> Children who spend a full day every day in day care are usually there to meet adult necessities rather than their own. This puts a psychological burden on day-care teachers and the parents they serve. The nursery school teacher can feel proud that she is supplying something that is her unique contribution to enriching childhood. The day-care teacher, particularly of children under three, can have no such confidence. Devoted teachers in most day-care centers may have confidence that they are giving the children in their care a good and enriching experience, but it is still viewed as a substitute for parental care (Platt 1991, 105).

The issue is further complicated by the fact that it is important that young children become attached to adults who care for them during so many of their waking hours in their parents' absence. But attachment is a mutual thing. And when two or more adults are attached to the same child, they frequently engage in "gate-keeping," a phenomenon described by Dr. Berry Brazelton as a subtle attempt to undermine the position of the other adult in relation to the loved child. It is no wonder that the ambiguous roles and responsibilities, complicated by emotional responses of competition, lead to an uncomfortable mistrust of the other that is usually not admitted or discussed. An acceptance of the differences and, perhaps, conflicts in the relationship of parents and teachers should not also imply an acceptance of distancing, mistrust, and hostility as inevitable. These responses result from a lack of communication and from mistaking differences for complete alienation.

More powerful influences than these ambiguous and emotional roles impel parents and teachers as they develop a working relationship. It is important to remember that when people come together, they do so as individuals whose personalities, past experiences, present needs, and situations all determine their perceptions and reactions. "Humans of all ages get caught in a powerful web spun of two strong threads; the way they were treated in the past and the way the present bears down on them (Hymes 1974, 16). Teachers need to examine sensitively the words and behaviors that pass between parents and themselves; to do so requires self-esteem and a sense of competence, or teachers will be reluctant to undergo so searching an examination.

Lombana suggests that most of the barriers of effective parent-teacher relationships can be separated into three categories: (1) those caused by human nature, (2) those caused by the communication process, and (3) those caused by external factors (Lombana 1983). It is worthwhile to consider these in more detail.

❖ Barriers Caused by Human Nature

There is a strong desire in most people to preserve their self-image; anything perceived as a threat to an individual's self-image serves as a barrier, as an individual avoids the source of the threat. It is interesting to note that the behavior that one person in the parent-teacher relationship might use to protect her self-concept might trigger an equally defensive behavior in the other person, setting up a cycle. For example, the teacher who remains coldly professional to hide her own insecurities and keep a parent at a distance may cause the parent to become hypercritical and demanding in order to get the teacher to pay attention to him. Several fears relate to protecting self.

Fear of Criticism

As John Reynolds expressed, many teachers dread parental criticisms and so avoid any possible source of these. This is particularly true of young teachers who fear that their position may not be accepted because of a lack of teaching experience or because they have not experienced parenthood firsthand. Teachers unsure of their own abilities fear any negative feedback that may confirm their inner doubts, dreading parents' discovery of their mistakes or inadequacies. They put an invisible "Do Not Enter" sign on their classroom door that conveys to parents that their presence and opinions are not welcome.

> Jennifer Griffin says: "I hate having these parents watching me—it's worse than the director coming in. They ask so many questions—it's as if they're just trying to find something I've done wrong."

Parents are also particularly vulnerable to criticism. Aware of the cultural myths and facts that place the burden for children's success and positive functioning squarely on parents' shoulders, most parents dread any indication that they are not doing a good job. With many parents uncertain that what they are doing is "right," yet feeling they must prove it is right in order to be accepted as fit parents, a defensiveness against any suggestion of change often results. If a teacher gives the impression of evaluating parents' efforts, it may be easier to avoid her or be defensive rather than hear the results of her evaluation. Hearing teachers speak of imperfections in their own child may seem like implied criticism of their parenting.

> Jane Weaver admits: "When I saw the teacher watching me scold Sandra the other day, I felt as nervous as a kid myself. You could tell by the look on her face she didn't like it. Well, I don't care—she doesn't have to live with her and I do. What does she know about children, anyway—she never had any of her own twenty-four hours a day."

Regardless of their personal outlook and how they view their parenting performances, most parents find it difficult to seek outside help, even under serious circumstances. It is incorporated into the self-image of most American parents that they should work things out for themselves as a sign of personal strength and parenting success. Therefore, for many parents, reaching out to share responsibilities with teachers is contrary to their self-image. For some parents, raising children is a private affair, and many parents consider that they know their child best and need no meddling in their matters by teachers.

Because of their strong attachment, many parents see their children as extensions of themselves; to comment negatively on one is like commenting negatively on the other. Teachers need to remember Katz's observation that it is not possible for parents to deal with information about their child from a rational and objective perspective. Their responses are emotional and intense.

> "It really bothers me when the teacher says Sandra is shy. I've always been pretty quiet myself, and it just hurts to hear her say that."

When children go to school, both parents and children are meeting their first big test: "How will he—and therefore we—do?" Parents have made a heavy emotional investment in their children and may avoid a teacher as a source of possible hurt and criticism.

Fear Hidden Behind a "Professional" Mask

An insecure teacher may depend too heavily on the image of the professional person who knows the answers and is all-important in the task of caring for children. This exaggeration of professional behavior intimidates parents and keeps them at a distance, which may be a teacher's unrecognized goal. Such a teacher has a hard time acknowledging the importance of parents' contributions or the right of parents to be involved. When one's sense of being in control is shaky, it is difficult to share power.

> "After all, I've been trained to do this. I frankly don't see why parents who haven't should be able to plan policies, make suggestions, or interfere with what I do in my classroom."

Exhibiting the aloofness of false professionalism or the unwillingness to recognize and respect parents' significant role masks a teacher's uncertainties that she hopes will go unchallenged.

Parents perceiving a teacher's self-imposed distance of excessive professionalism withdraw behind fear and resentment.

> "I'd like to ask her some questions, but she never seems to have time. The other day she frowned and suggested I make an appointment to talk with her. Why does she make it such a big deal?"

It is hard to communicate comfortably across this distinctly cold gap. Parents are reluctant to spend energy in a situation where they feel they are not really needed or wanted.

> "Who's she trying to kid? She really thinks she does a better job with them anyway—why does she even bother to ask parents to come in?"

Teachers who develop "territoriality"—resentment of having parents invade their turf—are often trying to draw lines that prevent fearful encounters with parents. Another possible reaction of parents faced with a teacher's excessive professionalism is to become aggressive in trying to bridge the gap, further alienating or frightening a teacher by demonstrating "pushy" behaviors.

> "There's no way I'm going to let these parents come into my classroom. Mrs. Randall called the other day and insisted she wanted to come sing some Christmas songs with the children. Next she'll be telling me what to plan. Give them a little power and they'll take over!"

Fear of Failure

Working with parents is an ongoing process; it takes time and effort to build a relationship, and that relationship is only the beginning. Teachers looking for immediate results from their efforts will be disappointed. If teachers are not prepared to accept the idea that it is an ongoing process and expect immediate evidence of effectiveness, they might be tempted to abandon all attempts, rather than leave themselves open to a sense of failure.

> Hear Dorothy Scott again: "Well, I'm certainly not going to bother planning another open house. Fifteen children in my room, and five parents show up. It's a big waste of my time."

Certainly no one wants to feel unsuccessful in her efforts, and teachers who define parent involvement only by numbers present at any one event may protect themselves in the future by withdrawing, rather than feel their time and effort are not yielding the results they want.

Fear of Differences

The majority of teachers are middle-class and have experienced little beyond middle-class life-styles, value systems, and ways of thinking. Teachers encountering parents from a variety of backgrounds, experiences, and viewpoints may fall into the all-too-human tendency to stereotype people, their conditions and actions. Even without deep prejudices or bigotry, assumptions made on the basis of stereotypes create barriers that preclude true openness to an individual and his actual personality, needs, and wishes. It is sometimes easier to criticize and avoid than to try to understand and empathize. The barriers may rise in as many directions as there are classes and cultures.

> Connie Martinez talks about some of her families. "Well, of course, the Butlers are college-educated and pretty well-off, so I expect them to do a good job with their children. They really don't need much advice from me." (The Butlers are inexperienced and uneducated in child development and guidance, and are very shaken by the breakup of their marriage. They hunger for advice and support.) "Sylvia Ashley's on welfare, so I don't suppose she'll make the effort to come to a parent conference." (Sylvia Ashley has never yet missed an opportunity to talk with any teacher who offered it.)

It is easy for human beings to attend selectively to information that is consistent with their beliefs and self-concepts and to screen out, ignore, or criticize those things that differ from their experiences and beliefs.

> Ignoring all the good parenting Sara Leeper and Ginny Parker do, Connie continues to complain, "I really don't see why they let them adopt a child. I certainly wouldn't have, if I'd been making the decision. What kind of environment can lesbians offer a child?"
>
> "And speaking of environments, Joshua's father lives with his girlfriend. I've heard Joshua refer to her that way: 'My dad's girlfriend.' Now what does that teach a child?"

Teachers who disapprove of family life-styles, or approach parents with a patronizing attitude because they are of lower socioeconomic status communicate a feeling of superiority, not helpful in forming relationships as equals. Parents, in turn, may avoid contact with teachers whose manner, communication style, and expectations are uncomfortably different from their own.

> "That teacher, I don't know, she talks too good," explains Mr. Rodriguez.
>
> "You know," says Mary Howard, "just because I'm black, she talks to me like I live in a ghetto or something."
>
> Nguyen Van Son is angry. "She's never tried to find out how our children live at home, what we want. I don't want my children losing everything from our culture, and if you ask me, she's ignoring the fact that we have a culture!"

In many school and programs, there exist these invisible (but not imaginary) lines based on race and class that prevent effective interaction. Often, there are real differences in background between teachers and parents, but these distinctions can be less divisive when teachers are careful to behave in ways that diminish the importance of the differences and make the effort to know parents as individuals, not as members of a particular ethnic group or social class.

❖ Barriers Caused by the Communication Process

Verbal and nonverbal messages sent and received by teachers or parents may be distorted through a filter of feelings, attitudes, and experiences. The words used or interpreted may widen, not close, the gap. (Chapter 7 will discuss ways in which the communication skills of a teacher can foster positive relationships with parents.)

Reactions to Role

Strong reactions are often aroused by the very role of the other. Parents have their own childhood histories of encounters with teachers and learning experiences. Some of these may be positive, causing the parent automatically to consider a teacher a friend. But, in many parents, painful memories of past school experiences cause unconscious responses to a teacher as someone to fear, someone who will disapprove, correct, or "fail" the parent (and child). With such an underlying assumption, many messages from a teacher may be interpreted more negatively than the sender intended. Some parents, particularly in lower socioeconomic classes, have had numerous encounters with case workers, social workers, and other figures in authority. A parent who has a history of dehumanizing or disillusioning experiences with professional people may already have erected barriers in the form of negative expectations.

Teachers need to realize how their unconscious reaction to parents is influenced by their relationships with their own parents. A teacher who has unresolved hostilities in the relationship with her own parents may have real difficulties relating comfortably to others who bear the label "parent." A teacher's experiences that have shaped her values about family life may conflict with the reality of parents with whom she works. For example, a teacher who feels that mothers really should be at home may not be able to relate sympathetically to a working mother. People alienated by unconscious emotional responses can never really hear or speak to each other clearly.

Other Emotional Responses

Parents may have fears of antagonizing teachers by their questions or comments, with the effect that a teacher could single out their child for reprisals when they are absent.

> "I'd like to tell his teacher that I don't like the way she lets the children do such messy art activities, but if she gets mad she'll just take it out on Ricky when I'm not around. I'd better not."

A study found that 50 percent of all parents, 59 percent of minority parents, were not sure how well their children would be treated when they left him in a center (Yankelovich 1977). With such feelings of uncertainty, it is not surprising that parents fear that speaking out might have a negative effect. (Interestingly enough, a recent study showed that teachers did not carry their disapproval of the parents into dislike or avoidance of the children. If anything, they seemed to compensate for that dislike by paying extra attention to the children (Kontos and Wells 1986).

Another fear promoting parents' feelings of being adversaries of teachers is the fear that they will be replaced by teachers in their children's affections. Attachment is a mutual process, and the affectionate relationship with their children satisfies many emotional needs of parents. Despite evidence to the contrary (Galinsky 1986), many parents fear this loss and are inhibited from forming relationships with teachers because of their feelings of jealousy and competition with teachers for their children's regard.

> "I'll tell you, it makes you wonder. She comes in to give the teacher a good morning hug, and not so much as a good-bye kiss for her own mother, who's going to be gone all day; I get pretty sick of hearing Miss Ha this and Miss Ha that, I can tell you."
>
> "How do you think I feel when she cries at the end of the day and just doesn't want to go home?"

There are often ambivalent emotions here: a mother wants her child to be independent and happy away from her, but resents the perception that a teacher is taking over in the child's regard. Feeling that she is losing her child to child care may threaten the mother's own identity.

Teachers themselves are not immune from competing for children's affections, especially if their own emotional needs are not being met in their lives beyond the classroom. A warm, affectionate bond with each child is important, but when a teacher finds herself thinking that she "can do a much better job with him than his own mother" or "would like to take the child home with me; he'd be better off," she has slipped into the dangerous territory of identifying with a child so completely she sees him only as a child she loves in the classroom, not as a member of the more important world of his family. Parents are the most important people in their children's lives and need to be supported as such. A teacher who begins to confuse her role with being a "substitute" for parents engenders fear and suspicion. A teacher who needs to feel more important to a child than his parents may find it too easy to blame the parents for the child's shortcomings and convey such an attitude in her choice of words.

> "The way you're reacting each time he has a temper tantrum is really causing Pete to have more outbursts."

Teachers need to realize that emotions of jealousy and fear of loss are hidden factors limiting much of what is truly said and heard. If teachers ignore the likely presence of these emotions, they may unwittingly fan the sparks into destructive flames.

> "Oh, she was just fine, Mrs. Weaver. She played as happily as can be all day and never asked for you once. You don't need to worry about her missing you."

This may be intended as reassurance, but will simply confirm the mother's worst fears. Most parents believe that no one else can do the job for their child as well as they can, and teachers who help parents feel they are not being displaced from this important position prevent barriers from being raised between them.

> "She did go to sleep well at naptime today. That was an awfully good idea you had to bring her blanket from home. I know she misses you especially then, and it helps to have that blanket as connection for her."

The world *guilt* creeps into many conversations when modern mothers have a chance to talk freely. The many demands on parents, along with an unrealistic image of perfection and a feeling of not doing what should be done, result in guilt feelings. This emotion may operate as a hidden barrier; parents feeling inadequate to the task may avoid all possible reminders of this, including the person doing things for their children that parents feel they should be doing.

Resentment can creep into the relationship from both teacher and parent.

Preschool teachers have extremely demanding jobs that use enormous amounts of energy, creativity, and emotion for long hours each day. In most cases, preschool teachers are paid much lower salaries and fewer benefits than their counterparts in schools for older children. They are accorded less professional status and recognition, even when they have completed the same number of years of training. Therefore, it is easy for teachers to feel they are taken advantage of by the community in general and parents in particular.

> "I don't see why they can't pick their kids up on time—don't they know I have other things to do in my life?"
>
> "Do you realize she had Easter Monday off and she went and played tennis and brought him to my classroom just like any other day?"

Parents have their own reasons for resenting teachers. It hurts to be removed from their children's lives. When it appears that teachers are making the decisions and setting the rules that exclude parents from classrooms and communication, parents are left with little recourse, but can seethe with resentment towards those teachers.

In most families where both parents work, child-care arrangements are the most critical components for the smooth running of the entire enterprise. This places parents in the ambiguous position of recognizing how important a preschool teacher is to their way of life, but resentful of having a person outside the family play such a necessary role. Contradictory, to be sure, but enforced dependence often breeds not gratitude, but resentment.

Parents and teachers who resent each other will be unable to communicate clearly. Thus it can be seen that the emotions of guilt, jealousy, and resentment may impede the process of open communication.

Personal Factors

Some teachers explain their lack of communication with parents as caused by their own personalities or their discomfort in social situations. These factors require special efforts on the part of teachers, and they should not be accepted as justification for failure to take the initiative in reaching out to parents.

> MiLan Ha knows that she doesn't have nearly as much contact with parents as many of the teachers in her center, but she says she can't help it. She says it shouldn't make a difference since she works so well with the children, but she does wonder what she might do to help the situation.

Teachers aware of their introverted personalities need to find ways of pushing their own efforts: perhaps setting specific goals, such as talking to a certain number of parents each day, or approaching a parent they have never talked with much, or saying one sentence beyond "Hello, how are you?" Teachers having difficulty getting started may need to pre-plan their comments to parents. (Thinking of one thing each child has done or been interested in may be a good place to start.) It may help to share feelings of discomfort with co-workers and be encouraged by their support. Some initial success in getting to know a few parents makes subsequent encounters a little easier.

Teachers need to remind themselves frequently that part of a preschool teacher's responsibility is to work with parents and that parents, because of a lack of familiarity with a school situation, may be far more uncomfortable than the teachers themselves. As the leader in a classroom, teachers are automatically placed in the role of hostess. Just as a hostess does not allow guests to flounder, unspoken to and uncomfortable, in her own living room, so a teacher must take the initiative to converse with parents.

Awareness will help; pushing oneself a little extra will help; a little success will help. Personality and social discomfort must not be allowed to interfere with the communication process.

❖ Barriers Caused by External Factors

As well as internal feelings and experiences, the external circumstances in which teachers and parents find themselves may act as barriers.

Time

Both parents and teachers are undoubtedly under time constraints. If school philosophies and administrative actions do not support working with parents, teachers may not receive either the staffing arrangements or the compensatory time that is needed to respond with flexibility to parents' life-styles and working patterns. Parents never have enough time for the demands of their lives, but they will find the time for parent involvement if they feel it is really important. There are ways to maneuver around time as a barrier (see chapters 9 and 10) if working together is perceived as important to parents and teachers. It is more productive to consider time as a real problem and search for creative solutions than to interpret the other's lack of availability as a lack of concern for the child.

"Busy-ness"

Another external factor that may function as a barrier is a teacher's appearance of being always busy. This may result from the realities of caring for the needs of a group of children or from an unconscious desire to keep parents at a distance. But, whatever the reason, the perception that a teacher has too much else to do to be bothered by a parent keeps many parents from more than the briefest greeting. As teachers try consciously to dispel this impression of being busy, there are things that can be done. At the beginning of the day, preparations for classroom activities can be made before the children arrive or by another staff member, leaving a teacher available to talk. Teachers need to plan, and have ready for use, activities that children may begin by themselves that require little supervision: puzzles on the table, dried beans and cups to fill in a basin; several lumps of play dough waiting in the art area. When children begin to play, parents and teachers will be free to talk. A classroom should be arranged so that when parents enter they have easy access to a teacher. Staffing arrangements and physical locations at the end of the day should provide enough teachers to care for children so that some are free to talk with parents. Planning and attention to details convey the message that teachers are there for parents.

Old Ideas of Parent Involvement

The changes in family structure and living patterns over the past two decades demand changes in the timing, content, and form of parent involvement, activities, and expectations. If a teacher or school continues to offer nothing more than the traditional forms and times for meetings, conferences, etc.—what Swap calls *institutionalized rituals*, which are so obviously unsupportive of good relationships (Swap 1993)—they are failing to recognize the current needs of families. Examples of *institutionalized rituals* are parent-teacher conferences scheduled at 4:00 P.M., on the teacher's break, or meetings held every first Tuesday at 6:30 P.M. Sometimes the old ideas are adhered to as an unconscious punitive attitude towards parents deviating from traditional life-styles—mothers who now work, instead of being available to come in for a conference at 10:30 in the morning. Directors and teachers must be aware that their own values and the weight of traditional practices may contribute to any reluctance to change forms of parents involvement. Schools and centers must examine their practices for evidence of outdated concepts of parent involvement and family needs.

Administrative Policies

Some schools and centers have policies that discourage or forbid contact and discussion between parents and staff other than supervisory personnel, perhaps on the grounds that unprofessional contacts may take place. The major difficulty here is that parents are denied the opportunity to build a relationship with a child's primary caregivers and that the designated supervisory personnel are often not available in the early morning or late afternoon when parents need to talk. Such policies effectively deter any meaningful parent involvement.

Administrative staffing policies that provide only a bare minimum of staff available at arrival and departure times also work against forming effective relationships. When the administration provides training and practice for teachers to learn how to form relationships with parents, lack of knowledge of how to work with adults is removed as a barrier. When administrative philosophy and policies support parent involvement, and parents are given clear guidelines of ways they can communicate with staff, parents know what is expected of them, and do not retreat because of confusion, anger, or frustration.

All of these external factors can be solved with concrete changes in the physical and social environment if they are identified as the cause of some barriers. Indeed, these are the easiest of all barriers to remove, needing only creative thought and perhaps a little money!

Personal Problems

From the parents' side, the pressure from personal problems can act as a barrier to the parent-teacher relationship. As much as a parent cares about his child and how he is functioning in the classroom setting, too many concerns about other life matters may require a parent's primary attention. This parent should neither be condemned for indifference nor ignored because of absence, but shown continued support and understanding from a teacher concerning the demands on parents.

This barrier for parents can be removed with community support and empowerment of attitudes. Jesse Jackson is credited with saying:

> Parents must make room in their hearts and then in their house and then in their schedule for their children. No poor parent is too poor to do that, and no middle-class parent is too busy.

In the same way, no teacher who believes in the importance of working as a partner with parents will find the problems so immovable as to abandon all attempts.

❖ Summary

The key to removing many of the barriers to parent-teacher relationships is a teacher's mind-set. When teachers believe that there is value in working with parents, they will find the time and energy to commit themselves to identifying and dealing with potential barriers. To sum up, these barriers "include the intense feelings, ego involvements, deeply held attitudes and values, past histories, and current concerns" (Chilman 1971, 124) that parents and teachers bring to the process of communication. It is an interesting reminder that each group sees the main obstacle in the other: teachers note parents' unwillingness, and parents note teachers' distant behavior (Tizzard et al. 1981). But, rather than blaming others, it is more productive to examine personal attitudes and behaviors. The barriers can be broken by "a bit more relaxation, a bit more empathy, a bit more recognition of the many complex factors that shape life for all of us" (Chilman 1971, 125).

❖ Student Activities for Further Study

1. As you work in your classroom or practicum placement, keep a journal of your experiences and encounters in working with parents. Use the journal to be honest about your emotional responses. How does your awareness compare with some of the emotional responses in the text?

2. Examine your own biases. Is there a style or kind of family with which you would be less comfortable working than with others? Discuss this idea in small groups.

3. Wherever possible, observe teachers and parents talking together. What nonverbal signs do you see of comfort and discomfort?

4. Talk with several preschool teachers. Ask them to recall negative experiences in working with parents. Afterwards, try to analyze which of the barriers discussed in the text might have been at work.

5. Talk with several parents whose children are involved in preschool programs. Do they recall negative experiences in relationships with teachers? Try to analyze which of the barriers discussed in the text may have been present.

❖ Review Questions

1. Identify three kinds of fears in parents and teachers, related to human nature, that may act as barriers to the development of effective relationships.

2. Describe four emotional responses that may break the communication process.

3. List four external factors that may act as barriers.

❖ Suggestions for Further Reading

Evans, J., and Bass, L. (1982). Parental involvement: partnership or prize-fight? in Brigham Young University Press (Ed.) *How to involve parents in early childhood education.* Provo, Utah: Brigham Young University Press.

Galinsky, E. (1988). Parents and teacher-caregivers: sources of tension, sources of support. *Young Children*, *43*(3), 4–12.

Greenberg, P. (1989). Parents as partners in young children's development and education: a new American fad? Why does it matter? *Young Children*, *44*(4), 61–75.

Herwig, J. (1982). Parental involvement: changing assumptions about the educator's role. in Brigham Young University Press (Ed.) *How to involve parents in early childhood education.* Provo, Utah: Brigham Young University Press.

Sarason, S. (1982). *The culture of the school and the problem of change.* 2nd Ed. Boston: Allyn and Bacon.

Travis, N., and Perreault, J. (1980). Day care as a resource for families. in L. Katz, (Ed.) *Current topics in early childhood education*, 3. Norwood, New Jersey: Ablex Publishing Corp.

CHAPTER 7

Foundations of a Successful Partnership

When administrators and teachers in early childhood schools and programs have decided that reaching out to include parents is an important part of their mission, they have taken a first step towards creating partnerships. Having made that decision, they then design the policies and practices to work with parents. Every program, responsive to what it knows about its particular population of families, will necessarily create methods of working with families that are unique; thus, many programs may look quite unlike each other in their approaches, and work very well in their own situation. Therefore, it would be impractical and not very helpful to set down a particular plan of action for working with families. But there are certain common elements that can be found in any program that has some success in reaching families. Some of these include attitudes of the staff involved. Others include the factors that support teacher efforts. By exploring these common elements, we will be able to determine the essential ingredients of successful partnerships. In this chapter, we will explore some of the attitudes, behaviors, and other factors that facilitate the formation of a productive partnership between parents and teachers.

OBJECTIVES

After studying this chapter, the student will be able to

1. discuss five attitudes or ideas of teachers that are conducive to forming a partnership with parents.
2. discuss concrete actions that are necessary in laying the foundation for a parent-teacher partnership.

❖ Teacher Ideas and Attitudes

> Jane Briscoe has become convinced that there are enough good reasons to merit really trying to form partnerships with parents. "Where do I start?" she wonders.

Since a teacher acts as initiator in forming the partnership, the starting place lies in an examination of some essential teacher ideas and attitudes.

Concept of Professionalism

Basic to the formation of a parent-teacher partnership is a teacher's concept of the professional teaching role. One traditional characteristic of professionals is keeping a certain distance between themselves and their clients to allow for more objective professional judgments, emotional protection from too many client demands, and enhanced status. But this separateness precludes an uninhibited social exchange between client and professional. With the traditional definition of the professional, teachers see their relationships with parents as a one-way process of informing parents and attempting to influence them. In such a relationship, parents are passive clients, receiving services, depending on the experts' opinion, in need of direction, and quite peripheral to the process of decision making. Such a concept implies that there is a deficit that the professional is trying to rectify, an idea that effectively makes shared understandings and responsibilities impossible. Inherent also in this stance is the idea that authority and power must rest with the professional: power over another. A partnership can develop only when teachers create a different mental concept of their role.

Teachers who can accept the partnership concept consider parents to be active members in making and implementing decisions regarding their children, and capable of making major contributions. These teachers share responsibility and power, believing that both teachers and parents have strengths and equivalent, though different, expertise. Such a belief implies reciprocity in a relationship, with parents contributing, as well as receiving, services. Parents are not viewed as a problem, but as part of a solution to common puzzles; power is shared with another.

The belief in partnership is a prerequisite to everything else. It requires teachers to define their professionalism in a new way, to see themselves as leaders of an educational team, using their special skills and knowledge to enlist the help of parents, expecting to exchange information with them, consider their opinions, and learn from them. (See Figure 7-1.) A partnership can be exciting and anxiety-producing, since teachers who function as partners with parents are frequently in a position where so much is untried and without guidelines. But, as partners, teachers believe parents are capable of growth, and in demonstrating this belief, they grow themselves. In a partnership, children, parents, and teachers grow and learn as they are drawn together by the same objective: what is best for the children.

Sense of Self

Teachers who are most able to move into a partnership with parents have a strong sense of self. They have learned to be in touch with, and can communicate effectively, their feelings. They are aware of their own strengths, weaknesses, concerns, and values; sure of their positions, they are not easily manipulated or threatened, nor do they try to manipulate others through fear. Because they respect themselves, they treat others with equal dignity, relate as one individual to another, and avoid stereotyping.

Teachers must consciously clarify their values to understand themselves. Jersild suggests that the crucial question to consider is: "What, in my

Figure 7-1 Teachers who believe in partnership can share responsibility. Courtesy Ellen Galinsky.

existence as a person, in my relations with others, in my work as a teacher, is of real concern to me, perhaps of ultimate concern to me?" (Jersild 1955, 4). As teachers identify their values, they also make opportunities for parents to consider and specify their own values. In a parent-teacher partnership, it is important for both to know themselves and each other, and to know also the areas of agreement and disagreement in their value systems. It is not necessary or desirable for teachers and parents to attempt to convince the other of the rightness of their beliefs. What is desirable is for both to feel comfortable expressing their viewpoints.

Humility

Another attitude of teachers related both to the concept of partnership and to the new definition of professionalism is humility, the ability to wait, be silent, and listen. Teachers who do not make impossible demands on themselves do not expect to understand immediately each question, or to have an instant response. This is not just a pose of hesitancy, but an ability to trust the outcome of the process of communication between individuals that is acquired only when teachers are able to dispense with some professional pretensions and keep a truly open mind. This may be called approachability; it is demonstrated by behaviors that suggest, "We're all in this together—help me out—what do you think?" (See Figure 7-2.) Teachers with humility are able to step outside normal frames of reference and find creative, novel ways to work with parents, because they are not limited by believing only the traditional methods will work. The attitude of humility also allows teachers to keep on trying when some attempts to work with parents have failed, to move "into new areas not because we know they're going to succeed, but because the element of success might be proportionate to the element of risk" (Fredericks 1989). The increased feelings of comfort resulting from continual contact with parents may help a teacher to relax and not rush the process.

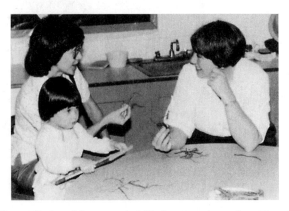

Figure 7-2 The attitude of "approachability" suggests real partnership. Courtesy CPCC Media Productions—Mike Slade.

✴ Compassion

Teachers who can work in a partnership display compassion for themselves and for others. As they attempt to understand parents, they try to realize not just what they are thinking, but also what they may be feeling. Such sensitivity is a first step towards the development of genuine mutual respect.

There is no question that teachers will encounter parents whose socioeconomic backgrounds, life experiences, and cultural mores are quite removed from theirs. One thing they can do is educate themselves about some of the general differences they may find in members of a certain class or ethnic group. For example, studies on differing expectations of lower- and middle-class mothers for their children's behavior and educational achievements, or on styles of family interaction in a particular cultural ethos, are helpful in preparing teachers to accept the variations in child rearing they will encounter. A useful resource for getting started on raising consciousness about differences that could separate teachers and parents is *Multicultural Issues in Child Care* by Janet Gonzalez-Mena. She reminds us that when teachers meet someone who obviously doesn't move in the same cultural framework that they do, they're jarred. An attempt to understand the ideas of parenting inherent in another's culture will lead to a more compassionate approach. But, just as they would not depend solely on textbook descriptions of typical three-year-old characteristics in teaching their preschoolers, nor will they depend on such general knowledge to guide them in understanding parents. Compassionate teachers attend sensitively to the unique reactions of each parent, no matter what the background.

✴ Respect for Others

Teachers who move into partnerships with parents express a genuine respect for parents, for their position as the most important people in their children's lives and for their accomplishments in child rearing. They respect the experiences, knowledge, and expertise that each participant brings to the situation. They also respect the rights of individual parents to define their own needs for the education and care of their young children. They convey this respect by treating them with dignity as individuals. Teachers try to find ways to meet the individual needs of parents. The respect becomes mutual as parents are encouraged to learn more about teachers and a center.

To summarize, teachers trying to move into a partnership with parents must work towards the following ideas and attitudes:

1. New image of professional role as partnership.

2. Strong sense of self.

3. Humility.

4. Compassion.

5. Respect for others.

❖ External Factors

Several other concrete, external factors are important foundations to the successful partnership in addition to the previously discussed attitudes.

Support Systems

Support systems are necessary for teachers striving to work with parents. Administrative support and leadership set the tone and atmosphere for a parent involvement program. It is fair to say that support for parent involvement needs to permeate the program from the top down; without wholehearted administrative belief in the importance of working with families, it will be difficult to convey to parents that their participation is a necessary part of the whole. Support may come in the form of a clearly stated philosophy in a parent handbook that values and welcomes the contributions of parents in the educational process; training of staff so they will be knowledgeable in techniques of working with adults; assistance, motivation, and appreciation of staff efforts; providing fair compensatory time and staffing arrangements to support efforts; and coordinating plans and strategies that emphasize parent involvement throughout a center. Such support sanctions and gives power to teachers' efforts. (See Figure 7-3.)

It is still possible for teachers to create an atmosphere for partnership and involvement on their own, but when the administration of a school supports and recognizes those efforts, they are far more productive. There are those instances where the administration actively discourages contact

Figure 7-3 Support systems from colleagues allow teachers to gain new perspectives.

between teachers and parents. If teachers choose to remain in such situations, their only recourse may be to work toward convincing the administration of the need to change its stance, through the positive experiences and proofs offered by research on the effectiveness of parent involvement (see references at end of chapter 4 for such data), by using community support and advocacy efforts (such as the NAEYC position statements on parent involvement in quality early childhood programs), and legislative movements (such as the requirements written into the Child Care and Development Block Grant for parent involvement), and possibly enlisting the efforts of parents to press for their own involvement. It can also be useful to point out to directors that there are advantages from a commercial viewpoint, since working closely with parents may improve retention rates! (See this viewpoint expressed in Meservey 1989. If you can't lick them, enlist them!)

Even with administrative support, working with a cross section of parents with individual needs, responses, and demands on teachers' time and energy can be stressful. Teachers can benefit from personal support systems, including colleagues and supervisors, that offer the opportunity to recognize and vent feelings of frustration or strain, and gain new ideas and perspectives.

Communication Time

One of the most crucial components in the foundation of a parent-teacher partnership is time for teachers and parents to communicate freely together. Communication time with parents may be made available by a flexibility in teachers' time options that fits parents' schedules, such as offering evening conferences, prearranged phone conversations, weekend home visits, and early morning coffee discussions. In order to have this flexibility, teachers should have their "after hours" work compensated for in release time. When teachers are allowed compensatory time, this is a tangible indication of administrative support for their efforts. Additional staff members or staggered coverage may be required to cover this release time, as well as to free teachers to talk with parents at the times communication takes place—when children are dropped off and picked up. Since the frequency of casual communication has a direct bearing on the quality of a teacher-parent relationship, it is worthwhile to set up patterns in staffing arrangements and classroom planning, and a variety of opportunities that allow teachers the freedom to talk. (See Figure 7-4.) Teachers and centers can become advocates for businesses and employers to allow working parents to have time necessary to attend conferences and school functions. In some communities the Chamber of Commerce has clearly stated that employers should support any efforts of parents to become involved in their children's education. Such a stance helps ease the problem of parent unavailability. Time may be an expensive commodity, but worthwhile to the effort of forming parent-teacher partnerships.

Figure 7-4 Teachers can gain time to talk with parents when they plan activities children can involve themselves in without assistance. Courtesy CPCC Media Productions—Mike Slade.

Variety in Parent Involvement

Another factor facilitating parent-teacher partnerships is to offer a variety of forms of parent involvement. A program reflects its understanding and responsiveness to the various needs of parents by allowing parents to select when, where, and how to participate. Flexibility in timing increases the variety. A program ready to meet individual needs, concerns, and interests indicates respect for parents and their value within the program. Someone within the program must take the time to find out what parents need and want, what they have to offer and are willing to share (See Resource Files, chapter 12 and Surveys, chapter 13), and evaluate the effectiveness of various methods of involvement. Asking parents for their evaluative feedback on particular plans, and using suggestion boxes or other formats to encourage parent ideas about the program facets that would be helpful to them, encourages parents to see this program responsiveness to their needs. Such variety in parent involvement opportunities allows parents to accept what is useful and reject what does not match their needs. (See Figure 7-5).

Information

For a constructive parent-teacher partnership, a clear understanding and knowledge of what is expected or possible in any program is required. Parents who clearly understand their responsibilities and obligations in a school are more comfortable. Routine encounters such as conferences and home visits will lose the apprehension that sometimes accompanies them if parents are familiar with the procedures and their role in them.

Figure 7-5 A variety of forms of parent involvement that allows parents to choose when and how to participate builds parent-teacher partnerships. Courtesy Connie Glass.

Many schools offer this information to parents in the form of a parent handbook, which is discussed as a parent receives orientation information and may be referred to later. Directors and teachers understand that much that is presented orally may later be forgotten, so the reinforcement of written material is essential. A parent handbook should define the general philosophy and services of a program as well as the specific philosophy concerning parent involvement, so parents understand both the work of a school and how they can be involved. Information is needed regarding a program's policies that concern parents, such as admission requirements, the daily schedule, hours and fees, attendance policies, late pickup policies, health and safety regulations, and children's celebrations. Many handbooks include general information on the developmental characteristics of young children and ways parents can help nurture development. A handbook should also describe the methods that teaching staff use in the classroom and in reporting a child's progress, lists of supplies parents may need, ways parents may be (or are obliged to be) involved in a center's activities. Some well-chosen examples illustrating parent roles can be added. Other information to include: dates of scheduled meetings; names and phone numbers of parent advisory committee members; facilities for parents in the school such as bulletin boards or parent lounge. Clear statements about when the school can be of assistance to parents is helpful. It is important that both limitations and choices for parents are explicit, as well as clear mechanisms that exist for parents who wish to raise concerns.

We welcome parents to enlarge the children's world by sharing an interest (job-related or hobby), ethnic, or religious traditions. Last year two parents helped us learn a Hanukkah song. Another parent helped us prepare a simple Vietnamese dish. A truck driver daddy brought his truck to school, and the mother of a new baby let us look at the baby—toes and all! Please come—what experience can you bring us? At the last parent work night, some of our handy parents fixed three broken tricycles and two limbless dolls. And some of our less handy parents helped us organize the housekeeping area. Please come on the next scheduled night.

In order not to miss important information when developing a parent handbook, it is helpful to ask parents whose children are presently in the school what they would like to have been told before their children started, and to ask teachers what they would like to tell parents.

The handbook needs to be concise, attractive, on a basic reading level, and clearly organized, in order to be usable. (See Figure 7-6.) It must be translated into every language represented by the center population. Much of the information will be reinforced later in newsletters and personal conversation, but it is helpful initially to answer all possible questions for parents, to help

Figure 7-6 Parent handbooks need to be designed to meet parents' reading and language abilities. Courtesy CPCC Media Productions—Mike Slade.

them feel comfortable in the new relationship without the concern that there may be surprises forthcoming. A parent handbook is also a concrete example of administrative support for parent involvement.

Communication Skills

Teachers attempting to create constructive partnerships with parents need to develop their communication skills. Many teachers are fortunate to have opportunities to speak with parents frequently. However, frequency of communication does not guarantee increased understanding or improved relationships. Unless teachers are aware of different styles and purposes of communication, of how to communicate verbally and nonverbally, to listen and convey attentive caring, and interpret messages from parents, miscommunication can create real barriers to a partnership. (See Figure 7-7.)

Some communication styles are almost certain to produce defensiveness: ordering, warning, blaming, advising, extensive questioning, and lecturing. Effective teachers learn to avoid these ways of talking. In addition, teachers will practice skills of listening and interpreting, of reading the behaviors in others that indicate the communication is causing them discomfort.

Four basic communication styles have been identified, each carrying its own amount of risk and value in sharing information (Flake-Hobson and Swick 1979).

Style I

The Superficial style ("What a pretty dress you've made!") uses informal small talk to get to know others on an informal basis. There is little risk involved, but little beyond "ice-breaking" is accomplished in a relationship.

Figure 7-7 A teacher's communication style is important in establishing a comfortable relationship. Courtesy CPCC Media Productions—Mike Slade.

Style II

The Command style ("Why are you not firmer about bedtime?") is riskier, because the authoritative tone that can be used effectively in some group situations often creates defensive reactions in an individual, providing little personal or factual information.

Style III

The Intellectual style ("Research studies indicate that the style of maternal interaction is definitely correlated with cognitive abilities and educational achievement.") is used to convey objective information and is therefore low-risk, though excessive use of this style can create the barrier of too impersonal a relationship.

Style IV

The Caring style ("I am concerned about Ramon. He frequently seems lonely. I wonder if his language understanding is keeping him apart.") openly shares personal information. The caring style requires the use of four sets of skills: listening, sharing self-information, establishing shared meaning through clarifying information received and sent, and making a conscious commitment to care for the self and others that requires the individual to risk self in relationships (Flake-Hobson and Swick 1979).

Lee Canter, who has developed a program on communication skills for teachers (Techniques for Positive Parent Relationships) suggests that teachers who can communicate their concern for a child will be most effective in eliciting parent support (Canter 1989). He suggests also that teachers will be effective by using assertive communication skills that do not apologize, minimize, or belittle the teachers' abilities and concerns.

With experience, teachers will discover that some words convey different meanings to some parents, and they will become more precise in their statements and descriptions. Teachers recognizing the social and cultural experiences of their listeners make adaptations accordingly and strive for unambiguous, descriptive words with no emotionally loaded connotations. They avoid professional jargon that may alienate or intimidate: words like *cognitive, fine motor, affective*. They reflect tentatively a parent's statements and their own interpretations—"What I hear you saying is:"—to elicit genuine feedback from the parents to check out their understandings. They focus on parents' statements or questions to clarify their primary issues—"I'm confused about. . ."; "Could you explain that problem again, please?" They use verbal reinforcers—"I see"; "Yes"; "Mm" the parent's name, to indicate they are listening and following what a parent has to say. They practice listening at least 50 percent of the time when they are engaged in discussion or conferences with parents. They realize that open-ended attempts to obtain more information—"Let's talk about that"; "I'm wondering about. . ."—are more effective than "who," "what," "how," "when" questions that may threaten the parent. They summarize for parents the ideas discussed.

Teachers need to remember that the verbal message they send account for only a small fraction of communication between people. Mehrabian claims that facial expressions have the greatest impact on the receiver: 55 percent of the message; that the impact of voice tone is next: 38 percent of the message; leaving only 7 percent delivered by words alone. What's more, in situations in which the sender's facial expression is inconsistent with the words (such as when a teacher says "I'm glad you could come for this conference," but her face shows apprehension or indifference), the facial expression will prevail and determine the impact of the total message (Mehrabian 1981).

Eye contact plays an important role in opening or closing channels of communication. Looking at the partner in communication conveys the physical impression of listening, or of seeking feedback, or desire for the other's speech. Looking away may indicate a desire to avoid contact, to hide some aspect of inner feelings, or an attempt to process difficult ideas. Because of the intensity of the emotional bond between parents and their children, teachers may notice that tears are often close to the surface in both fathers and mothers when the conversation touches important issues, including very positive issues. Many parents are uncomfortable with this display of their emotions and look away to hide the tears. Teachers sensitive to the amount of eye contact offered by parents may be able to perceive when their communication is too painful, or too difficult, and can alter the message accordingly. Teachers who realize how closely their own eye contact conveys evidence of listening and acceptance can make conscious attempts to improve this aspect of communication.

Other nonverbal communication for teachers to monitor in themselves and others that may produce effects of distance and discomfort include: learning towards (or away from) the other person; tone of voice similar to the other person; occasional head-nodding to indicate attention and approval; occasional gestures; smiles; speech errors and higher speech rates that can indicate anxiety and uncertainty. Even a teacher's style of dress may be sending a message that could help or hurt the development of rapport.

Such nonverbal cues are sometimes missed if the receiver is inexperienced, temporarily not paying attention, preoccupied with his own internal messages, or from another culture where cues may have different meanings. People are likely to base their response to messages on their perception of the source, rather than on the message content. Therefore, a prerequisite for effective communication is to relate to one another as individuals and avoid stereotyping. (For further exploration of communication techniques the student is encouraged to refer to Knapp 1980; Mehrabian 1981; McCroskey et al. 1971.)

A final word to all teachers who are anxious to start developing parent-teacher relationships. Parent-teacher relationships, as we have seen, are complex things, uniting two sets of internal experiences, needs, and responses with two sets of external circumstances. Teachers who expect total success will be disappointed if they measure complete success as full participation by every parent. Parents have unique responses to parent involvement opportunities; some parents are reached in one way, others in another. And some may be reached at another time, after the seeds of one teacher's efforts have long seemed to bear no result. So the measure of success lies not in the numbers responding to any initiative, but in the quality of interaction; not in total agreement, but in continuing dialogue. Teachers will discover they are in long-term relationships with parents. When children are in a preschool for a number of years, parents and teachers may learn to recognize each other informally before a child is actually in a particular teacher's classroom and maintain ties of friendship after a child moves on to the next classroom. Such an extended period of contact allows for the growth of comfort and communication, as well as the acceptance of ideas. The teacher realizing this is less likely to become frustrated and abandon all attempts.

❖ Summary

There are concrete steps that can be taken and skills that can be developed to help lay foundations for parent-teacher partnerships. These are:

1. Administrative support to provide collaborative philosophy and tangible assistance with staffing arrangements and time provisions; emotional support systems for teachers.

2. Time, created by allowing teachers to interact with parents at crucial points in the work day and compensating them for offering flexible options for parent involvement beyond normal working hours.

3. A variety of forms of parent involvement allowing parents to select where, when, and how to participate.

4. Clear explanations of policies, expectations, and openness to welcome parents into the educational program.

5. Developing and practicing effective communication skills.

For teachers like Jane Briscoe, who want to create partnerships with parents, these are some starting places. A variety of techniques to involve parents will be explored in Section III.

❖ Student Activities for Further Study

1. Contact several preschools in your community. Ask for copies of handbooks or printed materials meant for parents. Examine the material to discover any stated or implied philosophies of working (or not working) with parents.

2. With your classmates, work on creating a parent handbook that clearly conveys information parents want to know and the attitude of welcoming

parents into specific participations. (Each student might take a segment, after the necessary information and format have been decided.)

3. With your classmates, generate a list of words such as those discussed on page 154 that might convey different meanings depending on the cultural or environmental experiences of the receiver.

4. Imagine you are a teacher beginning employment at a child care center. What kinds of guidance, support, and training do you feel you need to become comfortable and capable in areas of working with parents? Devise an appropriate in-service training plan.

5. Observe a teacher you feel works well with parents. What personality characteristics and behaviors do you see? What do you notice regarding the teacher's nonverbal communication?

❖ Review Questions

1. Identify any three out of five attitudes of teachers conducive to forming a partnership with parents.

2. List five external factors important in laying the foundations for partnerships with parents.

❖ Suggestions for Further Reading

Bolton, R. (1979). *People skills.* NY: Simon and Schuster.

Braum, L., and Swap, S. (1987). *Building home school partnerships with America's changing families.* Boston: Wheelock College Center for Parenting Studies.

Davies, D. (1991, Jan.) Schools reaching out: family, school, and community partnerships for student success. *Phi Delta Kappan, 72*(5), 376–382.

Decker, C.A. and J.R. (1991). *Planning and administering early childhood programs* 5th ed. Columbus: Charles E. Merrill Publishing Co., (information on parent handbooks).

Ellenberg, F.C., and Lanier, N.J. (1984). Interacting effectively with parents. *Childhood Education, 60.5,* 315–320.

Hunt, D.E. (1987). *Beginning with ourselves in practice, theory, and human affairs.* Cambridge, MA: Brookline Books, Inc.

Kasting, A. (1994, Spring). Respect, responsibility and reciprocity: the 3 r's of parent involvement. *Childhood Education, 70*(3), 146–150.

Stone, J.G. (1987). *Teacher-parent relationships.* Washington, D.C.: NAEYC.

SECTION III

Techniques for Developing Partnerships

Having examined the importance and challenges of working with parents, it is time to consider the various methods teachers can use to develop communication and interaction with parents. There are a variety of techniques, and teachers should probably use a wide repertoire of methods in order to adapt to individual needs and personality preferences. Chapter 8 describes the process for establishing relationships with parents and children as they begin a program, and helping them with separation difficulties. Chapter 9 discusses a number of informal techniques for communicating with parents, such as newsletters, telephone calls, and bulletin boards. Chapter 10 takes teachers through steps in conducting effective parent conferences. Chapter 11 explores the topic of home visits. Chapter 12 considers involving parents in the classroom. Chapter 13 describes several approaches to parent education. And chapter 14 identifies ways that teachers and parents work effectively together within the larger community. All of these separate topics are important facets to study as teachers develop their skills for communicating with parents.

"Excellent communication skills. Poor choice of words."

CHAPTER 8

At the Beginning with Parents and Children

There is nothing more exciting and more touched with nervousness than children's first days in early education programs. For children, there is the challenge of leaving the security of parents and home, and moving into the company of a group of peers, new routines and activities, and a relationship with a new adult. For parents, there is the ambivalence of marking another milestone of development in their children's lives, the insecurities regarding the decision they have made about the program, and the uncertainties of their own roles in helping their children move into an educational program. For teachers, there is the excitement of meeting new children and families, and the challenge of making sure all the relationships get off on the right foot. Understanding the normal separation process and being able to support both parents and children through it is crucial for teachers in beginning the formation of trust and communication that will lay foundations for relationships. Chapter 8 considers initial steps to take in establishing a partnership between home and school, and between parent, teacher, and child.

OBJECTIVES

After studying this chapter, the student will be able to

1. identify several steps helpful in establishing a relationship prior to the child's entrance into the classroom.
2. discuss benefits associated with each step.
3. discuss strategies associated with each step.
4. describe the separation experience for children and parents, and discuss a teacher's role.

❖ Initial Contact Between Teacher, Parent, and Child

First impressions can have a lasting significance. Early attitudes and behavior patterns will determine later limitations on a relationship or what direction it will take. Parents and teachers who begin working together with particular expectations and understandings are likely to continue in that mode. Because it is often difficult to change patterns or behaviors once they have become habitual, it is important to involve teachers, parents, and children in a program of gradual orientation, information exchange, and increasing familiarity. No matter what their age, new school experiences are crucial steps for children. If these steps are facilitated by the adults around them, it is to the children's benefit, and therefore indirectly to the benefit of the adults as well. Between the time when parents first contact a school and the time when their child finally settles in is an important period when teachers have the opportunity to lay the foundations for successful parent involvement. There are several purposes for an orientation process: to make a child's transition to school as easy and pleasant as possible; to demonstrate to parents that they are welcome in the educational program and can learn to feel comfortable there; to help parents understand the school's goals and practices; and to give teachers a chance to learn from parents about a child and family situation (Tizard, et al. 1981).

The text will consider some ideas to involve parents as Connie Martinez first meets Sylvia Ashley and Ricky. In any situation, time and family circumstances may dictate modification of these ideas, but teachers striving for effective relationships with parents and children will see them as a goal to work for.

Choosing a School

The first contact between parents and a school or center is generally initiated by parents in their search for an appropriate facility for their child's care. The school, usually represented by the director, has the dual responsibility of encouraging parents to make the most appropriate educational choices for their children and sharing information about the school's philosophies and practices, so parents can see if this particular school matches their needs (Townsend-Butterworth 1992). Information concerning parental responsibilities and opportunities for participation should be included at this time as well.

In selecting a school or center for the early years, parents need to consider more than the usual consumer issues of convenience and cost. If this is their first experience in early childhood education, they may not yet be aware of the variations in educational goals and practices, licensing levels, discipline practices, parental rights and involvement, etc., existing in preschools within any community. Some child advocacy groups and schools offer parents a guide for questions and observations to emphasize their key role in making this decision. In many cases, parents feel panicky about finding care for their children in time to begin employment, and are willing to assume the best, rather than closely examining and evaluating situations. "Whether from desperation or a lack of knowledge or money, parents are accepting the unacceptable" (Hoyt and Schoonmaker 1991, 82). The task of early education programs is to give parents the information they need to make thoughtful decisions, and the encouragement to see their responsibility in making them.

Sample Guide for Parents

THE STAFF   YES   NO

Are staff members friendly and enthusiastic?
Do staff members seem to like and relate well to the children and to each other?
Are staff members required to have special training in child care?
Is there a staff in-service training program and/or other opportunities for continuous skill development?
Are parent conferences held on a regular basis?
Do staff members welcome questions and inquiry?

THE PROGRAM   YES   NO

Are teachers required to make daily lesson plans?
Is the daily schedule posted?
Is the program schedule balanced between active and
    quiet periods?
Are there varieties of materials and equipment ready for
    use and accessible to children, both indoors and out?
Do children have choices about activities?
Do the activities foster the children's physical, social,
    intellectual, and emotional growth?
Do the children know what to do?

YES   NO

Do the children receive individual attention from the caregivers?

Does the center have a policy on discipline?

Do you agree with it?

Are records kept on children and their development?

Are snacks and meals nutritious, well-balanced, and menus posted?

Are the parents linked to the daily life of the program?

THE PHYSICAL SETTING   YES   NO

Are there comfortable, relaxed areas for resting and naps?

Is the center bright, clean, comfortable?

Are the outdoor and indoor areas safe and free from hazards?

Is there enough space for free, easy movement?

Does it allow for both group and individual activities?

Does it provide possibilities for privacy?

Is there appropriate, clean equipment for different age groups?

Quality care provides:

- a caring, pleasant atmosphere.
- care by an adequate number of well-trained, nurturing, and affectionate caregivers.
- a program that responds to each child as an individual.
- experiences that facilitate exploring, skill development, and learning.
- support for, communication with, and involvement of parents.

Consider what is best for your child. If you are not satisfied with the care found, continue your search. You are the parent: the choice is up to you. (Adapted from Child Care Resources Inc., Charlotte, N.C.)

In many centers, parents are invited to observe a teacher in action with her present class before deciding whether to enroll their children. Such a practice sends two clear messages to parents: (1) the center respects their judgment and obligation to know exactly what arrangements they are making for their children; and (2) the center is proud of what it does, and wants parents to see it for themselves. Parents are justified in being suspicious of a center where such visiting is not encouraged or allowed.

It is preferable to enroll a child whose parents have carefully considered the issues important to them and their child, matched them with all the available options, and chosen a particular school on the basis of meeting needs, rather than parents who made a hasty decision based on whether or not they have to cross the line of traffic to reach the parking lot. Too many decisions are based on cost alone. Schools for young children have a responsibility to help parents realize the full extent of their decision-making role. Once parents choose a school, their next contact moves beyond the director as general spokesperson to meeting the specific teacher(s) where their child will begin.

Let's look at the beginning for Sylvia Ashley and Ricky.

> In Sylvia Ashley's case, social services had suggested the center for Ricky, and Sylvia went to look it over and talk to the director. As always, she had Ricky with her. "We're delighted that Ricky will be entering our school, Mrs. Ashley. Since he'll be entering our group of three's, let me take you down to meet Connie Martinez, our lead teacher in that class. Then you two can find a convenient time to get acquainted further."

First Encounter—Teachers and Parents

The first conversation between parents and a teacher is best scheduled for a time when parents can come without their child. At that time, parents are free to talk without concern for their child's response in a new situation, and a teacher can concentrate her efforts on helping parents become comfortable without her attention divided between adults and child.

> Sylvia had told Connie Martinez that she had no one to leave Ricky with, so Connie was not surprised when Ricky walked in with his mother. Connie got two puzzles, a book, crayons, and blank paper, and helped him settle in a corner distant enough that he could see his mother but not overhear the conversation. As Connie thought about it later, she realized that was the first time she'd ever conducted that first conversation with the child present. It certainly was far from ideal, but she'd at least had some time to talk freely with this new mother.

This meeting has several purposes. One is to permit a parent to share initial information about an entering child. Many schools ask parents to fill in a questionnaire about their child's personal and social history. Parents may fill this out at home and bring it to the meeting. In practice, if teachers and parents talk their way through a completed questionnaire, parents often supply additional information in a more easily remembered way. What are some questions teachers might like to ask parents? Here are some samples. What are you most proud of about your child? What worries or concerns you about your child? What is your child's favorite place to play? What roles does your child frequently engage in during play? What activities do you most like to share with your child? Is there a favorite friend or relative your child might talk about, real or imaginary? What does your child do when he is upset, and how is he best comforted? Does your child have fears or worries that we should be aware of? Is there something that your child has just learned that is important to him? What would you like your child to get out of this year's program? (Adapted from *Scholastic Early Childhood Today*, Aug./Sept. 1993, 41). As parents talk, teachers can gain an impression of the relationship between parent and child, of how a child has reacted to other new situations, and of how parents feel about enrolling their child in the program. (See Figure 8-1.) This also establishes a precedent of cooperation, of sharing information, with parents making important contributions and teachers listening. Teachers can also use this opportunity to acquire parent history and resource information. When asking questions, teachers must let parents know how this information will be used.

Figure 8-1 For happy a first day, teachers need much information from parents. Courtesy Chapter 1 Program, Charlotte, N.C.

Selection of Sample Questions

<u>Information on Routines</u>
  <u>Eating</u>
  As a rule, is your child's appetite:
  excellent   good   fair   poor _____
  Does child eat alone or with family? _____
  List favorite foods _____
  List foods especially disliked _____

  <u>Sleeping</u>
  Approximate time child goes to bed _____
  Approximate time wakes in morning _____
  Attitude at bedtime _____
  Usual activities before going to bed _____

  <u>Elimination</u>
  At what age was training started for:
  Bowel control _____ Response to training _____
  Bladder control _____ Response to training _____
  What words does child use when stating need for
      elimination? _____

  <u>Other Information</u>
  What do you enjoy most about your child? _____
  _____
  _____

  How does your child usually react to new situations?
  _____
  _____

  Pleasures your family enjoys most? _____
  _____
  _____

  Has child been separated from either parent for a long period
  of time? If so, how did child react? _____
  _____

  What things repeatedly cause conflict between parent and child?
  _____

  Is child happy playing alone? _____
  List age and sex of child's most frequent playmates
  _____

  Favorite activities _____

Many of the ideas discussed may be helpful in increasing a new child's comfort in the first days in school.

> "I see here that you mentioned Ricky likes to sleep with a favorite teddy bear. Do you suppose you could bring that along to leave in his cubby for nap time? It might feel good to have something so familiar. Pictures of you and his brother to put in his cubby might help too."

This first meeting allows parents to ask specific questions about the classroom.

> "Yes, there are four other boys who have entered the classroom quite recently, so he won't be the only really new one."

> "Well, our morning snack is really a hot breakfast, served before 9:30 each day, so if he doesn't eat much in the early morning at home he won't have to wait too long."

Parents can help prepare the child for becoming comfortable in the classroom if they have some accurate knowledge about what will happen and what to expect.

It also allows parents and teachers an early chance to know each other on a one-to-one basis.

> You're going back to school—good for you! That's great. You'll certainly be busy, but I'll bet you'll find it's worth it when it's all over. I'm taking some classes at night too, so we can complain about it together."

This is a good time to establish clearly what teachers and parents will call each other. If this subject is never discussed forthrightly, there is often an awkwardness, with the result that neither calls the other anything.

> "I prefer that parents call me Connie, though the children call me Miss Martinez. Then may I also call you Sylvia? Are you comfortable with that? I'm just more comfortable with first names."

During this time a teacher can inform parents of the rest of the orientation schedule, fix a time for the next visit, and discuss separation patterns that children and parents frequently experience. This establishes the precedent of a teacher casually informing and educating, as well as empathizing, with parents.

> "It's a good idea to get Ricky started the week or so before you have to start your classes. You know, we find a lot of our three-year-olds

take a couple of weeks or more to feel comfortable letting Mother leave. Please feel free to stay in the mornings as long as you can, but if he's upset when you leave, don't worry, we'll give him lots of special attention. I know it's hard for mothers too, but we'll help each other along.

By raising the issue of separation in advance, a teacher gives parents the opportunity to prepare themselves and their children for the transition. Studies show that parents' verbal explanations are the most important influence in how well children adapt to the new situation (Powell 1989).

In situations in which a school begins an entire new class of children at the same time, it works well to have an orientation meeting for all new parents to cover the common information all will need. This enables a teacher to offer information to the entire group and enables parents to meet each other right from the beginning. It can be very reassuring to talk to other parents and find they are not alone in their concerns about leaving their child in a new environment. (See Figure 8-2.) Still, individual meetings between parent and teacher offer opportunities to gain specific information on a child, answer personal questions a parent might not raise in a group, and establish the parent-teacher relationship.

So this first brief meeting of parent and teacher establishes the patterns of relaxed communication, of mutual informing and asking, that are important for the working relationship to grow.

First Encounter—Teachers and Children

For the first meeting between child and teacher, it is preferable to have it where a child is most comfortable—at his home. Whenever a child has to get used to a new concept, such as school and new adults caring for him, he

Figure 8-2   Teachers may hold group orientations for parents. Courtesy Barbara Stegall.

can adjust when fortified by the security of familiar people and surroundings. This first visit, scheduled at a family's convenience, may be very brief—fifteen minutes or so—but a child will have a chance to briefly socialize and observe his parents doing so. Any teacher who has experienced such an initial home visit will remember the comfort this gives children timidly entering a new classroom and recognizing an already familiar face. "You've been to my house." Children's feelings of security are enhanced by seeing that their parents and teachers are forming a relationship.

Parents too are reassured by watching teachers' sensitive approach when children are timid. When teachers speak quietly and get on children's eye level (being sensitive to cultures where eye-to-eye communication is not respectful), parents recognize that their children are being treated as special people. Parents pick up on that caring, "and it is conveyed back to the child" as "parents feel appreciative that someone has taken the time to help their child feel comfortable" (Johnston and Mermin 1994, 64). (Home visits are discussed further in chapter 11.)

The brief visit also offers a teacher a glimpse of the parent-child relationship and a child's home learning environment.

> Sylvia had been reluctant to have the teacher make a visit to their apartment, but when Connie Martinez explained it might help Ricky feel more comfortable with her (so far she wouldn't speak to this stranger), she agreed. Connie scheduled the brief visit for late afternoon, after learning Ricky's big brother would be home. And that did help. Terrence talked to the teacher and encouraged Ricky to show her their bedroom. Ricky smiled and waved good-bye when she left.

When home visits are absolutely not possible, teachers can write a letter to the family, and include something special for the child, perhaps her photo. This can be a tangible tie for the child and this new person (Jervis 1987).

First Visit to a Classroom

During a home visit, a teacher can arrange a time for a parent and child to visit the classroom. It is most desirable that a child have a chance to visit before the first time of coming to the classroom to stay. This visit also will be brief, a chance for a child to see and become interested in a new environment.

> Ricky and his mother came in mid-morning, two days after the home visit. He said hello to Connie and let her show him around the room. He especially liked the big fire truck. When the other children came in from the playground, he clung to his mother, but watched intently. He turned down the invitation to come to the table for juice, but joined his mother when she sat near Connie and drank juice. He nodded when Connie told him that next time he could stay longer and play with the fire truck.

It is often overwhelming for a young child to enter a classroom full of other children busy with activities. For this reason, it is a good idea to schedule this visit for a time when children from the classroom are outside, playing in a gym or other area with another teacher, or at the end of the day when fewer children are present. Then a child is free to be welcomed by the teacher he's met, shown that he will be a part of this classroom (having a cubby with his name and picture on it is a good idea; see Figure 8-3), and given a chance to investigate the toys and equipment on his own. It works well to have a visiting child join the group briefly for a snack or cup of juice. He can then enjoy the eating experience and have a chance to see other children without being called upon to participate. The parent stays in the classroom during this visit, offering his child a secure base from which to move and sharing his pleasure in new discoveries. Parental concerns may be allayed by observing the teacher and child interact and seeing how the classroom functions. This visit gives the parent specifics to discuss at home to continue to prepare his child for this new experience.

School visits are essential. If necessary for the family's schedule, the visit could be at 7:00 A.M. or at 6:00 P.M., to allow the parent to stay throughout. This step is too important to skip. A visit is in the child's best interests, and ultimately in the family's, even if it is perceived as inconvenient.

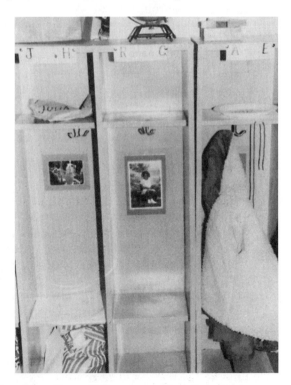

Figure 8-3 A cubby with a child's name and picture gives a sense of belonging. Courtesy CPCC Media Productions—Mike Slade.

If an entire class of entering children is new, teachers may schedule brief opportunities for a group of five or six children to come in for "tea parties" and a chance to look about the classroom. Breaking a class down offers teachers a chance to interact with each child while saving teacher time.

Child's Entry into a Classroom

The groundwork is laid for a child's entry into a classroom. Teachers and parents need to remind themselves of how much there is for a child to become accustomed to in a school experience: the "how's" of interacting with a large group of children; the new rules and practices of a classroom; the leaving of parent and becoming comfortable with another adult. (It is also important that teachers let parents know that children faced with all this may act out afterwards, in the secure environment of home.)

Since these adjustments can be exhausting for a young child, his first days in a classroom need to be as abbreviated as possible, allowing for the family's schedule. For example, if a child is beginning a full day child care program, it is helpful if he is picked up at the end of the morning for several days, then slowly extend the day to include lunch, nap, and then the afternoon. Children entering a half-day program will benefit from attending for half the morning at first. A school that enters its whole class at one time can shorten the entire schedule for the first week or so, gradually extending from one hour to three. The people most inconvenienced during this easing-in period are parents, so it is important they understand the rationale for this approach and its benefit for their children in building feelings of comfort and security. (See Figure 8-4.) Some centers offer a place where parents can have a cup of coffee during these shortened days, as a place to wait and converse with other parents. In the next section, we will discuss helping parents know what to do if they decide to stay in the classroom.

> After the teacher suggested it, Sylvia had decided to let Ricky stay for two mornings before she left him for the whole day. The first morning he cried hard as she left; Connie encouraged her to stay a little longer if she wanted, but she just hurried away, feeling a little sick herself. He was very quiet when she went back to get him before lunch, but after his nap he told her and Terrence a little about playing with the fire engine. The next morning he cried for about ten minutes, but as she stood in the hall, she heard him stop. The third day she and Terrence went together to get him after his nap. Connie said he'd had a hard time falling asleep, but she'd rubbed his back until he drifted off. Sylvia was starting to think Ricky might be all right.

Parents as well as children need special attention during this transition time. A teacher's evident concern and specific comments do much to further a sense of partnership as she takes the time to communicate with parents before and after school. (See Figure 8-5.)

Figure 8-4   There is a lot for a child to become accustomed to in the new school experience. Courtesy Chapter 1 Program, Charlotte, N.C.

Figure 8-5   Parents and children both need special attention during beginning times.

Every day when Sylvia came back to get Ricky, she looked eagerly for the teacher. Connie always tried to leave the children with her assistant briefly and come to tell her what Ricky had played with and how he seemed to feel.

Teachers should make every effort to accommodate family needs and pressures by modifying steps and timing, at the same time explaining the importance to the child of the visits and easing-in. Many parents will find the time, even if they didn't originally believe they could do so. At the same time, there will be some children left "ready or not." For those parents who cannot or will not stay, teachers should do what they can to help trust form. They may send preliminary notes or talk on the telephone. Teachers may suggest that the family bring transitional objects and pictures into the classroom, and may recommend that parents find a family member who might be free even if parents aren't. If teachers believe this process is important, they will convey this impression to families.

Through the orientation process, no large amount of parent time is spent; most of the visits are one-half hour or less and can be worked into a parent's employment schedule. For a teacher, the time can be scheduled into a normal teaching day with coverage from an assistant. Both adults need to realize the priority of a child's growing security and try to fit in as many of the steps as practicable. In addition to a child's security, it is important to set patterns of teachers and parents working together in home-school transitions and discussing a child's needs. As they work together, parents and teachers will get to know each other and start to build a trust that will help in the future. A good beginning for all.

"You know," says Sylvia, "Ricky is going to get along all right in the school. I really like the teacher; she's helped me a lot to get used to things. I won't have to worry so much."

(For further discussions of easing-in patterns and suggestions for specialized school settings, see Jervis 1987; Balaban 1985.)

❖ Dealing with Separation Experiences

The emotional responses to a new school experience may be heightened by the separation anxiety experienced by most children and parents. The mutual parent-child attachment, developed during the early years of a child's life, means that both adult and child feel more secure in each other's presence. A removal from each other's presence causes concern and changes in behavior for both.

What behaviors are expected of children experiencing separation? Many children up to age three or so will cry and be sad when a parent leaves. But even older children may find the initial leaving difficult. (See

Figure 8-6 It is just as hard for many parents to leave as it is for children to say good-bye.

Figure 8-6.) Sometimes this sadness continues off and on for a good part of the day; some children continue this pattern of crying for weeks. A child may come in quietly in the morning, and then begin to cry later. Such delayed reactions may occur days, or even weeks, later. Some children find times like mealtime or naptime particularly hard as they are reminded of home routines. Many children experiencing separation difficulties cling to a teacher and participate very little. Separation problems are also demonstrated by an increase in dependence or disruptions and changed behavior patterns at home, such as resisting bedtime, out-of-bounds talk with parents, new and assertive ways of behaving, and "games" that play on parents' guilt. Some children demonstrate regressive behaviors, reverting to thumbsucking, wetting, or other behaviors from an earlier time. (See Figure 8-7.) And some children exhibit "very good" behaviors, no signs of upset, just controlled passivity.

These behaviors are considered usual for a child experiencing separation, and the duration of the behaviors varies with each child. While they require special considerations, the behaviors are not cause for alarm. Teachers need to be matter-of-fact in their expectation of these behaviors so they reassure parents of both their normalcy and temporary nature. Experiences, circumstances, and temperaments are different for each child. Children who have rarely been left by parents may react quite differently from those who have had lots of baby-sitters or group encounters. The child

Figure 8-7 Thumbsucking and an increase in dependence may be part of the child's adjustment. Courtesy Mark and Denise Stephens family photos; Deborah Triplett, photographer.

who approaches each new situation with zest and enthusiasm may leave parents without a backward glance, while the child who is slower to warm up in new situations may appear unhappy for weeks. Most young children have this period of stressful adaptation to supplemental child care away from their parents. But once they understand that regular separation from parents does not imply their loss, the problematic behaviors subside.

Parents often have a difficult time with separation too. This is a time of ambivalent feelings: satisfaction that their child is more independent; fear of becoming displaced in their child's affections; and sadness at the changing status in their relationship. Parents may feel concern that their child no longer needs them and jealous of the person he appears to need. They may be concerned about how their child is cared for in their absence and about this change being too disruptive to their child's life and their own, as evidenced by the upset behaviors.

"Look, I thought it was going to work out fine at this center, but now I'm not so sure. Janie screams every morning when I leave and clings to my neck. I can hear those screams all day. I'm afraid of her changing; she's always been such a happy child. And I worry—wonder whether anybody's looking after her when she's so upset. I miss her too. But I'd hate to think I was one of those clinging mothers who can't let their kids go."

A parent may be struggling with more than her own separation feelings. If she's beginning a working situation, she may be feeling great pressure for her child to adjust to the care situation as quickly as possible. Getting her child adjusted is not an option; it has to work!

A teacher is in an important position to help parent and child deal with separation emotions and behaviors. The basic aim is for a teacher to remember that she is doing not just what works best, but what best strengthens a child. Teacher's attentions need to be directed to both parent and child, "for the way you treat the child affects the parents, and the way you treat the parents affects the child" (Balaban 1985, 71). Some basic strategies follow.

Prepare Parents for Separation Behaviors

Prepare parents in advance to accept separation behaviors and emotions as normal. Parents are more open about their concerns if they realize that a teacher is not judging their child or themselves negatively for experiencing separation anxieties.

> "Most children Janie's age have quite a hard time at first saying good-bye to parents. We expect it. You're the most important person in her life, and it will take a while for her to realize she can be fine when you're gone. In fact, though they don't show it as freely as children, most parents find this a fairly major adjustment too. I'll be here to help you both however I can. These are concerns we'll talk about each day."

Welcome Parents into a Classroom

Help parents feel welcome to stay in a classroom as long as it is helpful to a child. Some teachers have found it helpful to prepare a handout for parents suggesting some things they could do in the classroom during those first few days. The handout clearly says "You're Welcome to Stay!", and suggests that parents can help the child go through the morning rituals of putting things in cubbies, finding name tags and moving them to a designated spot, reminding children where the bathroom is, looking around together at the toys and activities on display. The handout may clearly state that parents are welcome to stay as long as they wish, and are free to drop back in any time they wish. A reminder of the importance of saying good-bye may be included. Both parents and children may benefit from not having a rushed good-bye in the morning, by slowly helping a child get interested in the classroom activities, and by having a parent see her child receive a teacher's attention. This approach will help a parent feel a part of her child's school world. (See Figure 8-8.)

Figure 8-8 Coming in may get a little easier when parents have a few extra minutes to help their child slowly become involved and comfortable with the teacher. Courtesy CPCC Media Productions—Mike Slade.

"Janie, maybe you'd like to show your mommy the puzzle you did yesterday" conveys such a welcome.

"We've got some nice, soft play dough on the table over there. Maybe that would be fun to do together for a few minutes."

"Perhaps you'd like to find a book to read together before you say good-bye."

Parents look to teachers for cues about what their role should be in helping their child settle in. As teachers provide direction to parents, parents will be able to act confidently with their children.

Allowing a child to decide when parents should leave the room—"Shall Mom go now, or after our story time?"—may help a child experience self-confidence.

Teachers can help parents and children plan together for the next day's parting and move toward establishing a regular morning routine.

"The two of you might like to decide before you come tomorrow whether she'll give you a hug at the door, or after she's put her things in her cubby."

In general, teachers must let parents know they will follow their cues concerning their desire or ability to stay. But an alert teacher picks up on the times a child is ready to move away from his parent who is lingering on, perhaps due to her own needs. Here a teacher can help a parent leave.

> "Mrs. Smith, since Janie's starting to play, it might be a good time to tell her good-bye. You and I can watch her from outside, if you'd like."

It is important that teachers make decisions regarding the timing of actual separation in such cases where a child's readiness precedes a parent's. When parents are feeling ambiguous and shaky, they may need or appreciate such help. However, when a parent is unable to respond to such a direct approach, it is probably an indication that the point of personal readiness for separation has not yet arrived, and teacher patience and support are necessary. It is also important for teachers not to become impatient with the process and arbitrarily set their own time limit. "Two weeks is long enough for any child or parent to get used to this!"

Should parents stay away? Some children don't seem to need their parents' presence at times of transition as much as others do, although they are usually quite agreeable to their presence in the room. However, there are also those children who get so habituated to a particular pattern, like parents staying at school, that it becomes even harder for them when their parents finally do leave. Parents of these children might do well to concentrate efforts at home to prepare for the leave-taking. The best policy seems to be one that would allow parents to stay as long as is necessary and helpful to the child. (See Figure 8-9.)

An important concept for teachers and parents to consider is that parents must see their own anxiety as separate from that of their child's; in other words, the reactions of a parent may not be identical to a child's feelings, and it is important not to project those feelings onto a child. It can set up long-lasting problem patterns if a child learns to give a parent a demonstration of his reluctance to be left before a parent feels satisfied that he will

Figure 8-9 Parents should feel free to stay as long as is necessary and helpful to the child. Courtesy © 1990, Washington Post Writers Group.

be truly missed. A parent may be more able to deal with personal emotions with an awareness of whose problem it is.

(A) Develop Children's Trust in Parents

An important step in a child's working through the separation process is to learn to trust that parents will reliably leave and then return. Teachers may need to help parents become aware of behaviors that can foster this sense of certainty.

Though less painful at the time, it is not a good idea for parents to slip away unnoticed while a child is distracted. A child can't help but become a little dubious about a parent's trustworthiness. Teachers can help parents realize the need for a definite leave-taking.

> "I know it bothers you when she cries as you leave, but it's really better for her in the long run to know she can rely on you to go and come just as you say you will. I'll help her say a quick good-bye to you."

In the same way, parents may not realize the importance of picking up a child at a predictable time. Clock time means very little to children, and even a short time elapsing after a parent's expected arrival will seem like a very long time. (See Figure 8-10.) It is best for parents to equate their return with a scheduled event and absolutely keep to it, especially during this transition time.

> "After you eat your snack, I'll be back to get you."
>
> "Remember, Sally, Dad told us this morning that he'd come back to get you after snack. I know you're missing him. Come with us while we have our story, and then we'll be getting ready for snack."

Figure 8-10   It is important to a child's sense of security to be picked up on a predictable schedule.

Discuss Separation Experiences

It is helpful to discuss and validate the emotional responses of separation openly, with empathy. Such an approach frees both child and parent to realize their feelings are recognized, accepted, and can continue to be communicated. Keeping "stiff upper lips" is too costly in terms of emotional health.

> "I know you're sad when your Mom leaves, Janie. It's a little scary too. But I'll be here to look after you until she gets back, and we can have a good time too."
>
> "It will take a little while to get used to our classroom, but I'll help you, and so will your new friends.
>
> "Most parents have some pretty mixed feelings about their child starting off in school. It can be kind of sad and scary, I'm sure."

Small touches can demonstrate to parents and children a teacher's empathy: a phone call in mid-morning to let a parent know that her child who was screaming when she left is now happily playing with play dough; an extra minute to share the day's events fully with a returning parent; talking with a child throughout the day about what they'll have to show Daddy when he returns; taking dictation for a note the child would like to write to an absent parent. All of these can show children that teachers are there for them, that they can listen, understand, and help.

Teachers who understand separation anxiety and its manifestations will not become irritated and offended by the behaviors of children or parents. They will not take the tears or anxieties personally, as indications that their classrooms are not good places. They will not scold crying children, nor ignore the tears and sadness. They will understand that time and support will solve most separation problems.

Special Attention to Parents and Children

Special attention to both parents and children is warranted at this time. Teachers may choose special children's books about separation and new experiences to read to children. (See Figure 8-11.) They may stay close to children, holding their hands at transition times, holding them on their laps when they are sad, talking with them often. Teachers should talk about what will happen next in the classroom and where parents are now. They will hold monologue-type conversations, not pressuring children to respond. They may write notes from children's dictation to the absent parent; this helps ease the child's feelings and shows that teachers can listen and help. They will encourage children to hold a transitional object from home or parent—holding Mom's scarf is reassurance that she will return. All of these techniques help children learn that teachers are there for them, and that sadness is accepted and can be channeled into work and play. They

Books about Starting School
for Young Children

Ahlberg, J. and A. *Starting School*. Gryphon House.

Barkan, J. *Anna Marie's Blanket*. New York: Barron's, 1990.

Barkin, C., and James, E. *I'd Rather Stay Home*. Milwaukee, WI: Raintree, 1975. After being hesitant to participate, Jimmy builds blocks and finds a friend.

Blue, R. *I Am Here: Yo estoy aqui*. New York: Franklin Watts, 1971. A book in English with Spanish phrases, about a child who finds an aide in the classroom who can talk with her, as well as new experiences and fun.

Bram, E. *I Don't Want to Go to School*. New York: Greenwillow, 1977. A kindergartner's fears about the first day and a wise mother.

Breinburg, P. *Shawn Goes to School*. New York: Crowell, 1973. After wanting to go to school, Shawn cries when he gets there, but slowly gets happy.

Cohen, M. *Will I Have a Friend?* New York: Macmillan, 1967. The beginning of school is lonely and hard, but Jim has a friend by the end of the day.

Crary, E. *Mommy Don't Go*. Seattle: Parenting Press, Inc., 1986. Enjoyable ways for children to think about separation.

Hamilton-Merritt, J. *My First Days of School*. New York: Julian Messner, 1982. Photos show child taking her bear along to school, then making friends, so Bear can stay home.

Henkes, K. *Owen*. Gryphon House. What to do with Owen's fuzzy blanket when he starts school?

Howe, J. *When You Go to Kindergarten*. New York: Knopf, 1986. Focus is on helping a child understand exactly what to expect in kindergarten and how it differs from nursery school and day care.

Hurwitz, J. *Rip-Roaring Russell*. Nursery school difficulties are replaced by friendship.

Johnson, D. *What Will Mommy Do When I'm at School?* Gryphon House.

Kantrowitz, J. *Willy Bear*. New York: Parents' Magazine Press, 1976. A little boy's fears and feelings about going to school are discussed with his bear, who stays home.

Molnar, D., and Fenton, S. Albert Whitman. *Who Will Pick Me Up When I Fall?*

Rockwell, H. *My Nursery School*. New York: Greenwillow, 1976. The environment and activities of nursery school are described by a child who is happy to be there.

Rogers, F. *Going to Day Care*. New York: Putnam, 1985. The day-care experience is presented in a clear way, with emphasis on the feelings, both negative and positive, that children may have.

Simon, N. *I'm Busy Too*. Albert Whitman, 1980. Mikey, Sara, and Charlie's first day in child care, while parents work, with time to share at the end of the day.

Soderstrom, M. *Maybe Tomorrow I'll Have a Good Time*. New York: Human Sciences Press, 1981. A little girl who doesn't want her mother to go to work and just watches all day.

Tompert, A. Albert Whitman. *Will You Come Back For Me?* Every child's question in starting day care.

Warren, C. *Fred's First Day*. Nursery school is just the right place for a middle child, too small to play with big brother and too tough to play with baby.

For more titles, a good reference to consult in the library is *Books to Help Children Cope with Separation and Loss* by Joanne E. Bernstein (R.R. Bowker Co.).

Figure 8-11 Books about starting school for young children.

will make opportunities for parents to tape record brief messages to leave in the classroom for children to listen to, and encourage parents to bring family photos to school, for a special book or to hang in the child's cubby.

Sometimes teachers are concerned that this special attention to the new child will shortchange the other children. It is useful to remember that individualizing responsive care for children means not always giving the same thing to all the children at the same time. The other children likely don't have such acute needs at this time. Further, they are learning valuable lessons about compassion, feelings, and adult trustworthiness.

They may call parents during the day with positive information to reassure them: "Jon has a new friend. He's been playing in the block corner with David all morning." They may take Polaroid pictures of the child involved in activity, and send with a note describing the activity and naming the children playing with their child. All of these gestures indicate to parents that teachers care enough to make sure they are being included in these first adjustments.

Some teachers find that in order not to foster dependency, some of this special attention and support can be supplied by pairing a new child with a special friend, someone who has already adapted to the classroom and has a personality that would enjoy helping to nurture a new child. A new parent can be introduced and provided opportunities to converse with a parent who has weathered the stress of separation. But dependency is less of a concern than fostering feelings of comfort and confidence.

All beginnings are important. The long-term effects of establishing parent-teacher relationships with clear patterns of empathetic communication, as well as a child's successful adaptation, justify taking these careful steps.

❖ Summary

Good beginnings include the following:

1. A meeting with a school's director to consider what a parent is looking for in a preschool and how this matches with a school's philosophy and practices.

2. An introductory conversation between a parent and individual classroom teacher. Specific information on a child and classroom is exchanged. Further orientation plans are formed.

3. A brief home visit so a teacher and child can meet on a child's secure home base.

4. A brief visit of parent and child to a classroom, specifically planned for a time when a teacher is free to interact with the child.

5. An easing-in schedule, so a child can slowly adjust to classroom life on less than a full-time basis.

6. Teacher assistance to parent and child during peak separation stress.

❖ Student Activities for Further Study

1. With your classmates, role-play the following situations, with one of you being a teacher who is trying to get to know, support, and establish a relationship with a parent who is enrolling a preschool child in your center.

   a. Parent says the child has never been left with anyone else in three years.

   b. Parent seems very reluctant to answer any questions about the child.

   c. Parent asks if she can stay until child stops crying—"It may take a while"—parent seems very tense.

   d. Parent says she really doesn't have time for the teacher to visit or have an extended conversation with the teacher, or allow the child to visit or "ease-in."

   e. Parent seems very frightened of the teacher.

2. Role-play the following situations and have your "audience" discuss a teacher's role in helping both parent and child during separation stress.

   a. Teacher with a parent whose child is screaming and clinging to the parent's neck—parent started a new job two days ago.

   b. Teacher with a parent whose child is screaming and clinging to the parent's neck—parent starts new job next week.

   c. Child says good-bye happily; mother stands at door looking very sad.

   d. Two hours after parent left, child begins to cry and says, "I want my Daddy."

   e. Parent begins to sneak out while child is distracted with a toy.

3. Ask several parents how they chose their preschool center: did they visit; were there particular things they were looking for; what convinced them this was the place for their child?

4. Look at the information forms that parents fill in at your center and several others. Do the forms really allow the parents to begin to share their particular knowledge of their child? What additional questions might be helpful?

❖ Review Questions

1. Describe an ideal process of orientation to a center for a child and his parents.

2. Discuss why each step of the orientation process is beneficial and what strategies a teacher may consider with each step.

3. Identify several behaviors typically associated with separation problems in preschool children.

4. Discuss several teacher behaviors that are helpful in assisting parents and children in adjusting to separation.

❖ Suggestions for Further Reading

Balaban, N. (1987). *Learning to say goodbye.* New American Library.

___. (1989, Aug./Sept.) Separation: helping children through the process. *Scholastic Pre-K Today, 4*(1), 36–42.

Daniel, J. (1995, March). New beginnings: transitions for difficult children. *Young Children, 50*(3), 17–23.

Duggins, L. (1985). Start from a safe place. *First Teacher, 6*(9), 2.

Epstein, C. (1985, Oct.). Kids and separation: books that help. *Parents,* 202–205.

Gottschall, S. (1989). Understanding and accepting separation feelings. *Young Children, 44*(6), 11–16.

Kleckner, K.A., and Engel, R.E. (1988). A child begins school: relieving anxiety with books. *Young Children, 43*(5), 14–18.

Montanari, E. (1993, March). Keeping families happy—communication is the key. *Child Care Information Exchange, 89*, 21–23.

Mundorf, N.K. (1994, Nov./Dec.) Bye-bye's with fewer tears. *Early Childhood News,* 20–21,

Viorst, J. (1986). *Necessary losses.* New York: Fawcett.

Waterland, L. (1995). *The bridge to school: entering a new world.* Columbus, OH: Stenhouse Publishers.

CHAPTER 9

Informal Communication with Parents

Relationships that work are built on trust and open communication. Finding methods to communicate regularly with parents is a challenge for teachers who already have many responsibilities within their classrooms. Obviously, face-to-face conversations are most important in communication, and we will explore how to provide opportunities for these. But in addition, there are other techniques that help keep information flowing both ways. Chapter 9 examines a variety of methods of informal communication that teachers can utilize to build relationships with parents.

OBJECTIVES

After studying this chapter, the student will be able to

1. identify eight techniques a teacher uses to convey information, interest, and support to parents.

2. discuss details for implementing each communication technique.

❖ Communication Techniques

As teachers begin to work with parents and children, it is important to open and keep open lines of communication. As previously discussed, the initiative for opening a dialogue should come from teachers. By approaching parents, teachers demonstrate their willingness to adapt to individual differences in personality, preferences, and time constraints that may result in different responses to the same method. For example, a busy parent may barely glance at the parents' bulletin board while rushing by, but enjoy reading a newsletter at home, while a quiet parent who does not usually talk much to the teachers may eagerly read everything offered on the bulletin board. For this reason, teachers should utilize as many of the communication techniques as they can. Most techniques are not time-consuming; a few minutes a day to work on ideas for the next newsletter or bulletin board, or for writing several individual notes or making a few telephone calls may be sufficient.

Communication techniques can be a one-way or two-way endeavor (Berger 1991). One-way communication from a class or school can inform parents about events or plans, or attempt to education parents. While this is important, since parents have a need and desire to know what is going on, a real sense of partnership grows through two-way communication that encourages and facilitates true dialogue, with parents actively reacting and responding. Devices can be incorporated into many communication methods that are normally one-way communication to expand them to two-way communication. In fact, expanding many ideas that have been traditionally used may make them interactive.

No matter what other informal techniques teachers use as alternatives for establishing communication with parents, it must be remembered that these techniques should not replace personal contact. Nothing is as important as personal, face-to-face conversation for building relationships.

Daily Conversations

> Connie Martinez says, "I don't have time for too much else, but I do a lot of talking to parents every day."

Frequent daily conversations when parents drop off and pick up their children are extremely important in building trust by fostering a sense of familiarity. A study of frequency of communication between parents and caregivers indicated that the highest frequency of communication occurs at the "transition point" when parents leave and pick up their child at a center (Powell 1978). There is an obvious problem when children are brought by car-pool drop-off or bus; teachers in these situations have to work harder to maintain regular contact by telephone calls or notes. (See Figure 9-1.)

Important things happen during these brief exchanges. Parents want to know that their child is known and recognized as a person. To see a teacher greet their child personally by name is reassuring. Parents also want to be greeted by name themselves.

> "Good morning, Pete. You look ready to play today. I've put some of those new little cars that you like in the block corner. How are you this morning, Mrs. Lawrence? Pete's been telling me about his new bedroom—you must be pretty busy at home these days."

This can be a time for brief but substantive exchanges on child- and family-related issues. Studies indicate that these conversations may be the most frequent form of parent involvement, although the substance of the conversations may not progress beyond social niceties (Powell 1989). The topics discussed most frequently are child-related, including child-peer relations and child-caregiver relations. However, when communication is frequent, the diversity and number of topics discussed by parents and teachers increases, pointing to the need for frequent conversations to build relationships. With greater frequency, the number of family-related topics discussed increases. More than social conversation is needed; quality care demands that home and center coordinate their efforts and exchange information on a regular basis. Extensive dialogue between parents and teachers is necessary for such coordination. The 'hellos' and 'how's it goings' are not to be diminished in importance; many significant messages may be

Figure 9-1 When children are dropped off by carpool, teachers have to work hard to maintain regular contact with parents. Courtesy CPCC Media Productions—Mike Slade.

transmitted in interactions that are direct and that outwardly appear shallow in substance. When these indirect messages constitute a significant portion of parent-caregiver interaction, however, their clarity and impact are questionable (Powell 1978, 687).

But nothing happens if there is no contact. A recent study (Endsley and Minish 1991, reported in Doherty-Derkowski, 1995) found that the average length of conversation between caregiver and parents at transition times was twelve seconds! Sixty-three percent of all "conversations" were greetings or other small talk, no real exchange of information. And in nearly half of the situations observed, the parent and caregiver did not even greet each other. Clearly, this is no way to begin or to build a relationship.

The frequency and quality of these daily contacts depend primarily on factors in classroom routine and center policy that can be planned and regulated. Staffing patterns need to provide an optimum number of staff available to talk during times when parents arrive at the beginning and end of the day. Preparing materials before parents arrive, or saving cleanup for after parents depart, keeps a teacher's attention from being diverted away from the door as parents arrive. If teachers display simple, open-ended materials that children can use with no need for adult assistance, neither parents nor teachers will have to devote full attention to the demands of children. When both members of a teaching team are in the classroom, making definite assignments for either child care or adult conversations clarifies expected behaviors for both teachers and parents. It is a good idea for the teachers in a team to take turns being responsible for conversations with parents, so parents develop relationships with both and do not feel they have no one to talk with in the absence of one teacher.

The atmosphere created by teachers and staff can either open or close opportunities for informal chats. The teacher who says, "Hello, how are you?" and turns to busy herself elsewhere indicates her unwillingness to prolong the contact. A teacher who asks a broad question that invites response—"Looks like you've had a busy day"—and stands by the parent, obviously ready to continue, creates an expectation of conversation. (See Figure 9-2.)

Some teachers complain they can never think of anything to say when a parent comes in. For these teachers, it might be helpful to consider what they most enjoy about a child and share these observations. It is difficult for most parents to resist a conversation that begins by focusing personally on their child. What else can teachers use to initiate conversation? Parents would love to hear about a favorite song, book, or activity; about new things their child is interested in; about who their child plays with; what the areas and materials in the classroom are called. Get started—other ideas will come.

Teachers striving for daily contact with all parents are helped to perceive their own patterns by keeping an informal tally (on a file card in the pocket or on a paper taped to the wall) briefly recording who was spoken to, for how long, and the topic of conversation. This often identifies a parent who was slipping in and out unnoticed, or with whom the teacher never felt comfortable enough to progress beyond the "How are you" stage.

Figure 9-2 When teachers create the expectancy for conversation, parents usually respond. Courtesy Connie Glass.

One study indicates that almost 30 percent of day-care parents do not enter a center when leaving their children for the day (Powell 1989). A clear and firm center policy about parents accompanying their children to a classroom is needed, stressing to parents both the need for safety and a child's emotional security, as well as the importance of making daily contact with a teacher. (See Figure 9-3.) The same study showed that as the frequency of communication between parents and teachers rises, communication attitudes become more positive. A policy that facilitates and supports this contact is beneficial.

One center posts a sign-in sheet on the parents' bulletin board just by the door. Rather than signing in the time of their child's arrival, which some centers do, this sheet provides a space beside each child's name for parents to fill in the phone number at which they can be reached that day. Space in the last column allows for parents' regular comments. A device like this makes routine the concept that parents will come in each day.

Teachers may need to help sensitize parents to the concept that conversations about children do not take place over children's heads, as if they cannot understand the meaning or the fact they are being discussed. By modeling such respect for children's feelings, teachers help parents grow in their understanding of children's needs and emotions. It is appropriate to direct conversations that turn to specifics involving children or families to another time or place.

Figure 9-3 A school policy stating that parents accompany their children to the class-room facilitates daily contact with teachers. Courtesy CPCC Media Productions—Mike Slade.

> "I'd like to talk more about this with you—could we step outside for a minute?"
>
> "This is important information that I'm not comfortable talking about right here—can we find a few minutes when you come back this afternoon to talk more privately?"

Some teachers are afraid that by encouraging parents to talk, they will begin a flow of conversation that they will be unable to cut off, and that the conversation will interfere with a teacher's accomplishing certain tasks and operating the classroom smoothly. In most situations, this is not the case, as parents' own pressing demands limit their available time. In those situations where parents completely accept an invitation to talk and spend long periods of time in a classroom, teachers should realize these parents are showing a need for companionship and feelings of belonging and try to find ways to meet this need. Teachers may suggest that parents join in an activity or find a way of linking one parent with another.

"I've enjoyed talking with you, and I must get busy mixing the paint now. If you can spend a little more time with us, I know the children in the block corner would enjoy having you be with them."

"Mrs. Jones, let me introduce Mrs. Brown. Your boys have been very busy building together this week; have you been hearing about these adventures at home?"

When parents ask teachers for lots of detailed information at a busy dismissal time, teachers may answer briefly, then set up an arrangement to give more information later, by note or telephone call. If these dismissal requests happen repeatedly, it may help the parent to become aware of classroom needs if teachers have children almost ready to leave when the parents arrive.

If a teacher realizes that daily conversations are valuable, she is more likely to find creative ways of dealing with potential problems like this, rather than cutting off all forms of communication.

Occasionally, teachers can encourage parents to spend a few extra minutes in the classroom with their children and teachers by making a cup of coffee available at the beginning or end of the day. No elaborate preparation is necessary for teachers or parents. Children can show things to parents or play as parents chat with teachers and other adults. Such an occasion offers a brief chance for everyone to relax together and is supportive for both parents and teachers.

Although daily conversations are probably most important in the context of other plans for parent involvement, they should not be seen as an end in themselves; other arrangements are needed to ensure the development of trust and full communication. In studies of groups of parents, it is uncertain

Figure 9-4 Daily notes and telephone calls may help when children ride a van and teachers do not see parents daily. Courtesy Bethlehem Center, Charlotte, N.C.; Peeler Portrait Studio, photographer.

whether trust develops solely on the basis of informal conversations or is instead a by-product of parents being impressed by the many efforts of teachers to be open to them (Tizard, et al. 1981). Nevertheless, beginning steps towards openness are perceived in daily interaction.

Telephone Calls

For teachers who cannot be in daily contact with parents, the telephone offers an opportunity for personal conversation. (See Figure 9-4.) Sometimes teachers use phone calls to indicate concern if a child is absent for several days.

> "Hello, Mrs. Rodriguez. I just wanted to let you know we've missed Tony at school. Has he been sick?"

Another important use of the phone call is to share personal observations about a child.

> "I thought you'd like to know. Lisa has been working so hard on the new climbing apparatus, and today she got to the top with no help at all! Was she pleased!"
>
> "I know you've been worried about Ricky's appetite, so I wanted to let you know I've been noticing him doing much better at lunch today. Today he ate two helpings of macaroni and cheese."

Such phone calls take only a few minutes each, but they let parents know of a teacher's interest and knowledge of their child and go a long way in establishing positive teacher-parent relations. The telephone facilitates two-way communication. Parents may be comfortable asking questions about progress or behavior they might not otherwise raise. Using the telephone is especially important for regular contact with those parents who are not in frequent contact with the teacher, either because of work schedules or transportation arrangements. These are "no problem" telephone calls, to offer positive attention. It is not a good idea to initiate conversation on the telephone about problems that teachers and parents need to address. Without being able to see parents' facial expressions, it is difficult to get their full response. These conversations are best handled face-to-face.

Communication opportunities can be further increased by the establishment of a telephone hour when parents can feel comfortable calling a teacher. One teacher chose an evening hour once a week; another chose a nap-time hour when other staff were available to supervise her children (Swap 1987). When the teacher has some control over when telephone calls will occur, they intrude less into her personal life. And when parents know about this regular opportunity, they will usually respect the appointed time.

An innovative use of the telephone to increase interaction and communication between school and home is being used presently by several schools in Alabama, Georgia, and Tennessee. Each teacher records a one-to-three minute message at the end of the school day, summarizing learning assignments, stating homework assignments, and including suggestions to parents for home learning. Parents can call and hear the message at any time, and can also leave a message for the teacher. This "Transparent School" concept has been found to substantially increase numbers of parent contacts with the school. Students from the "frequent user" homes showed a significant increase in homework completion. (For more information, see note in references at the end of the book.)

Personal Notes

Sharing positive, personal observations or anecdotes can also be accomplished by a teacher sending a personal note home with a child. Notes tend to be perceived as one-way communication, but a teacher may design them to invite response.

> "I wanted to let you know I've noticed Ricky is eating more at lunch lately. Have you also noticed an increase at home?"

Some teachers use pre-printed "Happy-Grams," filling in the blanks:

> "<u>Pete</u> has been doing a good job at <u>cleanup</u>."

However, this lacks a personal tone. Personal notes take only one or two minutes to write. If a teacher sends out two or three a day, each child in a classroom might take one home within a week or two.

Sometimes the note can accompany a sample of the child's work, to explain or expand on the idea. For example, for parents who are new at appreciating the stages of art young children move through, it might lead to more productive conversation between parent and child if the teacher makes a comment.

> "This is the first time Seth has made a closed scribble with his paint brush. That shows his small muscle coordination is really improving. He enjoyed the red paint today, as you can see!"

Notes back and forth may be exchanged in a notebook kept in each child's cubby.

Personal notes of appreciation to parents who have shared materials, time, or ideas reinforce a teacher's expression of pleasure. A tape recording of a child talking about a new experience or talking with a friend at snack time can be sent to parents, along with the tape recorder if necessary.

Figure 9-5   Bulletin boards can help parents learn about community resources.
Courtesy CPCC Media Productions—Mike Slade.

Bulletin Boards

Bulletin boards offer another form of reaching out to parents. Powell found in his study of day-care parents that those he characterized as "independent" had a low frequency of communication with staff and used non-staff sources of information, such as bulletin boards (Powell 1978).

A bulletin board needs to be clearly visible in an area well traveled by parents, preferably just outside a classroom, so parents make a clear connection between the information offered and the teacher as the source. It needs to be labeled for "Parents," so parents realize this is information meant for them. Eye-catching materials, such as snapshots of children, classroom activities, and samples of work, invite closer attention. Using different colors of paper or fabric as backgrounds is a visual indication to parents that there is a change in bulletin board offerings.

The information offered by a bulletin board will be decided upon by a teacher as she listens to parents' questions and comments or finds areas where they need resources or help. (See Figure 9-5.) Occasionally, bulletin boards may offer guidelines on choosing books or toys, on childhood diseases and immunization needs, nutritious menus appealing to children, suggestions for movies, television or local events, developmental information, or solutions to family problems, handouts or recent articles that prepare or follow up on a topic under discussion at a parents' meeting. Sometimes a sequence of bulletin boards can be planned. For example, one on how to choose good books for children, followed by one on library resources for parents and children. A third board on using books to help deal with childhood problems can be planned. Longer articles, recipes, or directions for making things can be mimeographed and offered in a folder of "take-aways." (See Figure 9-6.) (The empty folder offers proof to a teacher that a bulletin board is used.)

Figure 9-6   Longer articles can be offered in a folder of "take-aways."   Courtesy CPCC Media Productions—Mike Slade.

Bulletin boards can offer support to parents in the form of a wry cartoon or two reminding parents that a teacher understands the childhood foibles confronting them.

A bulletin board, or part of one, can be provided for parent contributions such as offers to babysit, exchange outgrown snowsuits, or requests for carpool drivers. The bulletin board may be used for interactive communication if teachers ask or encourage parents to ask questions that demand others' answers.

If a teacher wants to have a bulletin board used, it is necessary to change it frequently; a board that stays the same for weeks teaches parents not to look at it. When a teacher does put new material out, it helps to emphasize it by a visual change—new pictures or background colors. (If a teacher has the dilemma of choosing to spend time on elaborate changes or new information, it is preferable to pick the latter and keep it neat, simple, but, above all, new.) Material too long to be read in a few minutes needs to be offered as a "take-away" or it won't be used. Keep a board's appearance simple and uncluttered; it is better to offer one important point than so many that a busy parent feels it will take too much time to absorb the information.

If a center has enough room, a separate area for parents close to the main reception area can be provided with comfortable chairs, a coffee pot, and interesting periodicals This is the area for storing resources available for parents to check out, such as parenting books, children's books and toys, videos the teacher has taken of the class, and so on. (If space is a problem, such materials can be stored in a rolling cabinet which is placed in a central spot during pick-up and drop-off times.)

Having a space for parents is a concrete reminder that parents are welcome to stop, relax, and enjoy what a school has to offer.

Daily News Flash

"What about the parents who are in and out quickly?" wonders Dorothy Scott. "Is there any way of making contact with them?"

There are a number of ways of connecting with parents who are too busy for conversation. A daily news flash is one method of letting parents know what's going on and information that teachers want parents to know. (See Figure 9-7.) In a prominent place outside the classroom door or near the main entrance for parents waiting in the carpool line is a large board—perhaps a chalk board, a bulletin board, or a corner of one—that briefly describes one thing children have done or talked about that day.

This morning we blew bubbles outside.

We learned a new song today about squirrels.

Tommy's mother had a new baby boy last night, so we talked a lot about babies.

Classroom daily news flashes are not earth-shaking, but offer something tangible from the day that parents can pursue with their children. Most parents are grateful for these bits of news that make them feel a part of the day.

Figure 9-7 A daily flash may be part of the bulletin board—in another eye-catching spot.

Some centers post a board or memo pad for teachers to write personal reports on each child's day. This can be especially useful if there is a change in staff during the day, so that parents have reports from all staff involved with their child.

Tommy	A busy morning, great block building Very sleepy after nap time
Sarah	Quiet this morning Enjoyed talking with Jamie at lunch
Seth	Sad for a short time after Dad left, then busy with play dough Hard time sleeping at nap time, so rested, then read a book.
LaTonya	Loved our new song "Alice the Camel" Discovered broccoli is all right!

All such efforts convince parents that teachers are paying some personal attention to their children and that teachers are really trying to keep in touch.

Newsletters

Another communication technique involves sending regular newsletters to all parents. Newsletters have four main objectives: (1) to keep parents informed of classroom activities and plans; (2) to give parents insight into the educational purposes underlying classroom activities; (3) to enhance children's and parents' abilities to communicate with each other; and (4) to reinforce and extend learning from school into the home (Harms and Cryer 1978).

Parents are often frustrated when attempting to learn directly from their children what has gone on in school, and newsletters will solve this problem. (See Figure 9-8.) Content of the newsletter could include events that have occurred since the last newsletter, upcoming activities and themes, and ways parents can help with them, or practical examples of how parents can reinforce learning at home.

With the holiday season approaching, we will be discussing families—how many people are in our families and the things families do together. If you have an old family snapshot we could use for making a book together, we'd be grateful for you to share it.

Figure 9-8 Parents enjoy reading news of classroom activities.

We had a exciting snack time last Thursday. The children watched in amazement while the popcorn popped—right out of the popper onto a clean sheet spread on the floor. The children enjoyed their snack of popcorn and milk. We are trying to emphasize healthy snacks now. If you would like to join us for snack or have an idea which would be fun and healthy for snack, please share with us.

I know some of you have been frustrated in trying to understand the newest songs your children have been singing this fall. Enclosed are some words so you can sing along. (Words added.)

Dear Parents,

Here are some things we have done in the last two weeks to introduce the sense of smell to the children.

1. We made smell vials using cloves, peppermint, coffee, cinnamon, garlic, chili powder, vanilla, and perfume. We put each ingredient in a vial, poked holes in the lid, and covered them with nylon to keep the ingredients inside.

2. We roasted peanuts and used them in making peanut butter.

        2 cups roasted shelled peanuts
        2 tablespoons salad oil
        Salt

First we shelled the peanuts and put them in a meat grinder. This is much more fun for the children than a blender. Then we added the oil and salt.

3. One day we made collages of magazine pictures of things that smell.

4. Another day we cooked play dough using oil of wintergreen. It sure smelled good!

5. We also learned "The Smelling Song." Tune: "Did You Ever See a Lassie?"

Have you ever smelled a rosebud, a rosebud, a rosebud?
Have you ever smelled a rosebud?
Oh, how does it smell?

The children suggested substitutes by themselves, and responded verbally after each verse.

These are some basic understandings we were trying to teach:

a. We smell through our noses.

b. We learn about things by the way they smell.

c. Some things smell good; some things smell bad.

d. Animals find things by smelling.

e. Smelling some things warns us of danger.

This might be fun to carry on at home. Ask your child if he can close his eyes and identify foods in your kitchen or on the dinner table. Let us know how the game went.

Newsletters need to be fairly short—one printed page is about enough—so that parents do not set them aside, unread, thinking they are too time-consuming. Newsletters sent regularly, monthly or bi-weekly, will not get too far behind on current activities. They need to be neat, attractive, and display care for grammar and spelling. They can be made visually interesting with headings, graphics, changed typeface, or content divided into sections. Care with details indicates planning and effort on a teacher's part, further evidence of a teacher's concern.

It might be interesting for teachers to suggest a question parents could ask their children to trigger the children's memories of classroom events.

Ask your child what we saw when we visited the dairy last week. Something special was being packaged!

Sometimes anecdotes from children or use of children's names capture parent interest.

We have some new toys we're enjoying. Maria and Lisa have been busy mothering the new dolls. Seth, Tony, and Matthew have been fighting fires with the new fire truck, and Justin and Isaac enjoy outside time when they can ride the new hot wheels.

Recognition of special parent involvement and announcements of family events may build feelings that the classroom sees itself as a link for connecting parents.

> We especially enjoyed Mrs. Rodriguez's helping us build a pinata for the Christmas party.
>
> We're all waiting, along with Pete, for the arrival of his new baby. Fanny Lawrence will be taking a few months off from her teaching job after the baby arrives.

While there is no substitute for the personal classroom news that each parent wants or the addition of simple explanatory comments for subtle education from a familiar teacher, busy teachers may occasionally find that they want to insert an article produced by another professional. Some of these are available commercially (see Hymes, n.d.; Parent and Preschooler Newsletter).

To elicit two-way communication, teachers sometimes add a question for parent response and include the responses in the next newsletter.

> Would you please share ideas with other parents of activities and places you and your child have recently enjoyed in the community on weekends? We'll include these suggestions in our next letter.

Parents may be encouraged to run their own idea corner, with a parent editing this section. A regular feature for the newsletter could be a question and answer section, with parents encouraged to ask questions that teachers could answer for all. This might also be the section that is used for education and for reminders about community events.

Some teachers find that newsletters offer an opportunity for self-evaluation, as they answer the questions asked by parents concerning what they have been doing and why. Others use a collection of the newsletters for the orientation of new parents, since the pages present a summary of classroom activities throughout the year (Harms and Cryer 1978).

Traveling Suitcase and Libraries

Teachers can make contact with parents by sending home with a child a "traveling suitcase." On a rotating basis, each child has the privilege of overnight or weekend use of several items selected from the classroom. A child may choose a favorite book to have her parent read, or a puzzle he has just mastered to show. Depending on a teacher's knowledge of the socioeconomic background of the families involved, one or more of the items might be to keep—a lump of cooked play dough, with a recipe for making more later, construction paper for using at home, or a teacher-made matching game. Some teachers include a class-made book with pictures and names of each child in the class; parents enjoy associating faces with the names they hear from their children and seeing the visual record of classroom daily life.

Most children are very pleased to be able to show their parents something that has been enjoyed at school, and a child's enthusiasm often guarantees that the materials will be used and discussed. Children who have been taught that the "traveling suitcase" is a special privilege are also usually very responsible about the care of these "school things."

The bag can be used to exchange teacher and parent notes as well. A teacher may suggest "homework assignments" that parent and child can enjoy together. "Help your child find a picture of something big and of something little." "Help your child count out two crackers to bring—one for him and one to share with a friend."

Offering parents the opportunity to borrow materials they can use with their children is further evidence of caring. A stock of paperback children's books, perhaps those no longer used in classrooms or homes, may be borrowed for use at home. Numerous classrooms are using a rotating system to encourage family literacy. Good children's books are sent home one at a time in a ziplock bag. When the book is returned to school the next day, another book is selected from the collection until all the children in the classroom have read each of the books and then a new collection is begun. The excitement generated among the children about being able to take home a book that a friend has already enjoyed translates into real family interest. Literacy benefits from this variation on the traveling suitcase (Jordan, personal communication; Brock and Dodd 1994). Parenting books can also be available on loan. In the same way, children's toys can be available for loan by parents and children.

Another idea for circulating materials between home and school is to have classroom videos available for check out (Greenwood 1995). Teachers record classroom activities such as a cooking activity or story time, special visitors and events, and conversations. Children check out the videos to share at home with their families, with an attached "Comment Sheet" on which families can respond. Their comments are then shared with all the children back in the classroom. (Greenwood also comments that the videotapes may be used in other ways, such as for open houses, for parents who are sitting in the parent lounge, and to play over local-access cable stations during the Week of the Young Child.)

Another circulating form of communication could be letters sent home by teachers and children, especially in the early school years, and answering letters from their parents (Manning, et al. 1995). Teachers add a letter to all children's circulating notebooks each week about classroom learning activities. Then children add their own drawings and written letters, and parents respond. Not only does the growing notebook document the varied learning and writing progress during the year, it also provides children with meaningful opportunities to develop their own communication skills, and draws parents into seeing the real evidence of their children's learning.

Suggestion Boxes

It is useful for teachers to devise several methods of obtaining feedback from parents about the classroom, their goals, and the methods of involving them in the program. Various tools can be designed for parent evaluation, from checklists, to fill-in-the-blanks, to rating scales. For example, "Check which of the following have been useful to you this month: newsletter, bulletin board, daily flash, daily conversations." Parent interests can be surveyed—we'll talk more about this in chapters 12 and 13. A suggestion box should be prominently located and its use encouraged. Some parents are reluctant to raise issues with teachers directly, and may be more comfortable with the anonymity of forms or printed material. Other parents, less comfortable with literacy, may prefer to communicate through a designated parent representative for the classroom, who can then neutrally raise the issue. In whatever form, it is a demonstration of openness to parental input that teachers want to encourage.

If teachers list the good ideas contributed by parents in newsletters, parents realize that their ideas have been read and appreciated. Newsletter references to the suggestions also provide a means of explaining when or how the suggestion will be acted on, or explanations as to why some things may not be possible.

❖ Summary

The ideas discussed in this chapter are not time-consuming, and most don't require a great deal of formal planning. Teachers who use newsletters and bulletin boards often keep a file of ideas, articles, and clippings for future use and save things from year to year. Moreover, these efforts convey to parents that teachers are paying personal attention to their children and are really trying to keep in touch. What is important is for teachers to realize is that these contacts provide vital ongoing links between parent and teacher that are irreplaceable for building knowledge of and comfort with one another and evidence for parents that their involvement is welcome.

To summarize, a parent-teacher partnership is strengthened as teachers utilize the following informal communication methods with parents:

1. Daily conversations.
2. Telephone calls.
3. Personal notes.
4. Bulletin boards.
5. Daily news flash.
6. Newsletters.
7. Traveling suitcases, library, and other circulating materials.
8. Parent suggestion box and evaluation methods.

❖ Student Activities for Further Study

1. If you are in a classroom situation, keep a tally of the parents you speak to at drop-off and pickup times each day for a week. (A file card in your pocket can be used conveniently to jot down names.) Are there any parents you are missing contact with? Do you know why? Are there any parents you have little conversation with, beyond "hello" and "goodbye?" Do you know why? What circumstances create difficulties in finding time to talk in this particular classroom situation? Are there any alternatives that could help solve the problem?

2. Observe the encounters as teachers and parents meet each other at drop-off and pickup times. What nonverbal clues of comfort or discomfort do you note? How do teachers use space to convey messages of welcome or distance? Are names used? What topics are discussed? What are children doing as parents and teachers talk?

3. Write and distribute a newsletter for your classroom. (Let parents know what has happened recently and why it happened, or how the children reacted to it.)

4. Design a bulletin board with a theme that you feel would be helpful to a group of parents.

5. Plan a brief, personal note that you could write to each parent, sharing something positive about their child.

❖ Review Questions

1. Identify eight techniques teachers may use to convey information, interest, and support to parents.

2. For each technique identified, discuss two ways to implement it.

❖ Suggestions for Further Reading

Andrews, P. (1976). What every parent wants to know. *Childhood Education, 52*(6), 304–305.

Bell, R.A. (1985). Parent involvement: how and why. *Dimensions, 14*(1), 15–18.

Bundy, B.F. (1991, Jan.). Fostering communication between parents and preschools. *Young Children, 46*(2), 12–16.

Duff, R.E., Heinz, M.C., and Husband, C.L. (1978). Toy lending library; linking home and school. *Young Children, 33*(4), 16–24.

Edmister, P. (1977). Establishing a parent education resource center. *Childhood Education, 57*(2), 62–66.

Sclan, E. (1986, Fall). Twelve ways to work with parents—how to set up communication lines that stay open all year. *Instructor's ECE Teacher,* 39–41.

CHAPTER 10

Parent-Teacher Conferences

Besides regular informal contact and conversations, teachers need to provide opportunities for purposeful in-depth conversations with parents in parent conferences. In such structured meetings, there are opportunities for both parents and teachers to discover additional information, to assess their progress towards mutual and separate goals for children, and to continue to develop their relationships. But such benefits do not occur without planning and preparation on the part of teachers and parents. Because these conversations cover a wider range of topics than the briefer daily encounters, teachers need to ready materials, questions, and observations to make good use of the time. Arrangements will also need to be made for parental time and participation. With preparation, practice, and care in communication, parent conferences need not be a matter for apprehension. In this chapter, we will examine techniques that can be part of a teacher's attempt to structure productive situations for the exchange of information and plans.

OBJECTIVES

After studying this chapter, the student will be able to

1. identify four reasons for holding regular parent-teacher conferences.
2. list eight factors that facilitate productive parent-teacher conferences.
3. list six pitfalls to avoid in parent-teacher conferences.

❖ Importance of Regular Conferences

Casual conversations are extremely important, but the more formal arrangement of parent-teacher conferences offers additional opportunities for parents and teachers to work as partners. Yet conferences are often not used by many teachers or centers unless there are problems. The reasons for this include both fear and misunderstanding of the purposes of conferences.

The hearts of many parents and teachers may be filled with anxiety when it is time to schedule conferences. Part of this negative feeling may come from the fact that an infrequent parent-teacher conference may be virtually the only contact between them. Ideally, a parent-teacher conference offers an opportunity for the free exchange of information, questions, and ideas, and can be accomplished best after a relationship is already established. Conferences can help a relationship grow, but cannot function optimally if participants are not already comfortable with each other. All of the earlier contacts and communications are helpful prerequisites for a successful conference. Teachers should make it a goal to have some type of contact with every family before parent conference time. In some cases, circumstances may prevent the formation of a prior relationship; this is no reason to avoid scheduling a conference to begin the communication process.

Unfortunately, many parents and teachers view conferences as a last step in dealing with negative behavior. If it is assumed that parents and teachers meet only when behavior is a problem, no one can anticipate such a meeting with pleasure. Parents' history of conflict or success in their own early school situations may lay the ground for this assumption. Some will recall negative experiences when their own parents were called in for conferences. In fact, most of this reluctance probably comes from the fact that for many years, in the school systems for elementary-aged children and beyond, the only parent-teacher contacts were infrequent conferences where virtual strangers came together rather defensively to clear up some difficulty. As early childhood education programs and child care centers began to work with parents, teachers had little except these negative conference models to work from. (See Figure 10-1.)

To be productive, it is important that conferences be seen as a routine and necessary component of the ongoing coordination of information and efforts in a teacher-parent partnership.

Figure 10-1 Many parents are apprehensive about parent conferences. Courtesy Barbara Stegall.

"Oh sure, I understand how important it is for parents and teachers to talk," says Connie Martinez, "but I don't really see the need to get so formal as to have a conference. I talk to most of my parents every day. And these are, after all, preschoolers. It's not like we have to talk about reading and math test scores or anything. So why should I have conferences?"

There are several reasons why holding regular parent-teacher conferences is important, regardless of a child's age.

To Provide Developmental Overview

Conferences provide an opportunity to examine the overall progress of a child in a detailed and organized way. In daily conversations, particular accomplishments or aspects of development may be discussed. This may be a new ability—such as climbing up the slide—or a different behavior—such as a decrease in appetite at lunchtime. Particular problems may catch the attention of a teacher or parent—a new tendency to cry when Mother leaves or an increase in toileting accidents; such matters are frequently discussed in daily exchanges. But a complete look at a child's development is not possible in these brief encounters. Conferences provide opportunities for both parents and teachers to move beyond the daily specifics to an objective examination of total development.

To Provide Time and Privacy

Conferences provide uninterrupted blocks of time and an atmosphere of privacy, two essentials for facilitating the sharing of information and the formulating of questions and plans. (See Figure 10-2.) Regardless of a preschool teacher's commitment to talk with parents, the demands of caring for a group of young children may emphatically pull a teacher away from a conversation. She can't stand and discuss toilet training techniques at length while two children in the block corner are boisterously trying to knock down the tower of a third.

Parents often postpone talking about their concerns because of their awareness of the demands for a teacher's time.

> "I've been wanting to talk to Miss Briscoe about helping Pete get ready for this new baby," sighs Pete's mother. "But I hate to interrupt her—she's always got so much to do. I thought I'd go in a few minutes early this afternoon, but then a child upset some paint and another was crying when she got up from her nap, so it just didn't seem like a good time again."

Knowing they have time for just talking is important for both parents and teachers.

Figure 10-2   Conferences give teacher and parents time to talk away from the demands of classroom and listening children. Courtesy CPCC Media Productions—Mike Slade.

Privacy is also needed to facilitate comfort in talking. Teachers who are trying to model sensitivity and respect for children's feelings usually prefer not to discuss them within their hearing or the hearing of other children. While there are occasions when teachers feel it is appropriate to include a child in a parent-teacher conference, every conference would have to be considered separately, thinking of the individual child and the material for discussion (Bjorklund and Burger 1987; Readdick et al. 1984; Freeman 1986). Many teachers feel that a child's presence can seriously inhibit the parents' willingness to discuss family matters.

Parents are often understandably reluctant to ask for help in parenting skills or to discuss relationships where they might be interrupted by other adults. The privacy of a conference situation makes important discussion easier.

To Increase Mutual Knowledge

The unhurried flow of conversation in a conference setting allows for an exchange of questions and information that brief contacts at the beginning or end of a classroom day simply cannot.

"You know, it wasn't until after we'd gone through the developmental checklist and Mrs. Butler saw how well Sam compares with the average for four-year-olds that she told me how worried she's always been that he'd be slow. Seems he resembles a cousin in her family who has a learning disability, and she was afraid Sam might have inherited the same problem. It really helped me understand why she's been asking so many questions about getting early academics started in the classroom, and doing so much at home. It was a relief for both of us to be able to talk about how really well Sam does and to know what she really wanted to talk about was the best ways to stimulate learning in the preschool years."

Misunderstandings and concerns can only surface in longer conference conversations, with time to reflect on what each other is saying. Conferences offer opportunities for clarification and deeper explanations of many issues.

To Formulate Goals

Conferences can provide an important basis for formulating future goals and working plans.

"She decided, during our conversation, that maybe her teaching sessions with Sam at home weren't the best idea. I said that in the classroom I was trying to provide lots of books about dinosaurs, his current interest, and was trying to be available to read one to him each

> day. She thought she'd try something like that at home. We decided to get back together in three months and see whether this method was helping him enjoy books more."

Conference situations contribute to a sense of mutual knowledge and respect and to the enhancement of a parent-teacher partnership to a child's benefit.

Four Reasons for Regular Conferences

1. To facilitate a balanced examination of all aspects of development.
2. To provide uninterrupted time and privacy for conversation.
3. To facilitate a free-flowing exchange of questions and information, to increase mutual knowledge and respect.
4. To provide the opportunity to formulate and coordinate goals and plans.

❖ Groundwork for a Successful Conference

Such goals are not met without effort. There are important components to successful parent-teacher conferences.

Explain the Purpose of a Conference

Administrative policies and explanations help clarify the routine nature of parent-teacher conferences and the responsibilities of the participants. In both teacher job descriptions and parent handbooks, a statement about the purpose of regular conferences, an indication of when they will occur, such as November and May, and a description of probable content will make this a better understood procedure. Offering examples of the topics that will be discussed and questions parents may want to ask helps to destroy any misconceptions about conferences. Parents who are informed during orientation when they enroll their children that conferences are part of a program do not immediately assume there is something wrong when asked to a conference, nor are they afraid to take the initiative when they want a conference.

> Parent conferences are a routine part of our center life. A parent conference does not mean that your child is having a problem in the classroom. A parent conference is a time for parents and teachers to

> exchange thoughts and ideas, as well as a progress report from the team of teachers on all aspects of your child's development. The teachers may ask you questions about how your child plays at home, any special friends, etc. You will be able to ask the teachers about any aspect of his care or development in or out of the center and share any information that would help the teachers. (Sample from hypothetical parent handbook.)

Plan for Uninterrupted Time

Carefully selecting conference times is important, as parents and teachers both have needs to be considered and must have a voice in choosing the time.

Teachers should first decide when they are most free to leave a classroom under the care of another teacher or aide. Nap time is often a convenient time. Other possibilities may be early morning, when children filter in slowly at different times, or late afternoon, as children's departure times are staggered and there are fewer for whom to care. Some teachers find they are available during outdoor play time, when other adults can supervise on the playground. With families where both parents work, it may be necessary to offer the option of evening or weekend hours. This may sound like a great inconvenience for a teacher, but being flexible enough to meet parents' needs indicates a real commitment to the idea of parent involvement. It is desirable to have both parents present from a two-parent family, so that questions and information are not dealt with secondhand. In too many cases, mothers come for conferences alone. Specific invitations to fathers and accommodations to their schedules demonstrate that teachers value the participation of fathers and increase the probability that a conference will be fruitful. (See Figure 10-3.) Any adults who have primary care for a child should be included; this may mean grandparents, stepparents, and other adults in the household.

In team-teaching situations, it is rarely possible for both teachers to be free to join in the conference. It is a good idea for teachers to alternate responsibilities for conferences, so that parents do not come to think of only one teacher as the one with current knowledge of the child. It is also important for members of the team to schedule time to discuss information to be shared, as well as what is learned during each conference.

Having decided upon available conference times, teachers may suggest to parents that they find a specific time convenient to their own schedule. These invitations can be made in person or by telephone. Merely posting a sign-up sheet eliminates the personal touch and tends to de-emphasize the importance of a conference, as well as missing carpool parents. Personal contact also helps teachers find out if there are scheduling problems. When a sheet is posted, after a spoken invitation, it should make obvious the abundant choices of days and times, allowing for different working schedules,

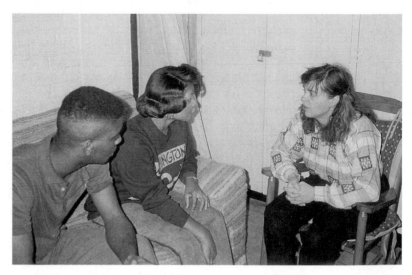

Figure 10-3 The presence of both parents at a conference is extremely valuable.

days off, and giving employers advance warning for a long lunch hour, etc. Teachers need to make it very clear, from conversation as well as a sign-up sheet, that they are anxious to be as flexible as possible in accommodating the needs of parents. If teachers are clearly willing to adapt a schedule to parents' needs, they will find responsive parents.

A sign-up sheet might look like this:

NOTICE

It's time to get together to discuss your child's development. Please sign up for a time convenient to you. If you can't find one here, let's find one together.

Nap time 12:30–2:30 P.M.
Arrival time 8:00–9:00 A.M.
Departure time 3:30–5:00 P.M.

I can also arrange to be available from 6:00–7:30 P.M. on the following days:
M-13, T-14, W-15, Th-16, M-20, T-21, W-22, Th-23

Tommy
Lisa
Seth
Jenny
Isaac
Akwanza
Pete

Let's look at a sign-up sheet that is less of an invitation to a parent.

Time to Sign up for Conferences

Any Monday, Wednesday, or Thursday between 4:00-5:00 P.M.

Do you see the problems here?

For parents who cannot be off work between 4:00 and 5:00 P.M., it looks as if they have no other possibility, and the teacher doesn't much care to be either understanding or helpful.

For busy parents, it looks as if this conference may be scheduled almost any time, so there's no motivation to set an appointment now.

It's too easy to walk by and leave blank a sheet of paper that doesn't seem specifically meant for you. It's much harder to ignore the message when your child's name is there with a space beside it.

As stated earlier, teachers certainly should not depend on words on a sheet to make an invitation clear. When frustrated by parents' seeming indifference, teachers might well consider these details.

Teachers and parents must remember that young children are sometimes upset by a change in the routine. Especially for very young children, it is valuable to schedule conferences for times when children can leave with their parents, rather than see the parents leave again without them.

Plan for a Private Location

Planning for a quiet, private location is important. In a center or school, this may mean coordination among staff members for use of available space—staff room, conference room, empty classroom, or another arrangement. All that's really needed is two or three comfortable, adult-sized chairs, perhaps a table on which to spread papers or coffee cups, and a door that can be closed and posted with a sign—"Conference in Progress. Do Not Disturb." Teachers need to be aware of conveying a firm impression that the conversation will be strictly confidential.

The physical environment probably least helpful to the conference goals is a formal office, with the teacher sitting behind a desk; the separation of one participant from the other by a desk conveys avoidance. A desk can act as a barricade between parent and teacher; it implies that the person seated behind it is dominant. These are not the nonverbal messages teachers want to send as they try to establish a partnership with parents. Remember that parents will arrive at the conference feeling nervous and fearful. A relaxed setting can help put both them (and the teacher) at ease.

Plan Goals to be Discussed

In preparation for a conference teachers must set their goals and devise plans for meeting each goal.

Since one goal for every conference is undoubtedly to share information for a developmental overview, teachers need to accumulate the resources they will use to guide this discussion. A simple developmental evaluation tool, such as the LAP or Minnesota Child Development Inventory, or Minnesota Preschool Inventory, or one that has been devised for a center's needs, is useful here. (Note: information on the Learning Accomplishment Profile can be obtained from Chapel Hill Training-Outreach Program, Daniels Bldg., University of North Carolina at Chapel Hill, Chapel Hill, NC 27514; information on the Minnesota Inventories can be obtained from Behavior Science Systems, P.O. Box 1108, Minneapolis, MN 55440. Both of these assessment tools evaluate children's accomplishments in several areas, including gross motor, fine motor, language, concepts, self-help skills, social skills.) The use of a developmental assessment tool in a conference with parents ensures that the conversation covers all aspects of development: physical (including self-help skills), cognitive, language, social, and emotional development. The checklist also offers concrete examples of what is usually expected at a particular stage of development, therefore educating parents as well as helping them to consider their child's behavior in an objective way. (See Figure 10-4.)

Figure 10-4 It may be helpful for teachers to use lesson plans and developmental checklists to illustrate information.

Other materials may be used to reinforce this developmental information visually and concretely for parents. Samples of art, collected over a
period of time, illustrate the refinement of small muscle skills, new concepts,
or a new stage in a child's art. Samples of writing or lists of books read may
demonstrate emergent literary skills. Snapshots of classroom activities may
indicate children's interests or interactions. Many teachers today, aware of
developmentally appropriate practices, are maintaining portfolios on children over time, to be able to assess their development and learning broadly,
with natural methods, rather than by artificial test situations. Sharing the
portfolio at conference time provides real evidence to parents of the process
of learning (SACUS 1991). Sharing of brief anecdotal records also helps to
make the discussion of a changing child more vivid.

To say simply, "Tony is doing well with the other children" conveys little a parent can learn from. Vague statements are not helpful to a parent and
give the impression that a teacher has learned little specific information
about a child.

To check "Yes" to three questions about social development on an evaluation scale offers more.

	YES	NO
A. Takes turns without objection		
B. Can begin playing with other children without adult initiation		
C. Plays with other children often		

Sharing reports of actual incidents that reflect social growth is probably most meaningful.

> You know, each day I try to jot down things that may be interesting to
> look back on. Let me show you some notes about Tony that show how
> he's progressed this year in his relationships with other children.
> Here's one—Sept. 30th—the beginning of the year.
>
> Tony was playing by himself in the block corner, pushing two trucks
> down a ramp he'd made. When David came over and wanted to play
> too, Tony grabbed the cars and held them tightly. When I went over and
> suggested they both could play, Tony lost interest and wandered over
> to the puzzle table.
>
> Playing with other children and taking turns was pretty new and hard for
> all our children then. For some it's still pretty hard. But let me read you
> a later note, which suggests how Tony's doing in this area now.
>
> Feb. 15th. Tony began to build a gas station. He looked around, saw
> David, called him to come over. Said: You can help me build this gas sta-
> tion. David said: I know, let's build a fire station and I'll be the fire chief.
> Tony said: OK, and I'll drive the fire truck and make the siren go.

Teachers should present impressions from observations in such a way that parents will feel encouraged to comment on or react to them. Parents are not told precisely what an observation might imply about a child, but the data are presented for mutual discussion and consideration.

Anecdotal records are also useful in describing to parents, and not evaluating, aspects of behavior that are of concern. One of the best reasons for using such records in a conference is that they offer tangible evidence of how well teachers have paid attention to a particular child—important to every parent.

In addition to planning what to share, teachers should prepare a list of the questions to ask so they will be sure to learn from a conference.

> To ask:
>
> Bedtime routine and time?
> Which friends he talks about at home?
> What are favorite home activities?
> Which parts of day are discussed at home?

Making a brief outline of the topics to be discussed is helpful to both teachers and parents. A teacher will not forget items of importance as the conversation continues. An initial sharing of the list of topics with parents and asking for their additions indicates to parents that they have more than a passive listening role to play and may prevent them from beginning too quickly to discuss problems, before a balanced overview is achieved.

If there are delicate issues to be raised, teachers will want to particularly plan how they will talk about these subjects. A mental rehearsal of the conference plan will help teachers be more confident.

> "Let me tell you some of the things I plan to cover today. We'll go through the center developmental checklist, so you can see how Pete's doing in all areas of his development. I also wanted to tell you about some of his favorite classroom activities and friends. There are a couple of areas we're particularly working on—his participation at group time, and doing things for himself—so I'll tell you how that's going. Now let me add the questions you've brought in today. This will help us make sure we get it all covered."

Some teachers find it helpful to send home a form to parents to ask for specific things they want to talk about in the upcoming conference. In this way, the teacher is aware of parent concerns and can plan to discuss those issues and have available materials that relate to the parents' concern.

The organization of anecdotal records and developmental assessments in preparation for a conference should take a small amount of time, since these are materials that should be part of a teacher's tools used for individualized goal setting and planning. A last review and organization of the materials will help teachers see they are prepared; pencils and paper should be added for teachers and parents to use for any notes. Being confident in their preparation leaves teachers free to initiate the social interaction of a conference.

Teachers may also suggest ways parents can set goals and prepare for a conference. This may be accomplished in two ways.

A handout to stimulate parents' questions may be displayed near the conference sign-up sheet, or mailed to carpooling parents. A suitable handout may resemble the following:

Parents usually have lots of questions about their children and school. Why not consider which of these might be helpful for us to discuss at our conference?

    —Why we do what we do in the classroom?
    —Your child's interests?
        —Reactions to others?
        —Sleeping patterns?
        —Eating patterns?
    —Your concerns about discipline?
        —Your child's adjustment to school routines?
        —Ways you can reinforce learning at home?
        —Any new behaviors you've noticed?
    —What else have you been wondering lately?

Whatever form it takes, the clear message is that parents can expect to talk about any issue or concern.

Another idea is to suggest that parents spend a brief period observing in a classroom before a conference—perhaps joining a group for lunch before a nap time conference or coming in earlier for a late afternoon appointment. (See Figure 10-5.) Here again, a simple list with a few questions can guide parents in watching their child, the activities in which he's involved, his interaction with others, a teacher's methods, etc. Such observation often stimulates immediate responses or questions or may allow parents to see some of the behaviors that a teacher will later discuss.

Groundwork for a
Successful Conference

1. Teacher and parent understanding of the purpose and their roles.
2. Planning for uninterrupted time, agreeable to teacher and parent.
3. A relaxed and private physical environment.
4. Planning of goals and organization of materials.

Figure 10-5 It may be helpful for parents to observe their child in the classroom setting before a conference. What might teacher and parent be able to talk about after seeing this scene? Courtesy Connie Glass.

❖ Strategies for a Successful Conference

Preparation for conferences has been discussed at length because setting attitudes and atmosphere conducive to full partner participation is vital. Now let's consider the conference itself.

Help Parents Feel at Ease

It is a teacher's responsibility to help parents become comfortable and at ease. Teachers are on familiar territory; parents are not. Unless parents are made to feel comfortable, their discomfort may be such a distraction that communication is hindered. A few minutes spent in casual conversation is time well spent. An offer of juice or coffee may be appreciated by a tired parent, as well as creating more social ease.

"I appreciate your taking the time to come in today. Pete's been telling me about your camping trip plans. Sounds like you're going to cover a lot of territory!"

While teachers need to recognize parents' likely fears when entering the conference situation, it should also be stated that most teachers also feel some apprehension when approaching conferences. Certainly the advance preparation and thinking through of goals, questions, ways to phrase things, and possible conflicts will lessen this, as will experience. Getting to know parents as people will also make conferences less formidable. Awareness and acceptance of inevitable nervousness on the part of both teachers and parents will help teachers be sensitive to the emotional atmosphere.

Begin with a Positive Attitude

As teachers turn the conversation towards the child, they begin with a positive comment about the child. It is important to indicate to parents at the outset that you like and appreciate their child. Parents are more likely to accept later comments, even constructive criticism, if the conference begins with both adults clearly on the same side and with a teacher's clear indication that she has paid specific attention to a child and knows them well. A positive opening comment also removes any lingering concern a parent may have about the purpose of a conference.

> "I'm enjoying having Pete in my classroom. I think one of the things I most enjoy is his enthusiasm about everything! I wish you could have seen him this morning when he was talking about the plans for your trip—eyes sparkling and words just tumbling out!"

Encourage Parent Participation

Although teachers clearly guide the conversation through the planned topics, they should be continually aware of the principle of partnership and try to draw a parent into participation at all times by frequently asking open-ended questions.

> "So he's achieved all of these self-help skills except for shoe tying, and we're working on that. What kinds of things do you see him doing for himself at home now?"

The use of questions will help a parent expand on a statement, so they can both get a clearer picture.

> "When you say you're having problems with him at mealtime, could you tell me a bit more about some things that have been particularly troublesome at dinner recently?"

Teachers who want to help parents assume the role of "expert" on their child use questions to guide parents towards thinking about possible courses of action, instead of telling them what to do.

> "What are some of the things you've tried when he's begun play-ing with his food?"
>
> "What else have you thought might be causing him to lose inter-est in his meal?"

They encourage parents to continue talking by *active listening*. Active listen-ing refers to the technique of giving sensitive attention and picking up a speaker's verbal and nonverbal messages, then reflecting back the total message empathetically, for a speaker's verification. (See Figure 10-6.) Tech-niques involved in active listening include paraphrasing and reflecting.

Paraphrasing involves restating what another person has said in slight-ly different words. This is a useful method of checking whether the other's meaning has been understood, as well as eliciting more information.

> Parent: "We've always believed in eating with the children, but late-ly Pete's been giving us such problems that I'm tempted to give it up."
>
> Teacher: "Mealtime with Pete has been unpleasant lately? It sounds to me like mealtime has become a time of day you really don't look forward to."
>
> Parent: "Oh, it's been nagging to get him to eat, and fussing about his dawdling—awful!"

Reflecting offers feedback on the emotional meaning of a message. It is necessary for teachers to put themselves into the position of the other per-son, to be able to feel as he does, and to see the world as he is now seeing it. This involves accepting the feelings of a parent without judgment and reflecting the feelings back to him in a way that lets him know that the teacher understands. When a teacher is not just quietly attentive, but is responsive to the feelings behind the other person's words, active listening encourages fuller communication. As a teacher reflects her understanding of a parent's message, the parent is often stimulated to continue talking about a situation, allowing for a deeper understanding of feelings for both teacher and parent.

> Teacher: "It really seems to concern you that he's not developing good mealtime habits."
>
> Parent: "Well, you know, it does bother me. I guess because I used to be something of a food fusser and I remember some very unpleasant mealtimes as a child. I want to avoid it developing into a real problem with Pete, if I can."

Active listening has the advantages of sending a message of clear acceptance, defusing hostile behavior, and assisting in identifying real problems. (See Gordon 1975 and Briggs 1975 for a fuller study of active listening concepts.)

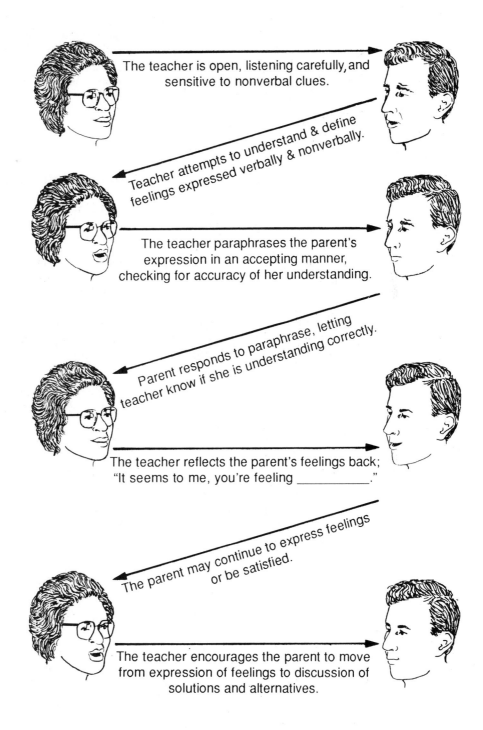

The teacher is open, listening carefully, and sensitive to nonverbal clues.

Teacher attempts to understand & define feelings expressed verbally & nonverbally.

The teacher paraphrases the parent's expression in an accepting manner, checking for accuracy of her understanding.

Parent responds to paraphrase, letting teacher know if she is understanding correctly.

The teacher reflects the parent's feelings back; "It seems to me, you're feeling _____."

The parent may continue to express feelings or be satisfied.

The teacher encourages the parent to move from expression of feelings to discussion of solutions and alternatives.

Figure 10-6 Active listening involves reflecting and paraphrasing.

Throughout a conference teachers depend heavily on questions and reflective statements to indicate they have much to learn from a parent. Asking, not telling, is an important indication of partnership and respect for the parent's opinions, as well as a good way to obtain information. Parents who sit through a conference and listen to a teacher talk are less likely to think about ideas that come through a one-way flow—or to come back for another conference.

Summarize for Parents

There is much to talk about when parents and teachers get together. But teachers must be mindful of the time pressures on busy parents and keep a conference to the scheduled time. If more areas arise that need to be discussed, it is preferable to make a second appointment. Too much information at one time may be burdensome and not fully absorbed.

As a conference ends, it is again a teacher's responsibility to summarize the main points discussed, as well as any projected plans. It might be useful to offer a parent a written copy of any assessment tool that the teacher discussed, and to offer writing materials for the parent to make final notes. If the teacher also makes notes of the summary, it will make it easier to write the conference summary later. It is a good idea for both parent and teacher to leave the conference knowing each has a specific action to perform. Parents need to leave a conference feeling their time was well spent; a summary to reinforce the discussion is useful. Once again, it is especially appropriate to be positive about a parent's efforts and contributions. (See Figure 10-7.)

> "Thank you for coming in today. I've certainly appreciated your sharing so much helpful information about Pete. As you've seen from our assessment, he's doing very well in every area. I'm particularly glad to know of your concern about mealtime so I can support your efforts here. Your plan of trying a time limit sounds good—do let me know how it goes."

These general strategies can help to achieve a successful conference.

Strategies for a Successful Conference

1. Teacher taking initiative in putting parent at ease.
2. A positive beginning and ending.
3. Give-and-take in conversation, facilitated by a teacher's questions and reflective listening.
4. A summarizing of areas discussed and action to be taken.

Figure 10-7 Ending a conference on a positive note is productive for continuing the parent-teacher relationship.

❖ Pitfalls to Avoid for a Successful Conference

In addition to paying attention to these strategies, there are specific pitfalls that teachers need to be aware of and avoid.

Avoid Using Technical Terminology

When teachers explain developmental progress to parents, they must be careful not to use jargon or technical terms that are not easily understood and can create distance between the adults. Parents are not likely to listen to someone talking over their heads and are understandably reluctant to ask for clarification of terms.

> NOT: "He functions well in the Piagetian sensorimotor stage!"
>
> RATHER: "He is a very active explorer. Every time we offer him a new material, he examines it very carefully, from every angle."
>
> NOT: "She did fairly well on her Denver."
>
> RATHER: "We use this set of questions to see how the children are doing at their developmental level, and she did well, as you'll see."

Avoid Role of "Expert"

Teachers should be careful not to set themselves up as experts on any child. Such a stance prevents the growth of a working partnership; many parents feel shaky enough at the business of parenting without being faced with a teacher who seems to "know it all." Rather than peppering their comments with advice that focuses on "shoulds" and "musts," teachers need to avoid such authoritarian dogmatism. The implication that if one disagrees, one is wrong, will inhibit discussion.

To avoid the appearance of being a dogmatic expert, teachers need to be cautious about the phrases they use as they share knowledge. Many teachers say "lots of parents find" or "some of my parents have told me;" they find these phrases more easily accepted than "I think," which sounds too authoritative. Teachers need to help parents realize that there are few absolutes in child guidance.

Certain areas of concern to a parent may be far beyond a teacher's scope of knowledge and competence. It is necessary for teachers to be straightforward in admitting this and to know when to refer a parent to an expert.

> "I appreciate your concern about Billy's language. Let me give you the number of the people at Speech and Hearing. They can answer your questions far better than I."
>
> "You know, I'm not quite sure about those admission test score systems. Suppose I check with the school and let you know."

If teachers feel questions could be answered better by another, they may invite the director, social worker, or co-teacher to join a discussion. Contrary to what some teachers believe, when they confess their limitations it tends not to demean them, but earns them respect in parents' eyes for their honesty.

Avoid Negative Evaluations

Knowing how closely parental self-esteem is tied to others' perceptions of their child, teachers must be sensitive to avoid the appearance of being critical or negative about a child's capabilities. Certain key words trigger defensive feelings in parents, and parents who feel defensive are unable to communicate and cooperate fully. Some words to avoid are:

> problem—"I'm having a *problem* with Jimmy."
>
> behind—"Jimmy is *behind* in language."
>
> immature—"Jimmy is more *immature* than the rest of the class."
>
> never, can't—"Jimmy *never* finishes lunch with the others; Jimmy *can't* do most of our puzzles."
>
> slow—"Jimmy is *slow* at learning."

Any labels, such as hyperactive, learning disability, etc., should also be avoided. Many of these terms have been adopted and over-used by the general public. Since teachers do not have clinical training, it is not appropriate for teachers to hypothesize diagnoses.

> labels—"Sometimes I wonder if Jimmy isn't *hyperactive.*"

Comments that are objective observations rather than subjective characterizations are more helpful and more easily received.

> NOT: "Jimmy doesn't like art." (Subjective)
>
> RATHER: "Jimmy rarely participates in art activities." (Objective)
>
> NOT: "Jenny is not a very friendly child." (Subjective)
>
> RATHER: "Jenny usually plays by herself in the house corner." (Objective)

When teachers merely describe behavior, parents are left to draw their own conclusions. This offers information in a neutral way, without implying evaluation or criticism. Teachers have a responsibility to help parents think positively about their children, and negative judgments are simply not helpful. Any parent would react emotionally to hearing these. Parents need teachers who can help with realistic and constructive, not destructive, comments.

"One of the things we're working on with Jimmy is . . ." A comment such as this does not imply negative evaluation, such as being behind or a problem, but states action that can be taken. Because behavior is complex, it would be impossible, as well as unproductive, to assign reasons or blame for a particular behavior.

> NOT: "Jimmy's having so many temper tantrums because your husband has been out of town so much lately."

The statement is not necessarily true, certainly not helpful, and so personal and pointed it could alienate a parent from a partnership. An observant teacher watches parents' body language to notice if there is an emotional reaction to what she has said. Some body messages to watch for include facial expression, tightening or withdrawal of the body, the degree of relaxation of hands and body posture, change in position.

Avoid Unprofessional Conversation

Teachers need to be sure a conversation remains professional, though warm, and centered on the adults' common concerns related to a child.

Teachers never discuss other children and parents in a conference with another; to do so would make parents question how confidential their own conversation is.

> NOT: "You know, Mrs. Smith has been having an even worse time with Janie—she had a terrible tantrum the other day."

> This might have been intended as a reassurance, but is probably unsettling to the other parent who hears it!
>
> RATHER: "Many parents find that four-year-olds can get quite out of bounds."

Teachers should not ask personal questions except when they are absolutely related to a concern being discussed about a child.

> NOT: "How do you spend your spare time on the weekends?"
>
> RATHER: "I've been wondering what time Jimmy goes to bed—he's been very sleepy in the mid-morning."
>
> NOT: "Just how do you and your ex-husband get along?"
>
> RATHER: "Are there occasions I should know about when Sally will be in contact with her father?"

When parents turn a conversation to personal matters not directly related to their child, teachers need to make it clear that their only role is to listen supportively if the parent needs to talk—of course assuring confidentiality—and to refer to more expert community resources if a parent seems interested.

> "I'm sorry to hear that you and Jimmy's father have been having some difficulties. If it helps you to talk about it, I'll be glad to listen. I can also suggest a couple of agencies that could be really helpful during a difficult time."

It is inappropriate to cut this parent off completely; teachers are sometimes so oriented to children's problems that they do not realize that parents have their own exhausting problems that must be dealt with.

Sometimes, especially in a conference with two parents present, teachers can get caught in the middle of a family disagreement.

> "Mr. Jones, my husband and I just don't agree about disciplining Bobby. He spanks him whenever he misbehaves but I just don't believe in spanking kids. What would you say?"

There could only be future difficulty in working with this family if the teacher were to take sides. His answer needs to be helpful and neutral.

> "Discipline's a broad subject, and even many experts don't agree. I think families have to make up their minds and do what's right for them. If it would help, I can tell you some of the things we do in the classroom and why."

Teachers' awareness of their roles as professional persons may help them avoid these pitfalls. Professional ethics also require that teachers not share personal family issues with other teachers except when necessary to understand children's behavior or situation. The information teachers learn about families must be protected both within the center and within the community.

Avoid Giving Advice

It is easy for teachers to make the error of giving unasked-for advice to parents, since teachers may see a need and have a fairly good idea what could help. But advice from others is seldom effective; it is only when parents reach a personal conclusion that they become committed to a course of action. Just because a parent mentions a problem, a teacher should not conclude that the parent is asking for a solution to that problem. A teacher is likely not to know the full complexity of the situation and may give inappropriate suggestions. It seems inappropriate for a teacher to tell the parent what to do at home, when the teacher will not be there to help in the carrying out of the course of action. Giving advice tends to distance a teacher from the parent. Parents might quietly listen to this advice while inwardly fuming:

> "Who does he think he is? A lot he knows about it anyway—this is my child, not his."

Giving advice may usurp the parent's right to decide, and may also detract from parents' feelings of competence and self-worth. Giving advice may also be dangerous; when the "expert's" suggestions don't work, the expert gets the blame and future mistrust.

A more effective teacher role may be to help parents move through several steps in problem solving and discovering options that they may follow.

1. Identify the problem, including agreement that there *is* a problem.

2. Identify options for responding to the situation. Multiple solutions can be generated by parent and professional brainstorming together, with neither's suggestions being ignored or put down. Teachers will have to set the stage for openness and encourage parent participation.

3. Discuss the advantages and disadvantages of each option.

4. Teachers and parents choose a solution to try first.

5. Discuss a plan to help implement the idea.

6. Agree to meet again to evaluate how the option is working. (The six-step plan for helping parents find their own solutions is discussed further in Johns and Harvey 1987.)

Teachers should remember that time spent helping parents find their own best solution is time well spent for enhancing parental competence and avoiding disrupting a relationship or partnership.

It's easy to fall into the trap of giving advice to parents when they do ask for it—probably because it's a good feeling to know you have the answer someone else needs! The best way to avoid such a pitfall is to make several suggestions and turn the thinking process back to the parent.

> "Some of the things we've tried in the classroom for that are: . . ."
>
> "Let me pass along some ideas on that that have worked for other parents. . . ."
>
> "Do any of those sound like something that could work for you?"

It's appropriate to help parents understand that, in guidance, there is seldom one right answer. Parents should be encouraged to come up with their own plans, which they are more likely to carry out than a plan handed to them. If teachers remember that one of their goals is to enhance not only parenting skills but also parental self-esteem, they will realize how important it is to be speculative in offering suggestions, not dogmatic in giving advice. "If I were you, I'd . . ." is definitely not the most helpful phrase, since it implies such an absolute and sure position.

Avoid Rushing into Solutions

Another easy error for either parent or teacher is to feel that all problems must be solved and conclusions reached during a designated conference period. Changing behaviors and understanding is a process that takes time and cannot be artificially rushed to fit into a brief conference. It is better to suggest the need for time:

> "All right, then both of us will try to watch and see when these outbursts occur. Maybe then we can work out some appropriate response. Let's plan to get back together and talk again next month."

It is also a mistake to assume that parents and teachers will always be able to agree and work together, and that a conference is a failure if the teacher is unable to "convert" a parent to her understanding. Different experiences, personalities, value systems, and needs influence how readily each can agree with the other's viewpoint. A successful conference is one in which there is an exchange and acceptance of various insights, including those that conflict.

Every teacher encounters conference situations that deteriorate as a parent expresses anger, hostility, or blame. If parents have trouble accepting information, it is not uncommon to employ the defense mechanisms of projection—"if only you could teach better he wouldn't have this problem"—or denial—"Don't you dare tell me my son has a problem." If parents become verbally abusive or irrational in anger, it is impossible to communicate effectively. At that point a teacher's task is to defuse the anger so that communication can begin. To do this, it is crucial that the teacher not become defensive or angry in return. Retaliating verbally, arguing, and retreating from the parent's anger are not helpful responses. A teacher needs to remain calm, speaking softly and slowly; to do some active listening that will allow parents to see their own words and feelings from the other's point of view; and to demonstrate an acceptance of the parents' rights to their opinions. Handling an expression of hostility this way will help a teacher work with a parent on the areas of disagreement, instead of losing the issues in personal attacks or emotional responses. (Working with hostility will be discussed further in chapter 17.)

Pitfalls to Avoid
for Successful Conferences

1. Too technical terminology or jargon.
2. Playing the role of an "expert."
3. Negative and destructive evaluations about a child's capabilities.
4. Unprofessional conversation—about others
   —too personal
   —taking sides.
5. Giving advice—either unasked for or asked for.
6. Trying to solve all problems on the spot, or trying to force agreement.

❖ Conference Evaluation

Soon after a conference is over, it is a good idea to summarize the new information gained and plans made.

2/1/96. Conference with Pete's mother. (Stepfather unable to come due to work schedule.) She is concerned about Pete playing with food at meals.

Topics discussed: LAP assessment. Preparation for new sibling due 5/2. Pete's readiness for kindergarten. Mother's concern about Pete playing with food at meals.

Plan: 1. Share information with co-teacher.
2. Observe Pete at lunch—move seat near mine.
3. Talk with mother again in two months.

It is also useful, for a teacher's professional growth, to evaluate her own participation in the conference by asking herself questions such as:

- How well did I listen?

- How well did I facilitate parent's participation?

- Did I offer enough specifics?

- Was I positive in beginning and ending the conference?
- How comfortable were we in the conversation?

With experience, teachers grow in their ability to facilitate an effective conference.

It is appropriate for a preschool teacher to hold conferences to discuss developmental progress and goals at lease every six months, since change occurs so rapidly at this time. For the needs of particular families and children, conferences may be held more frequently, at the request of either parent or teacher.

It should be remembered that non-attendance at a conference does not necessarily indicate disinterest in the child or the school. Instead, it may be a reflection of different cultural or socioeconomic values, of extreme pressures or stress of family or work demands. A teacher's response to non-attendance is to review the possible explanations of non-attendance, see if different scheduling or educational actions will help, persist in invitations and efforts, and understand that other methods of reaching a parent will have to be used in the meantime.

❖ Summary

Parent-teacher conferences provide the time and opportunity for parents and teachers to consider together all aspects of a child's overall development, including any particular interests, needs, or problems that may concern either parents or teachers. Such an opportunity will help further a sense of working together with shared information and common goals.

A teacher has the responsibility for setting the tone of a partnership in such a conversation by informing parents of the purpose for conferences, preparing parents for their participatory role in a conversation, guiding a conversation, and encouraging more parent participation by the use of questions and active listening.

Being sensitive to the dynamics of interpersonal relations in general, and more specifically to parental reactions, will help a teacher avoid communication errors that can block real understanding or inhibit the growth of a relationship. Careful planning and evaluation of conferences will help teachers grow in the skills necessary for effective parent-teacher conferences.

❖ Student Activities for Further Study

1. With your classmates, set up a role-playing situation in which one of you is a teacher, one a parent. Remember to concentrate on facilitating a dialogue in the conversation by the teacher's questions and active listening. Your "audience" can help you evaluate and suggest other possibilities. Try these situations, and any others you have encountered.

    a. A mother asks how to prepare three-year-old for new baby.

    b. A teacher is concerned about coordinating toilet learning efforts.

    c. A mother comments that her four-year-old son is being very "bad" lately.

    d. A teacher is concerned about a recent increase in a child's aggressive behavior.

    e. A father is concerned about his son who is in your classroom; he feels he is not as advanced at four as his older brother was.

    f. A mother asks you what too do about her toddler biting.

2. With a partner, brainstorm many possible teacher responses to these comments and questions from parents. Then decide which is most appropriate, and why.

    a. I honestly don't know how you do it—kids this age drive me crazy.

    b. What I want to know is, when are the kids in your classroom going to do some real work, not just this playing?

    c. Do you think my Sarah is slow—she doesn't seem to me to be talking right?

    d. Well, I don't agree with your soft approach—I say when kids are bad, they should be spanked.

    e. I don't know if I should tell you this, but my husband has left us and I don't think he's coming back.

    f. What's the best way to get a child to go to bed?

3. After reading the following record, develop an outline for sharing this information with parents during a conference.

Judy is three years and six months, much smaller than the other children in her classroom. She speaks indistinctly, and often not more than two words at a time. She plays by herself most of the time, and in fact seems to shrink back when other children or most adults approach her. She has well-developed fine motor skills and is extremely creative when she paints. Despite the well-developed fine motor skills, her self-help skills lag behind, and she often asks for assistance in the bathroom and in simple dressing tasks. She enjoys music and often sits for long periods listening to records with the earphones.

❖ Review Questions

1. Identify three of four reasons for holding regular parent-teacher conferences.

2. List five of eight factors that facilitate productive parent-teacher conferences.

3. List four of six pitfalls to avoid in parent-teacher conferences.

❖ Suggestions for Further Reading

Abbott, C.F., and Gold, S. (1991, May). Conferring with parents when you're concerned that their child needs special services. *Young Children, 46*(4), 10–14.

Canady, R.L., and Seyfarth, J.T. (1979). *How parent-teacher conferences build partnerships*. Bloomington, Indiana: Phi Delta Kappa Educational Foundation.

Davis, D.H. and D.M. (1981). Managing parent-teacher conferences. *Today's Education, 70*(2), 46–51.

Galinsky, E. (1988, March). Parents and teacher caregivers: sources of tension, sources of support. *Young Children, 43*(3), 4–11.

Hauser-Cram, P. (1986). Backing away helpfully: some roles teachers shouldn't fill. *Beginnings, 3*(1), 18–20.

Nielsen, L.E., and Finkelstein, J.M. (1993, Aug./Sept.) A new approach to parent conferences. *Teaching K-8*, 90–91f.

Rotter, J.C. (1987). *Parent-teacher conferencing. What research says to the teacher*. Washington, D.C.: National Education Association.

Studer, J.R. (1993/1994, Winter). Listen so that parents will speak. *Childhood Education, 70*(2), 74–76.

Young, M.E. (1992). *Counseling methods and techniques: an eclectic approach*. New York: Merrill.

CHAPTER 11

Home Visits with Parents and Children

Perhaps one of the least used methods of working with families is that of teachers making visits to the family's home. This is not really surprising, in that home visits place both teachers and families in unusual positions, making all participants initially wary. Home is the place of family privacy, and everyone is concerned lest this privacy be violated. In full-day early education programs, it is difficult to arrange the time for staff to make visits, especially to families who are themselves busy with work and family responsibilities.

Nevertheless, when teachers have found their way around these obstacles, they have discovered that there are benefits for all concerned: children's feelings of self-worth are reinforced as they are able to take the initiative in entertaining the teacher; parents are reassured about the teacher's real commitment to working with the family; teachers learn even more about children's lives. In this chapter, we concentrate our attention on the occasionally home visits made by a classroom teacher as part of the effort to build parent-teacher-child relationships. Varying aspects of home visitation programs, or home-based educational programs are also described. (See chapter 8 for a discussion of the initial home visit as part of the orientation process.)

OBJECTIVES

After studying this chapter, the student will be able to

1. discuss several purposes for home visits.
2. discuss points to consider in undertaking home visits.
3. describe advantages and disadvantages of home visits.
4. identify the general purpose and techniques of home-based programs.

❖ Purposes of a Home Visit

A home visit often presents scheduling difficulties for both teachers and parents and is therefore one of the components of a parent involvement program that is most frequently left out. However, a home visit adds a dimension that is not possible via other methods.

The prospect of a home visit may be frightening for a teacher who has not yet discovered how rewarding this encounter can be for everyone.

> John Roberts is frank in expressing some of his reservations to his co-worker. "This whole thing makes me nervous. I'm not all that familiar with the Rodriguezes; the father never drops Tony off, and his mother doesn't talk much. I have a feeling they're pretty old-fashioned. And I never even go over to the side of town where they live. I'm always afraid I'll get lost and hardly anybody talks English over there. Who knows what I could get into when I knock on their door?"
>
> The Rodriguez family has their own reaction when the note about the home visit first comes home.
>
> "What does Tony's teacher want to come here for?" wonders Mr. Rodriguez. "Has he got some problem, do you think?"
>
> "He said not, but I don't know. You've got to try to be home from work when he comes—my English is too bad for him. I wish we had some better chairs in the living room; I don't know what he'll think."

It is only natural that both participants have these concerns. A home visit takes teachers out of the familiar classroom world for which they are trained and directly into the diverse worlds in which the children live. Parents are in similarly uncharted territory, wondering about their function and perhaps concerned that the home and family "measure up" to a teacher's standard.

With such apprehensions on both sides, it is easy to overlook the reasons for the visit. But the reasons can be seen in this parent's comment after a home visit:

> Please continue doing this. It really makes a child feel important and special. It also continues my feeling about her school as a "family

away from home" and further reinforces the tie between family at home and the "family feeling" at school (Fox-Barnett and Meyer 1992, 50).

The most important aspect of a home visit, as this parent expresses, is the strong evidence that a teacher cares enough to move beyond the territorial confines of classroom to reach out to a child and his family. (See Figure 11-1.)

The visit of John Roberts to the Rodriguez family corroborates the value for both parents and teachers. After the visit is over Mrs. Rodriguez comments to her husband, "Well, that was nice. He really does like Tony, doesn't he, and he's not a bit stuck up like I thought he was. Maybe I will go in to the classroom to do some Spanish cooking with the children, like he said."

Her husband agreed. "I'm glad to have had a chance to meet him, since I never get to go to school. He must be a good teacher, to go to such trouble."

One teacher said she had thought of home visits as just another means of talking with parents that was probably not as effective as a conference at school, since one cannot talk as well in front of a child at home. But from the reactions of children and parents after her first visits, she realized

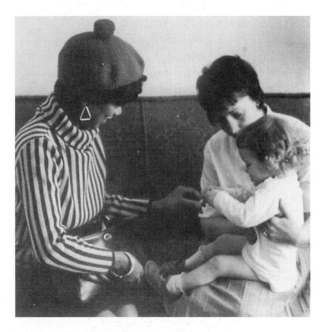

Figure 11-1 Teachers indicate their willingness to reach out to families with home visits. Courtesy Head Start Bureau.

> what should have been obvious all along, that the home visit should be chiefly for the child, and that what could be conveyed to the parents is that the teacher likes and is interested in their child, and therefore would like to see his toys, his cat, where he lives, etc., or to meet other members of his family (Bromberg 1968, 79).

The only purpose for a child-centered home visit is for teacher and child to spend some time together in the child's home. There is no "hidden agenda" of parent education or evaluation; child-centered visits just make children and parents feel good about themselves. For children, home visits offer opportunities to feel very special, with teacher and parent attention focused on them individually. Seeing a teacher in his home helps build greater feelings of trust and intimacy for a child as well.

Parents at home have opportunities to communicate more comfortably, on their own territory. They often gain the sense that "school is a more approachable place should they need contact or help in the future" (Fox-Barnett and Meyer 1992, 48.)

It is difficult for parents to be adversaries of teachers when they show such interest and concern.

For a parent who finds it difficult to get to school because of job or family responsibilities, a home visit offers the only opportunity for face-to-face contact with a teacher. A home visit allows this parent the chance to feel involved in the educational process and offers a reassuring look at teacher and child interacting.

To continue to ally themselves with parents as they indicate their interest and caring for a child is the primary purpose for classroom teachers to make home visits. Their efforts to make a visit and their warm concentration on a child during a visit helps to create a sense of partnership with parents.

Of course, a home visit is important to teachers also, in providing first-hand information about a child's physical environment. Information about a home setting and family can be learned by the teacher's observations; this information and its implications are usually not conveyed by a data sheet filled out at a center. Because the home environment is a place where children learn probably more than in school, it is important for teachers to understand that part of a child's life. Learning about the "whole child" includes learning about every family member who is important to that child. Entering a child's world helps them understand why he behaves as he does in a classroom. When teachers have a feel for what parents are doing with their children at home and why they are doing it, their own efforts can complement and supplement the home efforts. Carol Hillman says she gains a sense of the parent-child relationship during home visits as she notices whether parents allow their children to take her to their room by themselves (Hillman 1988).

John Robert's experience points out these benefits for teachers. "I haven't taught many Puerto Rican children. I've been worried about Tony's shyness in the classroom. After I visited his family at home, I realized that their expectations for a preschooler are that he not take the initiative when speaking with an adult. He really does have beautiful manners—I saw that when he was with his parents; it's not really shyness, just the respect he's been taught. I also discovered that only Spanish is spoken at home, which helps me realize some of his language needs in the classroom. It was fun to see Tony at home—he was obviously very proud to see me there. All this week since, at school, he's been coming to me more."

Because home visits allow teachers to learn about the children they teach and to continue to develop comfortable relationships with parents, it is important for both teachers in a classroom team to be involved, if at all feasible. (See Figure 11-2.)

For children, home visits offer opportunities to feel very special, with teacher's and parents' attention focused on them individually. Seeing a teacher in his home helps build greater feelings of trust and intimacy for a child as well. (See Figure 11-3.)

❖ Undertaking Home Visits

While home visit can be beneficial for children, teachers, and parents, it is not accomplished without effort and planning. Here are some points to consider.

Figure 11-2 It is helpful if both members of the team are able to make a home visit. Courtesy Chapter I Program, Charlotte, N.C.

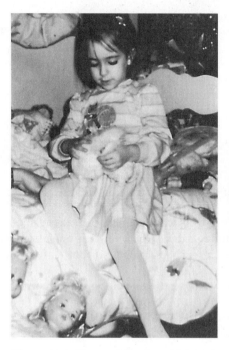

Figure 11-3 Home visits give children the chance to show their favorite things to the teacher and gradually become comfortable with her. Courtesy Tamar Meyer.

Explain Purpose in Advance

Parents need to receive a clear explanation of the child-centered purpose of a home visit in advance. Although the parent handbook and orientation discussion should do this, a reminding note from a teacher before a visit is reassuring. Such explanations may decrease the threatening aspects of a home visit, especially with parents who are accustomed to official visitors evaluating or judging their home, financial matters, and functions of family members.

> The reason for this visit is to help the child and parents to get to know the teachers away from the child-care center. It also helps to establish a relationship that is both open and friendly. Teachers' visits are mainly social; if you have concerns about your child or the child-care center we will be glad to discuss these at another time when your child is not present. (Sample from hypothetical parent handbook)

Arrange Time with Parents

A teacher needs to make clear arrangements regarding the date and time of a visit at parents' convenience by sending a note home with a child and following up with a telephone call. An unexpected visit does not permit parents to feel at ease and in charge of the situation. Some parents like to make a visit a social occasion and prepare refreshments and tidy their house. To be caught off-guard does not facilitate a relaxed atmosphere.

> Mrs. Rodriguez reported to her husband, "This is the day Tony's teacher is coming to visit at 5:30. Can you be sure to be home from work by then? He called and said I should say a time when we'd both be here, so I said 5:30. He said he won't stay long, but I made some pan dulce. This is nice of him to come. Tony's all excited."

Behave Like a Guest

Despite the fact that teachers take the initiative to set up a visit, they are still the guests in another's home. Actually, this puts them in a desirable position of having to follow another's lead. This aspect of a parent involvement program gives parents the clear advantage in feeling comfortable, even though both parents and teachers probably experience some discomfort when faced with the unfamiliar. This is a new role for the classroom teacher who is used to being in control. As visitors, teachers graciously accept whatever hospitality is offered by a family, whether this includes sitting on a sagging chair from which the family cats have been hastily removed or sampling an unfamiliar food. There should be no indication, no word or expression of surprise or disdain for the family's environment or life-style. They are not there to evaluate, but to indicate support. One of the most essential ingredients for a successful home visit is flexibility on the part of the teachers, an ability to accept variations in family behavior and conditions that are different from what they have experienced themselves.

A teacher's way of dressing may be important; a style of dressing that is either too casual—old jeans—or too fancy—a new designer suit—may indicate presuppositions about the family's life-style and make all participants uncomfortable.

Teachers should begin the visit in a friendly, relaxed way.

> "I see you have quite a vegetable plot out front, Mr. Rodriguez. Who's the gardener in the family?"

They let parents share whatever family mementoes or anecdotes they'd like, but avoid leading conversation into personal issues themselves.

> "Oh, I'd love to see your pictures of Tony and his big sister."

They listen respectfully to both children and parents.

> "Tony, I do want to see your kitten. Let me just finish looking at these pictures with your Mom."

In short, teachers use all their social skills of tact, sensitivity, and interest to help both themselves and family participants feel at ease with one another and accomplish the overall goal of enhancing a parent-teacher-child relationship.

Be on Time

Teachers need to be sensitive to the demands on a family's time. Teachers must be very careful to arrive and leave on time, allowing enough time to find unfamiliar locations. Scheduled visits should be canceled only when absolutely necessary, as the family will likely have made advance preparations. A visit should last from fifteen to thirty minutes, certainly not much longer, unless they have been invited by the parents for a particular social event.

Expect Distractions

Teachers must remember that they have left the institution in which they might be able to control the environment. When they are in a private home, controlled by the parent, it is the teacher who must adapt to the distractions that normal households offer. "It is the parents' phone that rings . . . , the parent's friend who drops in unexpectedly, and the parent who decides whether the television is to be on or off and whether the dog is to be in or out" (Powell 1990, 68). When the baby cries or the child being visited scrapes his leg, teachers have to adjust to distractions with grace.

Post-Visit Responsibilities

After a home visit, there are several things for a teacher to do to build on what has been accomplished.

Thank-You Note

Send a thank-you note to a family for allowing a home visit to take place. By including positive comments on some aspect of the home environment and comments directed particularly to a child, a teacher further indicates his interest and appreciation of a family.

Dear Mr. and Mrs. Rodriguez and family,

Thank you for making time in your busy schedule for me to visit you at your home on Thursday. I did enjoy the chance to see Tony at home and to see some of his favorite things. Tony, your kitten is very pretty, and you are doing a good job of looking after him.

Thank you also for those delicious pan dulce, Mrs. Rodriguez. I hope you can come soon to the classroom and cook with our children.

Sincerely,

John Roberts

Follow-Up

In the weeks and months that follow, a teacher must continue to be in touch with parents about the information learned and issues discussed during a home visit. For example, if a teacher discovered ways that parents can act as classroom resources, a teacher should make an arrangement promptly.

> "Mr. Rodriguez, when I visited your home and talked about your garden, we said it would be fun for you to visit the classroom with some of the ripe vegetables. Could you come one day next week? We're talking about harvest season."

Evaluation

A teacher needs to evaluate the home visit to learn how effective it was in strengthening the parent-teacher-child relationship, and how his own participation helped meet this goal. A statement summarizing the teacher's learnings should be added to the child's file, to document the home visit and to help the teacher record the information that will be useful in future assessment and planning for the child.

> 3/9
>
> Visit to Rodriguez family. 392 So. Main St.
>
> Present: Mr. and Mrs. Rodriguez, Tony, sister Sandra, age 8.
>
> Learned home language is Spanish only. Tony very well behaved and quiet.
>
> Resource ideas: Mrs. Rodriguez enjoys Spanish cooking, Mr. gardens.

❖ Advantages of Home Visits

Home visits provide positive impetus to a family-teacher relationship. Realistically, there can be advantages and disadvantages to this method. Let's first examine the advantages.

Increase in Trust

Parents and children usually feel more comfortable and secure in their familiar home environment. In most other aspects of the relationship, a teacher has the advantage as the professional person, of knowing what to do and how to do it. During a home visit, parents can take more initiative in furthering the relationship. A young child who sees his teacher welcomed as a guest into his home gets positive feelings about his parents' acceptance of his teacher. A sense of trust is increased among parents, teachers, and children.

Firsthand Insights

A teacher gains not only the rewarding experience of feeling accepted by a family, but also the firsthand insights afforded by a chance to see parents and child interact in their home environment. (See Figure 11-4.) Home visits can thus enhance and extend the classroom experience, as a teacher uses his knowledge to modify skills and plans to match individual children's interests and learning styles, and utilizes parent resources learned about during his visits. Teachers may also increase their sensitivity to cultural diversity and discover ways of responding to the varied backgrounds of children.

❖ Disadvantages of Home Visits

Although the advantages are more important, there are definite disadvantages to home visits that need to be overcome.

Additional Time Involved

Time is no doubt the greatest disadvantage. Not only do home visits take time, but it is often difficult to schedule a visit during a teacher's normal daytime working hours, especially in a full-day program. (In a part-day or part-week program, a teacher can often use some of his planning and preparation time for visits, when a child is at home.) In a full-day program, even if coverage for a teacher in the classroom can be arranged, parents are

Figure 11-4 Home visits offer teachers the opportunity to experience a child's home environment and relationships firsthand. Courtesy Chapter I Program, Charlotte, N.C.

often at work and the child at the center. School administrators may offer compensation time to teachers who use some of their own time off.

Both teachers and parents must be convinced that they will gain from a visit before they will give up time after work, during evenings, days off, or weekends, to schedule a visit. A teacher's explanations and persistence as he tries to schedule a convenient visit should be an indication to parents of how valuable a teacher perceives this activity to be.

As a parent, the author has been impressed by teachers' evident caring for her children, to care enough to visit in the late afternoon and on Saturday morning. As a teacher, the author's most productive visit came, after weeks of trying to set it up, at 9:30 A.M. before both parents went off to late morning jobs. The visit came after weeks of trying to find a convenient time. After this visit, they consented to visit in the classroom for the first time; their little daughter blossomed. Scheduling time is a definite disadvantage, but one that is worth overcoming. Expense needs to be considered too; it seems fair for teachers to be paid mileage for home visits.

Children Misbehaving

Another possible disadvantage is that during this exciting, unfamiliar event children may become overly excited and act out-of-bounds. Then comes the question—who is in charge? This can be an uncomfortable position for both parents and teachers. Teachers will be understandably reluctant to intervene in the parents' home, and parents may hesitate lest they show themselves in a negative light.

Advance preparation and explanation for children may help prevent some of this. Teachers familiar with particular personality characteristics of a child may anticipate this possibility and discuss strategies with parents in advance. Teachers may have to be flexible enough to cut the visit short, if it proves too stressful for child, parents, or teacher.

Possible Negative Feelings

Another major obstacle to overcome for a successful home visit is the negative presuppositions of each participant. Many parents feel suspicious and threatened by an "official" visit, and it takes sensitive, open efforts by schools and teachers to educate parents and remove these fears. It is probably after the experience of a visit that much of this concern is allayed, so teachers must take care to do nothing during a visit that appears to be official scrutiny or to be judgmental. Teachers' care to focus on the positive is necessary.

Teachers must honestly scrutinize their own attitudes and prejudices. In making home visits, they frequently find themselves in neighborhoods and life-styles quite removed from what they are accustomed to, and they must become aware of their biases. When faced directly, personal biases are less destructive than those not admitted, which will manifest themselves in behavior. By focusing their attention on the children and parents' concern for their children, teachers can find positive things in a home situation, rather than focus on those aspects that are different from their experiences. There is no question that emotional responses are complex things to deal with, but teachers who are conscious of these dynamics of the relationship are more likely to be effective.

Home visits offer:

- to parents, evidence of the teachers' interest and caring for their child, and an opportunity to play a more comfortable and dominant role in the home setting.

- to teachers, another chance to reach out to families, and opportunities to experience the child's home environment and relationships first-hand.

- to children, a chance to build a deeper personal relationship with the teacher in a comfortable home setting.

❖ Home-Based Educational Programs

This text assumes that most teachers are part of traditional, school-based learning situations and that they consider home visits to be a useful technique to use in building a parent-teacher working relationship. But it may be interesting to note also that home visitation programs have developed over the last thirty years that focus on teachers educating parents and children in the home.

The goal of most home-based programs has been to help parents become better teachers of their children and improve the quality of life for individual families. Typically, home-based programs serve those families who are isolated physically or culturally or who would have problems attending a center. Frequently, disadvantaged families are involved in home-based programs; Head Start began its Home Start Component in 1972. Programs serving handicapped children also frequently use home visits; there has been recent attention to visits to families of infants and toddlers with special needs (Powell, 1990). Some of the recently established family support and resource programs have home visits as one of the available options for parent contact. A 1988 survey found over 4,500 home visiting programs nationally, typically operating through schools, health departments, and mental health agencies (Powell 1990).

Various policy and program design decisions determine the content of the home visit. Some programs focus primarily on the child, and others include attention to parent and family functioning. Where the home visitors concentrate their efforts on working with parents rather than children, they often teach parents how to use everyday care-giving or household situations as opportunities to stimulate learning. (See Figure 11-5.) When a teacher works with a child, it is a way of modeling appropriate teaching behavior to parents present and involved. All home-based programs

Figure 11-5 Home visitors encourage parents to use household objects and activities to stimulate learning. Courtesy Head Start Bureau.

assume that parents are the most important teachers of their children during the early years, and the skills they are taught have a long-term impact on all children in a family. Parents are expected to add the responsibilities of learners, and then teachers, to their roles as parents and family members. In multiple-focus programs, the assumption is that "pressing factors operating in the environment or parent often interfere with the parent's ability to attend to the child and to other information and suggestions of the home visitor" (Powell 1990, 67).

The home visits in these programs require different skills and techniques in addition to those necessary for working with children. In these programs, home visitors are parent educators. The importance of a strong interpersonal tie between parent and home visitor is emphasized in most programs. In several programs, successful home visitors are trained paraprofessionals. (See Gordon and Breivogel 1976 for a description of Gordon's program in Florida; and Gray 1971 for the DARCEE program at George Peabody College in Tennessee.) This has several advantages, including the economic factor; it is less expensive to use paraprofessionals. Another advantage to the use of trained paraprofessionals is that residents of the same community may be used. A resident of the community may already have established rapport with a family and understand the values and attitudes of the area.

What is taught in each home-based program varies with the goals, but in most programs time and activities are used to build trust and communication between parents and the home visitor, to improve parent-child interaction and learning situations, and to improve home and family life.

Parents who feel isolated and burdened with the demands of young children respond to visitors who treat them with concerned interest. The Home Start guide lists criteria for selection of home visitors that include the ability to listen with empathy and sensitivity, to relate effectively to many different people and to adapt one's personality to meet varying needs. Home visitors spend time at each visit talking informally about whatever concerns parents wish to discuss, as well as having sociable chats.

Home visitors are also observant of family needs and spend time helping parents discover resources and methods of improving home practices, such as nutritional information and classes, financial planning, or recreational opportunities in the community. But the majority of time is spent in helping parents become sensitive to the development characteristics and needs of their children, and in teaching and demonstrating activities and techniques that parents can use with their children at home. Sometimes home visitors bring toys and books and demonstrate how these can be used to stimulate communication and creative play. Often these are left as "gifts" and encouraged to be used between visits. Home visitors develop activities or help parents improvise toys from the home environment. Home visitors will individualize activities according to the circumstances, often including ideas for younger children and ideas that other family members can also carry out. They may encourage parents to find their own ways of stimulating learning—perhaps by having a child participate in a household task such as washing dishes or folding laundry, or undertaking a routine caregiving situation with an infant in such a way as to create a learning game.

The following are some of the well-documented home visitation programs:

1. DARCEE, from the George Peabody College in Tennessee, that developed home visitation techniques and activities for mothers of preschoolers, hoping to provide mothers with the coping skills and assurance they need to be their child's sole preschool teacher (Gray 1971).

2. Verbal Interaction Project by Levenstein, based on the idea that parents can be taught to stimulate their children's intellectual development through verbal interaction about specific toys and books brought by the "toy demonstrator," as these home visitors are called (Levenstein 1971).

3. Ypsilanti-Carnegie Infant Education Project and the Wisconsin Portage Project, which work with parents of particular children (infants and handicapped preschoolers) (Lambie et al. 1980; Shearer et al. 1976).

4. Home Start Projects, added in 1972 to extend the operations of the center-based Head Start programs, by making the home the base and

helping parents become the teachers of their children (U.S. Dept. of HEW 1974 and 1976). Head Start currently is concentrating efforts on center-based programs.

Several of the comprehensive family support and education programs developed more recently, such as those in Minnesota and Missouri, use home visits as part of their outreach. Powell (1990) makes the comment that the full potential of home visits as an effective method of working with young children and parents has yet to be realized.

❖ Summary

Home visits offer evidence of a teacher's interest in and care for the parents' child, and an opportunity for parents to play a more comfortable and dominant role while in their home setting. For teachers, it is another chance to reach out to families and an opportunity to experience a child's home environment and relationships firsthand. For children, it is a chance to build a deeper personal relationship with a teacher in a secure home setting. Much has been learned from the home-based educational programs, and any community deciding to investigate or institute such a program has an abundance of resource information to draw from. Some of the references at the end of this chapter can help a student who wishes to investigate these programs further.

❖ Student Activities for Further Study

1. Role-play, then discuss the dynamics in the following situations a teacher might encounter during a home visit.
    a. A mother is fearful lest her husband be awakened from sleep—he's a third-shift worker.
    b. A child begins to "show off"—mother is embarrassed.
    c. A mother begins talking very negatively about her child's behavior as her child sits in the same room.
    d. A mother appears very shy—virtually tongue-tied.
    e. The parents keep watching a television program after a teacher sits down.
    f. The parents seem very ill at ease—they keep asking if their child is doing anything bad.
2. Discover whether there is any kind of home-based program in your community. If so, try to arrange to visit along with the visitor.
3. Discover whether there is a Head Start or other preschool program in your community where teachers make regular home visits. If so, try to arrange to visit along with a teacher.

❖ Review Questions

1. Identify several purposes for teachers making home visits.
2. Discuss several points to consider in undertaking home visits.
3. Name one advantage and one disadvantage of a home visit.
4. Identify the general purposes and techniques of home-based programs.

❖ Suggestions for Further Reading

(1983). *Community self help: the parent-to-parent program.* Ypsilanti, MI: The High-Scope Press.

Goodson, B.D., and Hess, R. (1975). *Parents as teachers of young children: an evaluative review of some contemporary concepts and programs.* Stanford, CA: Stanford University Press.

Gray, S.W. et al. (1983). The early training project 1962–80 in Consortium for Longitudinal Studies. *As the twig is bent: lasting effects of preschool programs.* Hillsdale, NJ: Erlbaum.

Karnes, M.B., and Zehrbach, R. (1977). Educational intervention at home, in Day, M.C., and Parker, R. (Eds.) *Preschool in action: explaining early childhood programs.* Boston, MA: Allyn and Bacon.

Meyer, T. (1990, Spring). Home visits: a child-centered approach to an old concept. *Day Care and Early Education, 17*(3), 18–21.

Nedler, S.E., and McAfee, O.D. (1979). *Working with parents.* Belmont, CA: Wadsworth Publishing Co.

Packer, A., Hoffman, S., Bozler, B., and Bear, N. (1976). Home learning activities for children, in Gordon, I., and Breivogel, W. (Eds.) *Building effective home-school relationships.* Boston, MA: Allyn and Bacon.

Scott, R., and Thompson, H. (1973). Home starts I and II. *Today's Education, 62*(2), 32–34.

Scott, R., Wagner, G., and Casinger, J. (1976). *Home start ideabooks.* Darien, CT: Early Years Press.

CHAPTER 12

Parents in a Classroom

One of the traditional ways parents have been involved in their children's education has been as volunteers in the classroom. The parent cooperative preschools that began in the first decades of this century believed that including parents in nursery school classrooms would educate them as parents, and would extend the learning experiences available to their children. Certainly, bringing parents into the classroom does this, as well as give them opportunities to understand the program through firsthand observation. But in too many cases, parent participation in classrooms has deteriorated into assignments of unattractive tasks, rather than seeing their participation as another method of developing positive relationships and working partnerships.

There are many roles parents can play within the classroom, from observer to teacher. This chapter examines these roles and considers ways teachers can make their participation enjoyable for everyone, including their children. Planning, preparation of all participants, and a positive attitude will help teachers draw parents into the educational process of their young children.

OBJECTIVES

After studying this chapter, the student will be able to

1. discuss several advantages and potential problems of working with parents in a classroom.
2. identify methods of encouraging parent visitations.
3. discuss methods to facilitate parent observation.
4. describe methods of utilizing parents as resources in a classroom.

❖ Advantages and Potential Problems

> There is a lively discussion going on in the teachers' lounge. Jane Briscoe has just announced she has a parent coming in to play the guitar at group time. MiLan Ha says nothing; she's never had a parent in, but Anne Morgan has told her she's just asking for trouble.
>
> "It's a disaster when a parent comes in; the whole routine gets turned upside down, and worst of all, I guarantee you the parent's child will act up dreadfully."
>
> Connie Martinez agrees. "One of my parents last year came in and brought a cake and balloons for everybody when it was her daughter's birthday. When the birthday girl's balloon broke, she burst into tears and her mother slapped her. I was furious, but what could I do? Now I just ask them to have parties at home." Jane looks thoughtful, and a little worried too.

There is no question that bringing parents into a classroom adds responsibilities for teachers as they cope with various aspects of behavior and reactions. Teachers often object to having parents in the classroom for reasons both professional and personal.

Involving parents in a classroom for any reason demands extra time and effort from a teacher as there are plans to make and fit into the routine. The best use of parents' time and skills must be determined, and both children and parents must be prepared for their roles in the unusual event.

> Jane Briscoe admits it took several conversations with Mr. Butler to learn of his guitar-playing skill, and then more to convince him that the children would enjoy having him come, and that he would know what to do when he got there! She's also had to reschedule the visit twice to fit around his working schedule, and has spent considerable time helping Sam understand his dad will be coming for a visit, but that Sam will be staying at school and not leaving when his dad goes back to work."

Teachers often have professional reservations about parents' functioning in a classroom. Teachers may be convinced that parents who do not have a professional teachers' education will behave inappropriately with children, especially with their own children, and, therefore, put teachers in the awkward position of observing unsuitable adult actions in their own classrooms.

> Connie Martinez sighs. "I could have predicted that child was going to get overexcited with that whole birthday party hoopla. What I didn't know was that her mother would react so angrily. I was embarrassed not only for that child, but also that the other children saw that happen in my classroom."

Teachers may be concerned that parents will behave unprofessionally in other ways, such as discussing children with others outside of the classroom.

Another concern of teachers results from their knowledge of children's reactions when adjusting to changed routines. Some teachers who perceive a child's overexcitement or distress when a parent leaves the classroom after a special event feel the experience is too disruptive to be beneficial.

> "Look, it's a nice idea, but in practice it's too upsetting. Children can't understand why their parents can't stay the whole time, and it undoes a lot of adjustment."

Teachers may also have personal qualms about parents being on hand to observe their actions for an extended period of time. Whether it is true or not, many teachers feel that they are constantly watched and evaluated when parents are present, and therefore feel uncomfortable throughout a visit, feeling the need to perform.

> MiLan says, "Frankly, I don't need the additional stress of having a parent watch me through the whole morning."

Considering these objections, are there reasons for including parents in the classroom that outweigh the disadvantages? There certainly are great benefits for parents, children, and teachers.

For parents, spending time in a classroom is the best way to understand what is going on in a program. (See Figure 12-1.) Parents have often equated school with purely cognitive learning and are surprised and dismayed to learn that early childhood classrooms do not emphasize overtly academic learnings. Seeing what is actually happening gives them more respect for the developmentally appropriate learning that is taking place.

A   **B**

Figure 12-1 For parents, spending time in a classroom is the best way to understand what is going on in a program. (A) Courtesy Barbara Stegall; (B) Courtesy Bethlehem Center, Charlotte, NC; Peeler Portrait Studio, photographer.

> Mr. Butler, the guitar-playing father, helps explain this. "It was good to see what they do at their group time. Those kids are really learning to listen, to take turns talking and participating. Then they had their snack. Several children were responsible for getting the tables set, and they did it just right. And they poured their own juice, and not a drop spilled. Then they all tried these vegetables in a dip; at home, Sam would never have touched the stuff, but there with his friends he did."

Such firsthand knowledge provides a ready basis for discussion with teachers.

In a classroom parents can see how their child is functioning with his peers and other adults. They can also observe typical behaviors and skills for a cross section of children the same age. This may also enable parents to see the kinds of problem behaviors that teachers want to discuss later.

> "You know, it's kind of reassuring to find out that most two-year-olds grab things from each other. I'd been thinking mine was particularly aggressive."

Being in a classroom also gives parents a feeling of satisfaction as they contribute to a program, are welcomed by a teacher, and are recognized as important adults by their child and his or her friends—a real ego boost.

> "I'd never play my guitar for a group of adults, but the kids loved it, I must say."

Children also feel special and important when their parents are in a classroom. (See Figure 12-2.)

> "That's my Daddy," beams Sam as his dad leads the singing with his guitar.

Figure 12-2 Young children feel special and important when their parents are in the classroom. Courtesy Connie Glass.

Such good feelings probably have a more lasting impact than the transitory distress caused by a parent saying good-bye twice in one morning.

Children's feelings of security increase as they see parents and teachers working together cooperatively, each respecting the other's contribution. Children also benefit as parents gain in understanding the process of learning and children's interaction skills.

Teachers as well as children gain through the expanded opportunities for learning that other adults bring into a classroom. Parents' skills, knowledge, interests, and talents add up to lots of possible resources for curriculum learnings.

> "I really like to give them as much music as I can, but I don't have a musical bone in my body. There's no substitute for having a real instrument in the classroom. From me they get a lot of records."

Having an extra pair of hands in a group of young children often allows for activities that just aren't possible without enough adults. (See Figure 12-3.)

Classroom visitation by parents gives teachers another chance to see parent-child interaction and parental attitudes.

> "It's interesting to me to see Sam and his dad together. Mr. Butler is very comfortable in the nurturing role."

Teachers perceive parent involvement in a classroom as evidence of support of their efforts as parents gain empathy towards a teacher and the problems of working with a group of young children. It is professionally

Figure 12-3 When parents go along to help, a special trip to the farm is possible.
Courtesy Barbara Stegall.

and personally rewarding to deepen a parent-teacher partnership through
such cooperative efforts.

> "I really enjoyed having Mr. Butler with us, and I appreciated his
> interest in sharing some time with us. It makes me feel like I'm not the
> only one who cares what goes on in this classroom. You know, when
> he went home, he shook his head and said he didn't see how I do it,
> all day, every day."

It is true there are potential problems when parents are involved in a
classroom. Teachers may have professional concerns for the possible reactions of children and/or parents in a classroom, or they may have personal
concerns about performing before an adult audience. And extra time and
effort are needed on the part of teachers and parents to plan ahead for the
event. However, the following advantages make it worth the effort:

- Parents gain firsthand experience of a program, of their child's reactions
  in a classroom, and feelings of satisfaction from making a contribution.
- Children feel special when their parents are involved, feel secure with
  the tangible evidence of parents and teachers cooperating, and gain
  directly as parental understanding and skills increase.
- Teachers gain resources to extend learning opportunities, observe parent-child interaction, and can feel supported as parents participate and
  empathize with them.

❖ Getting Parents Involved

There are many different ways to involve parents in early childhood
classrooms. Non-working parents can be regular volunteers assisting teachers in parent-cooperative nursery schools, Head Start programs, or other

programs set up to educate both parents and children. When parents regularly assume auxiliary teaching roles, it is advisable to prepare them for this experience with a training program. Then issues of teaching philosophy and goals, children's behavior and learning styles, and appropriate adult guidance and interactive techniques can be explored so parents entering a classroom clearly understand their expected roles. A training program may include classroom visits, workshops, orientation discussions, handbooks, and guided observation. (For a synopsis of one director's orientation program for parents who participate regularly, see Knowler 1988.)

Many other parents, particularly those who work and whose children are in child care programs, may visit a classroom infrequently for planned social events, opportunities to observe, or as an extra resource. There are a number of ways teachers can facilitate parent involvement in the classroom.

Exploring Resources and Needs

Before establishing any plan to bring parents into a classroom, teachers need to gather information about the families to discover which family members can be involved, interests and experiences that can be shared, and time resources. Some of this information can be gathered informally, as teachers learn about families during initial interviews and home visits, during casual conversations with parents and children. Other information may be gathered more formally by the use of questionnaires and application forms to acquire written responses to specific questions.

A brief background questionnaire may inquire about the following:

1. *The names and ages of other children and family members in the home*, to learn whether grandparents or teenaged siblings are available to come in occasionally, or if young children keep a parent too busy to visit. (See Figure 12-4.)

Figure 12-4 A father's musical instrument may add a resource to the classroom.

Figure 12-5 Visiting a father at work (in this case a pasta store) can make an exciting trip. Courtesy Connie Glass.

2. *Occupations,* to learn a little about working hours and days off, to see if there is available time; jobs that are of interest to young children or that can provide scrap materials and expertise for classroom use or to help out other parents. (See Figure 12-5.)

3. *Interests and hobbies, pets, travel, cultural or religious backgrounds.* (See Figure 12-6.)

Figure 12-6 An older brother can visit to give bike rides. Courtesy Connie Glass.

A wealth of resources is obtained by these few questions. As teachers accumulate information, it is a good idea to organize it into a resource file, with a card or page for each family. This file can be easily updated as new information is accumulated. Tentative plans for using these resources throughout the year can be noted, along with times parents are free to come to school.

Butler, Bill and Joan (divorced)
Other child: Lisa-3, (in center)
Bill: Salesman, Angel Stone, 8:00-5:00 P.M.; can be flexible in morning
    sometimes; out of town Wed. and Thurs. usually
Joan: Secretary, South West Telephone; 8:30-5:00 Mon-Fri; access to
    old computer sheets, discarded telephones
Interests: Joan-tennis, needlepoint, Chinese cooking
           Bill-plays guitar, golf
Possibilities: Bill-play guitar
               -Chanukah celebration (Dec.)
         Joan-ask for paper
             -stir-fry vegetables (Spring)
Note: No social for parents on Wed. or Thurs.

Weaver, Bob and Jane
No other children
Jane: homemaker
Bob: production in furniture factory, 7:30-4:30, Mon-Fri.
Other: Grandparents in neighborhood, retired. Grandmother likes to
    cook.
Interests: Jane-gardening, sewing
         Bob-volunteer fireman
Possibilities: Jane-help with planting (spring)
             -cloth scraps
             -free most days (field trips)
        Bob-wood scraps
             -bring firetruck or uniform (Community Helpers Unit,
             Feb., late afternoon)
        Grandparents-invite grandmother to cook with us.

Ashley, Sylvia
Terrence-9
Sylvia: job training program, 9:00-4:00, for next 9 months
Interests:
Possibilities: Invite for late afternoon time.
        Come in to read informally with children.
        Invite Terrence to throw ball with children on playground.

Encourage Informal Visits

How do teachers get parents into a classroom? At first, casual, unstructured visits are often best as parents feel no pressure to perform a role and no demands on their time. If allowed to get comfortable in a classroom, they will enjoy interacting with the children, other parents, and teachers.

Reserve Time

One morning or afternoon a week open for visiting creates a welcoming atmosphere. Parents are encouraged to spend an extra few minutes while dropping off or picking up their child—or more if they can stay—to join in or observe some free-play activities and perhaps have a drink or snack prepared by the children. Parents enjoy coming to a center to briefly participate in their child's work. Such a regular occurrence demystifies for children the idea of having parents in a classroom and allows parents to stay occasionally, as their schedule permits. These visitations require little effort on a teacher's part, beyond the usual setting up of free-play choices that require little supervision or assistance so teachers are free to move about. The casual nature of such visits means that only a few parents at a time are in a classroom, therefore avoiding the overcrowding that may be too stimulating for children. There is also less chance of children feeling "left out" if their own parents are not there, since play activities go on as usual, and many other parents are absent as well. The clear message of just sharing an ordinary day is relaxing as well as reassuring to parents that the classroom is always open for their viewing.

Birthday Celebrations

Most centers have a special way of celebrating children's birthdays. Inviting parents to be present for the celebration can make it even more special. (See Figure 12-7.) This may mean having the celebration at a time suited to a parent's schedule. Most parents enjoy an event that centers on their child. When classrooms have specific guidelines for celebrations, parents will not be drawn to compete in parties or make decisions deemed unsuitable for the group of children.

Personal Invitations

Some teachers include a "Family of the Week" component in their classroom plans. Specific, personal invitations made to an individual family may include siblings and other family members. The child whose family comes is host for the day, getting chairs for parents and siblings, serving them drinks and snacks, showing them around the room, discussing the art on the walls, etc. Parents are asked to share something about their lives with all the children, whether it's talking about jobs or other interests, or something that the family enjoys doing together. When each family is invited in

Figure 12-7 Parents may enjoy visiting for parties and special events. Courtesy The Crier, magazine of the Junior League of Charlotte, Inc.

turn, parents will make a special effort to come, as their child is honored. Not only is this a useful way to draw parents into classroom life, but it is also a concrete model for all the children of demonstrating multicultural diversity and uniqueness of all families.

Lunch Invitations

Parents can be invited for lunch in their children's classrooms. Most centers do not require too much advance notice to set an extra place for lunch; this offers another chance for a social visit and a special treat for a child. Having Mom or Dad just theirs for lunch, away from other siblings, may be fun. Parents get an opportunity to see firsthand how teachers help children develop appropriate table behavior, self-help and conversational skills, and encourage tasting a variety of foods.

Special Occasions

Whether a parent tea party, early morning coffee, or a picnic lunch, most parents respond to invitations made to a whole group of parents. With various family structures, it creates problems or discomfort when invitations are made to "fathers only" or "mothers only." Parents with particular work schedules may be unable to accept, and children who do not have the specified parent living at home will feel left out. Certainly special personal invitations can be made to fathers to make sure they are included. Involving children in the party preparations and invitations often gives parents an extra motivation to attend. The time selection should match a teacher's information about work schedules as far as possible.

Zoo Day

A "zoo" day where parents are asked to bring pets provides a good situation for getting parents to share and volunteer their resources. (See Figure 12-8.)

Parents often find their own ways of becoming involved in classroom life when allowed to take the initiative. One center reports that when parents come to take their children out of a classroom for appointments or a special lunch, they come back in time for the toothbrushing ritual or to read stories to their own children and some friends before helping a teacher settle everyone for nap—satisfying for everyone. Informal occasions such as these may be the only times some parents come to the classroom. (See additional notes on social occasions in chapter 13. For some creative events for teachers to plan that include families, see Horowitz and Fagella 1986.) Other parents may get involved in additional ways.

Encourage Parent Observations

Parents who are comfortable in a classroom may accept an invitation to spend a short period observing. This is beneficial for all parents, and partic-

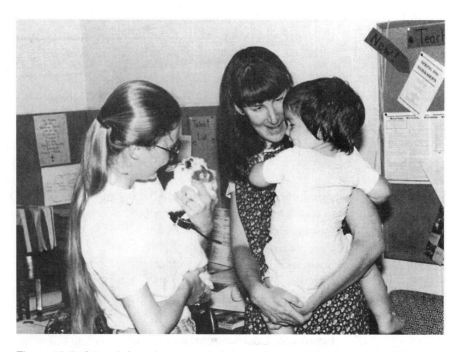

Figure 12-8 A "zoo" day when parents bring pets may help some parents begin to share and volunteer resources. Courtesy CPCC Media Production—Mike Slade.

ularly for parents with special concerns about their child or questions about a program, in anticipation of an extended conversation at a later conference.

Observation periods are most productive when parents and children are prepared for their roles. Teachers may explain to children that parents will be coming "so they can see all the fun things we do in the classroom." Children can also be told that the visiting grown-ups will probably want to sit at one side and not play, for a time. (It is ideal to have an observation booth or window where visitors can observe undetected. Since not many schools boast such an opportunity, both parents and children will have to accustom themselves to the others' presence.)

Both parents and teachers should be wary that children may act differently in the presence of parents. It is helpful to discuss this openly and to suggest that parents observe on several occasions, to accustom their children to the practice. Parents should also feel comfortable leaving if their child is having difficulty with their presence. Teachers can reassure parents that such behavior is normal, and that the parent can try coming again at a later time.

Observing during outdoor play is a good first step for both children and parents. Outdoor play may offer more natural opportunities for children to play freely, without feeling they're being watched. Parents who seem hesitant about the observer's role may also be more comfortable outdoors. (See Figure 12-9.)

Many parents feel uncertain about their role as an observer and may feel more secure when given both verbal and written guidelines for helpful classroom behaviors and points for observation. The following is a sample form that may be used.

Figure 12-9 Observing on the playground may help a parent and child become comfortable with the process of observation. Courtesy CPCC Media Production—Mike Slade.

Welcome to Our Classroom

1. The children will be delighted to see you and may need a gentle reminder that you've come to see them play. A crowd could make it difficult for you to observe or jot down questions.

2. Observe your child and as many others as you can. This can be a learning experience about
   • your child and how he relates to other children and the classroom activities,
   • what children the same age as your child are like,
   • how the teacher guides each child.

3. Observe your child and several others. Notice how they
   • respond to other children,
   • use language,
   • choose activities and how long they stay with each activity,
   • solve problems and obtain assistance.

4. Observe your child's particular interests and interactions.

5. Observe the teacher in a variety of activities. Notice how the teacher
   • relates to each child,
   • handles difficult situations,
   • prevents problems and guides behavior.

6. Write down any impressions, surprises, suggestions, or questions you would like to discuss later.

A parent with particular concerns should be given individual guidelines. Parents who observe on several occasions will appreciate having an observation booklet with specific points on each page.

Parents as Classroom Resources

As teachers get to know the families they work with, they become aware of parents' wealth of experience that can be used to deepen children's understanding of the world around them. It should be noted that parents are invited into classroom experiences to involve and include them, not to merely exploit them as an extra pair of hands to complete the grubby chores in the classroom. Parents' competence, creativity, and knowledge should be respected, so they will be involved in tasks that are worth doing, from which they can gain a sense of accomplishment and make real contributions. Parents may be invited to find a time convenient for them to visit a classroom and share an experience. When appropriate, children may be able to visit a parent at work or at home.

Parents are resources in a variety of ways.

Jobs

Many parents' jobs are interesting to young children when demonstrated along with the "tools of the trade." Visitors may be a dental hygienist with a giant set of teeth and toothbrush, a truck driver complete with a truck, a hair stylist, or a carpenter.

Even parents who have more prosaic jobs sometimes work in places that make wonderful field trips. A tall glass office building with an exciting elevator ride up to see the view, a company next to a construction site, a shopping mall, a neighborhood store, a bus terminal: all may have a cheery parent to greet the children as they explore the different places people work.

Hobbies

Parents with particular interests and hobbies may offer fascinating substance to a curriculum. A guitar player, an avid camper with back pack and pup tent, a gardener, a cook, an aerobic dancer, a cyclist, rock-hound, or carpenter: all have enthusiasm and skills to share with the children. A parent who enjoys using his video camera may take film of children busy at play, fun for the children to see re-played and interesting for parents to view later at a parent meeting. Most adults, even if initially hesitant, enjoy themselves thoroughly as children respond with zest to the new activities. Sometimes hobbies that appear to be strictly for adults create interesting situations as children relate to them in their own way; one parent who shared tapes of his favorite classical music was delighted to watch children spontaneously improvise movement and dance. (See Figure 12-10.)

Cultures

Multicultural experiences are promoted within good early childhood classrooms. Children need to have the opportunity to learn respect and value for the unique differences among people. Parents may help the teacher offer firsthand experiences for children in exploring customs, foods, or celebrations of a variety of cultural or religious traditions. Chanukah songs, games, and foods from a Jewish parent; a Chinese parent demonstrating use of a wok and chopsticks; Spanish children's songs taught by a Puerto Rican parent; the sharing of some family treasures by a Vietnamese parent; an African American parent explaining the traditions of Kwanzaa celebrations; an American Indian parent sharing a craft artifact; mementoes brought back from a vacation trip; such activities woven into a classroom curriculum enrich and stimulate learning for children. More importantly, inviting parents to share aspects of their lives and cultures provides an opportunity for teachers to demonstrate respect for the diverse family backgrounds in a classroom. Both children and their parents receive a boost to their self-esteem when a representation of their own lives is shared. All children benefit, as they learn to enjoy and accept the aspects of uniqueness and universality in multicultural experiences. We'll talk more about this in chapter 15.

Figure 12-10 Many parents will enjoy sharing their interests with children.

Extended Family

Knowing the makeup of each family will help teachers find resources beyond the parents. A retired grandmother who enjoys reading stories to children, a teenaged brother who can help with ball-throwing on the playground, a baby who can be brought to visit for a bath or feeding; other family members can provide additional experiences. (See Figures 12-11 and 12-12.)

Time

One resource provided by many parents is time. A parent coming into the classroom is helpful when an extra pair of hands is needed. Walks or field trips, classroom parties, or more complicated projects are undertaken when teachers can count on additional assistance from parents. Sometimes parents are more comfortable offering to share time instead of demonstrating a talent. As parents interact with children, they are often drawn into an activity they have done as parents—supervising cooking experiences, carving a jack-o'lantern, playing a game. (See Figure 12-13.) The parents' presence alone offers a learning experience for children as they see, for example, men nurturing and doing classroom tasks such as pouring juice and cleaning tables, roles more commonly associated with mothers (Hopkins 1977). (See

Figure 12-11 Other family members, such as grandparents, may have time to spend in the classroom. Courtesy Barbara Stegall.

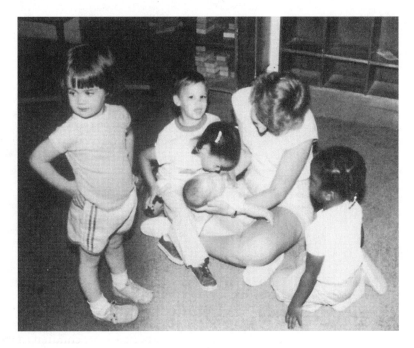

Figure 12-12 A baby sister may come to the classroom for a visit. Courtesy CPCC Media Production—Mike Slade.

Figure 12-13 Parents may be willing to share everyday experiences they are comfortable with from their homes. Courtesy Barbara Stegall.

Figure 12-14.) It is also important that parents' time not be wasted. Teachers need to have materials ready for their use, and be efficient in explaining classroom routines and activities, so that parents do not feel they are just waiting for something to happen. Sometimes parents would rather use at-

Figure 12-14 A father coming to read a story is a special event. Courtesy Nancy Pierce.

home time to support classroom activities. At home, parents can launder and mend dress-up clothes and toys, use personal computers to type newsletters, make phone calls to remind parents of meetings, or prepare simple classroom games.

Materials

Parents who are unavailable to come into a classroom may still provide resources in the form of materials to be used in classroom activities. Scraps and throwaways from jobs (computer paper, styrofoam packing bits, spools from a cotton mill), scraps and discards from home (kitchen utensils, dress-up clothes, magazines, fabric pieces), all make a contribution that allows both parents and teachers to feel a sense of cooperation. Some teachers regularly post a list of "Treasures Wanted" via a newsletter or bulletin board. For example:

Contributions from Home

Throughout the year we can always use:
- Writing supplies—envelopes, paper, postcards, small notepads, any sizes of paper, including computer paper
- Appliance boxes and cardboard boxes of all sizes
- Yogurt containers for paint
- Discarded clothing for dress-up
- Small appliances for taking apart
- Wood for the workbench
- Fabric, yarn, large needles for sewing
- Ideas for local field trips

Parents outside a classroom will feel involved as they prepare materials for classroom use. Tracing and cutting out pieces for teacher-made games is something a homebound mother can feel important doing.

In some communities, it is possible for parents to host an "Open House" for their children's classmates. The children may visit a child's home for a snack or a picnic lunch.

Special Skills

Parents may have skills or knowledge that can be drawn on as resources beyond the classroom, to support a center or to offer to other parents. Architects, builders, or landscape designers can contribute to playground design; accountants or business people can help with budgets, insurance, and tax matters; medical personnel can set up first-aid kits and procedures; particularly handy parents can repair toys as needed; "bargain hunter" parents can aid the person who purchases for a center, answering such questions as

"Where can we get the best deal on sand?" Knowledgeable parents are possible resources for parent meetings or workshops: a high school counselor leads a discussion on communication techniques; parents who have successfully negotiated divorce and remarriage share insights on stepparenting; a lawyer discusses tax tips for working parents.

❖ Teacher's Role

As teachers invite parents to participate in classroom learning activities, they need to concentrate on their skills for working with adults. Teachers need to be able to relax and enjoy the contribution of others to their classrooms and not feel threatened by any attention transferred from themselves to a visiting adult. It is important to remember that as more specific information is given to parents, parents will feel more comfortable knowing what is expected of them. Parents should know what time frame to plan on and that it is acceptable to leave or stay as their schedules allow. It is helpful to confirm all arrangements in writing, so that parents have a concrete reminder of an event to fit into their schedules.

> Dear Mr. Butler,
> We are looking forward to your visit to our classroom next Friday, Feb. 2, at 9:15 A.M. The children will have snack at 9:45, so that will give you about half an hour to sing songs with us. We'll probably have some favorites to request too! Please feel free to stay and have snack with us, if you're able. See you next week.
>
> Sincerely,
>
> Jane Briscoe

Teachers should immediately greet parents coming into a classroom and make them feel welcome, pointing out an area to sit or begin their preparations. Parents appreciate knowing beforehand exactly what they will be expected to do, not vague suggestions that they "join in." Even if parents are just coming to share time in the classroom, they will be more comfortable if teachers help them get started.

> "Our children love for someone to read to them. If you just sit in that chair in the book corner, I'm sure you'll have children joining you before long. There are two small chairs there too, to limit the number of children to two. Usually they'll move on to something else when they see the chairs are filled. There'll be about half an hour before we clean up for snack."

When parents come into the classroom frequently, it may be helpful to have specific work cards that indicate which part of the room to be responsible for, suggestions of questions or comments to facilitate learning, cleanup responsibilities, etc. Teachers should watch parents for signs of discomfort or indications of how much they want teachers to help them out in uncertain situations. When teachers prepare parents for potentially disruptive situations that could occur, especially if their own child is involved, parents are more likely to feel comfortable at school. Teachers help children of visiting parents understand that Mom or Dad will be helping all the children and will have special things to do today. This helps to clarify the visiting parent's role for the child. Occasionally a child of invited parents reacts by showing off or clinging and being possessive of his parents' attention. It is a good idea to warn parents ahead of time that this may happen and that a teacher is prepared for it and won't mind. Parents should also be reassured that a teacher will step in if necessary to remind a child of classroom rules so that parents will not feel the full burden of guidance is theirs, and perhaps react inappropriately because of embarrassment. In the classroom, teachers should enforce classroom rules. This understanding helps clarify adult responsibilities.

> "It's so special when parents come in that sometimes we get some unusual behaviors. No problem. If Sam forgets our rules, I'll just step in to remind him."

The unusual event may cause a young child to get upset when his parent leaves, even though separation is not normally a problem. A teacher needs to comfort him and to reassure the parent that the classroom visit was still a very good idea, even though there were a few tears at the end. The positive feelings for both child and parent far outweigh any brief distress.

Parents like feeling that they're making a valuable contribution to a classroom. Many parents will try to find the time for a visit if they feel truly needed and wanted. A note of appreciation from the teacher and children afterwards, pictures of the event displayed on a bulletin board, a mention of the event as a classroom highlight in the next newsletter—all these convey to parents that their time was well spent.

❖ Summary

Parents may become involved in the classroom as

1. casual visitors, to participate in classroom activities, meals, or celebrations,
2. observers, to extend their knowledge of children's functioning in a classroom, or
3. resources, to extend and enrich opportunities for the children.

❖ Student Activities for Further Study

1. If you are working or interning in a preschool classroom, gather information on parents—family composition, jobs and details of what is involved, hobbies and interests, religious and ethnic backgrounds.

Find out if parents have access to any particular materials that are useful in your classroom or have particular periods of time free. Organize this information into a resource file. (If you are not presently in a preschool classroom, use the fictional family information described in chapter 1 to make a sample resource file.)

2. Use your resource file to

   a. make a hypothetical plan for how you will use your resource knowledge to invite parents into the classroom for particular activities and/or events and/or curriculum topics throughout the year, and

   b. invite three different parents into your classroom, if possible. Remember it will be your role to prepare parents and children for what to expect; play hostess in making parents feel comfortable in the room and guide children's behavior. Use this as an opportunity to observe parents and children in the classroom and the effect of the visit on each.

❖ Review Questions

1. Describe at least one advantage for children, parents, and teachers when teachers work with parents in the classroom, and any one of three disadvantages.

2. List at least two methods of encouraging parental visits to the classroom.

3. Describe at least one method to facilitate parental observation in a classroom.

4. Discuss at least two ways parents can be used as resources in a classroom.

❖ Suggestions for Further Reading

Baskwill, J. (1989). *Parents and teachers in learning.* New York: Scholastic.

Brock, H.C., III. (1976). *Parent volunteer programs in early childhood education: a practical guide.* Hamden, CT: Shoestring Press.

Coletta, A. (1977). *Working together: a guide to parent involvement.* Atlanta: Humanics Press Inc.

Comer, J. and Haynes, M. (1991). Parent involvement in schools: an ecological approach. *Elementary School Journal, 91*(3), 271–278.

Fisher, B. (1991). *Joyful learning: a whole language kindergarten.* Portsmouth, N.H.: Heinemann.

Miller, B.L., and Wilmshurst, A.L. (1975). *Parents and volunteers in the classroom: a handbook for teachers.* Palo Alto: R and E Research Assoc., Inc.

Miller, S.A. and M. (1993, Jan./Feb.). Encouraging volunteer participation. *Early Childhood News, 5*(1), 9–10.

Tizard, B., Mortimer, J., and Burchell, B. (1981). *Involving parents in nursery and infant schools.* Ypsilanti, MI: The High/Scope Press.

CHAPTER 13

Parents in Meetings

One of the traditional ways of trying to reach parents in the school systems has been to hold occasional meetings. Generally, the meetings are designed to give information to large groups of parents. Frequently, parents will attend one of these meetings in order to discover what the meeting is all about, but the large-group aspects are usually unappealing, so future attendance may be less likely. This is unfortunate, because it continues the distance between home and school, and fails to function to give parents the assistance that may be truly helpful. Until children come with complete instruction booklets, parents will continue to need information and ideas to support their child rearing. Many parental needs for support, social contact, and increased information may be met in meetings. This chapter explores ways that early education programs can offer more than the traditional meeting, so that parents may be more likely to participate. In addition, parents may be involved in the decision-making aspects of a program. Teachers need to consider this facet of working with parents.

OBJECTIVES

After studying this chapter, the student will be able to

1. discuss a rationale for parent education.
2. identify several assumptions regarding parent education and corresponding implications for planning programs.
3. describe ways parents can function as advisors.

Anne Morgan and Dorothy Scott do a lot of things differently in their classrooms, but they do agree on one idea: neither of them wants to attend the center's parent meeting next week. Dorothy sounds quite cynical about it: "Look, I've been going to parent meetings for thirteen years, and it's always the same thing. A handful of parents show up, and always the same ones, the ones who are already doing a pretty good job and don't need to hear the guest speaker anyway. I'm just getting tired of the whole thing." Anne is also disappointed with the results of the last meeting she attended. "If there's one thing the parents need to understand, it's the terrible effect of television on preschool children. So after they listened to the man we invited to speak on that topic, do you think I noticed any difference in what my children tell me they've watched? It doesn't seem worth the effort." Even their director seems less than certain of the value of the parents meetings she continues to arrange. "It does seem there must be something else we could do to attract more parents."

These comments are frequently expressed teacher attitudes towards the attempts at parent education they have encountered. It would be interesting to hear the reactions of parents involved in the experiences and of parents who stayed at home; in all probability, additional negative responses would be heard.

Traditional parent education consists of various methods for giving to parents information deemed necessary by a professional. The traditional approach stresses information and training that is directly related to parent-child interaction. The model is that of a competent professional dispensing facts to a less competent parent. This one-way model implies a passive audience and a need to overcome a deficit in parental knowledge. Such a stance increased parental self-doubt; it is not surprising that parents frequently engage in these educational approaches with minimal enthusiasm or maximal avoidance!

Such a parent education program can make parents feel powerless and dependent on the advice of professionals. Research on learned helplessness reports that experiences and expectations of failure decrease the ability to learn and take the initiative and increase the tendency to turn to others for assistance. The more parents are treated as if they are not capable, the less they will try to do for themselves. The system through which they are educated is itself an important part of any parent-education program. The usefulness of many informational programs is hindered by procedures that point to the authority of professionals and the incompetence of parents.

In considering models that may be more effective, attitudes and practices that support and strengthen the parents' sense of competence need to be examined.

❖ What is Parent Education?

Although some programs refer to all efforts at parent involvement as "parent education," the term is usually used to refer to specific attempts to offer knowledge and support to parents in hopes of increasing parenting effectiveness. Parent education has taken many forms, for different purposes, with varying results.

Consider the following contrasts: Some programs focus on family-community relations while others teach parents how to stimulate a child's cognitive development. Some programs prescribe specific skills and styles for relating to young children while other programs help parents determine what is best for them. Some programs are designed primarily to disseminate child development information to parents while others attempt to foster supportive relationships among program participants. Some programs are highly structured while others let parents select activities they wish to pursue. In some programs the staff serve as child development experts while other programs adhere to a self-help model with staff in nondirective facilitator roles. There also are important differences in the use of professionals, assistants or volunteers, program length (weeks versus years), and program setting (group versus home-based).

Programs are operated by schools, hospitals, health centers, child-care centers, mental health agencies, churches, libraries, colleges and universities, and organizations that have parent education as their sole mission. Those served include first-time parents, expectant parents, future parents, teenage parents, single parents, parents of handicapped children, and grandparents (Powell 1986, 47). (See Figure 13-1.)

This listing of diversity could go on. Some of the divergent opinions involve differences in interpretation of the same phenomena; others seem to address different reference points. For parent education is a complex phenomenon. Its history and development have been and continue to be marked by major shifts in purposes, contents, and approaches (Florin and Dokecki 1983, 24).

Figure 13-1 Parent education programs must fit the needs of various family structures, including grandparents, teenage parents, and single parents. Courtesy USM Publications.

In the past decade a major direction for programs for parents has been the development of family support programs. This broad approach to parent education focuses on all of family life and emphasizes developing support systems for families. A goal is to help families prevent problems, believing that families receiving support are empowered on their own behalf. The Family Resource Coalition promotes this kind of program and offers information on local funding methods and organization models. (For more information on FRC, see chapter 4.)

Auerbach defines parent education as "intervention to help parents function more effectively in their parental role" (Auerbach 1968, 3). Swick expands this to "any effort to increase the development and learning of parents in carrying out the diverse roles they perform," including the personal dimensions of marital roles and relationships and personal needs as adults (Swick 1985, 4). Such efforts introduce new educational experiences that give parents added knowledge and understanding; cause them to question their habitual ways of thinking, feeling, and acting; and help them develop new methods (where new methods are indicated) of dealing with their children, with themselves, and with their social environment.

The term *education* is part of the problem since it connotes the formal study of facts associated with a narrowly cognitive academic world. In reality, the subject of parent-child relations and education is not so much concerned with facts and knowledge as it is with concepts, attitudes, and ideas. The content of any educational program may be less important than the methods of bringing parents together to widen their horizons and sensitize them to feelings in a parent-child relationship.

Perhaps the main functions of a parent education curriculum are (1) to stimulate parents to examine their relationship with their children more closely and (2) to encourage interaction among parents and between parents and program staff (Powell 1986). While the education of parents is primarily for the benefit of the children, the parent's own development can also be enhanced in the process of interacting with other adults.

A broader consideration of parent education implies a dynamic learning process in which parents are active participants, growing out of parents' interests and needs, and in which parents are able to participate as individuals. Research-based information increasingly suggests that the ways in which parents see their parenting roles and interact with their children directly influence the way young children learn to think, talk, solve problems, and feel about themselves and others. As teachers of their children, parents need the same awareness and skills that teachers have, so they can feel the same confidence in their ability to guide children to the fullest extent. Therefore, parent education needs to offer a broad variety of services designed to complement parents' responsibilities and knowledge, to increase their understanding of children and their competence in caring for them.

Samples of Predesigned Parent Education Programs

Several popular program models have been developed for widespread use, primarily with middle-class parents. These include Parent Effectiveness Training (PET), Systematic Training for Effective Parenting (STEP), and Active Parenting. (See Figure 13-2.)

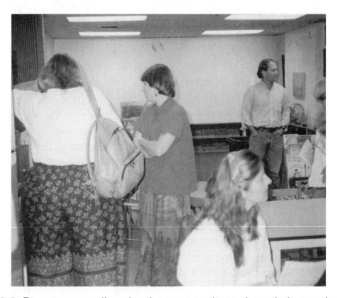

Figure 13-2 Parents generally enjoy the opportunity to share their experiences with other parents. Courtesy Connie Glass.

Parent Effectiveness Training

Thomas Gordon developed a course and wrote a book with this title. The method focuses primarily on helping parents develop communication skills that allow them to act as counselors to children regarding their behavior and feelings, and resolve conflicts between parents and children. Parents are taught techniques such as active listening, "I"-messages, and no-lose methods of conflict resolution. Studies on behaviors of parents who have attended PET sessions indicate increases in positive interactions with children and cohesion in the family, along with decreases in the frequency of family conflicts. (For more information on PET methods, see Gordon, 1975.)

Systematic Training for Effective Parenting

This program offers a structured curriculum represented in cassettes, parent manuals, and leadership manual, supplying material for nine parent group sessions, based on the child management principles of Alfred Adler and Rudolf Dreikurs. Communication methods and non-punitive discipline techniques such as natural and logical consequences are emphasized, along with skills for developing responsibility and decision making, and family problem-solving. (For more information on STEP methods, see Dinkmeyer and McKay, 1982.)

Active Parenting

Active Parenting, begun in the early 1980s, is a rapidly growing parenting program based on the use of videotapes and workbooks in six structured sessions with trained leaders. The program claims to "emerge from the concepts of psychologists such as Alfred Adler, Rudolf Dreikurs, and Carl Rogers, and goes beyond ground-breaking programs like PET and STEP to make parenting education easier to teach—and more compelling to learn—than ever before." (AP Newsletter) Concepts emphasized include "freedom within limits" and "democratic family units," with ideas for family council meetings. Tested techniques such as "I-messages," active listening, and natural and logical consequences are illustrated in the video vignettes, along with basic understandings of causes of misbehavior, formation of self-esteem, and helpful praise and encouragement in developing responsibility. (For more information on the Active Parenting program, contact Active Parenting, Inc., 4669 Roswell Rd. N.E., Atlanta, GA 30342.)

Such programs that appeal widely to middle-class parents may be quite unappealing for lower-income parents, or parents from cultural backgrounds that may not value democratic models and open expression of feelings.

Powell states that there have been major changes in the content and procedures of parent education programs in the past decade, with a new interest in matching programs with the intended parent populations, changing relations between program staff and participants, and paying attention to the social context of parent functioning (Powell 1989).

Matching Programs to Parent Characteristics

It has been noted that parent education methods often used with groups of middle-class parents do not necessarily transfer to low-income parents. For example, group discussion methods have limited appeal with these groups. Planned programs must recognize and respond to the needs and wishes of the individual participants. This suggests an active role for parents in determining content and method of learning.

Role of Professionals

There is an increasing trend towards equal relationships between program staff and parent participants. Dominant roles and decisions are not always played by directors or teachers. Professionals who work with parents take on a collaborative partnership role, rather than a professional-as-expert role. This puts staff into the role of facilitator of goals and activities that are jointly determined by parents and staff. Such an understanding focuses more on adult education within the relationship than on purely parent education, assuming that parents and teachers educate each other. Parents build on their strengths as individuals.

Attention to the Social Context of Parenting

Increasingly it is recognized that social networks and support are important for parents as a support for their performance in the parenting role. Families who receive adequate social support are more capable of supporting themselves. Traditional parent education programs rely on disseminating information to parents to affect behavior, but the parent support approach assumes that social ties will positively assist parent functioning. (See Figure 13-3.) Professionals who work with parents in groups facilitate the group members' ability to share ideas and experiences, and to support one another.

Parent education involves making available to all parents the necessary support and attitudes that

1. encourage them to use and depend on what they know,
2. encourage them to share their experience with other parents,
3. support what they are doing, and
4. expose them to new ideas they have not considered (Gordon and Breivogel, 1976).

These ideas eliminate the connotation that parent education is associated only with deficit models of parenting and emphasizes the need to support and help all parents.

In recent years, the number of programs working to help parents in aspects of their lives has greatly increased. Nevertheless, the value of parent education programs continues to be questioned by policy makers and

Figure 13-3 The social ties formed with other parents at parent education programs may be as important as the information. Courtesy Ellen Galinsky.

funders, who continue to believe that parenting is instinctive and only problem families need outside advice or help. Questions about effectiveness are raised by the wide variety of program types. What methods are most effective, and what are the desired outcomes? Assuming that the goal of parent education is to facilitate positive additions to parent-child relationships and to a child's functioning, evaluating whether or not such a goal is met is difficult to research. One reason why attempts to assess the effects of parent education yield inconclusive results is that many questions related to parent education imply a concern with long-term results of the increased knowledge, status, and altered behavior. Most methods used to study the effects preclude the wait for such long-term answers. It is also difficult to correlate the results of one program to another. Most studies of parent education programs have focused on children and found strong short-term effects on children. Effects on parents have been studied less frequently, but yield evidence of some immediate positive effects on interaction and attitudes. Family support types of programs have studied effects of parent involvement on families' socioeconomic and life circumstances, and found positive correlations (Powell 1989).

Assumptions Underlying Parent Education

A philosophy of parent education that involves parents actively in a dynamic situation assumes that

1. parents can learn. Parenting behaviors are not determined by the unfolding of instinctive reactions, but are learned behaviors that can be

acquired or improved with effort. The more parents know about child development and the effects of parent-child interaction, the more they examine what they do and why they do it, and the more skillful they become in displaying appropriate behaviors.

2. parenting is an area in which a knowledge base exists pertaining to effective types of parent behavior. Studies and research have indicated specific parental attitudes and actions that result in specific responses from children. It is important to state here that there is no unanimous agreement about what knowledge should be taught in any parent education program; however, the knowledge base is there for whatever areas need to be addressed.

3. knowledge alone is not sufficient to develop parenting competence. That is, all major efforts at parenting education deal in some way with emotions and attitudes. Feelings about family and parent-child dynamics run deeply and powerfully. Parents are sometimes fooled by the myth that parenting is always joyful and delightful and need to accept their own emotional responses of anxiety, frustration, and hostility. Attitudes about power, authority, reciprocity, and related issues are often more influential than facts. Parent education must provide a vehicle for dealing with both facts and feelings.

4. all parents, no matter how well-educated, well-adjusted, or fortunate in their social and economic arrangements, need help with learning how to cope with the parenting role. This need is intensified by current changes in living styles for some, as well as at particular stages of the family's life cycle for all.

5. parents want to learn. Parents do care about their children and will participate when they believe they are helping their children or are doing something that makes them better parents. It follows that, if parents do not participate in available education programs, they are not yet convinced of a program's value to their child or to themselves. It must also be considered that specific stresses in parents' lives must be alleviated if parents are to be able to involve themselves in learning and change.

6. parents learn best when the subject matter is closely related to them and their children. All parents have unique experiences in the relationships and circumstances of their lives and need to make specific applications of new ideas to their situations. This places the basic responsibility for growth and change within each parent as each identifies particular needs and motivations. (See Figure 13-4.) No person or agency outside the parent can decide what that parent needs.

7. parents can often learn best from one another. A negative expression of this idea is that parents are adults who don't want to be told anything by a stranger, even if he is an expert; parents also frequently resist being told things by experts they do know. Learning from the common

Figure 13-4   Parents want to learn and will come in to meetings that meet their needs. Courtesy Barbara Stegall.

experiences of other adults perceived as peers can be meaningful, as parents remind each other of what they already know and increase their feelings of self-worth as they empathize and understand.

8. parents learn in their own way. Basic educational principles point out individual differences in pace, style, and patterns of learning. A dynamic program offers flexible approaches that allow parents to proceed as they feel comfortable, to concentrate on what they find significant, and to participate actively to the extent that they are able. Professionals who work in parent education must understand principles of adult learning.

Some of the more typical problems that parent education programs have to address can be prevented or resolved with more attention to the implications of these assumptions. These problems include:

1. initial recruitment problems or lack of interest. Attention to program content and format, program time, transportation and other support services can all help here.

2. conflict in views and values. Collaborative discussion and planning can help turn differences in ideas and attitudes into stimulating situations that can cause parents to examine their own positions more deeply.

3. group management problems. Directors and teachers do have to learn skills necessary to work with adults. Part of the training should be a change from the professional stance of domination to group process techniques.

Recently the Family Resource Coalition has responded to the interest in new theories and techniques in parent education by offering summer institutes to train professionals. The training explores group process, peer support theory, dealing with diversity, curriculum and program models, and the role of the professional in social support networks. For information on the summer training institutes, contact the Family Resource Coalition (address in chapter 4).

❖ Implementing a Parent Education Program

Parents must be actively involved in planning the educational programs in which they will participate. A collaborative effort in which teachers and parents function as partners in needs assessment differs from the traditional approach of a professional making these decisions alone. There are numerous ways to facilitate this.

Initial Parent Involvement

Parents may come together first for purely social occasions such as pot-luck suppers, bag lunches, or parents' breakfasts. As comfort levels increase and relationships grow, the general discussion among the parents may narrow to particular interests and concerns. Teachers can help parents structure a program evolved directly from the discovery of common needs. Teachers are then acting not as "experts," but as resources, as families define their own needs. It is a natural progression for parents to become involved, because they already feel welcomed as a member of the group of parents.

To involve parents directly in the planning of parent education efforts, structure a meeting soon after the school year starts, specifically to generate and discuss ideas that parents are interested in pursuing further. At this initial meeting, parents can take an active role if staff members ask one or two parents to help plan and lead the first discussion.

Answering an assessment questionnaire or survey is one way of receiving input from parents on their interests and needs for future parent programs. A sample survey might look like this:

As we plan our parent meetings for this year, your ideas are needed.

1. Rate the following topics

	Interest		
	Great	Slight	None
Discipline			
Sibling Rivalry			
Nutrition and Children			
Getting Ready for School			
Choosing Good Books and Toys			
Sex Education			
Normal Development			

Please add topics of interest to you

2. Circle the day that best fits your schedule:

   M   T   W   Th   F

3. Indicate time of day that is best for you:
   Lunch hour
   Right after work
   Evening, 7:00 or 7:30

Thank you for your help. Watch for coming notices.

The disadvantage to using a survey form is that some parents may have difficulty with the reading and writing aspects of it and may not bother to return it. If the survey is also posted on the parent bulletin board, parents may stop and respond in the center. The form lacks the personal involvement of individuals in a discussion.   But at least a survey conveys the message that parents' ideas are needed and wanted. Parents will pay attention to subsequent announcements of meetings that they have helped to plan.

Teachers are often tempted to plan meetings based on what they believe parents need to learn. But unless parents are motivated by a current need to gain particular knowledge or skills, they may reject plans imposed by teachers, no matter how important the ideas are. It has been noted that parent education programs have a greater likelihood of effecting change if they are sensitive to and design activities around the basic assumptions and beliefs parents hold regarding child rearing (Sutherland 1983).   Recent reports of successful parent education efforts (Luethy 1991; Rose 1990) point out that in each case the curriculum is not pre-set and prescribed, but follows the interests and needs identified by parents. That is, programs should start where the parents presently are, rather than where teachers think parents should be. Only parents can accurately define this starting place by expressing their needs and interests. They can also keep the program responsive to differences of culture and class.

Selecting the Style of a Meeting

Group size and style of meeting must be considered when providing for parents' needs for comfort and an opportunity to talk with other parents. Studies find that the most important variable in terms of parent attendance and participation in meetings is group size; smaller groups create feelings of closeness, community, and ownership of the endeavor (Bauch et al. 1973). Other studies indicate that meetings involving parents of just one class are preferable to whole center meetings (Tizard et al. 1981); bringing together a dozen or so parents with children of similar ages facilitates the sharing of experiences and concerns. The advantage to large group meetings is that a timid parent can listen without feeling pressure to participate; the disadvantage is that individual needs are often not met, as all parents will not have the opportunity to ask questions related to their particular situations or gain the satisfaction of sharing with other parents.

Since parents learn from each other as well as from professionals, the style of a meeting should encourage such interaction. Greater changes may occur in parents' behavior and attitudes following discussions within a group of parents than following lectures. Powell refers to the importance of what he calls "kitchen talk," the informal conversation that occurs in the breaks of more formal planned education efforts, as both desirable and worthwhile (Powell 1989). This requires a reconceptualization of the roles of directors, teachers, and parents in parent education, emphasizing the importance of parents speaking to each other and putting professionals in the role of consultants, supporting instead of instructing. In some instances of successful parent education, nonprofessionals function well as group leaders. When parents identify a need that requires an expert, teachers can help locate and invite suitable resources.

Teacher's Role in Setting the Style of a Meeting

A teacher's role in a parent discussion group is first to provide a structure that helps establish a warm atmosphere of informality and friendly sharing, and then to function as a facilitator of group discussion. Such a leader displays acceptance, support, and encouragement for each parent in a group to express themselves; objectivity, to avoid taking sides in most discussions; tact, to protect each parent's right to discuss in a non-threatening environment; alertness of both verbal and nonverbal responses of group members, using that feedback to guide a discussion and maintain group morale.

It is only possible for a teacher or director to function this way when they have relinquished the attitude that only they know about young children. Such an attitude shows clearly in their interaction with parents and inhibits the formation of any informal group discussions. Heavy utilization of media or lecture techniques does not allow parents to participate, as do group discussions or working formats.

Teachers can structure the initial meeting of parents to ease interpersonal communication. Name tags, with reminders of whose parent this is, help parents make initial connections.

Icebreaker games or activities may start a conversation. It is important to remember, however, that teachers are now dealing with adults, not children, so an early childhood teacher must learn techniques that are appropriate for adults.

Teachers can demonstrate the philosophy that parent meetings are another way of working with the whole family by involving children in making refreshments or decorations during a classroom day, or asking parents to make a picture at the meeting to leave in a child's cubby for him to find the next morning. (See Figure 13-5.)

Figure 13-5 When parents come for Open House, children can leave notes for their parents asking them to do their favorite activity. This mother was asked to read ABIYOYO. Courtesy Connie Glass.

The prior existence of a social network of friends and relatives correlates with a lower level of attendance at regular group sessions and special events for parents (Powell 1983). In other words, parents without reciprocal ties with other adults are more eager for the support and interaction with adults in parent education settings. This may be especially true for single parents. The opportunities for social interaction and new relationships provide incentives for some parents to become involved in such a parent education group.

Selecting a Time for a Meeting

Other stresses and concerns of daily life may prevent some parents from involving themselves in parent education activities. Teachers need to be conscious of any accommodations they can make to help alleviate some of these problems.

Meetings are more convenient if parents help select the dates and times. Sometimes parents' attendance is precluded by child-care demands; providing child care may allow a parent to attend. This is why many successful parent education efforts of full-day programs occur during the lunch hour or late afternoon, while children are still in their classrooms. Transportation difficulties may keep parents from participating; parent committees can set up car-pools or arrange meetings in more central locations.

Some programs that are located close to parents' work sites, such as employer-sponsored child care, take the parent education program right into the office building during lunch hour (Luethy, 1991). Such assistance enables parents to become involved and is evidence that teachers understand some of the problems.

For working parents, evening meetings are often difficult to attend; after a long day at the job, then taking children home to prepare supper and getting through the evening routine, going back to school becomes quite unattractive. Many centers find success in providing an evening meal—a covered dish supper, or a spaghetti dinner—when parents come to pick up their children. Parents, children, and teachers relax together after a work day, enjoying a social occasion without parents having to worry about hurrying home with tired, hungry children. The children can play in another room while parents continue a more serious discussion. Parents and children are still able to get home early in the evening, after a pleasant and productive time for all. (See Figure 13-6 for a listing of books that might provide useful resources for teachers and parents planning discussions.)

Books to help teachers and parents planning discussions.

Ames, L. (1991) *Raising good kids: a development approach to discipline.* Rosemont, NY: Modern Learning Press.

Brazelton, T. (1983) *Infants and mothers.* NY, NY: Delacorte Press.

___. (1989) *Toddlers and parents.* NY, NY: Delacorte Press.

___. (1991) *Earliest relationship.* Redding, MA: Addison-Wesley.

___. (1992) *To Listen to a child.* Redding, MA: Addison-Wesley.

Calderone, M. and Ramey, J. (1983) *Talking with your child about sex.* NY, NY: Ballentine Books.

Carlsson-Paige, N. and Levin, D. (1990) *Who's calling the shots?* Philadelphia, PA: New Society Publishers.

Cole, J. (1986) *How you were born.* NY, NY: Scholastic Books.

Elkind, D. (1988) *The hurried child.* Redding, MA: Addison-Wesley.

Fraiberg, S. (1981) *The magic years.* New York: McMillan Publishers.

Ginott, H. (1976) *Between parent and child.* NY, NY: Avon Books.

Goldstein, R. (1991) *More everyday parenting.* NY, NY: Viking-Penguin.

Gordon, T. *Parent effectiveness training.* NY, NY: NAL-Dutton.

LeShan, E. (1978) *Learning to say goodbye.* NY, NY: Avon Books.

Rubin, T. (1990) *Child potential.* NY, NY: Continuum Press.

White, B. (1987) *A parent's guide to the first three years.* NY, NY: Prentice Hall.

Figure 13-6 Books to help teachers and parents planning discussions.

Schools centrally located to parents' workplaces find that asking parents to "brown bag" it occasionally for a lunch meeting brings parents together while children are cared for in the center. Such meetings recognize the many demands on parents' non-working time.

Busy, weary parents are more likely to attend meetings where the time frame, announced in advance, will not be much more than an hour and will begin and end promptly. It is helpful to announce meetings well in advance (a month, minimum), with weekly, then daily, reminders. Coordinating plans and arrangements takes time, so staff should assume parents are not able to come on short notice. Attention to physical comfort, with adult-sized chairs, refreshments, and a relaxed, uncrowded atmosphere creates optimum conditions for concentrating on a discussion.

As parent education discussion groups evolve, their purposes and goals will be more strictly defined by the participants. It is important to the ongoing success of such programs that parents and teachers occasionally evaluate whether or not activities are meeting the intended goals. It is important to remember that the effectiveness of any parent education program is not measured by how many people come, but by the effect the program has in changing attitudes and behaviors and increasing parental competence. An evaluation should center on how a program works for those who do come and what additional steps can be taken to include others.

For teachers like Anne Morgan and Dorothy Scott, who have been part of a traditional professional-giving-information type of parent education program, it may require a determined effort to accept the concept of parents choosing, guiding, and actively participating in a discussion. But such forms of education give strength and power to parents as they gain confidence in their own ideas and abilities.

❖ Parents as Decision Makers

Some programs involve parents as advisors and policymakers. Parent membership on parent councils or policy boards brings them into decision-making positions that may affect their children and the community they represent. The exact roles of decision makers may vary according to the regulations of the school or agency involved. (See Figure 13-7.)

Federally funded programs, such as Head Start and Title 1, have federal guidelines and local regulations to govern parental roles on advisory councils that have 50 percent parent membership. These roles are active, with the power to decide on budget matters, curriculum, and hiring positions.

Parent-cooperative schools generally allow their parent boards to make all policy decisions.

Other parent councils in some public and private educational settings may function as purely advisory bodies, with decision-making powers vested in professional personnel. A parent advisory council can be a first link to successful communication and collaboration between staff and parents. As

Figure 13-7 Parents are involved as decision makers in some programs. Courtesy Council for Children, Inc.

the staff works through the parents involved on the parent advisory council, there is less impression of "experts" advising or controlling the situation.

Many parents are eager to have a voice in their children's schools. Effectively involving parents in cooperative decision making can benefit everyone. Children benefit as programs shape their offerings to fit community character and need. Parents assuming leadership roles develop skills that benefit themselves and their communities, and increase their confidence in their abilities to shape their children's lives. They also may demonstrate more support for a school or center as they perceive a closer connection between its functioning and their own goals. Parents who feel they have a vehicle to voice their concerns will not withdraw or resort to negative methods of making themselves heard. As parents learn more about how a school functions and why, they learn more about children's needs. Directors and teachers benefit by the expansion of their viewpoints with the addition of parents' perspectives. They also may find their efforts are strengthened with the addition of parent understanding and support.

In poorly planned parent-advisory situations, a variety of problems may surface: conflicts about how to conduct the organizational process; power struggles between parents vying for control of a group; confusion about the responsibilities of group members; and disagreements over institutional philosophies and goals. But when an organization develops a trusting relationship among its members and helps develop group communication and planning skills, parents participating in the decision-making process develop important relationships between home and school. Specific guidelines for, and clear understandings of, parent action are most helpful. For example, rather than vague phrases like "the director will decide in conjunction with the parents," a more specific statement is desirable, like "the director will screen job candidates and present three choices, without recommendation, for final selection by the parent council." The real advantages of involving parents as decision makers should encourage professionals to find methods that avoid conflict and misunderstanding.

❖ Summary

Each early childhood education program has its particular characteristics, goals, and client populations, and each school or center must consider how it brings parents together for education, support, and/or advisory purposes in the total effort of parent involvement. Some early childhood programs even involve parents in the decision- and policy-making process. The following are assumptions that can be made if a philosophy of parent education is to involve parents actively.

1. Parents can learn.
2. A specific body of knowledge exists that can help parents become more effective.
3. Knowledge alone is not enough. Attitudes and feelings must be dealt with.
4. All parents need education and help.
5. Parents want to learn.
6. Parents learn best when the subject matter is closely related to their particular circumstances.
7. Parents can often learn best from one another.
8. Parents will learn at their own paces, in their own ways.

Teachers can structure meetings with parents in ways that facilitate parent participation, where parents will define for teachers their individual needs and wants. Meeting times should be decided according to when parents are available.

❖ Student Activities for Further Study

1. Attend a parent meeting at your own, or any other, preschool. Notice: efforts made to promote social comfort and interaction; physical arrangements and services, such as child care, seating, refreshments; planned activity and parents' response to it. Find out how and when the meeting was publicized. Discuss your findings with your classmates.

2. If you are working or interning in a preschool, devise a survey form to assess parents' interest and needs for making future program plans. After you obtain the responses, analyze the information and then devise several plans that match parents' expressed needs and wants. If you are not currently in a classroom situation, work in pairs to devise a questionnaire, then answer it as each of the hypothetical families in

chapter 1 might. Analyze the information and devise several education plans that match those needs and wants.

For the parent meeting you plan:

- list the purpose of the meeting;
- list the instructional strategies you will be using, and the materials and equipment you will need;
- describe the room arrangement you will use;
- list the tentative schedule, with approximate times for the events;
- list five questions you would expect parents to discuss about this topic;
- list five questions you might use to stimulate discussion about this topic.

3. Plan a simple "ice-breaking" social activity for the beginning of a meeting. Share with your classmates.

4. Contact several preschools in your area, including a Head Start or other federally funded program if one exists in your community. Find out whether parents participate in any advisory capacity.

❖ Review Questions

1. Discuss a rationale for parent education.
2. Identify five of eight assumptions regarding parent education.
3. For each assumption, describe a corresponding implication for planning parent education programs.
4. Describe how parents may act as advisors in a program.

❖ Suggestions for Further Reading

Anastasiow, N. (1988). Should parenting education be mandatory? *Topics in early childhood: special education*, 8(1), 60–72.

Braun, L., Coplon, J., Sonnenschein, P. (1984). *Helping parents in groups—a leader's handbook*. Boston: Resource Communications Inc.

Caldwell, B. (1986). Education of families for parenting in Yogman, M.W., and Brazelton, T.B. (Eds.) *In support of families*. Cambridge, MA: Harvard University Press.

Cataldo, C.Z. (1987). *Parent education for early childhood*. New York: Teachers College Press.

Diamondstone, J. (1989). *Designing, leading and evaluating workshops for teachers and parents: a manual for trainers and leadership personnel in early childhood education*. (4th Ed.) Ypsilanti, MI: High Scope Press.

Foster, S.M. (1994, Nov.). Successful parent meetings. *Young children, 50(1),* 78–80.

Harman, D., and Brim, O.G. (1980). *Learning to be parents: principles, programs and methods.* Beverly Hills, CA: Sage.

Kelly, F.J. (1981). Guiding groups of parents of young children. *Young children, 37(1), 28–32.*

Powell, D. (Ed.) (1988). *Parent education as early childhood intervention.* Norwood, N.J.: Ablex.

Rothenberg, B.A. et al. (1988). *Parentmaking: a practical handbook for teaching parent classes about babies and toddlers.* Menlo Park, CA: Banster Press.

Wetzel, L. (1990). *Parents of young children: a parent education curriculum.* St. Paul, MN: Toys and Things Press.

Wlodkowski, R.J. (1985). *Enhancing adult motivation to learn.* San Francisco, CA: Jossey-Bass, Inc.

CHAPTER 14

Teachers and Parents in the Community

Finally, as communities reel from the impact of families that are themselves crumbling with change and stress, the attention of the nation and its individual communities is drawn to the realization that healthy families are essential to every community. Furthermore, it becomes obvious that it is in the best interests of everyone within the community to support families to be effective in their childrearing function. When families, isolated and struggling, are left on their own to do what they can without the support of the larger community, it is the community that will bear the brunt of the family's failure. The entire village that it takes to raise a child that we have heard so much about in recent years has come to the certain knowledge that the vision that supports children, families, and the institutions that serve families is a vision that impacts us all. In this chapter, we examine the ways that the community at large impacts on early childhood schools and centers and the families they serve, and the ways that teachers and parents may function as advocates for child and family issues within the community. Together teachers and parents have a power to turn community attention to supports that will mutually benefit them and the children they care for.

OBJECTIVES

After studying this chapter, the student will be able to

1. discuss corporate involvement in family and child-care issues.
2. describe current legislative initiatives that shape policy affecting families and children.
3. discuss community linkages that support families and children.
4. identify and discuss advocacy roles for teachers and parents.
5. identify three ways the community can provide resources for teachers and children.

Children live in many worlds. Their lives are shaped by home and family, by schools and early education programs, by the neighborhood and community beyond. Just as every family is unique, so too is each community. In the best of circumstances, the many worlds of children are complementary and reinforcing, and each world is supported by the other, forming a circle of protection around children. However, the claim has been made that there has been an erosion of "social capital" over the past twenty-five years, both within the family and in the larger community. In the family, social capital refers to the presence and availability of adults, and opportunities for a range of parent-child communication about social and personal matters. In the community, social capital includes norms of social control, organizations for youth sponsored by adults, and a variety of informal social relations between adults and children that allow adults to support children in ways they might not seek from their parents (Coleman 1987).

As society has increasingly centered on advancing one's individual interests, there has been less attention paid to a sense of community responsibility for raising other peoples' children. (See Figure 14-1.) Certain government

Figure 14-1 Everyone in the community benefits when families are supported to give their children a healthy start. Courtesy Connie Glass.

actions during the past two decades removed visible support from some agencies within the community and left individual families to care for themselves as best they could. Most of this government withdrawal was done under the stance of non-interference in responsibilities that were stated to belong rightfully to families; in reality, families were left without necessary community supports and resources. It was during this same period that the numbers of children and families living beneath the poverty line increased dramatically. At the same time that the rhetoric of individualism and government withdrawal seemed to be withdrawing community attention from the family, other interests within the community re-focused attention on the family and its needs.

An examination of society's ills brings renewed awareness of the problems that arise when parenting roles are ineffective and the family unit is weakened. The community is left to face problems of high school drop-out rates with the results of illiteracy and under-prepared workers; of resulting high unemployment rates and increasing numbers of citizens living in poverty; of increasing numbers of adolescent and unmarried girls becoming mothers; of higher crime rates and drug addictions that accompany hopelessness and poverty; of family breakdowns and stress for adults and children that accompany changed family structures and different working patterns of parents. Considering how to deal with the primary causes of these problems has focused community attention on examining family situations and needs. Interest in child and family policy has been "accelerated by the timely collision of research, demographics, corporate concern, and presidential platforming in the late 1980s" (Kagan 1988, 33). These phenomena are still driving community attention as we approach the end of this century.

Families and early childhood programs exist within a larger community. The decisions and actions taken by that community impinge on the functioning of the family and the school. In turn, actions of parents and teachers can influence the community. Consider first some of the actions being taken within the community that have impact on families and schools.

❖ Corporate Involvement

The business community is having to deal with its employees as family members. Now that more than half of all mothers are in the work force along with fathers, employers are facing conflicts that arise between filing the roles of parent and worker at the same time. Concern about child care may interfere with an employee's productivity, as in the case of parents of latchkey children worrying through the work hours remaining after 3:00 P.M. Parents may have to be absent from work when child-care arrangements fall through, when a baby-sitter doesn't come, or when a child is sick and can't go to a center. Good employees may be lost because of the lack of helpful parent-leave policies. In fact, research has shown the business world that attention and assistance to parents' child-care needs pays off in recruitment, retention, productivity, absenteeism patterns, and morale of employees. The result is that, in the ten-year period between 1978 and 1988, there was an increase of 2,000 percent in the number of companies participating in some type of employer-assisted child care, to about 5,400 companies. The number of on-site child-care centers increased from 150 to 2,500. Another 1,000 or so employers offer referral services to help employees find child care. And about 2,000 have some sort of reimbursement accounts that allow employers to designate pre-tax dollars for child care. In addition, employers offer a variety of programs to assist families, including sick-care referral services, flexible scheduling, job sharing, and subsidized payments of child care.

The Conference Board, an international business research and information network, has a Work and Family Information Center, formed in 1983. This is a national clearing house of information designed to meet the needs of the business community, government agencies, and other organizations concerned with changes in work and family relationships. The center is concerned with the reciprocal impact of work and family interaction—how today's families are affected by what happens in the workplace and how the workplace is influenced by the special needs and resources that family members bring to their jobs. Seminars are held around the country to influence the thinking of business leaders as they consider their relationship to the families of their employees. (See Figure 14-2.) The center assists corporate leaders with individualized consultations, conferences on issues of family concern, information services, and research. For more information, contact the Work and Family Information Center, The Conference Board, 845 Third Ave., New York, NY 10022.

Figure 14-2 With corporate support, employees can volunteer time to work in community classrooms. Courtesy Connie Glass.

The increased awareness of child care and other family needs has brought corporate leaders into discussion and collaboration with other community organizations in efforts to improve services offered to families. Many communities have included corporate leaders in their child advocacy organizations. In Charlotte, North Carolina, for example, top executives from twenty of the city's largest corporations have become "Corporate Champions," cooperating on funding to explore child-care issues and upgrade available child-care quality. With awareness comes policy, such as the urging of a Chamber of Commerce to all local businesses to implement policies to release parents for necessary conferences with their children's schools, and for volunteering in the school system. As they become involved in ways to ease the stress of family care for their workers, employers are educating themselves about community child-care needs, and becoming collaborators in the private sector.

❖ Legislative Initiatives

The public sector also is increasingly aware of children's and family issues. In the early 1980s, the Reagan administration established policies that opposed government regulation of child care at any level. By the end of the same decade, Congress had finally passed and funded a first-ever comprehensive federal system for supporting child care, to address issues of affordability, availability, and quality.

The Child Care and Development Block Grants provide federal funds to states determined by a formula that includes the number of children younger than age five in the state, the number of children receiving free or reduced-price school lunches, and the state per capita income. The block grant offers a great deal of flexibility to states to determine how funds should be spent within the broad constraints of improving child-care affordability, quality, and availability.

More Affordable Child Care

The CCDBG give money to states to provide child-care assistance to low- and moderate-income families. Families are eligible to receive funds for child-care assistance if their children are younger than age thirteen and their family income is less than 75 percent of the state median income. Assistance may be provided through certificates and/or grants of contracts to providers. States must honor parents' choice of provider as far as is possible. The amount of assistance varies; families with lower incomes will get more help.

More Available Child Care

The law gives money to states to establish grant and loan programs for starting on renovating child-care programs; to recruit family child care providers; to develop local resource and referral programs to help link families to child-care services; and to encourage business involvement in child care. Emphasis is on developing more before- and after-school care and early childhood development services.

Better Quality Child Care

Under the law, states are required to meet basic child-care standards and help child-care providers meet the standards and to develop a plan for addressing the inadequate salaries of child-care providers. Monies given to the states are to be used to provide training to child-care workers, hire and train more staff, and strengthen consumer protection for families using child care. The bill includes specific references to the provision of family support services, giving a high priority for funds to those child-care programs that offer family support services.

Discussion about the bill itself directed national attention to the issues of needs of working families and the child-care community. For the first time, needs of children were discussed in the weekly news magazines and on television specials. With politicians and their constituents discussing the bill, the community at large became more knowledgeable about needs and problems shared by families and child-care centers. A broad-based coalition of about 100 national organizations, called the Alliance for Better Child Care, works to increase federal support for child care, while ensuring more coordinated delivery of services.

More Legislative Influences on School/Home/Community Functioning

In October, 1988, Congress passed a welfare reform bill, the Family Support Act, which significantly expands the federal funds available for care of children of AFDC (Aid to Families with Dependent Children) parents who are working or in school or training, and for parents leaving AFDC due to employment. A strong child-care guarantee is offered parents who are in the program and working, and some limited steps are taken by the bill to ensure the quality of child care reimbursed by these funds.

America lags behind most industrialized nations in parental-leave policies for care of children after birth in their earliest months. At a time when most European nations offer six to twelve months of paid parental leave, the U.S. is the only western country where an employer can legally fire a woman for being pregnant. There is no nationwide statutory provision that guarantees a woman the right to a leave from employment for a specified period, protects her job while she is on leave, and provides a cash benefit equal to a significant portion of her salary when she is not working because of pregnancy and childbirth. For several years in the late 1980s, the Family and Medical Leave Act, a maternity leave act, was discussed by legislators, with sponsorship by over 100 members of the House and at least 20 senators. In 1990 Congress acted to pass the proposal that could generate up to ten weeks of unpaid leave to care for an elderly parent, sick spouse, newborn, or newly adopted child, but President Bush vetoed the bill, stating he believed it would hurt the economy., The bill was finally signed into law in 1993. Unfortunately, the economic status of most families today means they are under financial hardship if they go for long periods without salary. Nevertheless, passage of this bill was a first step in indicating awareness of some community responsibility to support families in times of change.

About half of the states are now involved in funding some kinds of preschool education and family support services. (See the discussion of some examples in chapter 4. Be sure you learn what your state is currently doing or considering.)

It seems that the present is a time of increasing community attention at the legislative level concerning child care and family issues. At local, state, and national levels, economic and child-care policies are articulated that affect the quality of life that parents and teachers can provide for children.

❖ Linkings within the Community

In these times of enormous social problems and limited funding resources, many agencies within the community have found it productive to form linkages to support each other's services. "We can get more bang for our buck if we collaborate and cooperate . . . You're seeing more and more multiple-funded things that cross over and fertilize each other" (Washington et al. 1995, 28). Collaborations come in all shapes and sizes. "They can be a tool to increase accessibility for families, to consolidate or upgrade services, or to arrange new services that would be impossible to provide otherwise" (Washington et al. 1995, 29). For example, library systems may work with child-care centers and health departments run child health clinics in efforts to get parents involved in reading to young children. High schools, Planned Parenthood, health departments, and other civic organizations may unite their efforts to combat adolescent pregnancy. Connections strengthen attempts, as well as prevent wasteful duplication of services. Such linkages also heighten overall community awareness of the problems, as citizens and professionals from diverse backgrounds come together to discuss common concerns.

Teachers may play an important role in helping link families with the community agencies that can provide needed services. Every teacher should know what community resources exist for parent referral. A file of pamphlets and referral information can be accumulated and kept at the center for reference by all staff. Frequently parents learn of sources of help only through preschool teachers. (See Figure 14-3.)

A spirit of volunteerism may arise from raised awareness. In some communities, civic organizations and businesses have "adopted" schools, linking volunteers with a specific school or center. Senior citizens find helpful roles as "foster grandparents," working to give individual attention to young children in early childhood classrooms (Taharally and Smith 1990).

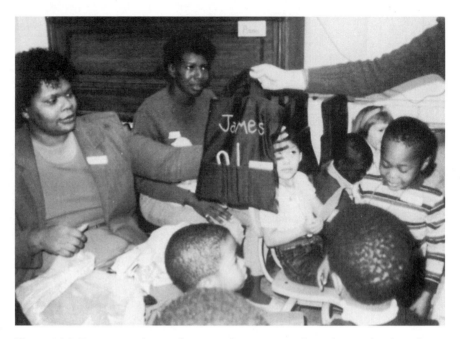

Figure 14-3 Parents can learn of community resources through preschool teachers. Courtesy Barbara Stegall.

"Mentor mothers" pair experienced volunteers with new adolescent mothers. Families and schools alike may reap benefits from such volunteer efforts.

The family resource and support movement discussed in chapter 4 is a graphic example of the power generated by community agencies forming linkages. Frequently the programs provide linkage to other community services rather than providing them directly. Such an arrangement is far more cost-effective, encouraging the optimal use of available resources. A community established "umbrella" organization has as its purpose to encourage linkages at the administrative level. This is accomplished by networking and providing coordinating mechanisms. Thus, conflict and fragmentation in the field are reduced, while training, funding streams, regulating mechanisms, and information are coordinated.

An example of an "umbrella" organization providing linkages to services within the community is Child Care Resources, Inc., of Charlotte, North Carolina. CCRI is a United Way agency established in 1982 at the recommendation of an ad hoc child-care committee, which had been appointed by United Way at the request of the county commissioners. The purpose of the program involves coordinating resources of industry, government, and the private sector to meet the needs of working families and their support services. CCRI provides services to parents, to child-care providers, to business, and to the community. (See Figure 14-4.)

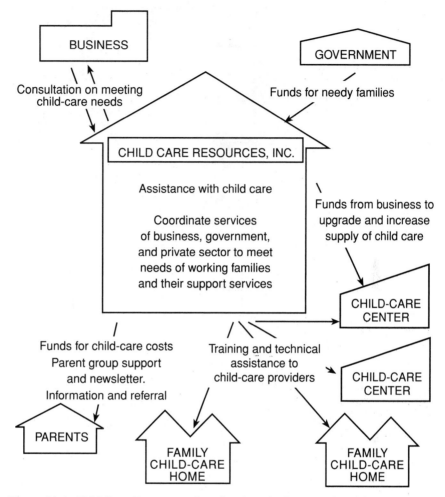

Figure 14-4 Child Care Resources, Inc.; Services for Parents, Child-Care Providers, Employers, and Government.

For Parents

An information service provides factual information about child-care centers, family child-care homes, and other child-care options within the community. Information specialists, trained in child development, provide consumer information on choosing quality child care. (See Figure 14-5.) CCRI publishes a quarterly newsletter, "Working Family," and sponsors a working parent support group. An eligibility and placement service assists parents with child-care costs, administering federal, state, and county funds as well as private scholarship funds for children whose parents are not eligible for help with government funds.

Figure 14-5 Parents are guided to choosing quality child care. Courtesy Child Care Resources, Inc.

For Child-Care Providers

CCRI offers training each year to thousands of child-care teachers and family child-care home providers. Technical assistance is also provided to help start new child-care centers and child-care homes. An annual award is given to the outstanding child-care teacher of the year, to raise public awareness about the child-care profession.

For Business and Industry

CCRI provides consultation to businesses about employer options for meeting employee child-care needs, including current information about local supply and demand for community planners. An offshoot of corporate involvement with CCRI is the development of the Corporate Champions Task Force, in which top executives of Charlotte's twenty largest companies were invited to come together to explore what could be done as a step in addressing child-care issues in the community. The twenty companies did two things: (1) contributed to a community fund a total of $110,000 each year for three years, and (2) developed guidelines with CCRI for the use of the fund to increase and upgrade the supply of child care in the community. The plans called for: start-up grants for nonprofit organizations to create new programs or expand existing programs; start-up and training grants for family child-care home providers; and nominal lease rates for twenty-five-year leases on publicly held parcels of land for providers who would build and operate child-care centers. Incentives were also offered by banks with innovative financing, recommending changes in zoning ordinances, and other public awareness activities. For more information about this community linkage organization, contact Child Care Resources, Inc., 700 Kenilworth Ave., Charlotte, NC 28204. (See Figure 14-6.)

Figure 14-6 Corporate champions promote and increase the supply of child care in the community. Courtesy Child Care Resources, Inc.

In both large and small ways, decisions made in business, government, and social/medical service agencies affect the quality of life for families and the ways schools can meet family needs.

❖ The Role of Advocate

From their positions, teachers and parents have the capacity and obligation to influence, both by separate and united action, those segments of the community that are making decisions that affect their lives. As those who best know and care about the needs of developing children, parents and teachers are uniquely suited to be advocates working to convince the community of what actions must be taken on their behalf.

Teachers and Parents as Advocates

As persons who see firsthand the everyday issues facing children, their families, and the early childhood community at large, teachers must become advocates within the community.

This is a relatively new role for many teachers of young children, who have often concentrated efforts on direct care of children, sometimes convinced that "no amount of advocacy would render change" (Kagan 1988, 32), or unsure of how to be an advocate. Other teachers have not acted, perhaps absorbing society's low evaluation of providers of child care in the earliest years, demonstrated by low wages and status. But, as Kagan states it, it is now essential to become advocates, since "the policy train has left the station, and if we want to influence its direction, we are forced to get on board" (Kagan 1988, 33). The community stands prepared to act; as those who best understand what is developmentally appropriate and supportive of families' needs and interests, it is necessary to become articulate proponents of what should be. As teachers advocate for improved conditions for young children and their families, they also advocate for their own profession and improving conditions in the welfare of early childhood personnel.

Where does a teacher/advocate start?

Be Informed

Community policies are developing rapidly and continually. Teachers need to keep informed of problems,issues, and proposals at local levels and beyond, and to know how these issues and proposals affect child care and family support. Students may desire to get on the mailing list for The Early Childhood Advocate, published quarterly by NAEYC's Public Affairs Division. (See address for NAEYC on page 304.)

There are many ways to become informed: newspaper reports of legislative and corporate discussion and action; bulletins and statements from professional and advocacy organizations; local hearings; staff meetings; discussion with colleagues; classes and workshops. Two helpful current publications are The State of America's Children—the annual yearbook, published by the Children's Defense Fund, and Issues and Advocacy in Early Education by Jensen and Chevalier. (See Suggestions for Further Reading at chapter end.) The important thing is to demonstrate professional willingness to stay abreast and learn what is going on.

Inform Others

Many people who are not directly involved with early childhood education or young families have no firsthand knowledge of problems and concerns. For example, most citizens probably could not accurately answer questions on why early childhood programs are important, what types of programs are offered in the community, the length of waiting lists, average salaries and turnover rates of local child-care workers, average cost of infant care, etc. Even many parents may not understand differences in state licensing requirements, legal adult-child ratios, or staff training requirements. Teachers who do have this information can perform an important service in helping others learn the magnitude of the problems and needs. Personal conversations, newsletters, letters to the editor are all important in raising community awareness of the issues. It is here that teachers can be joined by parents, who have also become informed of questions and solutions. Children's Defense Fund publishes An Advocate's Guide to the Media, to help individuals learn how to get media attention for their issues.

The National Association for the Education of Young Children sponsors the Week of the Young Child in communities across the country in April each year, to call attention to the critical significance of the child's early years. These individual community activities focus advocacy and information activities.

Join Organizations

Teachers become empowered as they unite with others to learn, support one another, define professional goals and standards, and wield political power. Increasingly, the National Association for the Education of Young Children is recognized as the professional organization that unites those from various occupations working in the early childhood field. With a membership of over 90,000, the organization has an annual national conference attended by about 20,000, with hundreds of workshops offering current research and practical knowledge. State and local liaison groups offer teachers frequent opportunities to meet with others concerned with children and families, share ideas and concerns, and network with professionals to build a united front within the community. The professional organization's publication *Young Children* is one way for teachers to become informed. The columns "Policy Alert" and "Washington Update" provide current information and calls for professional action.

Recent statements of standards by the organization have helped teachers and administrators define and evaluate appropriate curricula and services within centers. Standards for training and behavior of professionals have been delineated. All of these actions have compelled child caregivers and early childhood teachers to see themselves as part of a profession that is taking steps to prove its value to the community. In fact, the Code of Ethical Conduct adopted by the NAEYC Governing Board in 1989 includes a section on specific ideals and principles of the teacher's ethical responsibilities to community and society that says, in part,

> our responsibilities to the community are to provide programs that meet its needs and to cooperate with agencies and professions that share responsibility for children. Because the larger society has a measure of responsibility for the welfare and protection of children, and because of our specialized expertise in child development, we acknowledge an obligation to serve as a voice for children everywhere. (Code of Ethical Conduct, *Young Children*, Nov. 1989, 28–29.)

The political power of the NAEYC has been recognized at local and national levels. NAEYC was one of the original supporting organizations for the ABC legislation efforts of the late 1980s. Participants from the national convention in 1989 will recall then-president Ellen Galinsky reporting that Washington leaders were asking her to "call off her troops"; support for the pending legislation was jamming Senate phone lines! The political power of a large professional organization can yield results.

> A direction for our field must be political activity, not as an addition to what we do professionally, but as the very foundation of our work. By taking action in the world, together we can empower ourselves and be part of a transformative process that can benefit young children, their families, ourselves, and all humankind (Dresden and Myers 1989, 66).

(For more information, contact NAEYC, 1834 Connecticut Ave. N.W., Washington, D.C. 20009.)

There are other organizations in which membership may be an important part of a teacher's role as advocate. The Children's Defense Fund is a private organization supported by foundations, corporate grants, and individual donations to provide a voice for the children of America, to educate the nation about children's needs, and encourage prevention of problems. Its staff members include specialists in health, child care, education, child welfare, mental health, child development, adolescent pregnancy prevention, homelessness, and employment. CDF gathers and disseminates data on key issues affecting children; monitors development and implementation of federal and state policies; provides information, technical assistance, and support to a network of state and local child advocates; pursues an annual legislative agenda in the U.S. Congress, and litigates selected cases of major importance. CDF is a national organization with a main office in Washington, D.C. that monitors the effects of changes in national and social policies in towns and cities across the nation and helps people and organizations who are concerned with what happens to children. CDF has state offices in Minnesota, Mississippi, Ohio, and Texas, and works on cooperative projects with groups in many states. (For more information, write The Children's Defense Fund, 122 C. St. N.W., Washington, D.C. 20001.)

The Black Child Development Institute and the Family Resource Coalition are other organizations that can help teachers and parents feel united in their community efforts.

Many communities have their own local advocacy organization for child and family issues; a preschool teacher should find out if the local community has one. There is strength in numbers.

Parents can be encouraged to join these and other organizations. One organization has been established recently for parents to have a national voice, "a way to do something about the quality of life for parents and families in America." Parent Action, founded and chaired by Dr. T. Berry Brazelton, Susan DeConcini, Bernice Weissbourd, and Stevie Wonder, is established for parents to join together to encourage the nation's leaders to listen to their concerns and take action. Regular updates are sent to members on what is happening nationally and what parents can do to influence public policy. (For more information, write Parent Action, 2 North Charles St., Baltimore, MD 21201.)

As parents and teachers gain confidence in their ability to speak and influence others, they may find themselves able to link with other community representatives and committees: the local school board, the drop-out prevention task force, the council on adolescent pregnancy—whatever opportunities the individual community offers.

Contact Representatives

As concerned citizens, as professionals employed in specific capacities, and as members of professional organizations, teachers and parents need to contact their legislative representatives and state their positions, along with the specific reasons for their beliefs. Legislators can be influenced as they hear from large numbers of constituents regarding specifics about community needs.

Vote

Advocates follow up on their interests by learning what responsive actions have been taken by businesses, government officials, and others who can shape policy. With the power of consumer-buying decisions or voting decisions, teachers and parents can express their approval or disapproval of officials' actions. As private citizens, parents and teachers can support those leaders who publicly stand for policies favoring family and early education issues.

In analyzing successful efforts to improve conditions for early childhood professionals in New York, Marx and Granger highlight lessons for others who want to be successful in their advocacy efforts in other communities (Marx and Granger 1990). (See Figure 14-7.) The 1995 NAEYC publication *Grassroots Success!* documents specific successful programs of collaboration with various communities; read it for inspiration and ideas for your own community.

❖ Community as Educational Resource

Schools and centers exist within particular communities, and each community has much to offer as a resource to teachers planning curriculum for young children. Teachers need to assess what the community can provide. Resources may be categorized as natural resources, people resources, and material resources.

Natural Resources

Within reach from a center, teachers may find businesses, shopping areas, transportation systems and depots, construction sites, police and fire stations, parks and recreation areas, churches, zoos, museums, and residential streets. Each one of these offers countless learning experiences. It is a useful exercise for teachers to walk the areas within ten minutes walking

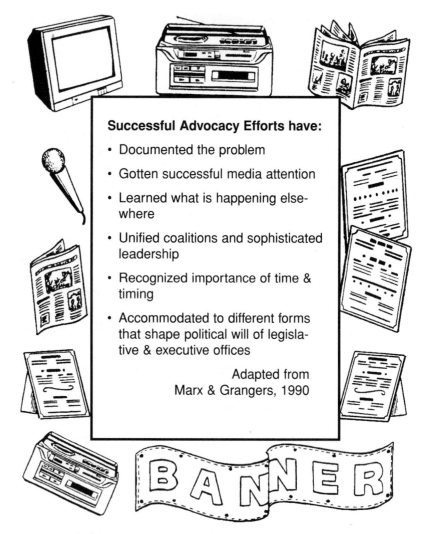

Successful Advocacy Efforts have:

- Documented the problem

- Gotten successful media attention

- Learned what is happening else-where

- Unified coalitions and sophisticated leadership

- Recognized importance of time & timing

- Accommodated to different forms that shape political will of legislative & executive offices

Adapted from
Marx & Grangers, 1990

Figure 14-7 Tips for successful advocacy efforts.

distance of their centers, to discover all the places that might be intriguing from a young child's point of view. (See Figure 14-8.) There might be, for example, a service station where children could watch cars being elevated in the service bay and see strange tools to examine, a bakery with a large oven for many loaves of bread, a grocery store where children could watch delivery trucks being unloaded before purchasing cooking ingredients to take back to the center, or an enormous construction crane working on a tall office building. Alert teachers use these natural community resources to design curriculum outside and inside the classroom.

Figure 14-8 Every community has interesting places for children to visit, whether the airport, a fish pond in the park, or a sculpture downtown. (a) and (c) Courtesy Christine Shamel; (b) Courtesy Connie Glass.

People Resources

Every neighborhood has its own socioeconomic, racial, and cultural composition. Teachers who familiarize themselves with the customs and life-styles of the people in the community surrounding their center may find richness and diversity to share with the children. (See Figure 14-9.) Parents themselves may be the link to assist teachers in learning the community's people resources, as they disclose aspects of their home lives. For example, teachers may find neighbors experienced in ethnic cooking or traditional music who could share their interests with the children. Many community service agencies have representatives prepared to explain the agency to young children: a fire-fighter, complete with boots, hat, and heavy coat, for example. (See Figure 14-10.) Teachers who notice the people in neighborhoods surrounding their centers may discover others who would have interest in spending time with young children: a retired grandfather who enjoys showing the children how to hammer nails in a woodworking activity, or a cub scout group that might enjoy sharing skills with the younger

Figure 14-9 People from the community may enrich classroom resources and offer positive role models. Courtesy Christine Shamel.

Figure 14-10 A policewoman visiting the classroom is an example of using community resources. Courtesy Bethlehem Center, Charlotte, NC; Peeler Portrait Studio, photographer.

Figure 14-11 "Foster Grandparents" are making a contribution in many communities. Courtesy Bethlehem Center, Charlotte, NC; Peeler Portrait Studio, photographer.

children. (See Figure 4-11.) People resources of all types can enrich the center. (See Figure 14-12.) (For more about parent resources, see chapter 12.)

Material Resources

Teachers who make "community connections" can find their classrooms recipients of many objects children can use. Fast-food chains may donate cups and napkins, and props for dramatic play. Lumber stores may provide scraps usable in woodworking. The telephone company may offer old telephone sets, more inviting for their realism. Large packing cases from

Figure 14-12 High school students may be community resources for child-care programs. Courtesy Child Care Resources, Inc.

the local appliance or furniture store can be transformed into storage or play spaces. The decorating shop's wallpaper sample books can be used in dozens of ways by creative teachers. Teachers should make lists of all community businesses and then brainstorm all possible material resources. Most businesses like to feel they can make a contribution. Parents are often helpful connections in identifying and obtaining material resources.

All of these "community connections" can enrich curriculum offerings, as well as convey evidence of community interest and support for teachers and families.

❖ Summary

There are three ways community agencies and actions affect families and schools:

1. Corporate involvement.
2. Legislative policies.
3. Linkages within the community.

Teachers and parents can work within their communities to support their best interests. There are five courses of action open to them.

1. Be informed.
2. Inform others.
3. Join organizations.
4. Contact representatives.
5. Vote.

Teachers and parents can also make "community connections" to use natural, people, and material resources to enrich curriculum offerings.

❖ Student Activities for Further Study

1. Obtain several copies of *Young Children* from your local college library or a NAEYC member. Examine the table of contents to find articles of interest for teachers of young children. Read the Washington Update and Public Policy Report columns. Discuss the current issues with your classmates.

2. Get information from your local or state NAEYC affiliate on program plans for the year and any legislative initiatives in your community that need your support.

3. Discover if your community has a child advocacy group, or an organization to coordinate services for families. Invite a representative to visit your class.

4. Create a community resource file. Obtain current pamphlets and referral information from the community agencies that offer services for families with various needs; i.e., economic, social, special medical and educational needs, recreation, etc.

5. Group discussion activity. You learn that proposed legislation in your state is not in the best interests of developmentally appropriate preschool programs. The impact of this legislation will create many problems for young children. How do you get parents together to pursue this issue? What steps could be taken to lobby for the rights of children? What could your center do to get support and help? How will you present this to the parents?

❖ Review Questions

1. Discuss ways that corporations are becoming involved in family and child-care issues.

2. Describe current legislative initiatives that shape policies affecting families and child care.

3. Discuss what happens within community linkages.

4. Identify and discuss five advocacy roles for teachers and parents.

5. Identify three ways the community can provide resources for teachers and children.

❖ Suggestions for Further Reading

Children's Defense Fund. (1989). *An advocate's guide to the media.* Washington, D.C.:

___ (1989). *A vision for America's future: an agenda for the 1990s.* Washington, D.C.: Children's Defense Fund.

___. (1995). *The state of America's children Yearbook 1995.* Washington, D.C.: Children's Defense Fund.

Edwards, P.A., and Jones Young, L.S. (1992, May). Beyond parents: family, community, and school involvement. *Phi Delta Kappan,* 72–80.

Fennimore, B.S. (1989). *Child advocacy for early childhood educators.* New York: Teachers College Press.

Jensen, M.A., and Chevalier, Z.W. (1990). *Issues and advocacy in early education.* Needham Hts., MA: Allyn and Bacon.

Kagan, S.L. (1988, January). Current reforms in early childhood education: are we addressing the issues? *Young Children, 43*(2), 27–32.

___. (1991). *United we stand: collaboration for child care and early education services.* New York: Teachers College Press.

Kamerman, S.B., and Kahn, A.J. (1987). *The responsive workplace: employers and a changing labor force.* New York: Columbia University Press.

Lombardi, J. (1988, July). Now more than ever . . . it is time to become an advocate for better child care. *Young Children, 43*(5), 41–43.

SECTION IV

Making a Partnership Work

In this section, we consider the challenges of going beyond techniques to particularize communication with individual parents. Every parent's situation is unique, so that teachers have to individualize their strategies and styles to fit different circumstances. In addition, parents who have particular needs because of life events create special challenges. Other challenges result from the attitudes and behaviors which teachers may find particularly troublesome. Even though committed to the concept of working with parents as partners, the complexity of working with diverse personalities, backgrounds, and situations frequently offers real challenges for teachers. Though it may be tempting to abandon the efforts, teachers have to persevere with professional skills. It is sometimes helpful to learn how other programs structure their parent involvement and communication. This section continues to consider the absolute necessity of teachers going beyond merely perfunctory gestures to ensure partnership works.

Chapter 15 explores the methods teachers can use to welcome families of diverse backgrounds into partnership. Chapter 16 considers the particular circumstances of families experiencing divorce, of families with children who have special developmental needs, of families with infants, of families who have experienced abuse or neglect, and of adoptive families. Chapter 17 discusses attitudes that create unique challenges, as well as behaviors that are frequent causes of tension. Chapter 18 describes several programs in the ways that they include parents.

"No use debating environmental versus genetic causes. Either way, it's your fault."

CHAPTER 15

Working with Families from Diverse Backgrounds

Teachers working in schools and child-care centers today frequently find that the families with whom they work exemplify the diversity typical at the end of this century in most parts of the world. Families can come with as many configurations, colors, cultural and class orientations, and communicate in as many languages as there are children in the room. Many western nations' cities report that students in the same school may speak close to 60 different languages, and that foreign-owned companies in most cities number several hundred. A recent study by the U.S. Department of Labor projected that by the year 2050, 75% of this country's work force will be people of color, and by that time, the U.S. population will include 82 million people who arrived in this country after 1991, or were born of parents who did. This will include two out of every five people in America. Canada and Australia experience similar increases in diverse populations.

These statistics make clear what classroom teachers already know: they must be prepared to live in a diverse society, welcoming and working with families from very different backgrounds. In this chapter, we explore how teachers can work with parents of very diverse experiences, respecting their uniqueness and supporting them in partnership, providing continuity in their child's early educational experiences.

OBJECTIVES

After studying this chapter, students will be able to:

1. discuss a rationale for working with parents from diverse backgrounds, identifying benefits for children, parents, and teachers.
2. describe several specific strategies for teachers welcoming all families.
3. identify methods of resolving cultural conflicts.
4. discuss common cultural issues that arise in classrooms.

❖ A Rationale for Teacher Attention to Diversity

Consider the children enrolled in Dorothy Scott's classroom this fall. Of the fifteen, five live with their biological mother and father, although two of these couples are not married. Two live with single, divorced mothers; one lives with his single, divorced father. Two live with one parent and a stepparent; one of these children was born in Asia and adopted by the mother and her first husband. One lives with her grandparents. One lives with a never-married mother, and another with two mothers. One moves mid-week between the homes and care of his divorced parents. The last child lives with his foster parents, the third home he has known in his four years. Of these families, nearly all the parents work, many in factory jobs, several in downtown offices, three in professional positions. Parental education levels range from several who have not completed high school to others with college and graduate degrees. One parent receives funds from AFDC, two others receive government assistance with medical and child-care needs. Eight are children of color, including African American, Hispanic, a family recently arrived from a Caribbean island, and the child adopted from Vietnam. Three of the families do not speak English in their homes. Six of the families own their own homes, three others rent a house, five rent apartments, and one lives with other relatives. Two of the children regularly fly long distances to visit grandparents and parents who live apart; six of them ride the bus to the center with their parents who do not own cars.

Dorothy Scott says that, in her mind, they're all children, and she never notices what color they are or what their families do. "They're all the same to me. I treat them all alike. Of course, some of these parents do a much better job of raising their children than others, and the ones who need the most help don't do a thing to get it."

What such a statement fails to recognize is that to treat all families as if they are the same is both unrealistic and disrespectful. It is unrealistic because it does not take into consideration what cultural values and experiences mean to people and how profoundly culture influences their approach to life. And it is disrespectful because individuals deserve recognition and acceptance of those separate things that create their unique identities. When teachers do not take the time to learn about the circumstances and experiences that shape each family, they effectively put up barriers to healthy identity formation for children and effective partnerships with their parents.

What is to be gained when teachers recognize and learn more about individual family cultural patterns and customs?

For Individual Children

"'Colorblindedness' ignores what we know about children's development of identity and attitudes as well as the realities of racism in the daily lives of people of color" (Jones and Derman-Sparks 1992, 13). (See Figure 15-1.) So too does failure to talk about the other differences that children perceive, such as differences in family structure, in socioeconomic status, in

Figure 15-1 Healthy self-identity results when children of all backgrounds find acceptance in their environment. Courtesy Christine Shamel.

customary ways of behaving. As young children develop a sense of who they are and who their families are in relation to others, they need to absorb positive attitudes towards that identity from the world around them. These attitudes need to be affirmations of their personal identity, clear messages from the larger society that who they are and who their families are is accepted and respected by others. When children find that the images of person and family with whom they identify are either responded to negatively or are oddly missing from the social images surrounding them, positive self-identity suffers. Teachers and parents who are concerned with healthy formation of identity in young children must ensure that children of all backgrounds find evidence of social acceptance of the characteristics with which they identity.

It is also not healthy for children of the dominant culture when recognition of diversity is absent. Children who can find only images of themselves and their families in the dominant social institutions are at risk of developing a falsely superior identity when acknowledgment of others is absent.

How can this experience become real to you? Imagine that you are learning to read using the primer that most adults used in first grade several decades ago. You would be exposed every day to the adventures of a white middle-class family. Father went off to work dressed in a business suit in a suitable automobile. Mother was also well dressed and busy caring for her well-appointed home and three blond and blue-eyed children. Dick, Jane, and Sally led the life that suburban children lead, with their varieties of toys, pets, and activities. But if your own life experiences suggested different family structures, different places to live and ways of living, and events with people who dressed and looked very differently, the implicit message received during that year of daily reading would be that this was the desirable, the norm, and that your experience was somehow deficient. While Dick, Jane, and Sally have fortunately disappeared, there are still too many occasions when children of all backgrounds are not given the clear message that their unique cultural circumstances are recognized and accepted. One of the easiest ways to do this is to reach out to parents and encourage full participation and offer a variety of ways to become involved.

For All Children

The kind of statistics that were presented in the beginning of this chapter make it evident that adults must prepare children to live comfortably in a world filled with diversity. Exposing young children to cultural differences and modeling appreciation and acceptance of the diversity enables children to grow up without developing the kind of prejudices and biases that are largely the result of fear and lack of experience. When differences are not acknowledged, talked about, explained, and seen as positive, children find them to be frightening, and respond to them negatively. Thus, does bias have its roots in children's early experiences. When adults provide an environment that allows children to explore differences and supports them in

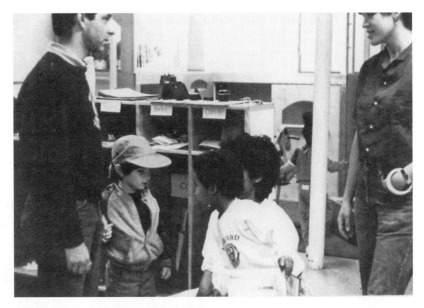

Figure 15-2 In an environment where children can comfortably explore both differences and similarities, children respond positively to diversity. Courtesy Olga Solomita.

discovering similarities as well as respecting differences in others' lives, children are more likely to respond positively to diversity. (See Figure 15-2.) When the true diversity of experiences of the families within classrooms is recognized and voiced, the curriculum can become richer. Utilizing the first-hand experiences that families provide allows children to experience culture, not just learn about it passively.

For Partnerships with Parents

Families transmit their culture to their children. Culture is "in its broadest sense a set of rules for behavior by which we organize and give meaning to the world" (Phillips 1988, 46). Each culture has its own values and beliefs that underlie parenting practices and ways of living, and that influence children's learning and communication styles. Culture determines how parents perceive their roles in relation to their children and in relation to society. Culture determines parents' age-related expectations of children, their expectations of a school and their relationship to the teacher, their ways of showing affection and giving discipline to their children, their attitudes about independence, cleanliness, attendance, achievement, desirable socialization of children, expression of feelings, and hundreds of other beliefs that are unconsciously absorbed within the individual culture. Culturally determined actions, behaviors, and ways of dealing with people are not thought about—they are automatic. (See Figure 15-3.)

Figure 15-3 Teachers and parents who come from diverse cultural backgrounds likely have very different views on children and expectations of school. Courtesy Connie Glass.

When teachers and parents who do not move in the same cultural framework meet, it is a jarring experience from both perspectives. Janet Gonzalez-Mena, in her important book on multicultural issues in child care (1992), describes what many do when faced with cultural differences.

Because my way seems right, even normal, I tend to judge others based on my own perspective. I may consider them exotic or interesting, or I may consider them weird. But being a polite person who tries to get along with others, I do what I can not to notice. Because my way is normal to me, it seems rude to make an issue of the fact that someone else is not normal. And because I have a whole society behind me giving me the message that "my people" are the standard by which everyone else is judged, I can afford to keep on ignoring what I choose to.

But can I? What does this attitude do to me? It shields me from reality. It gives me a slanted perspective, a narrow view. I miss out on a lot because of my perspective. . . . What does it do to those who are not "my people" if I continue in this narrow, slanted perspective, ignoring what I consider "not normal"? . . . Imagine the harm I can do both to "my people" and those whose differences I ignore when I carry out my job with this biased attitude. . . . What does it do to people who are different from me to have those differences defined as abnormal? What does it do to people who are different from me to have those differences ignored? (Gonzalez-Mena 1992, 1–2).

By ignoring the differences in behavior, communication style, and beliefs created by culture, teachers run the risk of creating real conflicts and barriers to effective partnership with parents.

It is far too easy for teachers who are of one culture to assume that children of another culture are culturally deprived, and that their parents need to be taught how to better accomplish tasks of parenting. There is a genuine challenge to teachers to improve their sensitivity to cultural and individual differences and increase communication across cultural divisions. This process is hard work, and takes time and effort. Nevertheless, the best early childhood programs continue to press for communication across cultural differences, to avoid eroding or conflicting with parental responsibility and value systems. True partnerships with parents come when teachers genuinely attempt to learn and understand the ideas that are central to each family's experience.

For Teacher Growth

The past experiences of every teacher are unique, and each teacher is a product of her own culture. Everyone has biases acquired in the early years. Nevertheless, professional experiences offer individual teachers the opportunity to reach beyond their limited cultural experiences, learning to understand and value diversity. "But I'm not prejudiced!" you may protest. The attitudes that we all learned beginning in childhood deserve honest examination; such examination offers teachers a chance for increased self-awareness and change. And by genuinely trying to explore the ideas, values, and customs that are meaningful to the families with whom they work, teachers are granted real opportunities for personal growth.

❖ Strategies for Teachers

To create an atmosphere in classrooms and centers that conveys welcome and acceptance of diversity, teachers and administrators can do many specific things. Some of these are discussed here.

Examine Personal Attitudes

Teachers must begin with genuine examinations of their attitudes and assumptions about children and families of diverse configurations and ethnic and class backgrounds. They must explore the stereotypes they have learned that are racist and ethnocentric, and find ways to change what they believe about themselves and others, about the way families are supposed to look and behave. This can be both difficult and painful, but it is a necessary prerequisite for successfully conveying an attitude of acceptance. Phillips suggests that teachers might begin these explorations "by discussing the stereotypes we know and hold, by looking at where stereotypes come from and what purpose they serve, and by identifying ways to confront each other about our divisiveness" (Phillips 1988, 46). Only through this process can teachers reach the point of genuine openness to others.

There will be times when teachers experience personal discomfort when faced with particular ideas and behaviors of others. It is vital that teachers work with this feeling, identifying what it is that makes them uncomfortable, and being very clear about their own values and goals that guide them. Accepting others' right to hold very different beliefs does not mean teachers have to let go of their own values. Teachers must accept that there will be different perspectives, and they may be equally valid to those who hold them.

Many teachers have found it helpful to develop a support group among colleagues who are interested in doing this kind of self-reflective work. Working with trusted peers can encourage a more honest examination and discussion of values, beliefs, and the accompanying biases and prejudices that are inherent. Support groups can also be valuable to teachers who are seeking ideas on how to reach out to families in order to become more inclusive of all cultures.

Learn about Other Cultures

When dealing with families whose culture is different from their own, teachers must become involved in educating themselves about the values, practices, and communication methods that are comfortable to the others. (See Figure 15-4.) How does this education take place? Reading books and articles may help; see the list of suggestions at the end of chapter 3. Perhaps the best resources for learning are the families themselves. Through careful observation of parent-child interaction during parent participation in the classroom, home visits or daily contacts, teachers will learn much about how messages are transmitted verbally and non-verbally, and about what is important to the family. Intercultural communication finds real differences in the proximity of people when communicating, in facial expressions and eye contact, in the desirability of touching another. (See Dodd, 1991; Samovar and Porter, 1994; Brown, 1991; and Brislin, 1993 for specifics about intercultural communication and culturally influenced behavior.) Showing a genuine desire to learn respectfully will help families become comfortable with demonstrating and discussing their family systems and style with the teacher.

Establish an Environment that Welcomes

When each family first crosses the classroom or center threshold, they should find evidence that their presence is recognized and accepted.

Figure 15-4 Teachers must educate themselves about other cultures, and intercultural communication.

Enrollment forms may be a first place to begin to learn about families, and to convey the message that diversity in family styles is expected. Rather than having blanks for "mother," "father," and "siblings," centers might change this to "adults in the home" and "children in the home" and "family living out of child's home." There should be a space to indicate which language is the primary language at home. Enrollment forms and information booklets should be in as many languages as possible; parents are often happy to help with translating the information if it has not already been done, and the center's invitation indicates genuine intentions of including all. Individual teachers may already have visited the family in their home setting, and have learned something about the family's neighborhood, work, and living conditions. Often teachers take a Polaroid snapshot of the family, or ask for a family picture to add to their family picture board, a sure way of including every family. (See Figure 15-5.)

Teachers use initial visits and survey forms to obtain information that will help both child and family feel comfortable in the new setting, and assist the teacher in working more effectively with the child. Learning what language is spoken in the home allows the teacher to obtain the services of an interpreter for the first conversations with child and parent, or to post a welcoming greeting in the family's native language. If the teacher does not know how to add this, parents will often willingly write it, if they feel their help would be welcome.

Figure 15-5 Pictures of every family send a message of welcome.

The classroom can appear "culturally safe" to both parent and child when materials, pictures, books, and room design reflect family and home experiences. Utensils and clothing in the home living center can reflect the items children might see in use in their own homes; a wok, garlic braid, or a string of dried chilies for pretend cooking; a pair of work coveralls for dress-up; and woven baskets for decor could reflect varied meanings from different homes. Dolls that represent the various racial and ethnic traditions of the classroom and community show awareness of differences. (People of Every Stripe! Dolls, P. O. Box 12505, Portland, OR 97212 (503) 282-0612 has realistic dolls in several sizes, with 11 skin tones, a variety of facial features, hair, clothing, and special-needs accessories, and also provides custom-order dolls.) Photograph posters that depict the ethnic heritage, social class, and family configuration representative of all children in the classroom convey messages of acceptance. (Lakeshore Learning Materials, P.O. Box 6261, Carson City, CA 90749 (800) 421-5354 has a Families Poster Pack that has nonstereotypical pictures of families from different backgrounds. Lakeshore also has People Colors tempera paints and crayons; Crayola has multicultural crayons that represent skin tones for self-portraits.) Displaying books that depict particular cultures or represent traditional literature and stories also conveys welcome. All of these additions to the environment help both children and their parents feel secure and accepted.

Asking families to contribute songs, tapes, musical instruments and recordings representative of their culture's music can help build the diversity of the classroom listening library. Exposing young children to different tonal patterns and rhythms can enhance their musical experiences and build positive acceptance of a wide variety of music forms.

Teachers can plan family get-togethers, scheduled for times that are convenient for all parents to attend. A potluck dinner where each family brings a favorite food helps parents meet their children's friends and families, and welcomes everyone into the program. (See Figure 15-6.)

Open the Door for Communication about Culture

Teachers need to send clear and constant messages that they are interested in learning how a family wants to have their culture represented and supported by the early childhood classroom. Remember that we are using the term culture here in its broadest sense to indicate the uniqueness of each family in its ideas, attitudes, and values. Some teachers seem to feel that if they are working with mostly white families who have lived in this country for generations, they do not have to concern themselves with culture. But every family is still individual in its beliefs and attitudes, its parenting methods, its celebrations and ordinary life-style. Teachers need to elicit from parents their wishes with regard to their children's care and education, and their ideas about how family experiences can enrich the classroom curriculum.

How do teachers open the door for such communication? Many teachers survey their parents at the beginning of the school year, either through conversation, written questionnaires, or both methods. They ask families about their goals for their children, and what they want their children to

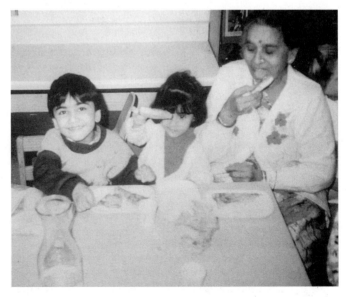

Figure 15-6 Potluck dinners allow families to meet their children's friends and families. Courtesy Connie Glass.

accomplish at school during the year. They elicit detailed information about family caregiving practices, such as toilet learning, discipline, and so on. They attempt to learn as much as they can about family activities and experiences. They ask parents what holidays the family celebrates in their homes, and how the center can support such celebrations without lessening the family's primary importance. They find out what parents would like to share from their family home life with all the children in the classroom. They find out information about home languages, places the family has lived, and experiences the children have had. (See Figure 15-7.) And with all this, they let parents know that their primary desire is to use this knowledge to preserve and enhance the family's culture, to support parents and their beliefs as the primary influence on the child's life. They empower parents with the knowledge that they can play an active role in helping the school or center better address the aspects of their cultural heritage that are meaningful to families, rather than smolder resentfully in silence while the institution imposes ideas and activities with which they disagree.

One important sensitivity for teachers is to not make any assumptions about a family based on limited knowledge. For example, one teacher asked a parent if she would come in to explain Kwanzaa customs to the children, assuming that the family would celebrate that holiday important to many African American families simply because the family was black.

Figure 15-7 Teachers must find ways to communicate across language differences.

Another parent, whose great-grandparents had been immigrants from Japan, recounted the story of the teacher who had asked if she could bring "a kimono or something to show the children." The mother firmly declined, saying she had no such items. Fortunately, the teacher was wise enough to ask the parent what she could share with the preschoolers. The mother, a nurse in a coronary surgery unit, visited to help the children understand what makes healthy hearts. Jumping to conclusions that arise from stereotyped assumptions about a family's culture should be avoided.

When teachers open dialogue about the issues that are meaningful to families, parents feel freer to ask questions, to talk about conflicts they perceive. As teachers work to see the parents' point of view, they model acceptance of differences.

❖ Negotiating with Cultural Conflict

It is inevitable and predictable that when teachers and parents from diverse cultural settings come together, conflict and differences will appear. Culture determines that both parents and teachers have very strong viewpoints about what is good and necessary for young children's development. Gonzalez-Mena (1992) identifies four possible outcomes to cultural conflicts. Three of them involve activity and change to resolve the conflict.

The first possibility is that the conflict is resolved through understanding and negotiation, with both sides seeing the other's perspective and finding a compromise. An example here might be the familiar situation where the parent objects to seeing her child messy and dirty, and the early educator provides many classroom opportunities for sensory exploration with water, sand and paint. As the teacher communicates with the parent about why cleanliness is so important to this parent, she learns that this family equates sending children to school clean and well-dressed with the parent's respect for education and with the family maintaining decent standards within the community. The teacher is also able to help the parent learn something about good early childhood education and the importance of sensory experience in early learning. The teacher agrees that she will change the child's clothes or cover them well during messy play. The parent agrees to allow the child to do messy play as long as the clothes are protected. Both parties feel they are right (and the other is unnecessarily worried about something that doesn't seem very important), but they feel that the compromise is satisfactory.

The second possibility is that the situation could be resolved when the caregiver learns a new perspective from the parent and subsequently changes her actions. The example Gonzalez-Mena offers is of a caregiver who is convinced that the best place for babies to sleep is in a crib in a quiet nap room; this seems to provide optimum rest for most infants. But a baby from a family who is used to sleeping in the midst of an active household is unable to sleep. When the parents express dismay that their child will be isolated and alone in his crib, the caregiver discovers their point of view, and works with the licensing consultant to accommodate parental requests and infant needs. The caregiver changes her actions because she recognizes and accepts the cultural difference.

A third possibility is to resolve the situation through parent education. Parents gain knowledge and learn ideas that might be different from their traditional cultural ideas, but that they come to see will provide optimum developmental environments for their children. This requires thoughtful, respectful sensitivity on the part of the caregiver, to be very sure that the education relates to ideas that seem essential for children's development, not merely to help the family conform to some arbitrary standard of what is "normal." Gonzalez-Mena's example regards the conflict between parents of infants whose cultural beliefs are that babies should not be left free on the floor to play with toys, but instead should be held and involved with human interaction. Rather than stopping floor freedom, the teacher helps parents understand the importance of physical freedom for muscle development and cognitive stimulation. When parents understand this importance, they are more open to learning how they can keep their children safely playing on the floor. The teacher displays cultural sensitivity to the parents' concerns, but finds the developmental issue important enough to pursue.

The last, and indeed fairly common, possibility in cultural conflicts is that there may be no resolution of the conflict. The worst case scenario here is for neither parent nor teacher to perceive or accept the other's perspective, and to persist in their separate beliefs and practices. Children caught in the middle of such separation may be very confused and uncomfortable when the practices in the school setting "are so very different from those at home that they represent in alien culture to them (Phillips 1988, 47). The term *culturally assaultive* has been used to refer to such negative experiences, since the family's culture is in fact under attack.

A better outcome would be for both parents and teachers to gain an understanding of the other's ideas which are treated with respect and sensitivity, but without change of the strong beliefs. The action is for parent and teacher to learn to cope with the differences, each in the way that is acceptable to the individual. With sensitivity, communication, and working at problem solving, teachers and parents may find ways of reconciling cultural differences, or at least becoming sensitive to separate perspectives.

❖ Common Cultural Issues that Arise in Classrooms

Linguistic Diversity

Communication with both parents and children is challenged when the primary language of a family is different from the teacher's and that used in the classroom. A vital attitude for teachers is to consider a "nondeficit perspective in relation to linguistic diversity" (Rosegrant 1992, 146). That is, it is not so much that the child or parent is limited in English but that they are proficient in their primary language, while learning a second language. Some specific things that teachers can do to show respect and to facilitate communication are:

- Learn greeting words in the family's native language. These can also be posted on the wall, so that other teachers and families in the classroom can use them, such as "Hello to Eleni and her family is 'Kalimera'. Good bye is 'Yia sou'."

- Provide written materials in the family's native language. Help with translation can often be obtained from others in the community, such as university faculty or students, English as second language programs, churches associated with particular cultures, school system personnel, representatives from foreign-owned businesses, international clubs, or bilingual members of the same nationality. Explore your community resources to help find individuals who can help with translating materials or interpreting conversations.

- Encourage the family to bring family members who can speak English to conferences, meetings, and classroom activities. If there are other parents who also speak the same language, be sure the parents meet. These other parents may be able to support the new families, and also act as a bridge for involving them in the school.

- Encourage parents to use their primary language with their child at home. Children will quickly pick up the second language in the classroom, and it is vital not to disturb the parent-child relationship, and the language in which they are primarily communicating. Both teachers and parents need to realize that interacting and working with children in their native language at home will help their children at school. When parents are encouraged to "practice more English at home," the quality of their interaction with their children may be limited. This hurts self-esteem and social competence, and ultimately affects their abilities to do well in school (Wolfe 1992).

- Label objects and pictures in the classroom with all the languages represented in the room. (See Figure 15-8.) Parents will be happy to supply the words. This will allow the teachers and all the children to enjoy learning new words in each others' languages.

- Make a photograph book that represents the daily life and routines in the classroom. Pictures tell the story when words are not understood. Another strategy is to make a video of the children during the day. Parents can interpret the actions even if they do not understand the work.

- Create many opportunities for two-way communication, particularly with face-to-face contact, such as home visits, conversations at the door, potluck dinners, conferences, classroom open houses. In this way the teacher's real attempts to include the families with primary language differences may be seen more clearly—and gestures and body language can help the communication process.

Figure 15-8 All the languages represented in the center should be used, as in this sign in the garden of a child-care center in San Francisco.

- Make a collection of take-home children's books in the children's primary languages. This will encourage parents to reinforce their native language as well as read to their children (Rosegrant 1992).
- Invite parents to teach songs or tell stories in their native language in the classroom. This will be welcoming of parents' contributions and a positive message about diversity to all children.
- Be sensitive to not assuming developmental delays or personality difficulties in children when behavior may be limited by the child's language understanding in the classroom, as well as by cultural differences. An example is a child who does not make eye contact with a teacher because of cultural teachings about respectful communication. Help children by demonstration, gestures, and support as they become involved in play activities. Also be sensitive to overlooking needs for special attention that can be masked by assuming that the problem is lack of understanding, or failure to assess children in ways that consider their cultural background. An example is a hard-of-hearing child who is assumed to be non-responsive because of the language difference.

Holidays

Because of religious tradition or cultural backgrounds, many families in centers or schools may celebrate their holidays in their own way, celebrate holidays that are unfamiliar to mainstream society, or not wish their children to participate at all in celebrations that are traditional in many schools and centers. Examples are a family who celebrates Buddha's birthday or Chanukkah; one who has never heard of Halloween or feels it is contrary to their religious views; one who only wants the religious aspects of Christmas recognized; one who is offended by the teacher's creation of a dragon to celebrate Chinese

New Year as though it were merely a tourist attraction; or one who does not want their child to participate in a Christmas story pageant.

Teachers need to be sensitive to the cultural diversity within their classrooms and must think long and hard about building much of their curriculum around holidays that may not be celebrated or valued by the families in their classroom. Exploring the issue with families and colleagues can help teachers gain different perspectives and develop new ideas for celebrations.

There is a point of view that suggests that early childhood programs may be inappropriate places to celebrate holidays, period (Neugebauer 1990). This approach points out that: (1) it is extremely difficult to give holidays meaning that is developmentally appropriate for young children. "Most holidays are based on abstract concepts that are beyond their comprehension" (Neugebauer 1990, 42). (2) Holidays challenge inclusiveness. The decision about whether to include holidays that represent all the family traditions in a center, or what to do if many other traditions are not represented in a center, or what to do when all families do not agree on the celebration or method of celebration of a particular holiday may jeopardize real inclusiveness. (See Figure 15-9.) (3) Many holidays are overdone in any case, with great emphasis on commercialization, leading to uncomfortable situations of competition and pressure on families of limited economic means, as well as trivialization of deeper feelings that families may hold.

Figure 15-9 This poster suggests a concrete and inclusive celebration of Father's Day, with pictures of fathers and grandfathers at work and play, both those living in the home and living elsewhere.

These are certainly points worth considering.

In the *Anti-Bias Curriculum* (1989), Derman-Sparks presents useful guidelines for thinking about the holiday question.

- Make sure that the holiday activities included in classrooms are related to children's lives. If not, such activities take time away from other meaningful curriculum.

- Holiday activities should be connected to peoples' daily lives and beliefs, to the specific families and teachers in the classroom. If holidays are meaningful to real people in children's lives, children can happily participate as "guests" in holiday activities that are not part of their culture. The participants whose holiday it is can share their feelings and memories about the importance of the holiday, as well as information.

- Encourage children and parents to talk about family traditions of holiday celebration, even of holidays that the teacher discovers are shared by the group. This increases children's awareness of the diversity even when the main holiday is the same.

- The holidays of every group that is represented in the classroom should be honored, with their agreement and active participation. Participation prevents the holiday celebration from becoming just a "tourist" experience, where the holiday is seen as exotic rather than regular. The participation of all concerned also allows the particular differences in the way individual families within a culture celebrate the same holiday to be respected and demonstrated. When holidays are celebrated without any connection to real people in the children's lives, or without anyone in the classroom having ever participated in this holiday before, the danger is that the holiday celebration may deteriorate into a rather trivial and superficial experience that actually works against developing respect for diversity. There is much more to Cinco de Mayo than eating tacos!

- Families whose beliefs do not permit their children to participate in particular holiday celebrations should be included in planning satisfactory alternatives for the children within the classroom. Teachers must guard against feeling sorry that these children are being deprived of some experience that the teacher believes is important. Such an attitude implies that the only desirable cultural beliefs are those tied in with celebration of that holiday—a truly ethnocentric error. By becoming knowledgeable about particular family beliefs and traditions, teachers can help support children in making the explanations to their peers.

> Henry's family doesn't celebrate Halloween, so that's why he decided he didn't want to help carve the jack o lantern. "He's going to help me wash and bake the pumpkin seeds for our harvest snack. Who would like to help us?"

- Think and rethink every classroom practice to be sure that everyone's traditions and beliefs are being represented throughout the curriculum.

Classroom Curriculum

An obvious way to draw parents of diverse backgrounds into their children's early education programs is by inviting them to enrich the classroom curriculum with their ideas and presence. Some parents are reluctant to come into the classroom, fearful that this will identify their child as being "different." Teachers need to be able to articulate the benefits for all children and families in becoming comfortable with their differences and similarities. What are some of the ways in which the cultural diversity of individual families can enrich the classroom? A first essential is obviously for teachers to learn about their families through the kinds of methods discussed earlier. Again, when teachers clearly open the door by indicating recognition and appreciation for individual family experiences, parents will likely become comfortable enough to offer ideas of importance to them. Teachers can avoid making assumptions about particular ethnic or religious backgrounds by allowing parents to decide on which aspects of their family life they will share. (See Figure 15-10.)

It is vital that teachers include *all* parents in enriching the curriculum, not merely the ones who present more obvious cultural differences. Parents from sociological groups that have not traditionally been involved in their children's schools or are called only when their children have problems may require particularly persistent invitations. The basic principle that teachers are trying to demonstrate is that all families are unique and special, and

Figure 15-10 A father chose to share his experiences growing up in a farming family with the preschoolers.

have their own richness of experience to share with others. Teachers can invite parents to:

- come and talk about what makes their family unique—what they enjoy doing together.
- bring records and cassettes, photos, folk art, and artifacts of their home culture into the classroom to share and discuss. Everybody has something that they treasure and that has meaning to the family.
- share their experiences with traditional celebrations, literature, dance, and religious ceremonies by activities, discussion, and display. Because these are important to the child and family, other children will gain an appreciation of the depth and breadth of human experience, finding similarities with their own experience, as well as appreciating the differences.
- cook and share recipes with the children. (Figure 15-11.) A cookbook of favorite recipes from each family could be compiled. When culturally diverse foods are shared regularly, children may learn new food experiences, see how foods relate across cultures, and feel comfortable sharing their own family traditions with others without fear of stereotyping. Parents can help explain religious or cultural food restrictions followed by children in the group.
- share maps and travel experiences with the children, to enliven social studies learning.

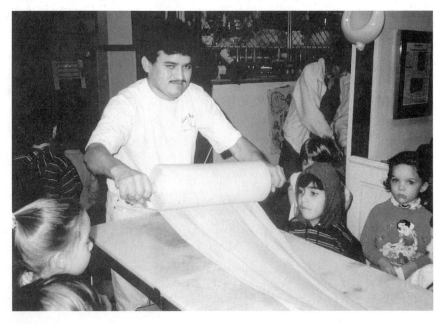

Figure 15-11 The class visits a family's Italian restaurant to watch pasta being made. Courtesy Connie Glass.

Figure 15-12 Parents helped the teacher create and evaluate the curriculum materials and activities as the children explored Native American culture.

- help teachers evaluate curriculum materials and activities to be sure that no stereotypical influences creep in, and to make sure that all children and families are fairly represented. (See Figure 15-12.) Conversations about curriculum will help make sure that individual needs are being recognized.

- help teachers interpret areas of similarity and differences to children. Learning about diversity takes thoughtful processing after experiences. As teachers and parents work with children, they can gradually help them sort out the experiences that join us together in humanity.

❖ Summary

Because culture has influenced us all in so many ways and without our awareness, working with parents of diverse backgrounds presents major challenges for teachers. Becoming sensitive to personal experiences and feelings is an important beginning point for teachers. Learning about individual cultural values through reading, conversation, and observation is important.

Figure 15-13 Parents and teachers worked together to create this mural that welcomes all the community residents to the child-care center.

Teachers must identify and use strategies to welcome each family fully into the school environment. (See Figure 15-13.) Cultural conflicts can often be resolved through sensitivity, communication, and/or education. Common issues that teachers face include dealing with linguistic diversity, deciding how to honor family feelings about holiday celebrations, and finding ways to enrich classroom experiences with the diversity of family experiences. Classroom teachers can get additional free information from:

African American Institute
School Services Division
833 United Nations Plaza
New York, NY 10017

Alternatives (information on Native Americans)
1924 East 3rd St.
Bloomington, IN 47401

Hispanic-American Institute
100 East 21st St.
Austin, TX 78705

Asian-American Studies Center
3232 Campbell Hall
University of California
Los Angeles, CA 90024

❖ Review Questions

1. Discuss a rationale for working with families of diverse backgrounds. What are some of the benefits for individual children? for the group of children? for parents? for teachers?

2. What are some of the specific things teachers can do to ensure that all families feel welcomed?

3. Identify and discuss the four possible outcomes in resolving cultural conflicts.

4. Discuss several common cultural issues that arise in classrooms, and possible teacher actions.

❖ Student Activities for Further Study

1. Evaluate the forms and written materials of a center or school to see how welcoming they appear of diverse family experiences.

2. Discover the resources available in your community to assist teachers working with parents with primary languages other than English.

3. Talk with teachers of early childhood programs to learn how they make their decisions about holiday celebrations. Consider whether what you learn indicates a real respect for families of diverse backgrounds.

❖ Suggestions for Further Reading

Burrell, S. (1991) *Families: explore family concepts in a caring classroom.* St. Paul, MN: Redleaf Press.

Church, E.B. (1992, Nov./Dec.). Celebrating families celebrating together. *Scholastic Pre-K Today*, 44–46.

Hildebrand, V., Phenice, L., Gray, M., and Hines, R. (1996) *Knowing and serving diverse families.* Columbus, OH: Merrill (Prentice Hall)

Jones, E. and Nimmo, J. (1994). *Emergent curriculum.* Washington, D.C.: NAEYC. (especially chapters 8 and 9)

Manfredi/Petitt (1994, Nov.) Multicultural sensitivity: it's more than skin deep! *Young Children, 50*(1), 72–73.

Thomson, B.J. (1993). *Words can hurt you: beginning a program of anti-bias education.* Reading, MA: Addison-Wesley Publishing Co. (especially chapters 2, 7, and 9)

York, S. (1991). *Affirming culture in early childhood programs.* St. Paul, MN: Redleaf Press.

CHAPTER 16

Working with Parents in Particular Circumstances

Every parent's situation is unique in its history, emotions, and demands. As such, there is no neatly prescribed package of services or supports that meets the needs of every parent at every time. Teachers find themselves working with parents who have specific needs at particular times. This chapter examines several of these circumstances and discusses helpful teacher responses.

One frequent occurrence in contemporary society is the dissolution of existing family structures due to divorce. At this critical time both children and parents need help in making the necessary emotional adjustments. Remarriage and the formation of stepfamilies is another stressful period when sensitive classroom teachers can help. Families who are providing for the special developmental or learning needs of young children whose development is not typical face continual stress and emotional adjustment. Parents who are adjusting to the demands of an infant and to leaving their little ones in the care of others also have unique needs. Teachers must also be aware of their responsibilities to children and parents when abuse and neglect is a family pattern. Lastly, families created by adoption have their own unique situation. Early childhood teachers are in a unique position to help them all.

OBJECTIVES

After studying this chapter, the student will be able to

1. describe behaviors in children and parents associated with the stress of divorce and/or remarriage and discuss ways teachers can be helpful.

2. describe possible emotional responses of parents of exceptional children and discuss ways teachers can work effectively with them.

3. describe some responses of parents of infants and discuss ways teachers can work effectively with them.

4. discuss factors that create an abusive situation, indicators that suggest abuse or neglect, and teachers' responsibilities in working with these families.

5. identify ways that classroom teachers can support adoptive families.

❖ Working with Families Undergoing Change Due to Divorce

> Dorothy Scott has recently noticed some disturbing behaviors in one of the children in her classroom. He has been quite out of bounds, almost defiantly breaking the group rules, and striking out aggressively at other children. She's also bothered by the quiet sadness she sees in him at other times. She knows his parents' divorce is now final, and she wonders what she might to do help the family at this time of change.

The family that concerns her is not alone. Mr. Rogers of the well-known children's television show has said, "If someone told me twenty years ago that I was going to produce a whole week on divorce, I never would have believed them." The norm of lasting marriage has been shaken. The rate of divorces in American marriages rose steeply in the 1970s and reached a plateau in the 1980s that shows no sign of decreasing. One of two recent marriages is expected to end in divorce. (See Figure 16-1.) Children born in the mid-1980s stand a 40 percent chance of having their parents divorce before they reach age eighteen. Because about 50 percent of all divorces occur in the first seven years of marriage, the children involved in divorce are often quite young. Five out of six men and three out of four women remarry after divorce, often creating stepfamilies. It is predicted that about 35 percent of all children in the 1990s are expected to live at least part of their growing up years in a stepfamily (Barney 1990).

One researcher correctly predicted that single-parent families and stepfamilies would outnumber nuclear families by 1990 (Visher and Visher 1979). Such large numbers have led to the societal acceptance of divorce; divorced person are no longer as stigmatized or considered deviant since "no-fault" divorce laws refrain from naming a wrongdoer. Though the societal stigma may be reduced, the pain experienced by children and their par-

Figure 16-1 Divorce affects about half of all American families. Courtesy Council for Children, Inc.

ents is not. In addition to real pain and disruption, there are still some pre-vailing ideas about the functioning of a "broken home" that may work to the detriment of many families undergoing this transition.

An important first step for teachers working with such families is to be informed about the facts concerning divorce and examine their own atti-tudes and expectations in order to avoid stereotyping.

A longitudinal study that tracked and studied divorced families one, five, ten, and then fifteen years after divorce has recently been published. This is the longest study on divorce ever conducted, and it contains many interesting implications for those in positions of support to those families experiencing divorce (Wallerstein and Blakeslee 1989).

Divorce, the second most stressful experience for families after death, is a critical experience for the entire family, affecting each member differ-ently. To some degree, all family members experience abandonment, trau-ma, rejection, loss of income, and a lower standard of living. Adults, how-ever, usually also experience relief to be finished with a difficult situation. No child in a recent study reported they were relieved that their parents were getting divorced, even if the parents were "often in violent conflict with each other" (Clarke-Stewart 1989, 60). Most adults, lacking an ade-quate model for single parenting, are confused in how to go about daily life. A single-parent family is not the same as a two-parent family minus one adult. The entire family system is strained When it comes to parents, two is usually better than one. "One parent can be in only one place at a time, and for parents going through a divorce, that place is most often work, therapy, or the lawyer's office" (Clarke-Stewart 1989, 60).

This is a time of bereavement for everyone in a family; the family they knew is gone. One parent usually leaves the home and is less available to a child, and sometimes siblings may leave as well. There are no proven guidelines for non-custodial parents. This is an unfamiliar parenting experience for those who move out and see their children on visits. A mother's working pattern may increase, and a family's living standard is likely to change with increasing economic stress. Recent studies have shown that in many states, a woman and her children suffer a drastic drop in income; this drop not only creates a new impoverished class, but is demoralizing as well. Each family member grieves in different ways peculiar to their roles and ages. The stages of grief are similar to the Kubler-Ross model for dealing with loss of death; initial denial is followed by anger and then bargaining to find a happy way out. Depression follows as ultimate realizations are made. The final stage is acceptance of the loss. It is important to be aware of patterns, but not to expect all children and parents to react similarly to divorce due to individual personalities, experiences, and outside supports, as well as varying developmental levels in children.

Wallerstein claims that divorce is almost always more devastating for children than for their parents, and that the effects of divorce are often long-lasting. While the conventional wisdom has been that the divorcing family goes through the stress of adjustment in about two years, the longitudinal studies indicate that "children's fundamental attitudes about society and about themselves can be forever changed by divorce and by events experienced in the years afterward" (Wallerstein and Blakeslee 1989, xii). Ten years after divorce many children felt less protected, less cared for, less comforted than children who have not experienced divorce. What they saw and experienced at the time of family break-up becomes part of their inner world. For example, violence witnessed at that time may dominate their relationships ten to fifteen years later. It is important, then, that the adults who are intimately involved with children realize what a critical point this is for their development.

Children are in particularly vulnerable positions at the time of divorce and subsequent changes in the family. As Wallerstein puts it, "In what other life crises are children used as bullets!" (Wallerstein and Blakeslee 1989, 6).

> In most crisis situations, such as an earthquake, flood, or fire, parents instinctively reach out and grab hold of their children, bringing them to safety first. In the crisis of divorce, however, mothers and fathers put children on hold, attending to adult problems first (Wallerstein and Blakeslee 1989, 7).

The mother and father may resolve this life crisis and move on to the next chapter. For children, divorce is not a chapter, but a long continuum of life experiences.

Children react with a variety of behaviors, related to their dependent position in a family and age level of intellectual development. In general, preschool children are the most frightened and show the most dramatic symptoms when marriages break up. (See Figure 16-2.) Their self-concept seems to be particularly affected, with an increased sense of powerlessness. Their view of predictability, dependability, and order in the world is disrupted. In their anxiety to be sure their needs are met, preschool children may show an increase in dependency, whining, demanding, and disobedient behaviors. In their fear of abandonment, they may have trouble sleeping or being left by adults. Other noted behaviors are regression to immature behavior; separation anxiety and intense attachment to one parent; guilt, shame, and anxiety about loss of love and bodily harm. The denial stage of grief is often expressed by young children in rhythmic behavior, such as bouncing, hitting, banging, kicking: children seem to keep moving so they don't feel the pain. Symptoms of emotional stress may take the form of nightmares, temper tantrums, bedwetting, and unusual fears. In their play, preschool children may be less imaginative, exhibiting less associative and cooperative play and more unoccupied and onlooker play. More aggression is frequently noted. Preschool children, because of the egocentric nature of their thinking, often feel responsibility for the divorce and

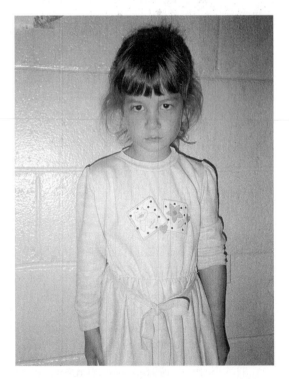

Figure 16-2 Preschool children are generally the most frightened and show the most dramatic symptoms when marriages break up.

behave "better than good," fearing to lose the remaining parent's love through more "bad" behavior. Sometimes the exact opposite behavior is seen as a child tries literally to test every limit, to see what it takes to lose the other parent. Even infants show behavioral changes such as sleeping and feeding irregularities, clingyness, and lack of trust, as they react to tensions felt at home. But, in the long run, "the younger the child is, the better the prognosis for a complete adjustment" (Clarke-Stewart 1989, 62). They have spent less time in a family under conflict; their experience in the family unit is less; and the parents themselves are younger and more able to recover easily.

School-aged children may show great sadness and despair, fears and phobias, anger, loneliness, shaken identity, and an inability to focus attention on school-related tasks. The growing ability to understand the feelings and perspectives of others allows them to be sympathetic and concerned for their parents. They may feel conflict in their loyalties to each parent. Other behaviors of school-aged children may include nervousness, withdrawal and moodiness, absent-mindedness, poor grades, physical complaints, and acting out behaviors. In Wallerstein's study, children in this age group were still functioning poorly ten years after the divorce.

Children react best when the open conflict between parents is limited and when children are able to maintain continued good relationships with each parent individually. The quality of the mother-child relationship is the single most important factor in determining how children feel about themselves in the post-divorce decade and how well they function. Other factors predictive of positive outcomes include the parents' flexibility and adaptability in redefining roles; availability of social support for family members; and provisions for a secure and predictable environment (Camara 1986).

Parents, at the same time, have their own difficulties. They often feel a double sense of failure for not living up to the American dream of happily-ever-after and for their unsuccessful efforts to make a marriage work. This decreases their confidence, self-image, and feelings of competence, while increasing feelings of anger, guilt, terror, and helplessness. Some of these feelings directly relate to their children as they worry that they have endangered them by their actions. In most cases, there is disorganization of the household; even meeting rudimentary needs seems overwhelming when an exhausted and anxious parent takes on more roles. Parents display a diminished capacity to parent in almost all dimensions, and children feel this most deeply in their heightened state of need. Frequently unavailable to the child, parents at this time exert less consistent and effective discipline, communicate less well, may be less nurturant, and make fewer demands for mature behavior. "In the first couple of years after the divorce, children have less regular bedtimes and mealtimes, eat together as a family less, hear fewer bedtime stories, and are more often late for school" (Clarke-Stewart 1989, 62). See Figure 16-3 for a glimpse of all the changes that may affect children's and parents' lives. In many instances, conditions in a post-divorce family are more stressful and less supportive than conditions in failing marriages.

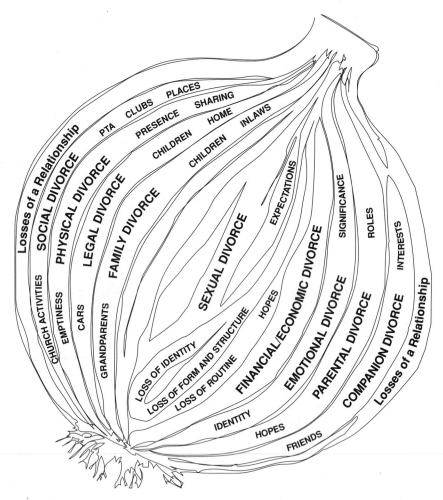

Figure 16-3 Families undergo many kinds of changes with divorce.

Wallerstein points out that parents and children have different tasks to work on during and after a divorce. Adult tasks include: ending the marriage; mourning the loss; reclaiming oneself; resolving passions; venturing forth again; rebuilding; helping the children. Children's tasks are understanding the divorce; strategic withdrawal; dealing with loss; dealing with anger; working out guilt; accepting permanence; taking chances on love.

Working with Children in the Classroom

A family overwhelmed by its own turmoil is greatly helped by the understanding and support of teachers and others outside the family. A teacher can help a child within the classroom and provide information and supportive guidance to a parent in a variety of ways.

Maintain Structured Environment

Children whose lives are in a state of transition are helped by the maintenance of a relatively structured and predictable environment. Some certainty is provided when a child's classroom world is unshaken. Keeping to familiar activities and a scheduled routine will lessen some of the negative effects of a stressful home environment. As a child perceives that his basic physical and emotional needs are being met, he may come to feel personally safe. Part of an environment's stability is demonstrated by consistent expectations. Teachers who firmly and gently maintain limits enhance a child's sense of certainty during this uncertain time.

> "I know you're sad today, but we do need to pick up our toys before we can have a snack. Shall I help you, or do you think you can do it by yourself."

Encourage Expressions of Feelings

Teachers' knowledge of specific areas where these children need attention comes from observing and listening to them in the school setting, rather than making assumptions about problems. A teacher can help children work through feelings by opening up an area for discussion, and understanding and accepting a child's reactions. (See Figure 16-4.)

Figure 16-4 Children are helped by being able to talk about their fears and feelings.

"It can be pretty scary not to have both your daddy and your mommy living in your house together anymore."

"Sometimes children get pretty mad at their mommy and daddy when they change a lot of things in their family."

Teachers who use active listening skills to listen empathetically can help a child release many pent-up feelings.

Teachers can also provide classroom activities and materials that offer acceptable opportunities to work through feelings: clay, water and sand play, paint, family figures and props for dramatic play, and books about various family styles may help. Several dozen children's books about divorce have been published in the past decade; a list of books for preschool children and information on others is included in Figure 16-5.

Privacy and additional opportunities to be alone may help some children.

Teachers may offer concrete evidence that a child is loved, with touch, hugs, smiles, but must be careful that a child does not become too dependent on them.

Teachers may discover that some children need additional help in understanding a family's changed situation; repeated, clear explanations of information supplied by the family may be appropriate. Teachers must remind parents that they need information to be able to help a child, not because they are curious. Parents will be more comfortable sharing information when teachers have previously established a caring relationship.

"Mrs. Butler, I know this is a confusing time for all of you. We find it helps children get used to changes if they get facts they can understand. If you let me know how you've explained the situation to her, I can reinforce it when she brings it up."

Encourage Acceptance

Teachers can guide children in accepting their changed family structure. In words and actions, teachers demonstrate their respect for each family, stressing how unique each family is. Books or pictures that show only traditional family groupings are not helpful. Teachers want to avoid activities for an entire group that make some children feel uncomfortable, such as making Father's Day cards or gifts. If this is just one of several choices planned for activity time, children can choose to participate or not. As a teacher becomes knowledgeable about family patterns, adjustments will need to be made.

Books to Read With Young Children

Adams, E. (1973). *Mushy eggs.* New York: C.P. Putnam's Sons.

Baum, L. (1992). *One more time.* New York: Mulberry Books.

Berman, C. (1982). *What am I doing in a stepfamily?* Secaucus, NJ: Carol Publishing Group.

Bienenfeld, F. (1980). *My mom and dad are getting a divorce.* St. Paul, MN: EMC Corporation.

Boegehold, B. (1985). *Daddy doesn't live here any more.* Racine, WI: Western Publishers.

Brown, L.K., and Brown, M. (1988). *Dinosaurs divorce.* Boston, MA: Little, Brown.

Caines, J. (1977). *Daddy.* New York: Harper and Row.

Girard, L. (1987). *At Daddy's on Saturdays.* Niles, IL: Albert Whitman Concept Books.

Goff, B. (1969). *Where is Daddy? The story of a divorce.* Boston: Beacon Press.

Hazen, B. (1978). *Two homes to live in: a child's-eye view of divorce.* New York: Human Sciences Press.

Helmering, D.W. (1981). *I have two families.* Nashville, TN: Abingdon Press.

Kindred W. (1973). *Lucky Wilma.* New York: Dial Press.

Lach, M., Loughridge, S., and Fassler, D. (1989). *My kind of family: a book for kids in single-parent homes.* Burlington, VT: Waterfront Books.

Lexau, J. (1972). *Emily and the klunky baby an the next-door dog.* New York: Dial Press.

Lindsay, J.W. (nd). *Do I have a daddy: a story about a single-parent child.* Buena Park, CA: Morning Glory.

Perry, P., and Lynch, M. (1978). *Mommy and daddy are divorced.* New York: Dial Press.

Roy, R. (1981). *Breakfast with my father.* Boston: Houghton Mifflin Co.

Schuchman, J. (1979). *Two places to sleep.* Minneapolis: Carolrhoda Books.

Simon, N. (1983). *I wish I had my father.* Niles, IL: Albert Whitman Concept Books.

Seuling, B. (1985). *What kind of family is this? A book about stepfamilies.* Racine, WI: Western Publishing Co.

Stanek, M. (1972). *I won't go without a father.* Niles, IL: Albert Whitman Concept Books.

Stein, S.B. (1979). *On divorce: an open family book for parents and children together.* New York: Walker and Co.

Stinson, K. (1984). *Mom and dad don't live together any more.* Annick Press Ltd.

Vigna, J. (1983). *Mommy and me by ourselves again.* Niles, IL: Albert Whitman Concept Books.

____. (1973). *She's not my real mother.* Niles, IL: Albert Whitman Concept Books.

____. (1982). *Daddy's new baby.* Niles, IL: Albert Whitman Concept Books.

(For a list of books for older children, see Skeen, P. and McKenry, P.C. (1980). The teacher's role in facilitating a child's adjustment to divorce. *Young Children, 35*(5), 3–14.)

Figure 16-5 Books for young children about divorce and stepfamilies.

Be Aware of Group Reactions

Teachers may find that other children in a group may express or experience anxiety about their own parents divorcing or leaving. It is best to remind children that all families are different; that when grownups have problems, they still love and look after their children; and that they need to tell their parents what they're worried about.

Working with Parents

As teachers become aware of parents' probable emotional reactions, they will understand some puzzling behaviors.

> "Honesty, I don't understand the woman. Every time I ask how Danny has been at home, like if he's having trouble sleeping there too, she changes the subject. Doesn't she even care that her own son seems upset?"

Because of the feelings of guilt and isolation, parents may be evasive or hostile when asked innocent questions about a child's daily routine. Often parents are so preoccupied with their own concerns that they are unavailable to teachers, as well as to their children. Teachers must remind themselves frequently that this does not mean they are disinterested.

When teachers are aware of parents' emotional state, they are less likely to become angry at parents' behavior and seeming indifference to their children's problems.

Reassure Parents

Teachers who empathize and demonstrate their caring are in a position to encourage parents in helpful actions with their children. Teachers can remind parents that an open and honest discussion of adults' and children's feelings will help, as will clear statements of the facts of divorce and a new living situation. Teachers can reassure parents about the amount of time needed for families to adjust; giving information regarding the grief process and positive outcomes may help alleviate parental guilt.

Teachers can provide books about divorce for both children and adults, such as those in Figure 16-6. Having a lending library of such books readily available in a center is useful.

Keep Requests Light

Teachers must be especially conscious of any requests they make. Asking stressed single parents to "Bring in two dozen cookies tomorrow" or "Send in a new package of crayons" may be overwhelming in light of the new strains on both time and budget.

Books to Suggest for Parents about Single Parenting and Stepparenting

Atlas, S.L. (1981). *Single parenting: a practical resource guide.* Englewood Cliffs, NJ: Prentice-Hall.

BelGeddes, J. (1974). *How to parent alone—a guide for single parents.* New York: Seabury Press.

Berman, C. (1986). *Making it as a stepparent.* New York: Harper and Row.

Bienenfeld, F. (1987). *Helping your child succeed after divorce.* Claremont, CA: Hunter House.

Burns, C. (1985). *Stepmotherhood.* New York: Times Books, division of Random House.

Dodson, F. (1987). *How to single parent.* New York: Harper and Row.

Francke, L.B. (1983). *Growing up divorced.* New York: Linden Press/Simon and Schuster.

Galper, M. (1978). *Co-parenting: a source book for the separated or divorced family.* Philadelphia: Running Press.

Grollman, E. (1975). *Talking about divorce: a dialogue between parent and child.* Boston: Beacon Press.

Kennedy, M., and King, J.S. (1994). *The single parent family: living happily in a changing world.* New York: Crown.

Klein, C. (1973). *The single parent experience.* New York: Avon.

Noble, J. and W. (1979). *How to live with other peoples' children.* New York: Hawthorn Books.

Salk, L. (1978). *What every child would like parents to know about divorce.* New York: Harper and Row.

Sinberg, J. (1978). *Divorce is a grown-up problem: a book about divorce for young children with their parents.* New York: Avon Books.

Visher, E. and J. (1982). *How to win as a stepfamily.* New York: Dembner Books.

Figure 16-6 Books to suggest for parents about divorce and remarriage.

Be Aware of Legal Agreements

Teachers should know the legal and informal agreements between parents regarding their child's care. It is important that teachers release children to only those persons authorized to take them. Joint custody is the newest family form, agreed to by parents and courts to soften children's loss. Sharing parenting responsibilities reflects the growing interchangeability of men's and women's roles in the workplace and in family life. Teachers need to be sure they are relating equally to both parents in a joint custody arrangement, rather than unconsciously giving more attention or information to one. For example, both parents in a joint custody arrangement may wish to arrange for joint or separate parent-teacher conferences.

Both parents should be invited to the Christmas party; it is up to parents to decide if either or both will attend.

Know Available Community Resources

Teachers should refer parents to community resources that can help families in times of stress. It is important that teachers remember their professional expertise is in working with young children. However caring and concerned they may be about family situations, their only role here is to provide emotional support, information, and an accepting listening ear. When parents need professional counseling to work out their problems, teachers should refer them to appropriate community agencies. Many communities have family and children's service agencies with qualified family therapists and counselors. United Way agencies may offer this information; teachers should be familiar with the appropriate agencies for referral in their own communities.

Teachers also may refer parents to agencies that help families in severe economic stress.

Another helpful referral is to organizations that provide support and social opportunities for isolated parents and children. One example is Parents Without Partners, an international organization of more than 200,000 full- or part-time single parents and their children, and single-parent education and support. Many churches offer similar programs. (For more information about Parents Without Partners, the national headquarters is 7910 Woodmont Ave., Suite 1000, Washington, D.C. 20014.) Parents may also be interested in discovering if their community offers an organization of Big Brothers and Big Sisters that provides opportunities for children of single parents to form relationships with interested adults to supplement possible missing relationships in a family.

Teachers should be knowledgeable about their specific community resources and have information ready for referral if the opportunity arises.

In working with families undergoing divorce, teachers need to be conscious of their own attitudes, values, and emotional reactions. These personal aspects can influence a teacher's ability to function well with parents and children and may cause a teacher to expect more problem behaviors than are really present. Truly helpful teachers do not get caught up in assigning blame or evaluating families negatively. Teachers should remind themselves that everybody is doing the best he or she can. Crisis is difficult, but it presents opportunities for change.

Working with Stepfamilies

A teacher notices that whenever Pete Lawrence's stepbrothers visit for the weekend, the Monday after is a disaster. Pete is frequently whining and demanding, and his mother always looks frazzled and exhausted. And when he was asked to draw his family last week, he drew his mother and sister, then his stepfather, then his "other" father, and then lost interest in the project. She doesn't know if she should be concerned with this behavior or not.

About 250,000 families are "recycled" every year—created after the breakup of old families; from one-third to one-half of these have children from either or both former marriages. Such family structures can be complex, as the number of possible relationships is multiplied, and the stepfamily is highly influenced by another adult or family, thus having less control over their family life. This complexity is the source of both the positive and negative aspects of a "blended" family. (See Figure 16-7.)

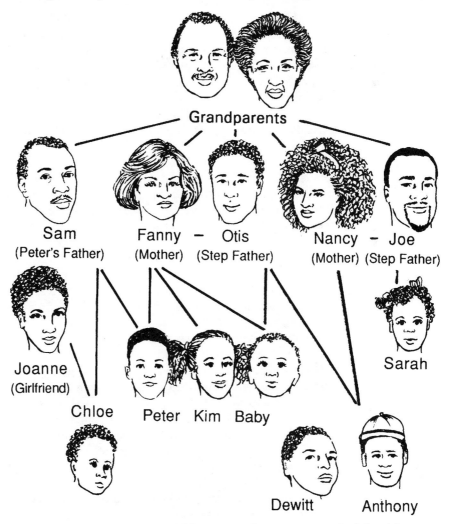

Figure 16-7 Stepfamilies offer children a complex assortment of relationships.

One of the major difficulties is that parents often feel ambiguity in their roles, unsure of when to step in or to stand back. Here again, the only role models offered are distinctly negative—everybody remembers Cinderella's very unattractive stepmother! Parents often expect to make up for the upset in the original family by creating a close-knit, happy family. The stakes are higher the second time around. For everyone it becomes more important to succeed.

> All children come to second marriages shaped by the earlier marriage and burdened by its failure. Children of divorce are more eager to be loved and more frightened of being rejected and pushed outside (Wallerstein and Blakeslee 1989, 246).

However, second marriages with children from a first marriage are more prone to divorce. Differences in child-rearing beliefs and methods, friction, conflicts with other parents, and children testing the entire situation result in a good deal of stress. In Wallerstein's study, half the children had experienced at least two divorces of their mother or father within a ten-year period.

Teachers may need to remind stepparents and themselves that there are also positive aspects for the children involved: they have multiple role models and an extended kin network; they may have happy parents, additional siblings, and a higher standard of living; a new family may offer experience with conflict resolution and flexibility.

In working with stepfamilies, teachers can provide similar kinds of emotional support and information that they offer to adults and children undergoing the transition of divorce. It is helpful to reassure parents that adjustment takes time, usually years, and to provide children with a secure, stable, classroom environment.

Many communities may have a local organization of the Stepfamily Association of America to offer information and support to these families. (Information can be obtained from the national office at 3001 Porter St. N.W., Washington, D.C. 20008.)

Teachers need to be sensitive to family name differences. If John Smith is the stepfather of Billy Jones, he may not appreciate being called "Mr. Jones." Again, teachers need to learn the legalities in each family situation, including who has the right to pick up children or give permission for their care.

Teachers can help a child adjust by accepting the multitude of family styles represented in a classroom. Attention to language and the message it conveys to children is important; what does it imply to talk about "real" parents? (Coleman et al. 1984). Teachers should not put stepchildren in awkward positions by promoting activities that cause confusion. "Mothers' tea parties" or "fathers' breakfasts" can cause problems about who gets the invitation. Designating "Parent" events might remove this awkwardness. (If teachers are concerned that fathers will be left out, they can make this clear through personal conversations.) If children are making Christmas gifts for mothers, encourage stepchildren to provide gifts for as many mothers as they'd like!

(It is worth noting parenthetically that many of the children's reactions and teacher's strategies would be similar for children experiencing the stress of loss of a parent through death, or even temporarily, through lengthy hospitalization or imprisonment. There are obvious differences in each situation, but sensitivity to supporting children and their families at these times of crises is necessary. Divorce and remarriage are dealt with more extensively here because of the statistics that indicate that most classroom teachers will likely encounter those phenomena more frequently.)

❖ Working with Parents of Children with Special Needs

> Sylvia Rodriguez presently attends the Cerebral Palsy Kindergarten in the mornings, but her mother has asked the child-care center if she can go there in the afternoons if Mrs. Rodriguez begins to work full time. The teacher in the afternoon program is rather concerned about this, as she has not worked with a physically disabled child before.

Since 1974, Head Start has been mandated by Congress to have 10 percent of its children be those who have disabilities (Community Services Act, PL 96-644). With the passing of the Education for All Handicapped Children Act of 1975 (PL 94-142), which directed that all children from three through eighteen must be provided with free and appropriate education in the least restrictive setting, many teachers besides those trained in special education are working with the children with special needs mainstreamed into their classrooms. The same law directed educators to involve parents in the development and implementation of Individualized Educational Plans (IEP) for their children. The Education for the Handicapped Act Amendments of 1986 (PL 99-457) lowered the age for intervention to birth and provided empathetically for significant involvement of and focus on families as essential collaborative members of the intervention team. (PL 101-576, The Individuals with Disabilities Education Act reauthorized the Education for All Handicapped Children Act in 1990, and emphasized the concept of the family as expert in creating the Individualized Family Service Plan—IFSP.)

The stated purposes of PL 99-457 are to enhance the development of infants and toddlers with special needs and to minimize the risk of developmental delays; to reduce educational costs by minimizing the need for special education and related services after these infants and toddlers reach school age; to minimize the likelihood of institutionalizing the disabled and maximize their potential for independent living; and *to enhance the capacity of families to meet the special needs of their handicapped* (Gallagher's word) *infants and toddlers* (Gallagher 1989).

Figure 16-8 Current legislation includes families in assessing their own needs and encourages collaborative goal setting. Courtesy Council for Children, Inc.

PL 99-457 requires a written Individualized Family Service Plan (IFSP) that addresses not only the needs of the infant, but also the strengths and needs of the family, related to enhancing the development of their child. Going beyond the IEP model, where goals were often based on the professionals' perceptions of the family's needs, the IFSP approach challenges professionals to develop practices that allow families to assess their own needs and encourage collaborative goal setting. (See Figure 16-8.)

Working with parents of children with special needs offers particular challenges to a preschool teacher, who must learn to understand the common emotional reactions, anxieties, and problems that these families face. Because it is now so very common for children with special needs to be included in most centers and classrooms, all teachers should prepare for working with this special group of families.

Emotional Reactions

Parents of children with developmental challenges undergo an adjustment process that is lifelong; its emotional stages resemble the process of grieving. (See Figure 16-9.) The shock of learning that one's child has special needs is frequently followed by feelings of guilt, of somehow being responsible. Many parents undergo feelings of denial that may take the form of shopping from one professional to another, always looking for a more optimistic opinion or magical solution. Sometimes denial takes the

Figure 16-9 Parents of children with special needs undergo a lifelong adjustment process. Courtesy Deborah Hefner.

form of projecting blame onto others or attempting to hide the disability. Anger often follows before acceptance finally takes place. These feelings are often recycled, as stages that were previously experienced reappear and influence behavior. This may happen in response to particular events in the lives of children or their families, such as beginning a new school year, or when a sibling is born (Gargiulo and Graves, 1991). Although most parents of children with special needs entering a preschool have probably been aware of their child's situation since birth, entering a classroom with children who do not have similar problems may be another reminder that the problem will always exist.

Other emotions frequently experienced by parents of children with developmental challenges are frustration, guilt, ambivalence, and a desire to overprotect.

For many parents, the realization that their child has a disability is a blow to their sense of self-worth. They are in difficult parenting situations with many unknowns and may feel less than capable. (See Figure 16-10 for a mother's words that describe the unknowns, as well as the growth experiences, of parenting a child with a disability.) Most parents of children with

---

WELCOME TO HOLLAND

I am often asked to describe the experience of raising a child with a disability—to try to help people who have not shared that unique experience to understand it, and to imagine how it would feel. It's like this. . . .

When you're going to have a baby, it's like planning a fabulous vacation trip to Italy. You buy a bunch of guide books and make your wonderful plans. The Coliseum. The Michelangelo David. The gondolas in Venice. You may learn some handy phrases in Italian. It's all very exciting.

After months of eager anticipation, the day finally arrives. You pack your bags and off you go. Several hours later, the plane lands. The stewardess comes in and says, "Welcome to Holland."

"*Holland*?!?" you say. "What do you mean Holland?? I signed up for Italy! I'm supposed to be in Italy. All my life I've dreamed of going to Italy."

But there's been a change in the flight plan. They've landed in Holland and there you must stay.

The important thing is that they haven't taken you to a horrible, disgusting, filthy place, full of pestilence, famine and disease. It's just a different place.

So you must go out and buy new guide books. And you must learn a whole new language. And you will meet a whole new group of people you would never have met.

It's just *different* place. It's slower-paced than Italy, less flashy than Italy. But after you've been there for a while and you catch your breath, you look around . . . and you begin to notice that Holland has windmills . . . and Holland has tulips. Holland even has Rembrandts.

But everyone you know is busy coming and going from Italy . . . and they're all bragging about what a wonderful time they had there. And for the rest of your life, you will say "Yes, that's where I was supposed to go. That's what I had planned."

And the pain of that will never, ever, ever go away . . . because the loss of that is a very, very significant loss.

But . . . if you spend your life mourning the fact that you didn't get to Italy, you may never be free to enjoy the very special, the very lovely things . . . about Holland.

Figure 16-10 A mother of a child with a disability describes her parenting experience.

special needs live with increased amounts of stress in their lives due to the increasing amount of time and energy spent parenting their child, often with no respite; the economic strain of medical expenses, therapy, and treatment; the strain of living with complex emotions and shattered dreams; the isolation that results as families either anticipate or experience social rejection, pity, or ridicule.

No parent is ever prepared for a child with special needs. There are no role models, no guidelines to assist parents in modifying their child-rearing practices to match their child's special needs. Parenting is a task that can make people feel shaky, even under the best of circumstances; parents of children with disabilities often feel most insecure in their position.

Parental reactions can best be understood by hearing them in the words of a parent of a child with a disability talking to a group of professionals.

"It's a strange life, because I don't consider myself an unhappy person, and I'm doing okay, but there's a part of every parent who has a child who is damaged which is in perpetual mourning. . . . What happens to a family when you have a handicapped child? I think that really it is a myth that tragedy brings families together. It does not. We grieve very, very privately, and men and women grieve differently. . . . There is a certain animosity that is just there between parents and professionals that will always be there because you have these intervention programs, . . . but you can't make our kids better. And when push comes to shove, that's what we really want. . . . The bottom line is, he can't be fixed. And that always makes a parent sad. And as a professional that's something you have to understand. . . . As a professional you should keep in a part of you the idea `I don't know what it's like, I have not been in this parent's shoes." And make yourself a little less judgmental. But there is this anger that we parents have because we're in the know, but you're writing out the IEPs [Individual Educational Plans], and you're making the judgments, and you're the one who's determining things. . . . There is a free-floating anger that has to do, very simply, with our children not being whole, and there's nothing really that you can do about that. . . . So sometimes when parents are aggressive and upsetting, I don't think you should take it personally. . . . I never had so many people (helping me). . . . And I can remember feeling that I didn't like it, that this was a real intrusion on my life and who I was as a mother . . . (but still) I really needed help. I need a great deal of help. . . . People who are in your profession have chosen it, and it is a profession that gives you a lot of self-esteem and a lot of good feelings. . . . *The parents have not chosen this.* No parent would choose to have a child that is anything less than normal and whole. And so while we both want the best for our child, the best program, we also have to realize that we're coming from different places. You're coming from a place that gives you a lot of self-esteem. A parent of a handicapped child does not have that self-esteem (Kupfer 1984).

Parents of a child with special needs find themselves trying to maintain the family's integrity as a group with its own developmental tasks while providing for the distinctive needs of their child.

When teachers increase their awareness of these particular emotional reactions and tasks, insensitive responses can be avoided.

Parent Relations with Professionals, Teacher, and Others

Many parents of children with disabilities already have an established history of relationships with professionals by the time they encounter a classroom teacher. Families of children with special needs learn to allow professionals into their lives to provide the help and knowledge they need. These parents also have learned how to enter a professional's world in order to equip themselves to better help their child.

Some of these earlier experiences with professionals may not have been positive. Parents of children with special needs relate stories of being shuttled from one professional to another, and finding a confusing lack of integration between these professional evaluations. Sometimes they feel they have only been partially informed of the findings and prognosis, and have not been given complete knowledge of the available resources.

The emphasis on the team approach mandated by PL99-457 means that parents and various early intervention professionals must now function interdependently and collaboratively. "Families are being viewed as competent decision makers who must be allowed to choose their level of involvement with an early intervention program according to their values, resources, strengths, needs, and supports" (McGonigal and Garland 1990, 27). This stance may help parents become less suspicious and hostile when interacting with professionals, including teachers.

A partnership between parents of a child with special needs and a preschool teacher is crucial to the child's optimum functioning. Only when teachers interact with these parents do they gain valuable information on the developmental and medical history, and social and emotional history. In addition, teachers can assist parents in obtaining the skills and information necessary for directly working with their children in the home. Continuity between home and school is crucial for the optimum development of a child with a disability; efforts to learn and coordinate similar techniques that can be used throughout a child's life are important.

How can a preschool teacher work effectively with these parents? Several ideas are important.

Treat Parents as Individuals

Parents of children with special needs want most to be treated as individuals. They do not want to be categorized, but treated with dignity. Teachers who know and respond to parents as individuals show such respect.

Teacher who examine their own attitudes towards children with special needs and their parents will avoid treating them as stereotypes. It should also be recalled that the culture of the individual family will influence a number of attitudes about the disability, including the meaning of the disability, the family's attitudes about professionals and about seeking and receiving assistance, their attitudes about children and about family roles and interactions. All of these culturally determined attitudes will influence an individual family's level of acceptance of the disability, and of their willingness to participate in their child's care plan.

Focus on the Present and Future

Teachers must be aware of parents' tendencies to project blame and feel guilty for their child's problems. Teachers should avoid discussing the past, the source of a child's disability, and focus conversations and plans on the present and future; what actions can best help a child and parent now and in the future. (See Figure 16-11.)

Figure 16-11 Teachers help parents focus on the present. Courtesy Deborah Hefner.

Clarify Information

Teachers may have to reinterpret or reinforce earlier communications from other professionals. Parents who are uncomfortable with medical and/or educational terminology may use a teacher to clarify the information. Teachers should remember that their function is to clarify, not comment on, the diagnosis. Preschool teachers working with children mainstreamed into their classrooms need to communicate regularly with other members of the professional team who are planning the overall care and methods of treatment.

Be Hopefully Realistic

Parents value a teacher's realistic approaches. It is only natural to want to comfort parents with optimism, but raising false expectations is unacceptable. Teachers should offer hope whenever possible and help parents rejoice in small successes. (See Figure 16-12.) Specific and frequent reporting to parents is helpful here. Teachers should be as positive as possible.

Help Parents Let Go

Parents must undertake the process of letting go, especially difficult when complicated by a desire to overprotect their child, a frequent reaction due to guilt feelings. Teachers can have an important role in supporting parents as they try to strengthen their child to function independently.

Figure 16-12 Teachers will help children with special needs see their small successes and rejoice with them. Courtesy Christine Shamel.

Separation and letting go are always hard, but in this case parents may experience real conflict as they perceive children's real or imagined dependence.

> "I know it must feel almost cruel to have her walk into the classroom on her own—it's such hard work for her. But the light of accomplishment on her face is worth it to see, isn't it? Good for you!"

Increase Parent Involvement in the Classroom

Recognizing that parents of children with special needs often feel impotent, teachers should provide opportunities for parents to contribute meaningfully in the process of helping their child. Opportunities to observe and participate in a classroom help parents feel included, as well as provide firsthand knowledge of their child's functioning and a teacher's methods of working with him. (See Figure 16-13.) As teachers help parents devise and follow through on plans for home training, parents are able to function more effectively with their children. Teachers must also remember that there already are many burdens and expectations on these parents, so they must feel free to become involved in ways that fit into their lives.

Figure 16-13 Opportunities to observe and participate in the classroom help parents feel included.

Know Available Community Resources

Teachers must be familiar with all community resources that can be helpful to families of children with special needs. Parents who don't know where to turn for assistance will need teachers' knowledge for referrals. The following national resources may be helpful:

Council for Exceptional Children
1920 Association Dr.
Reston, VA 22091
(703) 620-3660

National Information Center for Children and Youth with Disabilities
1155 15th St. N.W., Ste 1002
Washington, D.C.
(202) 785-4268

National Parent Network on Disabilities
1600 Prince St.
Alexandria, VA 22314
(703) 684-NPND

Exceptional Parent Magazine
P.O. Box 3000, Dept. EP
Denville, NJ 07834
(800) 247-8080

Help Reestablish Self-Confidence

Recognizing the social and emotional isolation of many families with disabled children, teachers should make particular efforts to help them establish social linkages with the outside world. Introducing and involving them in work or discussion projects with other parents, and arranging for other parents to take the initiative in approaching them are methods for helping these parents reestablish self-confidence in relating to others. (See Figure 16-14 for suggestions of books that may be helpful for parents of children with special needs to realize the common threads of their experiences.)

Teachers who recognize the emotional reactions and needs of parents of children with special needs are best able to support and strengthen these families' abilities to function optimally for their children.

❖ Working with Parents of Infants

Another group of parents that have particular needs requiring consideration are parents of infants.

> "Honestly, that Mrs. Black! Doesn't she think I know anything at all? You should see the list of instructions she left with the baby this morning—how much to feed, when to feed, what to do if she doesn't finish it all, what it might mean when she cries. I'd be furious, if it wasn't so funny."

Fewell, R.R., and Vadaszy, P.F. (1986). *Families of handicapped children: needs and supports across the lifespan.* Austin, TX: PRO-ED.

Pueschel, S., Bernier, J., and Weidenman, L. (1988). *The special child: a source book for parents of children with developmental disabilities.* Baltimore, MD: Paul H. Brookes Publishing Co.

Simons, R. (1985). *After the tears: parents talk about raising a child with a disability.* New York: Harcourt Brace Jovanovich.

Thompson, C. (1986). *Raising a handicapped child: a helpful guide for parents of the physically disabled.* New York: William Morrow and Co.

Wetzel, L.L. (1990). *Parents of young children.* St. Paul, MN: Toys N Things Press.

Figure 16-14 Books to offer to parents of children with special needs.

There are often strained feelings between the caregivers of babies and their parents. The inherent tension that exists between the individualized focus of parents on the well-being of their child and the generalized focus of the program on the well-being of all children is exacerbated by the particular aspects of parental development that are at work in the parents of infants. Teachers who are working with parents of infants need to consider the particular emotional responses characteristic to the first stages of parenting. Caregivers also must remind themselves how new is the phenomenon of many young mothers having to leave their babies early in the child's life. In 1950, it was so rare to have mothers of babies working that the Labor Department did not keep statistics on it! Currently, about 35 percent of mothers have returned to work by the time their babies are two months old. More than half are back at work by the infant's first birthday.

Reactions of Parents of Infants

The important process of attachment in the first two years of a baby's life is mutual; adults are becoming attached to their special babies, just as babies are becoming attached to the adults who care for them. This means that not only do they care for each other deeply, but they also feel more secure and comfortable in each other's presence. It is this feeling of a special close relationship with their babies that is crucial to the beginning parent-child relationship and the optimum development of the baby. But this is also the cause for parents' possessive feelings toward their babies. They do not want to be away from them for too long and are convinced that their baby isn't safe with anyone else. This is the reason that, for example, mothers leave long, explicit lists of directions that a caregiver may find insulting to her intelligence, or demand exactly detailed accounts of every minute of the babies' day away from them. It may help caregivers if they can respect parental anxiety as flowing positively from the attachment process. It is important to realize that parents are always anxious about putting their infants into substitute care. There are usually other emotions involved too. Most parents feel guilty, or at best ambivalent, about leaving their babies for someone else to care for, feeling that the baby might not still love them if someone else is caring for him.

Attachment leads adults to engage in what Dr. Berry Brazelton calls "gate-keeping"—strategies to keep rival adults distant from the adored infant. This happens within families, as well as other outside caregivers. Within the family gate-keeping may look like:

> Mother saying to father: "Don't lay him down like that. He likes to be on his tummy. Here, I'll do it."
>
> With the caregiver, a "gate-keeping" mother might say, "Well, she doesn't have any trouble sleeping at home on the weekends when I settle her down."
>
> A "gate-keeping" caregiver might say, "If you'd just burp her like I do, halfway through her feeding, you'd see that she won't spit up."

Any infant caregiver knows that you don't have to be related to become strongly attached to babies, so it is not surprising that tension between parents and teachers in an infant room may be present. (See Figure 16-15.)

Figure 16-15 When all the adults caring for a baby are strongly attached, rivalry may develop. Courtesy Council for Children, Inc.

Another factor to consider is that new parents are often anxious and tentative as they approach the unfamiliar tasks and decisions of caring for an infant. Parents are unsure of how they measure up to the expected standards in their new role. The confident behaviors of a very experienced caregiver may increase the parents' feelings of incompetence by contrast.

There are many life adjustments necessitated by adding a baby to a household: new demands on time and money; disruptions in the marital relationship and the smooth-running household and careers; physical exhaustion from attending to a baby's needs twenty-four hours a day, as well as returning to work outside the home. The parent of an infant is often emotionally and physically stretched with the stress of the new life-style.

> The growth spurt associated with the first year of parenting is probably the most intense, compact, and pressurized period of growth in a young adult life (Joffe and Viertel 1984, 319).

Dr. Berry Brazelton feels that many new parents are in deep emotional trouble, due to having to share their babies with others too soon in the development of the parenting relationship. He predicts two possible courses of action for these young parents. One is to protect themselves from forming attachments, because it will hurt too much to care; the second is to grieve. Grieving, he claims, may be manifested by blaming, anger, guilt, or helplessness, which may lead to the distortions in behavior that teachers see. Child care workers, then, have a special responsibility to help young parents so they will have an opportunity to move into attachment. (See Figure 16-16.)

> I would press for one more set of stipulations on day care for infants: that the care include nurturing of mothers. Unless a mother is included in the planning for her baby, she will feel shoved out and useless at a time when it is critical that she continue to feel important to him. If she is left out, she is likely to grieve about losing him and may begin to detach at an unconscious level in order to defend herself from her feelings about having to share him. This will make her raw and competitive with his care givers (Brazelton 1992, 190).

Teacher Relationships with Parents of Infants

Recognizing the emotional responses and needs of new parents, caregivers can do several things to form an effective partnership with these parents.

Support the Attachment Process

Competition over the child can be transferred into concern for the parents' degree of attachment to their child. Teachers can make sure that infant room practices facilitate the attachment process. The function of good infant day care is to support a family's developmental needs, and attachment is the

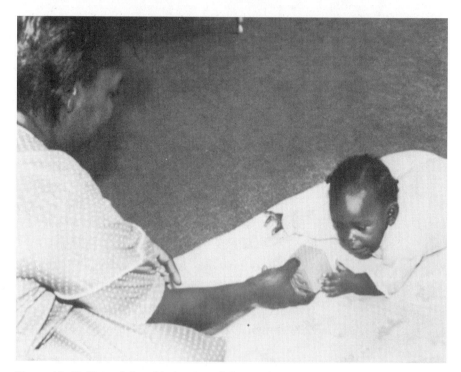

Figure 16-16 The relationship between infant and parent needs to be supported by the staff. Courtesy USM Publications.

primary need of both infants and parents. Caregivers should be given specialized knowledge about the attachment process (See Bowlby 1988; Karen 1994).

Parents should feel welcome to drop in whenever they want. (See Figure 16-17.) Many parents of infants will come and feed their babies during lunch hours or other free times during a day, if they feel welcomed. Mothers who want to nurse or offer a bottle should be provided with comfortable chairs and as much privacy for a one-to-one time with their babies as they would like. No matter what a caregiver's personal feelings about breast or bottle-feeding, caregiver's positive attitudes can be very important in supporting the mother's ability to continue to nurse even while her infant is in child care (Morris 1995). This is not an intrusion into an infant room routine, but an important time for parent and baby. The physical environment makes a statement of welcome; creating a parent corner right in the baby room, with soft chairs and an array of helpful books and pamphlets, conveys a warm message that parents are welcome to stay. It is also very important that caregivers and administrators make clear welcoming messages to fathers in the infant room, rather than ignoring them or only including them in a special and artificial role, rather than in the natural roles of a parent learning attachment roles and behaviors (Meyerhoff 1994).

Figure 16-17 Parents should feel welcome to drop in whenever they can. Courtesy Jakaret Veerasarn, Washington, D.C.

If parents feel that routines and regulations are not separating them from their baby, they will feel less possessive in their relation with a caregiver and reassured that their baby's care is satisfactory.

Standardize Informational Procedures

An important responsibility is to enable parents to share their information and so build their feelings of competence in parenting. Procedures for passing information back and forth between parent and caregiver must be standardized and clear. Many centers keep a written record of daily occurrences such as feedings, naps, diaper changes, activities, and behavior, as well as recording developmental progress. They offer parents additional forms and a chance to record information that can help a caregiver, such as the last feeding time, amount of sleep, unusual behavior, or home routine. Keeping this individual form conveniently located—on top of a baby's cubby, perhaps—means that its use is routine for all adults. When parents are convinced that an infant room staff wants to share with them fully and that the information they offer as parents is important to their baby's day, feelings of anxiety and rivalry often decrease. (See Figure 16-18.)

All About Me

My name is _____

I like to be called: _____

My birthday is_____

My parents names are _____

In case of emergency call_____

_____

I like to sleep on my side, tummy, back. (circle one).

I have/haven't a special blanket.

I have/haven't a pacifier.

I like to eat every _____ hours.

I am allergic to _____

I am afraid of _____

When I cry it helps me if you _____

_____

My favorite thing to do is _____

_____

I want you to know _____

_____

_____

Figure 16-18 Sample information sheet for parents to complete

Remain Objective

Caregivers of infants need to be conscious of their own feelings towards the infants in their care. This relationship is warm and nurturing on a caregiver's part, but brief, probably lasting only through the months of infancy. What these babies most need from a caregiver is support warmly offered to a total family unit as baby and parents work through the process of attachment. The family is at the center of things, with child care being just one of the satellite of services the family has chosen to use. There is no place in this relationship for caregivers who disapprove of the decisions parents have made, or who think how much better a job they do for a baby than his own anxious, inexperienced parents do. Parents are the primary people in an infant's life. With connotations of rivalry among adults, a baby will only suffer. It is important for caregivers to examine their feelings about authority, so they can become sensitive to ways of sharing power without abdicating their role. Loving caregivers realize that the best way they can help an infant is to support his parents' growth.

Introduce New Parenting Techniques

Teachers of infants should offer information and ideas to new parents. During their infants' first year, first-time parents are most open to learning basic parenting behaviors that have a lasting effect on themselves and their children. As their relationship develops, teacher should have frequent conversations in which it is appropriate to introduce ideas and answer questions subtly. (See Figure 16-19.) At the same time, teachers must guard against overt behaviors that suggest parental incompetence, contrasted with professional expert knowledge. A teacher in an infant room educates gently, as a friend.

> "Wow, we should really have a celebration today. When I noticed how hard it was for her to say goodbye to you this morning, I realized this was the first time she's done that. That crying when you leave is a good sign that she loves you very much, that all your hard work these past few months has paid off and she's become attached to you. That's a very special day."

Figure 16-19 Teachers can introduce new parenting ideas subtly.

Sometimes the meaningful communication can be done lightly by "talking through the baby."

> "Tell Mom how you like it when she wraps you up so securely."
>
> "It does make you feel good to see Mommy come back, doesn't it? See how she gets all your best smiles!"

Pamphlets, books, articles, and parenting magazines are made available for parents who prefer to get their information through printed matter.

As teachers educate, they should also be sensitive to the fact that ideas about parenting are borne from cultural contexts, and some practices that they would like to introduce may be quite alien or even unacceptable to parents from other cultures (Gonzalez-Mena 1992). It is important for teachers to hear parents' viewpoints as well as learn their child rearing philosophies, rather than focus solely on information they want to impart.

As an increasing number of infants are cared for by other adults outside their homes, these teachers will have important opportunities to support families and act as resources at this crucial point in their lives. Indeed, by establishing the pattern of sharing care, rather than handing a child over to the professionals to be educated, infant caregivers begin the precedent of reducing the distance and formality often found in school encounters.

❖ Working with Families When Abuse Occurs

> Every time Dorothy Scott reads an article in the paper about child abuse and neglect in her city, or any other, she shudders. "What kind of parents could do a thing like that?" she wonders. "Thank goodness we'll never have that problem in our school—not with our kind of parents."

Many teachers believe that in their communities, with their particular populations, they will never have to face this problem. But this is simply not so. Child abuse occurs in every segment of society, among families who are just like everyone else. In fact, it is likely that one in four teachers have experienced abuse themselves as children or know someone well who is a survivor of abuse. Although reporting of cases seems to have improved in recent years due to more public information and awareness, it is still difficult to quote reliable statistics on occurrences of abuse and neglect. Nevertheless, it is inevitable that classroom teachers will encounter abuse and neglect, and its effects on families. Teachers must understand the dynamics of abusive families and the indicators that suggest a problem may exist, as well as the legal obligations and possibilities for helping a child and her family. Perhaps even more importantly, teachers must be aware of their own emotional responses to the idea of abuse, so that they will be able to act in professional and helpful ways with the children and families involved, rather than merely react with personal emotion. It is vital that early educators perceive that they have several roles in relation to child abuse. These roles include a role of primary prevention, by modeling positive child guidance and enhancing the development of positive self-esteem in children, and by supporting parents in developing positive parenting skills. Caregivers play a role in secondary prevention when they identify suspected child abuse and report it to the appropriate child protection agency for investigation. They also play a tertiary role in child abuse prevention as they support both children and parents when child abuse has been confirmed (Pimento and Kernested 1996).

The Child Abuse Prevention and Treatment Act of 1974 defines abuse and neglect as "the physical or mental injury, sexual abuse, negligent treatment or maltreatment of a child under the age of eighteen by a person who is responsible for the child's welfare, under circumstances which indicate that the child's health or welfare is harmed or threatened thereby." Physical abuse includes the deliberate inflicting of injuries on children, often becoming more severe over time. Emotional abuse is more difficult to prove, lacking the more obvious evidence of physical injury. It should be obvious that emotional abuse will also accompany any other form of abuse or neglect, since the explicit and implicit message is always of the child's lack of worth and the resulting damage to a positive sense of self. Sexual abuse may include any involvement of children in sexual activities for the gratification of the offender, including sexual contact and exploitation of children for pornographic purposes. Neglect occurs when adults do not provide for the physical, emotional and social needs that are necessary for healthy growth and development. Adults who are entrusted with the care of children are responsible for their well-being. When this well-being is at risk, the law enables others to intervene on a child's behalf.

What forces cause parents to abuse their children? "Child abuse is always a misuse of power—a person with greater physical, cognitive, and/or emotional power and authority controls a child in a way that does not contribute to the child's growth and development" (Pimento and Kernested 1996, 374). Child abuse is a complex subject; many different factors or components in the environment may come together and interact. These include social, educational, cultural, economic, religious, family, and individual circumstances and ideas. Specifically, these factors may include the examples of adult control absorbed in their own childhoods, the cultural messages of the individual community about the responsibilities and styles of "good parents," the lack of child development knowledge and skills, the church teaching that children are inherently evil and must be broken in spirit, the isolation of a family that has moved too many times to develop supports to remove isolation, a rigid and demanding personality in a parent or a difficult child, and any other number of factors that you and your classmates may identify.

Precipitating Circumstances

In most cases, the personality potentials for both parent and child are present, but a crisis event is needed before a parent loses control and abuse occurs. Often a family undergoes too much change too fast, with no time to recover before being hit by a new crisis. The crisis may be economic—loss of a job, financial problems; it may be personal—desertion by a spouse or other marital problems, death of a family member or other transitional events; the perception that a child needs extraordinarily strong discipline; it may be environmental—a move, inadequate housing, the washing machine breaking down. Whatever it is, however remote from the child himself, this event is the last straw, and a parent loses control. Because these are circumstances that know no socioeconomic or cultural barrier, abusive situations are found in every stratum of society.

Indicators of Abuse and Neglect

There are four general groups of injuries that may result from physical abuse (Ayoub et al. in Pimento and Kernested 1996). These include injuries to the skin and soft under tissues, including bruises, abrasions, bites, and burns; injuries to the skeletal system from direct blows or from shaking or squeezing; injuries to the head and central nervus system from being shaken or choked; or internal injuries from being punched, kicked, or thrown.

Teachers might see:

Physical Signs of Abuse

- Bruises or contusions, especially those in places where a child's physical activity cannot account for them: backs of knees, upper back; those that are bilateral (matching on each arm); or those that indicate some agent made the mark (a belt buckle or loop of electric cord). Sometimes long-sleeved clothing inappropriate for the season may attempt to cover up such marks.

- Injuries reported to be caused by falling, but that do not include hands, knees, or forehead.

- Burns, especially small burns such as those made by a cigarette or match.

- Trouble sitting or walking may indicate physical or sexual abuse.

- Frequent injuries, especially those that do not seem to match the explanation offered.

Physical Signs of Neglect

- Need for medical attention, even after conditions have been drawn to a parent's attention.

- Clothing inadequate for weather, chronically unwashed or uncared for.

- Physical hygiene unattended to.
- Child excessively fatigued or hungry, missing breakfast constantly.

Behavioral Indicators

Abuse or neglect may be indicated by a variety of behaviors in children. Teachers may see a number of behaviors over time that make them suspicious of abuse. The following are some behaviors that should trigger teachers' watchful concern:

- Deviant behavioral systems, such as aggression, destructiveness and disruptive behaviors; or passive, withdrawn, extreme quiet, extreme compliance.
- Daydreaming.
- Fearful of adults and of parents.
- Unusual, sophisticated, sexual acting-out (contrasted with curious, exploratory behaviors usually associated with preschoolers).
- Regressive behavior.
- Lack of emotional attachment.

Teacher's Role

When a teacher suspects abuse or neglect in a family situation, there are several courses of action indicated. Information gathering and clarifying should occur continually as teachers try to determine if there is cause for concern. Teachers ask for explanations of injuries or appearances, neutrally inquiring, "What happened to your knee?" or "What did the doctor say about the bruises?" so that the child or parent may explain the situation without being put on the defensive. Parental responses may either confirm teacher suspicions or resolve the question. The director or principal should have an opportunity to observe the concerning injury or behavior.

Document Evidence

When teachers become aware of possible abuse and neglect, documentation of what they see must be kept. Such records indicate patterns for teachers and directors, and may determine their next actions. Documentation is to substantiate any suspicions with recorded evidence, and is useful to an investigator. Many centers will have devised their own forms for such documentation. Otherwise, simple, objective descriptions are all that is required, including the child's full name, and the date when the information was recorded, as well as the date when the observation occurred. Include also the verbatim conversations held with the child and/or the parent. If concerns are removed after clarification with the parents, documentation may be the only step to take at this time.

> Nov. 18th. Two large bruises, on each upper arm, including distinct finger marks.
>
> Dec. 3rd. Bright red welts on backs of legs. Child reports father was very angry previous night.

Report to Proper Agencies

Teachers are mandated by law to report cases of suspected abuse in all states and provinces and child-care workers in most. Preschool teachers should check their own region's regulations for current laws and the appropriate protective agency to whom to report. The burden of proof is not on teachers, but on the protective services agency to whom teachers must report; if a report of suspected abuse or neglect is made in good faith (contrasted with the malicious intention of a parent who is trying to discredit another in a custody battle, for example), the reporting adult is protected from liability.

There are instances of teachers and centers who try to close their eyes to the problems they suspect or see in families, perhaps fearing reprisals or parents' anger if they involve themselves in "family matters." Teachers need to accept their responsibility as perhaps the only people who know what is going on with some children and their families, and as the only advocates a child might have. Teachers need to realize their own legal and moral responsibilities, if they discover their center's policies discourage such active advocacy roles. The Code of Ethics makes it absolutely clear that early childhood professionals have a definite responsibility to act to protect children. When reports are made, they should include the child and parents' full names and addresses; the child's age, sex, and birth date; the name and address of the person making the report; and the name, address, and telephone number of the child-care center. Professionals should realize that less attention is usually paid to anonymous reports, according to some evidence.

Examine Personal Attitudes

Teachers need to examine their own attitudes to be able to work with these families. Many teachers feel great anger towards parents who are hurtful to their small children. It is important to recognize the existence of this anger and to work especially hard to get to know parents and the circumstances of their parenting, in order to develop true empathy for their situations. It is more appropriate for teachers to release some of their negative feelings in conversation with colleagues, rather than with parents, since parents are themselves in need of nurturing and acceptance, not expressions of anger. It is important to remember, however, that confidential material or statements that have not yet been confirmed must be treated professionally.

Create an Atmosphere of Trust

Teachers' concern and caring for children in these troubled families enable them to support children through very difficult times. It helps these children to know teachers care for them, are dependable and trustworthy, and are concerned enough to help them and their parents. Such an atmosphere of trust may free children to confide their problems and allow them to feel confident in the ability of other adults to help them and their parents. Children need allies in the classroom who can help them provide for their anger to be expressed safely (Caughey 1991). Play is a vehicle that helps build trust, as teachers accept the children's self-expression. These children do not need to hear condemnation of their angry feelings or of their parents, who are the most important people in their lives no matter how troubled at this time. Teachers can also comfort themselves in the knowledge that they are providing an important model for children, helping them to realize that not all adults are abusive.

Refer Parents to Support Groups

Many communities offer agencies and groups to support parents under stress. If teachers know these community resources, they can refer parents on a preventive basis or reassure them after a court's referral. Many agencies, such as the Family Support Center in Charlotte, North Carolina, offer support to parents in the form of therapy, a twenty-four-hour stress telephone line manned by trained volunteers, and reparenting education for parents who have abused. One method found very effective is to give families a "parent aide," a parent, trained in counseling skills, who makes home visits and models positive and appropriate ways to interact with children.

In recent years, courts have tended to be less punitive with parents and concentrate on efforts to help parents learn alternative methods of discipline and appropriate expectations. Teachers can wholeheartedly support such efforts. There are benefits for an entire family when parents learn new methods of parenting.

Support for these efforts can also come from parents who have experienced similar problems. Many communities have a local group of the national Parents Anonymous organization, whose members are formerly abusive parents who come together to encourage each other in their attempts to change their behavior. For more information about this organization, write: Parents Anonymous, 2810 Artessia Blvd., Suite F, Redondo Beach, CA 90278.

The reality is that child abuse and neglect is a problem many teachers will encounter. The best scenario is for teachers to be able to recognize signs of distress and problems, to know their legal and moral obligations and their community resources, and to support families through the agonizing process of evaluation and reconstruction. Building a caring relationship with parents is the best gift a teacher can give an abused child.

❖ Working with Adoptive Families

As we have discussed throughout this book, every family is unique in its situation, history, and structure. Adoptive families have been created by legal agreement, not by biological ties. Parents frequently receive notification of a child available for adoption with very little notice, often after long waiting periods, and even longer preceding periods of attempting to conceive a child. Sometimes older children who are adopted into families have already experienced difficulties such as death of parents, abuse, neglect, or abandonment, or leaving a home/country. Such circumstances create adjustment difficulties for the children and their adoptive parents. Although a minority, these families deserve sensitive and supportive responses from classroom teachers.

What are some things that classroom teachers can do?

Know the Facts

Teachers and directors need to support parents in the information they have given to their children. Programs generally need to explain that they are as open with children about adoption as about the myriad of other different situations that children live in and may have questions about. Nevertheless, they will be sensitive to information that individual families consider private. Admission information forms need to have a place to include adoption information about this child or other siblings that may be adopted. Teachers must also be sure to find out whether the child knows this, how questions have been answered at home, and whether people in the community are aware of information that the child is not aware of. This is obviously a sensitive area that some parents may be reluctant to answer; teachers must explain to parents their need for information to be sure they are supporting children's comfort and also not lying to children.

"Adopted children should know they are adopted. . . . They need to know as much of their history as is appropriate for their development, told in a way that is respectful of them, of their genetic parents, and of their adoptive parents" (Munsch 1992, 47). Teachers may have had personal experience with adoption through their own family backgrounds, and may need to focus on their own comfort level before helping children explain their circumstances to other children and adults. There are myths and fears about adoption, and teachers need to be sure they are doing nothing to increase these fears.

Include Adoption in the Curriculum

When topics such as babies, family trees, types of families and family resemblance arise in the early childhood classroom, teachers need to include adoption as a concept for children to understand, whether or not there are adopted children in the classroom. Children's books (See Figure

16-20.) about adoption can help children understand that all children deserve parents who can look after them, and that there is both joy and pain in adoption. Modern books focus on honest, sensitive approaches that look at both children's and adults' feelings.

Teachers should be aware that some adopted children will not necessarily have photos of themselves as babies, and plan accordingly when using family materials in curriculum. Some parents whose children are adopted from other countries or cultures may welcome the opportunity to include their child's native culture in classroom activities. These experiences expand children's thinking about the complex subject of families.

Talking to Parents

Heightening their awareness of parental feelings regarding adoption may help teachers prevent insensitive communication. These parents cannot have their relationship to their children affirmed by appearance, "Your son is certainly the absolute image of his dad." Instead, their relationship must be affirmed in less concrete ways: "The baby really watches you." "Your son really enjoys spending time with you."

Talking about "real" parents is insulting to adoptive families who *are* real parents. Instead, where necessary, teachers can refer to "birth" or "biological" parents.

Banish, R. (1992). *A forever family.* New York: Harper Collins.

Bunin, C. and S. (1976). *Is that your sister?* New York: Pantheon Books.

Girard, L.W. (1989). *We adopted you, Benjamin Koo.* Niles, IL: Albert Whitman.

Krementz, J. (1982). *How it feels to be adopted.* New York: Knopf.

Livingston, C. (1978). *Why was I adopted?* Secaucus, NJ: L. Strenck.

Meredith, J. (1971). *And now we are a family.* Boston: Beacon Press.

Rogers, F. (1993). *Adoption.* New York: Putnam.

Rosenberg, M. (1984). *Being adopted.* New York: Lothrop, Lee, and Shepard Books.

Sobol, H.L. (1984). *We don't look like our mom and dad.* New York: Coward-McCann.

Wright, S. (1994). *Real sisters.* Charlottetown, P.E.I., Canada: Ragweed Press.

See also Miles, S.G. (1991). *Adoption literature for children and young adults: an annotated bibliography.* New York: Greenwood Press.

Figure 16-20   Children's books about adoption.

Many adoptive parents have limited information about their children's backgrounds or their lives before adoption. Teachers should make it clear that they welcome any information parents can give them, but that they are focusing on helping the child and family in the current adjustment. Parents may understandably feel sad or even guilty that there are gaps in their knowledge of the child. In many of the adjustments that occur in families after adoption, parents may feel frightened, worried, angry, and stressed in the new situation. Teachers can help best by providing a supportive listening ear.

As newly adoptive parents are getting to know their children day-by-day, teachers can assist by sharing objective observations and specific information about what the child is like while under their care.

Talking With Children

Teachers should be emotionally and cognitively prepared to answer questions from children who have not been adopted as well as from adopted children.

Children might wonder:

- Why do parents give up their children?

- Will it happen to me?

- Will it happen again?

- Why don't I look like my parents?

- What was so bad about me that my mother didn't want me?

Phrases and responses that teachers might use include:

- "Being adopted means Lena had another mother before, but her first mommy couldn't take care of her, so Mrs. Peters is Lena's mommy now."

- "Children need to have parents who can look after them."

- "Real parents are the ones who feed you and put you to bed and take you places and live with you while you grow up" (Munsch 1992, 48).

Offer Resources

Knowledgeable teachers can assist family adjustment by providing books (See Figure 16-21.), information about support groups, and opportunities to meet with mental health professionals experienced with adoption issues.

Anderson, R. (1993). *Second choice: growing up adopted.* Chesterfield, MO: Badger Hill Press.

Bartholdt, E. (1993). *Family bonds: adoption and the politics of parenting.* Boston: Houghton Mifflin.

Berg, B. (1981). *Nothing to cry about.* New York: Seaview Books.

Canape, C. (1986). *Adoption: parenthood without pregnancy.* New York: H. Holt.

Chase, M. (1990). *Waiting for baby.* New York: McGraw-Hill.

Gilman, L. (1984). *The adoption resource book.* New York: Harper and Row.

Hormann, E. (1987). *After the adoption.* Old Tappan, NJ: F.H. Revell Co.

Jewett, C.L. (1978). *Adopting the older child.* Harvard, MA: Harvard Common Press.

Melina, L. (1989). *Making sense of adoption: a parent's guide.* Grand Rapids: Perennial Library.

Plumez, J. (1982). *Successful adoption.* New York: Harmony Books.

Siegel, S. (1989). *Parenting your adopted child.* New York: Prentice Hall Press.

Tukas, M. (1992). *To love a child: a complete guide to adoption.* Reading, MA: Addison-Wesley.

Figure 16-21 Books to suggest to parents about adoption

❖ Summary

Some parents with particular circumstances include parents experiencing separation, divorce, and remarriage; parents of children with special needs; parents of infants; abusive or neglectful parents; and parents who adopt. Teachers working with parents in these circumstances will be challenged to develop new sensitivities in understanding the dynamics and emotional responses of both parents and children in each situation. Teachers must also incorporate necessary classroom behaviors that can help children and skills and knowledge to support parents. In the process of such professional growth, teachers will be able to reach out to help the families who need them most.

❖ Student Activities for Further Study

1. Investigate and gather referral information and brochures on any agencies that exist in your community to:
   - assist or support parents and/or children undergoing separation and divorce, such as counseling services, Parents Without Partners, Big Brothers and Big Sisters, etc.,

- assist parents and their children with special needs, or help in the identification and early intervention process.
- offer support to new parents,
- assist, treat, and/or support in abusive family situations, and
- support adoptive families.

If there are a large number of such agencies, it is useful for each class member to visit one to gather information and report back to the class.

2. Find the state law that defines the legal responsibilities for professionals and paraprofessionals in preschool and child care in your state regarding reporting abuse and neglect. Learn about your local reporting agency. It is helpful to invite a representative of that agency to visit your class.

3. Investigate your library resources for parents and children with special needs. Compile a list of these to have available for parents.

4. If children with special needs are mainstreamed in preschool classrooms in your community, plan a visit to these classrooms or to any specialized schools. Learn what their parent-involvement policies and practices are.

5. Role-play and discuss the following situations:

   a. You are concerned by a four-year-old's aggression and regression in your classroom. The father moved out of the home two months ago. You want to discuss the child's behavior with his mother.

   b. A mother wants to tell you all about how terribly she and the children were treated by her ex-husband.

   c. A child in a recent divorce situation seems totally withdrawn and sad. Your conversation with the child?

   d. A child tells you, "He's not my real daddy, he just married my mother. I hate him." Your response?

   e. A child tells you, "My daddy hit my mommy hard. He scares me when he's so mean to us." Your response?

   f. A child has been observed in explicit sexual activity (not exploration). You want to discuss this with the parent.

   g. A mother of a child with cerebral palsy says, "The doctors say she'll never walk or talk right, but she seems so much better in your class. What do you think?" Your response?

   h. A mother of an infant says, "My mother visited this weekend and says for me not to pick the baby up so much, just to let him cry, so you shouldn't either." Your response?

   i. A mother of a three-year-old who was adopted as an infant requests that you not mention the adoption to other children and parents in the classroom. Your response?

❖ Review Questions

1. List several behaviors in both children and parents associated with the stress of divorce or remarriage.
2. Discuss three of four ways teachers can be helpful to children experiencing divorce or remarriage.
3. Discuss three of four ways teachers can be helpful to parents experiencing divorce or remarriage.
4. Identify three of five possible emotional responses of parents of children with special needs.
5. Describe four of seven ways teachers can work effectively with parents of children with special needs.
6. Discuss typical responses of parents of infants.
7. Identify three of four helpful behaviors for teachers of infants.
8. List two of three factors that can create abusive situations.
9. List any six indicators of abuse and neglect.
10. Identify three of five responsibilities of teachers in situations involving abuse and neglect.
11. Describe ways teachers can support adoptive families.

❖ Suggestions for Further Reading

A. On Divorce and Remarriage

Briggs, B.A., and Walters, C.M. (1985). Single-father families: implications for early childhood educators. *Young Children, 40*(3), 23–27.

Carlile, C. (1991, Summer). Children of divorce: how teachers can help ease the pain. *Childhood Education,* 232–234.

Heatherington, E.M., Cox, M., and Cox. R. (1982). Effects of divorce on parents and children. In M.E. Lamb (Ed.), *Non-traditional families: parenting and child development.* Hillsdale, NJ: Lawrence Erlbaum Assoc. Pubs.

Procidano, M.E., and Fisher, C.B. (Eds.) (1993). *Contemporary families: a handbook for school professionals.* New York: Teachers College Press.

Skeen, P. and McKenry, P.C. (1980). The teacher's role in facilitating a child's adjustment to divorce. *Young Children, 35*(5), 3–14.

Skeen, P., Robinson, B., and Flake-Hobson, C. (1984). Blended families: overcoming the Cinderella myth. *Young Children, 39*(2), 64–74.

B. On Parents of Children with Special Needs

Diamond, K.E. (1994, Spring). Parents who have a child with a disability. *Childhood Education,* 168–170.

Dunst, C., Trivette, C., and Deal, A. (1988). *Enabling and empowering families: principles and guidelines for practices.* Cambridge, MA: Brookline Books.

Gallagher, J.J., Berkman, P., and Cross, A.H. (1983). Families of handicapped children: sources of stress and its ameliorization. *Exceptional Children, 50*(1), 10–19.

Graves, S., and Gargiulo, R. (1989). Parents and early childhood professionals as program partners: meeting the needs of the preschool exceptional child. *Dimensions, 18*(1), 23–24.

Griffel, G. (1991, March). Walking on a tightrope: parents shouldn't have to walk it alone. *Young Children, 46*(3), 40–42.

Turnbull, A.P., and Turnbull, H.R. III. (1990). *Families, professionals and exceptionality: a special partnership.* 2nd ed. Columbus, OH: Merrill Publishing Co.

C. Working With Parents of Infants

Brazelton, T.B. (1984). Cementing family relationships through child care. In L.L. Dittmann (Ed.), *The infants we care for.* (rev. ed.). Washington, D.C.: NAEYC.

Galinsky, E. (1982). Understanding ourselves and parents. In R. Lurie and R. Neugebauer (Eds.), *Caring for infants and toddlers: what works, what doesn't, 2.* Redmond, WA: Child Care Information Exchange.

Greenberg, P. (1991). *Character development: encouraging self-esteem and self-discipline in infants, toddlers, and two-year-olds.* Washington, D.C.: NAEYC.

Lurie, R., and Newman, K. (1982). A healthy tension: parent and group infant-toddler care. In R. Lurie and R. Neugebauer (Eds.) *Caring for infants and toddlers: what works, what doesn't, 2.* Redmond, WA: Child Care Information Exchange.

Wieder, S., (1989, Sept.). Mediating successful parenting: guidelines for practitioners. *Zero to three, X*(1), 21–22.

D. Working with Abusive Parents

McFadden, E.J. (1986). Helping the abused child through play. In *Play: working partners of growth.* Wheaton, MD: ACEI.

Meddin, B.J., and Rosen, A.L. (1986). Child abuse and neglect: prevention and reporting. *Young Children, 41*(4), 26–30.

Wexler, R. (1990). *The real victims of the war against child abuse.* Buffalo, NY: Prometheus Books.

E. Working With Adoptive Families

Brodkin, A.M. (1992, Nov./Dec.). You don't look like your mom! *Scholastic Pre-K Today,* 18–19.

CHAPTER 17

Working to Resolve Troublesome Attitudes and Behaviors

Human nature being what it is, teachers occasionally find themselves dealing with parents whose attitudes and behaviors are difficult to deal with, no matter how positive the teacher's attempts have been. Stress or personality may cause some parents to display responses that range from belligerence to indifference, and either extreme is quite daunting to work with. In addition, any classroom teacher can tell you that particular situations with parents arise regularly enough to become sources of chronic irritation. Such encounters may be so discouraging or threatening that teachers retreat from future efforts to work with parents. But when this happens, children's well-being will suffer, so it is important that teachers develop skills and strategies to help counter the negatives. In this chapter, we will consider reasons for parents' behavior and strategies for approaching them. This does not suggest that there are magical solutions to these difficulties. Rather there are teacher and program responses that may get the teacher through the immediate encounter, and policies or procedures that may prevent recurrences. Perhaps most important of all is the teacher belief that partnership with parents is important enough to keep on trying.

OBJECTIVES

After studying this chapter, the student will be able to

1. discuss reasons for hostile reactions and considerations in dealing with them.
2. discuss reasons for apparent indifference and considerations in overcoming it.
3. discuss over-involvement of parents and ways of dealing with it.
4. discuss several frequent causes of parent-teacher tension and ways of dealing with them.

As professionals, teachers have the responsibility to keep working towards effective relationships with parents, even under very difficult conditions. Perhaps the most difficult circumstances arise when teachers and parents view a situation quite differently. These differences may center on pedagogical issues: differing opinions on appropriate educational goals, curriculum, teaching, or discipline methods. Parental expectations and behaviors may conflict with a teacher's view of her role. Differences arise when teachers try to help parents recognize a characteristic or need of their child that parents don't wish to accept. The uncomfortable feelings that develop in both teachers and parents may make it hard to continue the dialogue to the point where real communication or problem solving can take place.

In general, as a teacher contemplates such situations, it is important to analyze a situation critically from both teacher's and parents' viewpoints; define and break a problem into its component parts to see how each person perceives a situation. In some cases, there may be no solution to the vast differences in perspective or emotional response of teacher and parent; but in others a careful analysis of the dynamics and facts of a situation may help the parties find common ground on which to work together. An important thing for teachers to realize is that dealing with attitudes and values is a long, slow process. There are no instant solutions or successes. An understanding of human growth and development, not just child development, is necessary for a teacher working with a variety of adults at different stages of their unique lives.

❖ Hostility

> In a recent conference, the parent angrily burst out at the teacher, "My son has never had this problem before. If you ask me, there's something wrong with a teacher who can't get a young child to obey her. Don't tell me he needs limits! I think your director should watch *you* more carefully!"

As a teacher responds to this attack, it is important to consider several points.

Hostility as a Mask

Teachers need to realize that everything that seems like hostility may not really be so. Sometimes parents are motivated by genuine concern for their child and questioning the practices or evaluation is a form of healthy self-assertion. The intensity of concern may be expressed in voices that sound angry. Individuals who are not used to being assertive may go too far and appear aggressive instead. Sometimes parents who feel powerless attempt to grab power inappropriately.

Another emotion that may be masked by hostility is the grief parents feel when realizing that their child has a developmental problem or handicap. (See chapter 16.)

> Bearing in mind that a parent may be overwhelmed or upset by the staff's findings or interpretations, one should view parents' defensive reactions more as their method of coping with aroused anxiety than as an attempt to obstruct the proceedings (Losen and Diament 1978, 150).

Parents who feel defensive or guilty about their effectiveness as parents may strongly resist teachers' comments. It is essential that a teacher think about a parent's position before automatically labeling a response as "hostile."

True hostility appears as an individual reacts with anger when dealing with a person seen to be "in authority." A hostile person is defensive, suspicious, assumes that others have unfriendly intentions, and therefore feels impelled to strike the first blow. Such hostile reactions often indicate a carryover of childhood attitudes or earlier experiences with authority.

Hostility Inhibits Communication

When parents are verbally abusive or irrationally angry, it is impossible to communicate effectively. It is a teacher's task to defuse the anger so that communication can begin. Teachers need to avoid being caught up in parents' strong emotions, while making an effort to understand what is behind the feelings. The first step in working with an angry reaction is to accept it. An expressed feeling is real, no matter how distorted the perception of facts that caused the feeling. Accepting someone else's feelings does not mean giving up one's own perspective; it simply means being more sensitive to that of the other. By taking a parent's perspective, a teacher is able to show genuine concern and is more likely to respond appropriately. As a teacher reflects an understanding of a parent's point of view through active listening, a parent realizes that her feelings are recognized.

> "You're really very upset by my comments about Roger's behavior, aren't you?"

The teacher has listened carefully to the concern, asked herself "What is she feeling?", tried to define the emotion being expressed, and reflected that understanding back to the parent to see if she is right. Such feedback may eliminate a parent's need to show more anger because a teacher clearly has picked up on the message and may elicit a response that can clarify a concern in terms of specific details.

> "You bet I'm upset, and I'll tell you, I don't think it's fair to be talking about making him keep rules after all that kid has had on him. With his dad being so strict with him, and then leaving last year, he's had enough to get used to, without you being strict too."

When active listening does not evoke an opportunity to hear the reasons behind the anger, a teacher should continue to reflect back her empathic perception of a parent's response.

> Parent: "Of course I'm upset—anybody would be, to hear a teacher say such things about their child."
>
> Teacher: "It really troubles you to hear the kind of comments I made."
>
> Parent: "It certainly does. It's just not fair—what do you know about it anyway?"
>
> Teacher: "I know there's a lot about Roger I don't know, and I'm counting on you to help me understand. What can you tell me that would help me?" and so on.

Remain Calm

To be able to work through the anger, it is vital that a teacher remain calm in every way. The louder and more vehement a parent's voice, the softer and slower should a teacher speak, being careful that her body language remains open and positive, avoiding, for example, the crossed arms or lack of eye contact that suggest being closed to the parent's position. It helps teachers remain calm when they don't interpret the parents' approach as a personal attack, but as a code for expressing emotions that spring from the parenting role. It is very important that a teacher not become defensive or argumentative and not retaliate verbally, as in the following statement:

> "Look, don't you talk to me about my teaching. If you were doing a halfway decent job with parenting I wouldn't be having these problems in my classroom."

Defensive behavior suggests that the attacker is right and tends to escalate the tension. Responding to a parent's emotion with a teacher's emotion can only lead to an explosive situation. Remaining calm may not be an easy task.

> Professional skins are not significantly thicker than anyone else's. And there are limits to one's ability to remain nonjudgmental in the face of persistence in irrational or inappropriate behavior, despite our best efforts to understand it or tolerate it (Losen and Diament 1978, 150).

Nevertheless, a teacher must continue to maintain composure, and the best chance of doing so is to try to perceive a situation from a parent's perspective and identify with the emotional responses of a parent. Learning to support parents nonjudgmentally, without losing emotional control, is crucial. Professionals do not have the right to lose control with parents. By taking on the role of teachers, they commit themselves to working constructively with those who need assistance.

It is necessary for a teacher to analyze her own emotional responses, determining whether this has become a power struggle and why she feels so strongly about an issue; are there facts involved or only emotional responses?

Teachers, being human, sometimes overlook details or simply make mistakes in dealing with certain situations. This may become a source of hostility or anger in parents. Teachers need to be prepared to admit the mistake or responsibility openly and honestly to parents, empathizing with their frustration and anger, and then sharing a plan to ensure this will not occur again. Such honesty can mitigate the hostility.

> "I don't blame you for feeling so upset with me. This was my mistake, and I'm sorry for it. I'd feel angry too, if I were you. Here is what I plan to do so this doesn't happen again."

It is also important that a teacher not retreat from the anger by suggesting "You'd better talk to the director," or "I won't talk to you unless you stop shouting at me." The potential for communication and learning more about a problem is available here and now. As teachers help parents express feelings and perceptions, they both have an opportunity to see the issues from a different perspective.

Adhere to Facts

As a conversation proceeds, teachers must be careful that any disagreeing statements concern facts and issues, not personalities. In discussing different viewpoints, participants should use descriptive statements, not evaluative ones. It is easier to deal with descriptions, rather than labels. By being objective and factual in the statements made to parents, and by having written observations that support the statements, teachers will sound less judgmental or accusing.

> NOT: "Roger is a very undisciplined, out-of-bounds child."
>
> RATHER: "I'm noticing that it's hard for Roger to keep the rule about hitting others. This week when he was angry with Eddie on three different occasions, he hit him. Do you notice hitting at home?"

Parents would be more likely to respond to the second statement with information and suggestions, while the first statement would likely produce defensive, angry reactions.

Express Concerns Constructively

Teachers need to remember that angry outbursts may be triggered if they approach parents with problems so directly that the only recourse is to attack back in order to protect themselves. It is effective to use more palatable methods, such as "sandwiching" the meat of a problem between two slices of positive, supportive statements regarding a parent's interest and concern.

> "I appreciate how deeply concerned you are for Roger. There's no more important thing for a child than to know his parents care. I'm concerned about his ability to develop some self-control, and I feel sure this is an area that we can work on to come up with some things that might help him."

Using the communication technique of "I-messages" to express concerns allows teachers to express their feelings constructively and so indirectly encourage parents to do so as well. An I-message has three basic parts:

1. "When . . ."—a statement of the behavior that troubles a teacher,
2. "I feel . . ."—a statement of the feeling about the behavior or its consequences,
3. "Because . . ."—a statement of the reason for the concern. (For more on "I-messages," see Gordon 1975.)

So an I-message sounds something like this:

> "When Roger hits other children, I feel frustrated because I'm not able to help him understand our rule about everybody being safe here."
>
> "When Roger forgets our rules, I feel very concerned about his level of self-control."
>
> "When you refuse to discuss these problems, I get upset because the problems seem urgent to me."

Some of the potential explosiveness is removed when feelings are expressed in I-messages, rather than "You-judgments" that focus blame squarely on the other.

> "You're just not helping this situation."
>
> "You're refusing to admit there's a problem."
>
> "You always take Roger's side and refuse to listen to what's really happening."

Respect Parents' Concern

It is important that angry parents know their concerns are taken seriously. These problems are important to a parent and must not be minimized by a teacher.

One way to indicate respect for parents' problems is to write down every complaint, allowing them to truly vent their feelings. When they slow down, teachers can ask if anything else is bothering them, so their list of complaints is exhausted. If teachers then read back the list, using the parents' own words, it suggests that the teacher truly values the concern. Teachers can then ask for any suggestions that parents have for solutions to the problem, and write these down as well. This conveys a valuing for the parents' input, although the teacher is not necessarily committing to follow these courses of action. These actions say that the concerns are important and parents are being listened to. It is also valuable to state that educators don't have all the answers and need all the help they can get.

Reschedule Meeting

On those occasions when all attempts to reduce the amount of anger and facilitate communication fail, it may be wise to reschedule another meeting.

> "I'm not sure we can accomplish anything more today. Could we meet again next Wednesday at this time? Maybe some new ideas will occur to us in the meantime."

It can be useful to invite a colleague or supervisor to sit in on the next conference, since some participant at every conference needs to be free of emotional responses and have skills to help the other participants deal with their emotions quickly and fully. Checking out a situation with a colleague may help a teacher see it from a different perspective.

If the teacher and parent are able to come up with a plan for responding to their mutual problem, it is important to schedule another meeting promptly to attempt to follow-up on the original conversation as an indication of the teacher's sincere desire to work with the parent.

Anger is a powerful emotion, destructive if allowed to rage unleashed, but potentially a strong motivation to examine a situation and work together for understanding and change.

❖ Indifference

> Connie Martinez is concerned about a different kind of behavior. There are a couple of parents in her classroom that she simply can't reach. They seem apathetic, uncaring about their children's needs or the teacher's attempts to involve them in any way.

There are several possible reasons behind apparent indifference. One may be that the overwhelming pressure in parents' lives prevents them from focusing such attention on their child, as much as they care for him. Too many concerns abut basic physical needs may crowd in. A parent who worries that her resources will not stretch to cover both food for the rest of the month and the electric bill has little emotional energy left to care about higher emotional or social needs.

Pressure in parents' lives can come from the opposite end of the socioeconomic spectrum, from having two sets of career demands and the problems of meshing two schedules, relocating households when told to, and continuing to push up the ladder of success. Sometimes there is little time or energy left for personal relationships or development. Such parents are often more than willing to entrust child care to the professionals and to withdraw to more obviously gainful career pursuits.

Parents who feel particularly uncomfortable due to differences in social class or cultural backgrounds may withdraw from a situation and appear indifferent.   Noninvolvement or indifference may indicate an attempt to disguise illiteracy or other problems (Boutte et al. 1992). Some parents may have a high regard for teachers and education, but feel that education is a one-way street and that they have nothing to offer. Other parents may see teachers simply as employees in a low-status occupation and feel there is no need for their involvement in a "baby-sitting" arrangement.

Still other parents who seem indifferent may be adults who missed childhood, who are themselves products of abnormal parenting. Such parents spend their grown-up years attempting to have their own lost needs met by their children, and by doing so raise children whose own needs are never met.

Whatever the reason for parents' lack of interest or involvement, most teachers don't like not being able to reach them. As is human nature, teachers who feel unsuccessful in reaching particular parents often withdraw from them, thereby increasing the distance between them. It is common for teachers to shift the blame from themselves to parents.

> "Well, I'm sure I don't know what's the matter with them—goodness knows I've tried."
>
> "What kind of parents are they anyway—not even caring about their own child enough to come in for a conference."

These responses do not improve a situation. It is more helpful to adopt an attitude that parents are not unreachable, but that teachers have not yet found ways to reach them. Teachers cannot interpret inaccessibility personally. Rejection is something teachers must learn to manage. A positive way to look at rejection is that it is an opportunity to reconsider values or redirect energies. The key is not to give up, but to consider other ways of getting through, reminding oneself of specifics about this particular parent.

Teachers must assess the reasons for parents' unapproachability and consider various ideas to overcome it.

Personal and Economic Pressures

For parents overwhelmed by economic and personal pressures, there is little probability of their becoming involved or less "indifferent" to their children's needs as long as these external pressures exist. The most positive action for a teacher is to be an advocate for these parents, referring them to appropriate agencies for assistance. Such concern and help will lay the basis for trust in a relationship that may develop as these parents' other concerns are lessened.

Career Interests

For parents busy with their own career interests, teachers may emphasize particular techniques to reach them—newsletters that can be read at their convenience, occasional bag lunches with their children issuing the invitation and planned with plenty of advance notice. Opportunities to talk with other upwardly mobile parents may be appreciated as a source of support.

Cultural Differences

With parents who may remain distant because of discomfort with social or cultural differences, teachers must be warm friendly, and casual in their contacts. It may be important to consciously simplify speech styles and vocabulary.

Other parents from similar backgrounds who are more comfortable in a school setting can be helpful in making contact with these parents and personally inviting and accompanying them to informal events. Casual social activities or hands-on workshops (making toys for their children or materials for the classroom) provide less threatening experiences and give a sense of being important in their child's education.

Through genuine indications that a teacher needs and values parents' participation, those parents who feel they have nothing to offer may see that preschool education is not as formidable or as unimportant as they had believed. Persistence can pay off here.

Emotional Pressures

Perhaps the greatest challenge to teachers comes in attempting to reach those parents who are less sensitive to their child's and a teacher's needs because of their own overwhelming emotional needs. This can be any parent at any particular time of her life. Teachers must realize that their expectations for these parents to understand and be involved are often unrealistic. A truly helpful stance is

> to be prepared to accept these parents as they are and to offer them
> not what we need in the way of their involvement in our programs or

what their child needs in parenting, but what the parents need themselves to grow (Rundall and Smith 1982, 73).

What they need is nurturing. These parents need to be accepted for what they are, encouraged for whatever they have done, reinforced for any strength and efforts, and helped to feel understood. As teachers slowly establish a climate of trust with these parents, they should recognize that this relationship may help lessen parents' neediness.

In conversation, teachers focus the discussion on the parents, their concerns and interests. Where possible, teachers should provide services for parents—a cup of coffee when they're looking tired, an opportunity to trade outgrown clothes with another family—as an indication that teachers care for parents and understand their needs. In fact, teachers are creating a dependent relationship, not for the professional's needs, but as a way to assist a parent in establishing a trust relationship. Once a parent exhibits trust in the relationship, a teacher can gradually begin to set limits and demands that would have been too frightening before the relationship was secure.

It may be a long and trying struggle, but by responding to parent's needs, teachers may be able to reach parents who are "unreachable" in ways teachers had first expected to involve them.

❖ Over-Involvement

To teachers struggling to get parents involved in a program or even indicate an interest in their children's welfare, the predicament of over-involvement might seem a lesser problem. But a parent who is too involved in a school situation may hinder his child's move towards independence or do the wrong thing at the wrong time, disrupting his child and the class. This is sometimes the parent who "knows it all," and is full of recommendations or criticisms, or doesn't want to hear a teacher's observations of his child. Sometimes this parent just gets in the way of orderly classroom procedures as he lingers to talk indefinitely, despite a teacher's need to care for the children or set up activities. How does a teacher respond to these behaviors?

Understanding a parent's behavior is a first step to tolerating or dealing with it. A teacher must get to know a particular parent to assess the individual situation and motivation.

Reluctance to Separate

Many parents are overwhelmed because of their own reluctance to separate from their children. Being uncomfortable with separation is a natural experience in the developmental stages of parenthood, but a positive resolution of the conflicting feelings is important for both child and parent.

These parents need particular reassurance that their child is being well cared for. Regular and specific reporting of information helps, as will personal notes and phone calls to share personal anecdotes about their child.

This communication reassures parents that individual attention is paid to their child, and that they are not losing contact with him.

Empathizing frankly with a parent's feelings brings separation into the open.

> "I know there must be a lot of mixed feelings about seeing her grow up—rejoicing at all the new things, sadness at the idea of the baby left behind. It must seem to you sometimes like you're not as close as you once were. But it's just different, isn't it? Believe me, you're still the most important person in her world. Why, just the other day . . ."

Teachers should encourage parents to share their feelings and thoughts, and such communication allows teachers the opportunity to reassure and subtly remind of a growing child's needs.

> "Hard as it is for you, the most loving thing a parent can do is to allow the child some room to move on, feeling stronger about being able to function without you. She needs to know you have enough confidence in her that she can be all right, for a while, without your presence."

When presented with the idea that it is for their child's welfare, many parents try harder to let go.

Unmet Personal Needs

A parent who is over-involved because of unmet personal, social, and emotional needs benefits when a teacher responds with genuine appreciation and praise for his efforts. It is counterproductive to try to stop this involvement, since it is so important for a parent's emotional health, as well as potentially helpful to a school or center.

When a parent's over-involvement in a classroom becomes a problem to a child and teacher, his efforts can be redirected to other areas that are less disruptive—another classroom; working to involve other parents; preparing materials.

The particular strengths of parents should be identified and utilized fully, always with sincere appreciation for the value of their contribution. Positive ways to contribute may be found—an extra pair of hands at lunch time in the infant room, a cozy lap for an upset toddler, gathering the dress-up clothes that need refurbishing, or calling other parents to remind them of an upcoming meeting. Such efforts are not disruptive to a child's independent functioning and allow a parent to feel important to a program.

Insecurities

For a parent who "knows it all" and wants to share his knowledge, a teacher may need to indicate frequently that she considers a parent to be the real expert on his particular child. Sometimes a parent acts this way out of insecurities caused by real or imagined perceptions of a teacher's competence and dominance in a situation. When a teacher emphasizes partnership and defers to a parent's knowledge of his child, parental feelings of unimportance may diminish.

> "You know, parents really know their own children best. I need to know all I can about Johnny, and I appreciate your sharing your knowledge. What can you tell me about his playing in the neighborhood at home?"

Sometimes a parent's information can be acknowledged and shared with others.

> "That's a good tip about those children's books. Could you write that down so I can add it to next month's newsletter? I think a lot of parents would like to know."

Teachers have to realize and acknowledge that in many cases parents really are more knowledgeable than they are. As the parent's knowledge and contribution can be directed in positive channels, her urge to criticize and complain may diminish.

When the "know it all" parent is unable to hear a teacher's points, a teacher must exercise skills of assertiveness and state her position clearly without belittling a parent's ideas or antagonizing and hurting. Teachers who recognize the complexity of human behavior know that a situation may be perceived in a variety of ways, and it is healthy to air all perspectives. This realization often prevents becoming too aggressive in presenting one's views. Assertiveness in a discussion may be helpful; aggressiveness will likely be destructive.

If reluctant to accept the validity of another's viewpoint for information, a parent may be more susceptible to information conveyed by less personal means. Making pertinent articles available to parents allows them to absorb the ideas and make them their own; an exposure to new ideas is accomplished without the resistance that can be inherent in personal discussions.

Lingering to Talk

For a parent who lingers on indefinitely to talk, a teacher should draw clear limits while still making the parent feel welcome.

> After a few minutes of talk, when other responsibilities press, the teacher can say, "I enjoy talking with you, but right now I need to get over to those children at the water table. We'd love to have you stay if you have a few extra minutes. Perhaps you'd like to sit near the book corner—there's always someone looking for a story to be read."

This reassures a parent that his presence is welcomed and provides a chance for him to be useful in classroom life. If he is uneasy about leaving his child, it allows him to observe a teacher and see how busy she really is.

If such patterns continue, a teacher may need to say frankly

"I really want to talk with you, Mr. Jones. It's important to me to hear from you. But arrival time is so busy I'm not able to give you my full attention. Let's see if we can find some time to talk that's less hectic for me. I can be free at naptime, or at my break this afternoon at 3:30.

Specific guidelines help a parent realize the many facets of a teacher's responsibility.

In addition to these troubling attitudes and behaviors, there are several situations that frequently arise in centers and cause irritation for the staff involved. Let's consider some ways centers deal with these situations.

❖ Frequent Causes of Tension Between Parents and Teachers

Late Parents

Among recurrent problems that annoy teachers is the frequent late arrival of parents picking up their children. At the end of a long and tiring day, this becomes a final insult for hard-working teachers and is a cause of resentment and relationship breakdowns. If teachers confront parents at the time of lateness, there is potential for explosive responses on both sides.

This is one situation that is probably best handled by directors, rather than by teachers themselves. It is a good idea for timely pickups to be stressed in the parents' handbook and in orientation information. Some centers ask parents to sign a contract agreeing that, since staying with children after school closing times is a personal service to the family, late fees will be paid directly to the teachers who use personal time to stay and care for children. Others find that a late fee must be more than modest, since some parents find it worth it to pay a small fee and have extra time. A substantial fee, such as $5.00 every ten minutes, often eliminates the problem. With parents who are habitually late, some directors find it necessary to ask parents to make contingency plans or provide lists of people who can be called to pick up children when parents are late. Termination warnings and follow-through may be a final step. It is important for late policies to be strict, clearly communicated, and consistently administered by those in charge, leaving teachers and children free of the emotional issue.

Releasing Children to Adults Who are "Under the Influence" or Noncustodial Parents

A very uncomfortable and potentially dangerous situation arises when teachers are asked to release children under their care to adults they suspect to be impaired by drugs or alcohol, or to an adult who does not have legal custody of the child.

The best protection against such occurrences is to have written policies that are discussed at the time of enrollment. Complete information on persons permitted to pick up children should be on file with a verifying signature, and parents should understand that any changes must be made in writing, with the signature that can be compared. Identities should be confirmed with picture identification. Teachers should not hesitate to delay the departure procedure to confirm the legitimacy of any person's claim. Certified copies of court orders regarding custody should be made available for the center's files; verbal requests of one parent to prohibit access of another parent are not valid without a court document. Teachers should not be put in a position of having the responsibility to decide which parent has legal custody without such a document. If asked to release children to noncustodial parents, teachers should try to reach the custodial parent, and law enforcement if necessary, to protect all the children in the teacher's care as well as herself.

If a teacher feels that the adult picking up a child is not in a condition to be driving, he can: call other authorized adults; call law enforcement officials; or pay for a cab (a requirement for reimbursement can be part of a parent contract [Cohen 1993]). In either case, the concern is to protect children under teacher care.

Sick Children

Another frequent cause of home-school friction is parents' disregard for policies that exclude sick children. It is, of course, understandable that parents are sometimes overwhelmed by the difficulty of finding substitute care for sick children when parents feel that they must be at work themselves. Nevertheless, teachers cannot be expected to allow sick children into their classrooms, knowing the danger of the spread of infections and the special needs of children who don't feel well enough to participate in the usual routine. Clearly stated policies may help with this problem also. Parent handbooks and orientation information should state specific conditions which demand exclusion from the classroom, as well as expected parent responses when called to pick up sick children. It is probably useful to require parents to file plans and names of providers for sick child care during the application process. Many parents would not consider this eventuality until a time of crisis unless directed to do so at the outset.

Teachers can and should empathize with parents who are torn between child's and employer's needs, while gently focusing on the sick child's needs and holding firm to policies.

> "I know how hard it is to have to be at work when you wish you could be home looking after Jessica. I also know how difficult it is to

> find someone who will agree to look after a sick child. I wish we could help you, but our policy on her staying home for at least twenty-four hours after a fever is there to protect Jessica—she just won't feel up to being here and her health is extra vulnerable too."

It is important not to interpret parents' actions in bringing sick children to the center or reluctance to leave work to come and get a sick child as poor parenting or signs of indifference. It is more likely desperation at the role conflict of parent and worker.

As center staff discover community resources that can assist parents needing care for sick children, directors can post the information and notify parents. Care of sick children of working parents has become a community issue. Some companies and communities have created linkages between medical facilities and personnel and the child-care community to ease the problem (Jacobs 1992).

End-of-Day Problems

When parents, children, and teachers come together at the end of the day, there can be problems created by the transition, magnified by fatigue. Children sometimes test and evade parents, almost as if challenging them to take charge again. Parents sometimes demand information and answers from teachers, again appearing to challenge how the day has actually gone. From their side, teachers may have reports of negative behavior they feel are necessary to make. Fragile relationships can be stretched at this time.

What can teachers do to make the end of the day less stressful for everyone? Part of the solution may lie in preparation for the transition.

Quiet activities such as reading books or working puzzles should fill the last period of the day. This way both teachers and children have a chance to have a period of calm at the end of the day. While children are quietly occupied, teachers can be free to do some of the closing chores, so they are not feeling rushed in hectic clean-up when parents arrive. Teachers can post summaries of the classroom and/or individual child's day, so that parents can get some answers to their questions by reading the notice-board when they enter. If teachers help children gather their belongings or get partly dressed, this assists parents and children to be able to move toward home-going.

The end of the day is probably not the best time to discuss behavior problems. Parents who are continually given negative reports about their children at pick-up time are not being helped to feel positively about either their children or the teachers. Teachers need to avoid the temptation to give daily reports of negative behaviors when everyone is tired and least likely to be receptive to sensitive discussion. A better strategy is to arrange a sit-down discussion for a later time.

> "Mrs. Alexander, I think it would be useful for you and me to have a chance to talk away from the classroom. I know you've had questions about Roger, and there are some things I'd like to share too. Can we find a time this week? Perhaps if you'd come in twenty minutes or so before your usual time, I could arrange for Miss Phillips to be in the classroom."

Such a conversation is likely to be more productive than an at-the-door confrontation between harried parents and teachers.

Parents Who Ask for Special Treatment

Teachers are frequently annoyed by parents' requests for services or attention for their children that go beyond typical classroom practices.

> "Jane's father asked if we can let her stay in today when the other children go out to the playground, since she's just getting over her cold."
>
> "Jeremy's grandmother wants him not to take a nap today because they want him to sleep in the car when they leave for their trip. Now how am I supposed to do that—he'll bother everybody else."
>
> "Another toy from home—her Mom says she just wanted to let her bring it, even though she knows it's against our rules."

Rather than simply being irritated and refusing the requests arbitrarily, teachers may need to remember that early childhood centers are there to provide support services for families, and families have a right to define some of the individual services they need. Teachers should consider how the request might be provided, rather than immediately refusing. Could Jane stay in with another class? Could Jeremy spend some time with books in the director's office? A cooperative stance may find a solution satisfactory for everyone.

Those requests that have no solution need to be explained to parents, so they understand the problems their requests make for the center. Clearly communicated policies can offer support for the teacher's position.

> "We'll keep her toy in her cubby so it will be safe. But she can show it to her friends at group-time."

But it is most important to remember that families do have individual, unique needs, and arbitrary refusal of all special requests does not recognize this.

Disagreement over Readiness

A current issue which is emotionally charged for the parents and teachers involved is the issue of readiness for children moving on, usually into elementary school situations.

"I can't believe it. We've been planning all along for Tammy to start kindergarten this fall—her birthday is in August, well before the cut-off date. And at last I was planning to go back to my job full-time—both my boss and I have been counting on it. Then the teacher calls me in for a conference and tells me she's not 'ready,' all because they gave her some test and she couldn't tell the difference between upper- and lower-case letters. Letter, for Pete's sake. She's as smart as can be, and gets along just fine with other kids. I can't believe they can do this to us."

More and more parents are getting the kind of news that Tammy's mother just received. As school programs need to demonstrate improved quality and accountability, there is a growing tendency to use standardized test results to dictate placement decisions. School systems nationwide are using various types of tests to assess children prior to or after the kindergarten year. Unfortunately, this often leads to practices that are inappropriate considering the age and developmental level of the children involved. Testing narrows the curriculum, as teachers teach to prepare children to succeed on tests. Many important early childhood skills are not easily measured by standardized tests, so social, emotional, and physical development and learning are not given equal importance in making decisions about readiness. Standardized group and individual testing is inappropriate for young children, who often don't have good test-taking skills, such as sitting still, being quiet, and following a series of directions, often to write or make particular marks. Young children are growing and learning so rapidly that there is great potential for obtaining inaccurate test results, and thus mislabeling children. The concern narrows down to one central issue: "Should we expect young children to conform to the set expectations of the public schools, or should those schools tailor their programs to accommodate the needs of all children?" (Freeman 1990, 29)

The best information about readiness comes from systematic observations by trained teachers, along with information from parents, who know their children better than anyone else and should be active participants in the assessment process. What this means is that teachers as well as parents should work against practices that exclude children's own parents from providing meaningful input into decisions that affect families and the educational future and self-esteem of children. Together they can become advocates of developmentally appropriate practices that are not potentially harmful for young children.

If teachers find themselves working in situations that use arbitrary (and often proven invalid) test results to decide readiness, they must realize that parents will find the decisions painful and disruptive to the family's plans and image of the child. Discussions of the findings must be careful and specific, so that parents carry away no misunderstandings about future prognoses for learning.

Teachers can give parents specific information and guidelines about what is developmentally appropriate and what is not, perhaps helping them become advocates to work for change in community school practices. Teachers can convey support for the parents' perceptions of their child, always indicating that parents are the real experts on their children. It may help parents to hear of the evidence that many children, especially (but not always) boys, may benefit greatly by the additional time which the school system is giving them, although the gift is arbitrary and unappreciated at the time. Decisions made when the child is four or five may have great impact when the child is in junior high school, for example. If this sounds as if the recommendation is that the teacher should sympathize with the parent who is left out of the decision-making process and forced to accept the school's view of readiness, that is correct. Teachers should not lend support to practices that are developmentally inappropriate for children and families.

On those occasions when teachers find themselves in disagreement with parents' perceptions of children's abilities and developmental levels, it will be wise to bring in a third party to observe the child and join the conversation. Another perspective may help both parent and teacher approach the situation from a fresh viewpoint.

❖ Summary

Teachers may encounter troublesome behaviors and attitudes that are personally annoying and professionally discouraging. In each case, a teacher's first step should be to attempt to identify the feelings or circumstances that might be the cause. A stance that is directed towards solutions rather than accusations, is important. Meeting these needs constructively will eliminate some of the destructive reactions, including teacher frustration.

For a teacher who makes genuine efforts to understand and problem-solve, and still finds situations that seem to have no solution, remember that you are not alone. Any teacher has had similar experiences that sometimes linger in memory long after forgetting more positive experiences. It is important to learn as much as possible from these negative experiences and to keep on trying!

Many teachers find that recording their feelings, perceptions, and experiences in working with parents is an invaluable tool for their own growth. Informal notes or journal entries document concerns, needs, and progress, and pinpoint areas that need attention. Such personal notes, meant purely for a teacher's use, provide both an emotional release and evidence that her efforts are effective.

❖ Student Activities for Further Study

1. Role-play, and then discuss with your classmates, the following situations where teachers are faced with hostile reactions.

   a. Mother says, "I refuse to talk to you any more. You're just plain wrong about Sarah—she's a very bright child."

    b. "How dare you ask me so many questions about my child? It's none of your business."

    c. "I want to talk to your director. If you were doing your job properly, there would be no problem with Melvin. She should know how really incompetent you are."

    d. "If you ask me, you want me to do your job for you. You can't handle him in the classroom, so you want me to get tough with him at home."

    e. "As long as I'm the one paying the bill for child care, I want things done as I ask. I insist that you get busy and teach Barbara to read this year before she goes to kindergarten. Are you saying I don't know what's best for my own child?"

    f. "What is this stuff about readiness? I know my own child. I say she's ready for kindergarten, and I don't care what your test results say."

❖ Review Questions

1. Discuss possible reasons for apparently hostile responses.
2. Describe three of five considerations for teachers dealing with hostile reactions.
3. Discuss three of four possible reasons for apparent indifference; for each, identify a consideration for teachers' overcoming indifference.
4. Discuss three of four possible reasons for over-involvement; for each, identify ways of working with these parents.
5. Describe consideration for dealing with several causes of parent-teacher tension.

❖ Suggestions for Further Reading

Carter, M. (1988, March). Face-to-face communication: understanding and strengthening the partnership. *Child Care Information Exchange, 60,* 21–25.

Fredericks, A.D. (1988, Nov./Dec.). *Rejecting rejection.* Teaching K–8, 18–20.

Galinsky, E. (1988, March). Parents and teacher-caregivers: sources of tension, sources of support. *Young Children, 43*(3), 4–11.

___. (1990, July). Why are some parent/teacher partnerships clouded with difficulties? *Young Children, 45*(5), 2–3, 38–39.

Grollman, E.A., and Sweder, G.L. (1988). *The working parent dilemma: how to balance the responsibilities of children and careers.* New York: Harper and Row. (worth recommending to harried parents.)

Katz, L.G. (1992). Readiness: children and their schools. *The ERIC Review,* 2(1), 2–6.

Morgan, E.L (1989, Jan.). Talking with parents when concerns come up. *Young Children, 44*(2), 52–56.

___. (1988, Jan.). Prickly problems #1 the late parent. *Child Care Information Exchange, 59,* 16.

CHAPTER 18

Looking at Parent-Involvement Programs that Work

This text has offered a rationale for working as partners with parents in early education and has considered numerous strategies and practices that may open and enhance the communication process. It remains for teachers and programs to create their own parent-involvement programs, to respond in the ways that seem most appropriate to the particular needs of their populations.

OBJECTIVES

After studying this chapter, the student will be able to

1. understand the ways various early education programs function to involve parents in their programs.

Some of you may already know of some good programs for children and their families that exist around the country. Child-care programs vary a good deal in the way they look and function, depending on the needs of the populations they serve, amount of funding and staff available, philosophy, and goals. Each center must create its own patterns that work well for the staff and families concerned. As centers consider ideas to try, it may be useful to look at some programs that work effectively with children and families.

❖ Open Door School, Charlotte, North Carolina

Located in the building of its sponsor, the Unitarian Church of Charlotte, the Open Door School offers a rich, creative program for preschool children. The school was established in 1966 as a morning program for three-, four-, and five-year-old children at a time when no public kindergarten and little preschool education existed in the city. When no integrated schools of any kind were available, Open Door encouraged the enrollment of children of all races, religions, economic levels, and ethnic origins. More recently, Open Door was one of the first programs in the area to adopt the ideas of the anti-bias curriculum developed at Pacific Oaks by Louise Derman-Sparks. Teachers have kept parents involved in this process. As community needs evolved, so did the structure of the Open Door School. Several years ago, a parent-cooperative program for two-year-olds was added, as was a full-day program for three- and four-year-olds, who come together for lunch, nap, and afternoon activities from their morning classrooms. Open Door was also the first center in its city to be accredited by NAEYC, and has undergone two reaccreditations.

From the beginning, working with parents has been a part of the Open Door philosophy, and now parents who want to be actively involved in their children's preschool experience deliberately seek out Open Door, for themselves as well as their children. As one parent said, "We feel like it's our place too." (See Figure 18-1.)

How does this good feeling come about? The director says, "We work at it." For parents, Open Door's written philosophy states that the school "acts as a resource on a professional level: teacher to parent; educates parents about child development through workshops, discussion groups, and two-year-olds' Parent Co-op classes; alerts parents to events related to children, parents, and education; maintains a library of child development information of interest to parents; provides a support system of other parents: a basis for friendships; assists with tuition through Open Door's scholarship program for low-income families." For teachers, it is a stated part of

Figure 18-1 From the beginning Open Door has been a place where children of diverse racial and cultural backgrounds have come together—and where younger siblings can be welcomed to play. Courtesy Christine Shamel.

their job descriptions to "establish and maintain an open and healthy relationship with parents; to visit at his/her home, each child in the class before school starts or immediately thereafter; to hold parent/teacher conferences twice a year, once in the fall and once in the spring; to attend parent meetings." New staff members undergo an orientation week before school opens for each of their first two years that includes discussions on working with parents and a workshop on parent-teacher conferences. In fact, many of the staff are former or current parents.

The two-year-old program, meeting two consecutive mornings per week, initially involves parents by requiring them to participate in the classroom on a rotating basis along with paid teachers. Both fathers and mothers actively participate with teachers and children in the classroom, setting a pattern for a high level of involvement that carries over into the following years when such regular participation is not required, only invited.

Before they enter the two-year-old classroom, these participating parents are given a three-hour workshop that covers topics such as typical developmental behaviors of two-year-olds, what to expect in the classroom, what is forbidden in the classroom, and who does what, including who will step in if a child of an involved parent has a problem (the parent). Despite this preparation, many participating parents later admit they approached the experience with hesitation, wondering if it would work—would they know what to do, or get in the way, or do something wrong in front of the teachers. But after being in the classroom, the questions vanished. The director says she is frequently asked how it works to have the parent co-op aspect to the two-year-old program—"Don't you find the children cry or are clingy?" "Sometimes," she responds, "and that's ok." Parents and children together are learning to trust and be comfortable.

Open Door is a very comfortable place. Teachers, parents, and children are all on a first-name basis, and there is a drop-in atmosphere. When parents bring children in or pick them up, they linger and chat—with teachers, other parents, and other children. (See Figure 18-2.) A teacher new to the staff commented on how impressed she'd been in the beginning of school to hear parents comment—"Look how he has grown" or "Hasn't she settled down!"; their frequent contacts have brought them to know and care for each child. Parents form an extended family between families and the school, with parents arriving at the same time in late afternoon for relaxed conversation on the playground or to pick up another child with their own to take to a Children's Theater matinee, much as a relative would.

Casual as it seems, there is careful thought about what will work well for children and their families. Before children enter the program, teachers make a brief, informal home visit to get to know them. Parents fill in an acquaintance sheet with space for both mother and father to answer such questions as "What do you enjoy most about your child?" "What is your method of setting limits for your child?" "Where do you experience your greatest difficulty with your child?" Parents have a group meeting before school begins to introduce them to the school's philosophy and practices and to discuss issues of separation.

Open Door's gradual easing-in-program allows enough time for children and parents to become comfortable before parents move away. On the

Figure 18-2 Open Door is a comfortable place, where parents feel free to sit and chat with teachers. Courtesy CPCC Media Production—Mike Slade.

first day, the session is shortened and parents stay the entire time. There are several more shortened, small group sessions before the whole group comes together and stays for the full session. A coffee room is there for parents to meet each other and to be available if they are needed. Teachers are sensitive to parents' concerns and come out of the classroom to let them know how the children are doing: "He's crying, but I think he'll be OK," "It's not him you hear," "I think it might be a good idea for you to come back in the classroom for a while." One parent commented that this kind of experience really helped build her trust in the teacher, the idea that she could count on the teacher to tell her the truth. Teachers are also sensitive to parents who are just not ready to leave their children and allow them to take as much time as they need.

Communication is worked at. Though most children arrive by car pool, parents escort the two-year-olds and all-day children into their classrooms every day, as the school feels it is important to have a direct transition for these children. The car-pool pace is relaxed enough to allow for some interchange, and most parents come into the classroom two or three times a week. (See Figure 18-3.) The school feels it is important that parents make this connection and encourages them to do so. Parents are given teachers' home phone numbers and encouraged to call. The school sends out newsletters, individual teachers send out newsletters (often quite elaborate ones with wonderful anecdotes of what children have said and done). One teacher sends home personal letters about each child that are much appreciated.

Figure 18-3 An effort is made to make even the car-pool drop-off a time for relaxed communication. Courtesy CPCC Media Productions—Mike Slade.

On February 11th we looked out the nap room windows while getting up and saw rain drops forming as ice on the bushes.   Brendan announced decisively, "Those are called ice berries."

We got new sand.   Jonathan proclaimed, "It's almost like cornbread."

Jonathan's dad, Dean, and Uncle Jack set up a small tent and the next day we figured out how to make one with our old bedspread. Rae's dad, Brad, brought Otis, his synthesizer; we each improvised a tune and sang a cool round of "Rudolph" and "Jingle Bells."

We are creating a collection of pictures to look at each time we recall or plan for a trip.   Seth and Andrew have promised pictures of their mountain homes and Jonathan will get us one from his Wrightsville Beach first-time-in-a-motel-trip. When you travel away, please bring us a folder with a picture or mail a postcard to share a spare photo. If you have a picture (photo or something from a brochure, etc.) of a place your family is planning to visit, please send it in ahead of time; we want to share the anticipation as well as the memories.

A parent-school relations committee has been established to share information, not set policies or design curriculum. The committee is meant to be another option for parents to express themselves or get information for those who don't want to go through the current avenues of teacher or director. Two suggestions that have been acted upon include parents' wishes to have direct fund raising methods rather than sales, and so on, and the publishing of the Parent Council meeting minutes for all parents. Teachers convey the message that they care about each child and his family and value the communication with them. Parents respond by growing closer, by sharing information voluntarily—as one teacher said, "not because I'm the expert, but because I'm a member of the family."

This emotional response is reciprocal. As one teacher said, "I find myself investing lots more in individual children than I have at other places I've worked. Everything I do with William matters—I can't get rid of William in six months, he's not mine alone. I've got the whole family. I know the family is committed; these parents belong to the school. The parent is no longer an `it,' but has become a person. It becomes really hard when they're no longer with us." (See Figure 18-4.)

Most of the commitment to working with families is demonstrated informally, on a day-to-day basis. Organized events tend to be fairly low-key: a December holiday party for parents only, for which the children make cookies and punch and gifts; a Thanksgiving feast, again prepared by the children, which parents may attend; an end of the year pot-luck lunch on the playground. The parents in the full-day program have standing invitations for lunch and also have a pot-luck supper in the summer, which families who are both leaving and entering the program attend. Parents are invited to classrooms to share interests, time for field trips, and so on.

Figure 18-4 Open Door families really belong to the school. Courtesy Connie Glass.

Parent education meetings vary according to a needs assessment each year. Each class has an in-class evening parent meeting in October that continues the discussion of philosophy and practices and helps the individual teacher emphasize involvement.

One teacher found that by emphasizing the importance of father involvement at the fall meeting, she later had 100 percent of her fathers appear for conferences. Conferences are scheduled twice a year, fall and spring, at hours during the day and early evening that fit parents' schedules. One teacher scheduled conferences over a cup of coffee in a local restaurant when it proved to be a more convenient place to meet.

Parents volunteer labor for workdays. The director tells of a project a year or so ago when the playgrounds and equipment had to be moved due to an addition on the church. Most of the parents worked for four consecutive Saturdays in temperatures over 100 degrees. At the end of one of these back-breaking days, one parent thanked the director, saying it was the closest he'd ever been to a barn-raising, a wonderful experience of being together with others who have a common goal—"our children." (See Figure 18-5.)

The staff at Open Door is forthright about letting parents know how and what they can do—a "Talent" list and a "Wish" list hang in the office, along with volunteer sign-up sheets. A newsletter jokes every third sentence—"We can use anything." (See Figure 18-6.)

> Rae spent a large part of the afternoon dragging a ragged, stringy rope. (We use absolutely everything.) . . . Heath invented a game of rolling hickory nuts through the big, black plastic tube. (We make use of highly unlikely objects.) . . . Janelle stirred silently in the beat up cooker that has no handle. (We can find a use for . . .)

A booklet of loving, funny, and serious anecdotes about their children was sent home by the full-day program last summer. "The News from Late

Figure 18-5 Working together to build a playground created a sense of community for parents. Courtesy Christine Shamel.

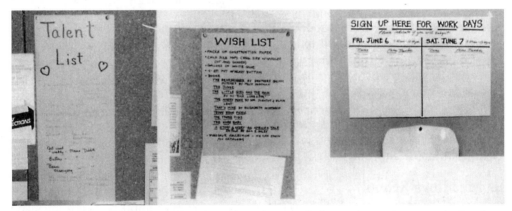

Figure 18-6 Open Door lets parents know how they can help—and parents respond. Courtesy CPCC Media Productions—Mike Slade.

Afternoon," organized under such slightly tongue-in-cheek headings as "Scientific Achievements," "Family and Society," and "Business and the Economy," must have delighted every parent, with the evidence of observing and listening to the children with loving care. It concluded with words that seem to speak for Open Door: "There is much more, but by now you should have gotten the message: you have enriched our lives by sharing your children and yourselves with us. That's why, instead of just "Goodbye," it's fun to be able to say, "We'll be right here tomorrow."

Open Door is finding ways to see parents and teachers as partners in the process of child rearing.

❖ Fair Meadows School, Converse, Texas

A pre-kindergarten program just outside of San Antonio, Texas, in the small town of Converse, has found ways to pull parents from segments of the population who are typically uncomfortable with teachers and school settings into involvement and participation. The Fair Meadows School in the Judson Independent School District evolved from an old elementary school to a setting with small groups of children with special needs. In the mid 80's the state mandated that pre-K programs be established and funded by local school systems for children from low-income backgrounds and/or those who use English as a second language. In fact the state mandated that three-year-olds be added in 1992.

The state guidelines did not include provision for parent involvement, but the teaching staff of the new pre-K program set up at Fair Meadows agreed that it would be "just putting on a band-aid" to try to do the task without including parents. Their goals for involving parents are two-fold: to help parents understand their children's developmental needs and to make school a comfortable place for both parents and children. The philosophy is that parents are the child's most important teachers, and helping parents understand and become comfortable in the school system is an important teacher's role.

Parents must take the first step by registering their children for the program. (Notices of registration are sent out from schools with older children, particularly those eligible for the free lunch program.) On registration day, parents bring their children to school where they meet the teachers, who arrange for subsequent home visits. Over 180 children are served in two three-hour, half-day sessions, morning and afternoon. Many of the children are from Hispanic backgrounds—Mexican and Puerto Rican—though there are Vietnamese, Russian, Hungarian, and Philipino families as well.

The home visits made before school begins are an important component in establishing the comfortable relationship with parents and children. Many parents are not comfortable with the teacher coming into the home. Often older siblings help with the conversation. When teachers dare to use their broken Spanish, many parents are a little more at ease speaking their imperfect English.

Teachers use the visits for two main purposes. One is to learn about families and the particular characteristics and interests of the child. On a form completed after the home visit (see Figure 18-7), teachers record pertinent information, such as the child's attitude towards the teacher, family members' attitudes, a description of the child's home—yard, room, play area, and other helpful hints. The second reason is to inform and prepare parents and children for the school experience. Teachers take a packet with a variety of written materials, including a copy of the child's schedule to "give you a good picture of his time at school, particularly when he shrugs and says he did 'nothing' during school time." A copy of the units of discussion helps parents see the topics children will be learning about. A list of

---

Record of Home Visit

Teacher's Name _____

Child's Name _____ Time _____ Date _____

Family members present:

Distinguishing characteristics of child:

Child's attitude toward teacher:

Child's home — yard, room, play area, etc.:

Pertinent information about parents or family members:

Family members' attitude:

Questions asked:

Helpful hints — interest of child, etc.:

Day child will start school:

Length of visit:

Comments:

Figure 18-7 Home visit report form. Courtesy Fair Meadows School; Dianne Jurek, Sharon MacDonald, Carol Vogel, Karen O'Connor.

supplies needed by children and an inventory for parent participation are included. One teacher has created a photo album of children involved in classroom activities to carry along, so she can talk parents and children through a typical day, showing children riding the bus, playing in various interest centers such as sand, paint, and dress-up, and showing parents acting as resources in the classroom, cooking tortillas and eggrolls.

As is true with many parents today, teachers at Fair Meadows have discovered that most parents have expectations for the education of young children that are often developmentally inappropriate, wanting to rush them into early academics. The classrooms at Fair Meadows reflect the belief that four-year-olds learn best through a variety of active child-initiated play choices. Attractive and creative materials are displayed in separate interest centers. From the beginning, through picture and conversation, the value of play is emphasized. The theory is communicated informally, and the emphasis is on building rapport that will allow parents to come to trust the teacher and the school.

Most of the children come by bus from widely separated geographic areas. This means that teachers have to work especially hard at keeping home-school communication going. Teachers give out their home phone numbers and encourage parents to call. Each week a folder containing the child's work is carried home on the bus. There is a sheet for parents to return, in the empty folder, with space for parent comments. Teachers send frequent newsletters, including both updates on classroom activities and ideas for activities to do at home. Teachers may drop by homes that seem to need more contact. Conferences are held twice a year at school, with teachers working with parents' needs to schedule them, and sometimes holding them at home if necessary. Social activities for the entire family are held: a party at Christmas and an end-of-year picnic in the park.

The real success story, however, has been in the parent club. During the program's first year of operation, the staff had offered an official "Parent-Teacher Government" type of association, complete with elected officers and dues. What they discovered is that this did not work with the particular parent population they served. Parents did not come. As staff investigated the reason for this lack of interest, they found there were several reasons for which solutions could be found. The logistics of work, transportation, and child care presented problems for parents, many of whom are young and single. The difficulties with work schedules and transportation were solved by offering the same program three times in the same day, at 8:15 A.M., 12:30 P.M., and 6:45 P.M. (See Figure 18-8.) That way, parents who attended the day segments could ride on the bus with their children. A connection was made with the child development classes at the high school to provide students for child care. (See Figure 18-9, page 414.)

Perhaps the greatest difficulty, though, was that these were parents from outside the mainstream who were not comfortable in schools and organizations. So the group was called a "Parents' Club," with no dues or officers or formality, but emphasis on friends, games, door prizes, and fun, with learning on topics suggested by the parents at the initial meeting in September. (See Figure 18-10, page 414.)

By learning theory in an informal setting and manner, parents who may be resistant at first come to find that it really works! Staff have considered using materials packaged for parent education groups, such as the STEP kit, but feel there are advantages to being able to custom design their program to parents' needs and interests. Parents are in charge of refreshments for the club and help coordinate necessary arrangements.

The club has truly become a place where parents can begin to strengthen their friendships with teachers and other parents. Many now carpool together, and lots of fathers come too. Some parents interpret for others. Because many families are new to the area, teachers act as an informal referral to community resources. One special aspect has been the inclusion of the parents of the special needs early childhood classes. In meeting together, the parents have discovered that the likenesses in their children are greater than the differences. This has been an important realization for those parents who might otherwise become focused on their child's disability.

Because the daytime meetings extend over the whole school day, there is time for additional activities for parents who come in then. Teachers take

Fun!   Prizes!   Games!

Learning!   Food!   Friends!

Preschool Parents Club

When?   Tuesday, January 30   8:15 a.m., 12:30 p.m.
                                          or 6:45 p.m.

What?   A speaker from Family Focus, Safety Through
                   Assertive Response will teach us how to help
                   our children with "tough issues" like kidnapping
                   and sexual abuse. A very important meeting!

Child care will be offered for the 6:45 p.m. meeting.
Children must be registered in advance for child care.
Please complete and return the attached registration form.

Please register the following children for child care on January 30.

Names (Including first & last name)   Ages

This form must be returned by Friday, January 26.

Figure 18-8 Offering the same programs at three different times allows parents to
come despite work and family responsibilities. Courtesy Fair Meadows School.

Figure 18-9 Child development students from the high school provide child care while parents meet. Courtesy Dianne Jurek.

Figure 18-10 The emphasis is on informal learning and social interaction. Courtesy Dianne Jurek.

turns through the morning and afternoon spending time and doing activities with parents for thirty minutes or so while the teacher assistant is in the classroom with the children. Frequently the staff help with "make it-take it" sessions where parents create books and games to use at home with their children. Classrooms are equipped with special observation booths so that parents may spend a period observing their children busy in the school setting. Six different parent observation guides are available, so parents may consider their child's progress in the areas of language development, creative expression, expression of emotion, and social interaction. (See Figure 18-11.)

Parent Observation
Evaluate Your Child in the School Situation

Note the behavior of your child when with a group of children.

What is his/her attitude toward other children? Note particularly: Evidence of courtesy, leadership, initiative, over-agressiveness, over-suggestibility.

What type of response does he/she show to authority?

Does he/she seek companionship? Does he/she appear to avoid it?

How far does he/she appear to stand up for his/her own rights?

How far does he/she seem to be influenced by the behavior of other children? Has he/she developed a sense of property rights or fair play?

To what extent will he/she cooperate with the group? Does he/she seek attention unduly? Is he/she shy?

Notice the behavior of your child with that of other children of the same age and realize the difference or maturity which he/she has reached in his social adjustments.

Figure 18-11   One of several guides for parent observation created by the staff. Courtesy Fair Meadows School.

What are the benefits of these opportunities for teachers and parents to build rapport and become comfortable as they share and learn new ideas? For parents, there is a chance to move away from being shy, hesitant, and lacking in knowledge of even basic things that can help their children function within the school system. For teachers, there is the excitement and satisfaction of watching this happen. As one parent described her relationship with a particular parent, "It all goes back to that home visit that establishes rapport. In her own home, she wasn't afraid, and she came to know that I'm her friend. It gives me an opportunity to slide in suggestions that she takes, because she knows it helps Don, it helps her, and she can help me understand Don. Other schools scared her off—she was afraid of them."

In the atmosphere of rapport and support, teachers are able to understand and work with the whole family more effectively. A teacher shared this example. "One of the girls in my classroom got her feet wet when the children were building a channel to direct the waterflow on the playground." (Fair Meadows has creative, permanent, outdoor learning centers in the warm Texas climate.) "I was disturbed to hear the next day that she had been spanked for this. Because I have a relationship with her mother, I was able to call to explore this. The mother explained she had indeed spanked the child for this, because she gets sick when her feet are wet." Despite the teacher's explanations of illness being caused by germs and not wet feet, the mother held firm to her culturally held view. When the teacher pointed out that the child did not always become ill when her feet were wet in the bathtub or swimming pool, the mother patiently explained this was because her head was wet too, and that balanced it out. The quick-thinking teacher offered to dampen the child's head at school the next time wet feet occurred. Mother gratefully agreed, and there have been no more post-water-play spankings.

Because teachers have been willing to be flexible and adapt to parents' situations and ideas, Fair Meadows School has been able to support young children and their parents towards success as they take their first important steps in the school system.

❖ Senate Employees' Child Care Center, Washington, D.C.

Within sight of the Capitol building in Washington, D.C. is the Senate Employees' Child Care Center, a nonprofit child development facility that is both a model for quality child care and proof that a parent-governed center (a variation on the parent cooperative model) can work successfully in child-care programs for busy working parents. Opened in February, 1984, the center is a result of efforts by working parents who are Senate employees, and some senators and their wives, who focused attention on changing family needs and the importance of employer-assisted child care. Parents and some Senate wives assist in fundraising and support. Parent involvement is mandated according to the by-laws. The center's philosophy states that parents will participate in the ongoing activities of the center and will assist as requested by the director in the operation of the center.

Though sponsored by an employer, the U.S. Senate, the center is a nonprofit corporation, owned and operated by its members, which include all parents of children enrolled in the center or on the waiting list, as well as other interested supporters. Members are represented by a board of directors, elected annually. It is the parent-governed model that makes the difference in both ensuring the quality of the center and bringing parents into involvement in such a way that a sense of community and shared enterprise is created.

Sixty children attend the center regularly, including some enrolled for fewer than five days a week. More than twice that number are on the waiting list. Various options for expanding are presently being considered. Children from eighteen months to kindergarten age are divided among four groupings, each with degreed and trained teachers and assistants. A group of ten five through eight-year-olds is added for a summer day-camp program of ten weeks each summer. The center is open from 7:30 A.M. to 6:45 P.M. (6:30 during long Senate recesses), and tuition covers the nine-and-a-half hours of child care daily that are recommended by the community. Fees range from $115.00 to $135.00 per week, with scholarship assistance available. Priority for enrollment is given first to siblings, then to children of Senate employees, then to the House of Representatives and other federal agencies, then to the community at large.

There are visible indications throughout the center of parent participation, cooperation, and sense of community. The entrance foyer opens into a large, central, multi-purpose area complete with several comfortable couches, a loft, and other play equipment. During the relaxed, slow, drop-off time in the morning, parents chat casually with teachers, other children, and parents. There are collections of family photos in the toddler room, a child information sheet for parents to jot down information daily, and a posted narrative of the day for parents to read. There is a home-like feeling as morning snack is prepared in the galley kitchen. (Snacks are served at 9:30 A.M., 3:30 P.M., and 5:50 P.M. for those children whose dinners will be late because of parents' working hours. A catered lunch arrives at 11:30. All foods are wholesome and are served family-style. Children and staff enjoy the social experience of eating together.)

There is a separate parent room with mailboxes for each family and staff member, a parent lending library, bulletin board, payment box, as well as the posted lists of volunteer jobs to be filled and the recording system for keeping track of parent participation. Besides a comfortable sense of community, there are specific obligations for each parent whose child is enrolled in the program. These are clearly enunciated in a variety of documents, including a twenty-eight page parent handbook that details every aspect of center operation and parents' corresponding obligations, from birthday parties (no chocolate, please) to health policies and late pick-up policies (very substantial fines), from parent-staff communication methods (many) to policies on bottles and pacifiers (discouraged in toddler classroom, though allowed if parent feels it important during the initial period; not permitted in the three older classrooms). The carefully stated policies give clear, developmentally based reasons and encourage discussion with the director and teachers if parents find individual problems with any policy. Policies are strictly enforced.

Parents wanting to learn about the center may take one of the scheduled bi-weekly tours and participate in a parent seminar. When called from the waiting list and accepted for enrollment, the director provides an in-depth orientation discussing the details of the parent handbook policies and the "Agreement for Child Care" contract that parents enter into with the cooperative. Parents agree in writing to certain conditions that include the child's schedule and tuition rates, acceptance of the operating policies of the center, and support of the program.

One of the conditions requires a commitment from the parents to provide three hours of volunteer time to the center each month (one-and-a-half hours for single parents). This time can be spent in many kinds of volunteer tasks from supervising nap time (needed daily, one hour credit), shopping (needed bi-weekly, two hours credit), taking home laundry (bi-weekly, two hours), typing and distributing snack and lunch menus (monthly, one hour), washing chairs and toys (weekly, time spent), or tallying sign-in and sign-out times up to the nine-and-a-half hours allowed each day (monthly, actual time.) A variety of tasks are needed on an irregular basis: field trip and party helpers, book repair, cooperative child care provided to other families during days the center is closed for snow or staff development (three hours for each child cared for), making flannel board stories or table games. Parents are also awarded the monthly quota of volunteer hours for serving on the board, as a member of the executive or chair of one of the committees (Budget, Fundraising, Personnel/Policies, Program Development, or Scholarship), or for serving as room representative, parent volunteer coordinator, or newsletter editor. Each parent must also participate in one of the three Saturday clean-ups held each year.

As the list indicates, parents are involved in most aspects of center management, thus freeing staff to concentrate on program quality. This also holds costs down. Parent volunteers perform many of the tasks that the director might undertake in other centers. The volunteer coordinator contacts those families who fall behind more than six hours in their obligation to the center, and works out the plan for correcting the situation. (If families are still six hours behind the next month, a second notice is sent, explaining that if hours are not completed they will be asked to remove their child from the center. If the situation is unchanged the next month, a third notice is given by the Board, stating that the child must leave the center within two weeks, and $10.00 for each hour in arrears is deducted from their escrow account.) A parent volunteer functions as a welcomer, calling all new parents prior to their child's entry. Parents have written the descriptions of all volunteer tasks and monitor their completion. Parents write the monthly news column that describes topics being studied, events, and favorite songs and books of each classroom that month.

Work-site child care does diminish anxiety, increase productivity, and reduce absenteeism of the parent employee. One of the advantages to having an employer-sponsored center so close to the parents' work site is that parents are able to stop by. This is, of course, very reassuring to parents in case of emergency, and also permits ready access for birthday parties or participation in other classroom special events. One newsletter described parents dropping in for a summer ice cream party in the afternoon. The handbook describes it as an open door policy, inviting parents to visit whenever they can: "Parents may come to read a story or tuck a child in for nap time, to take the child out to lunch, to share in a special activity set up by the center, or for other reasons."

A variety of methods of parent-teacher communication are used. Parents may telephone teachers between 1:00 and 3:00 P.M., or leave a message at other times. They may leave notes in mailboxes, use the notice boards in each classroom, or talk with teachers as they come and go. Formal conferences are scheduled twice a year during the parents' working hours for easy access.

Parent education is another aspect of the cooperative. There is a parent library in the parent room with books available for check-out. Monthly brown-bag lunches are held in a room in the Senate office building for parents of each age-group. The individual classroom teacher is responsible for the agenda of the informal discussion, which will include a discussion of the past month's activities, the coming month's curriculum, and a discussion of an appropriate article discussing particular developmental aspects, as well as lots of time for parents just to talk. One of the benefits of the lunch with parents, teacher, and director is that it gives parents a chance to get a whole different look at the teacher's capabilities and have the input of the director. This particular model works well with a seasoned director who is the facilitator of a link between parents, teachers, children and the agency. The director has the full responsibility of the educational component and the day-to-day operation and is skilled in human development, early childhood education, and administration.

Several social events are held each year. A family day tea party is part of the celebration of the Week of the Young Child each spring. A community party is held in December in one of the Senate hearing rooms. The parents are totally in charge of this pot-luck dinner, held primarily to honor staff. Entertainment includes skits, sayings, and limericks derived from each classroom. An annual anniversary party is held to commemorate the hard work of those who helped to get the center established.

What does this model of a parent-governed program with cooperative involvement bring to the parents, children, and teachers at the center? For parents, there is the opportunity to be concretely involved in the lives of their young children at school, even though they are busy with their own work. By collaborating and sharing responsibility with staff, they are making a real contribution to the quality of child care their own children receive. Teachers are able to concentrate their efforts on the children and curriculum and have ready access to concerned, interested parents. Through collaboration and trust, a feeling of community is created, benefiting everyone.

❖ Auraria Campus Child Care Center, Denver, Colorado

The Auraria Campus Child Care Center near downtown Denver is a department of the Auraria Student Services Division, which offers high-quality child care to meet the needs of students, staff, and faculty of the Auraria campus. (The Auraria campus is itself unusual in combining three institutions of higher learning on one campus: the two-year Community College of Denver, the four-year Metropolitan State College, and the University of Colorado, which includes both undergraduate and graduate schools.) Embedded in the Center's philosophy is the concept of not just providing child care, but of serving families, of being a piece of the picture that helps families work out what they need. Parents may choose from a variety of options of full day, half-day, or hourly care at the center, which is

Figure 18-12 Parents accompanied by their children make an extensive orientation visit to the center.

open from 7 A.M. to 8:30 P.M. for children from toddlers through kindergarten. There is a long waiting list for the center, which charges below Denver market rates, but it is a "real" waiting list comprised of parents who have already made an extensive orientation visit to the center, usually accompanied by their child. (See Figure 18-12.)

During the visit, lasting one to two hours, parents meet with the director to chat about what the program entails for children and parents. They are given a detailed parent handbook and enrollment forms, and tour the center, spending time in the prospective classroom for the child. (For preschoolers, this may involve looking at both classrooms, to make a choice.) Parents and children may stay and play in the room. The center is a casual, friendly place. Everyone is on a first name basis—teachers, parents, and children. Teachers and parents talk together generally on a personal level; the conversation is quite likely to be about how the morning's biology test went. Parents are recognized as unique individuals with other aspects of their life in addition to being the parent of this child.

Daily conversations are supplemented by a variety of written forms of communication. Each parent has a "parent pocket" hanging outside their child's classroom for teachers to leave articles and personal notes. (See Figure 18-13.) Inside the classroom there is a parent information area, which includes a sign-in sheet, the current lesson plan, lists of parent names, and a notebook for parents to jot brief, nonprivate messages that will be helpful for the teacher: "Grandma is in town this week, so she may be picking up": "I'll be traveling this week". (See Figure 18-14.)

Supervising teachers are free from 1–3 P.M. each day outside the classroom for phone calls, writing notes, private conversations. Each month the

Figure 18-13 Every parent has a pocket for teachers to leave personal communication and articles.

Figure 18-14 An available notebook for parents to jot messages allows teachers to keep up with individual family needs.

teachers write reports on each developmental area, about one and one-half pages for each child. These are helpful to have in the child's cumulative file, and are also used in parent conferences.

Classroom newsletters keep parents up to date with current events. A center newsletter is a much larger, typeset creation that helps parents hear the "bigger picture"; it includes articles on issues of quality care, community events and concerns, book reviews, and so on. Parents often write guest articles and commentary for this newsletter, as it is part of the center's philosophy that it is important to expand parent-to-parent communication and friendship, along with the attitude that professional staff are not the only experts.

The center recognizes that student parents have put together a patchwork of financial, emotional, and time resources to be able to make it, and that the center's role is to help and support with the aspect involving the children. The center offers parents places to sit, to relax, to study, to make phone calls. Parents who are on campus with pockets of time may be taking a nap on the couch in the workroom that parents and staff share (see Figure 18-15), chatting with a staff member in the conference room or the office support person whose desk is in the main hall, or reading a magazine or textbook in the library. (Parents may borrow books or videotapes on child rearing from the library.) They may also be volunteering in the classroom, reading to children, or throwing a ball on the playground. When they want to get involved, as a cook, carpenter, or pretzel maker, they do, as they have time. The director says it's all a matter of setting up the environment so that parents feel welcomed and that their talents are valued and genuinely appreciated. There is a true open door policy. Parents are encouraged to spend time daily; they are there for lunch "all the time."

Parents take things home from the center to do also—trucks that need fixing, books to be repaired. They also bring things from work—a lot are working and going to school at the same time. Field trips at the center often involve making trips to other parts of the campus, to enjoy facilities of the art, music, biology, or physical education departments so the children can experience their parents' lives away from them.

Formal conferences are held three times a year. Supervising teachers have two days out of the classroom to schedule conferences at times that fit

Figure 18-15 Parents and teachers share the staff room, so that parents may use it for rest or reading before picking up their children.

parents' schedules—"evening, what about next week then? Yes, you may bring your child."

All parents are voting members of the parent advisory board. The elected executive committee advises the director on center issues and assesses the program. The board constitutes a separate financial entity, and raises money through bake and candy sales to give room gifts, which may be used for things like a petty cash fund or tickets for a play. The parents also give a staff appreciation banquet, complete with flowers and gifts for staff.

The parent advisory board acts as a liaison to gather parent meeting ideas. Meetings (held monthly in the evenings in college facilities with child care provided) respond to parent needs for support and education in areas the parents designate in surveys. About half the meetings are for the sole purpose of parent support and friendship.

Parents who become comfortable with each other and with the staff and who are learning more about their children's needs begin to share advocacy roles with the staff, becoming involved and committed to doing things that will help the children. The parent advisory board has gone to the college administration to lobby for more staff money, and to the transportation department in Denver to get involved with the planning of a light rail system that could threaten the center's playground. One prime example of parent support and advocacy was the staffing of the center for two workdays to release teachers to attend the national conference when NAEYC met in Denver. (See Figure 18-16.)

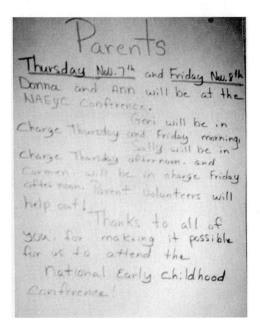

Figure 18-16 Parents support teacher development by staffing the center so teachers can attend a professional conference.

Figure 18-17 When parents feel comfortable in the center, their children do as well

Parents also become involved in the staff hiring process. The director helps write the criteria and job description, then appoints a search committee of seven or eight, usually including two teachers and the rest parents, representing as much diversity of gender and ethnicity as possible. The committee selects the most promising candidates from the applicants, and selects three or four for the final interviews by the director. Time consuming as the process is, parents involved in the search understand more about the program and have more invested in the success of the employee and the whole center.

Busy parents, supported at their own developmental stage of parenting and personal growth, work together with the staff at Auraria Campus Child Care Center to create a marvelous program for their children and themselves. (See Figure 18-17.)

❖ Summary

From these accounts of four different programs, it is evident that there is more than one method of working with parents. The common thread is the philosophy that parents deserve support and respect as they undertake the massive and vital tasks of parenting, and that teachers can work most effectively with children when they work closely with parents. Each center has worked to find the particular methods that best suit their program, with its specific goals, needs, and perception of the needs of the families served. There are some things that work well; in general, methods of working to ensure the fullest communication possible are important. The challenge is always there as teachers and centers continue to reach out to the families they serve.

❖ Student Activities for Further Study

1. Visit a local child-care center and/or preschool half-day program. Arrange to interview the director, a teacher, and a parent about their perceptions of how the parent-teacher relationship has been developed and how each participant feels about the degree of communication established. Learn what methods of communication exist and how parents become involved in the program. How do your findings compare with the descriptions of the four programs in the chapter?

2. Draw up a chart, with a column for each of the four programs described. Summarize the information given in the descriptions, under: Philosophy of Working with Parents; Orientation Procedures; Communication Methods; Parent Involvement in the Program; Parents as Decision Makers. What similarities do you discover? What differences?

3. Draw up a similar chart for the center where you are involved as a student, or where you work, and for the center you visited in Question 1. What similarities do you find with the chart of the four programs from the chapter? What differences?

❖ Review Questions

1. Using the chart you drew up in Question 2 above, compare and contrast the four programs regarding the ways each involves parents in the programs and in relationships with classroom teachers.

2. List those components and philosophies the four programs have in common.

❖ Suggestions for Further Reading

Note: Due to the nature of this chapter, the information was gained firsthand by interview or by reading the hand-outs from each center. Students may be interested in reading descriptions of several other types of programs, including the ways they involve parents. Such descriptions may be found in:

Driscoll, A. (1995). *Cases in early childhood education: stories of programs and practices.* Needham Heights, MA: Allyn and Bacon.

Appendix

❖ Resource Directory

Active Parenting
Active Parenting, Inc.
4669 Rosewll Road, N.E.
Atlanta, GA 30342

Advocates for Children's Issues
The Children's Defense Fund
122 C St., N.W.
Washington, DC 20001

Community Linkages
Child Care Resources, Inc.
700 Kenilworth Ave.
Charlotte, NC 28204

Community Programs
Family Resource Coalition
Dept. P, Suite 1625
230 N. Michigan Ave.
Chicago, IL 60601

For and About Fathers
The Fatherhood Project
610 West 112th St.
New York, NY 10025

For Parents to Have a National Voice
Parent Action
230 N. Michigan Ave.
Suite 1625
Chicago, IL 60601

Learning Accomplishment Profile
Chapel Hill Training-Outreach Program
Daniels Bldg.
University of North Carolina at Chapel Hill
Chapel Hill, NC 27514

Minnesota Inventories
Behavior Science Systems
P.O. Box 1108
Minneapolis, MN 55440

Professional Organization for the Early
Childhood Field
NAEYC
1834 Connecticut Ave., N.W.
Washington, DC 20009

Single Parent Organization
Parents Without Partners
7910 Woodmont Ave.
Suite 1000
Washington, DC 20014

Stepfamilies
Stepfamily Association of America
3001 Porter St., N.W.
Washington, DC 20008

Support Group for Parents at Risk of Abuse
Parents Anonymous
2810 Artessia Blvd.
Suite F
Redondo Beach, CA 90278

Work and Family Relations
Work and Family Information Center
The Conference Board
845 Third Ave.
New York, NY 10022

References

Chapter 1

Bigner, J.J. (1993). *Parent-child relations: an introduction to parenting.* 4th ed. New York: Macmillan Publishing Co.

Brazelton, T.B. (1989). *Families: crisis and caring.* Reading, MA: Addison-Wesley Publishing Co. Inc.

Bronfenbrenner, U. (1974). The roots of alienation. In N.B. Talbot (Ed.), *Raising children in modern America: problems and prospective solutions.* Boston: Little, Brown and Co.

___. (1991, March 29). Rush-hour children: an interview with Urie Bronfenbrenner. *Charlotte Observer.*

Coontz, S. (1992). *The way we never were: American families and the nostalgia trap.* New York: Basic Books.

Elkind, D. (1994). *Ties that stress: the new family imbalance.* Cambridge, MA: Harvard University Press.

Halpern, R. (1987, Sept.). Major social and demographic trends affecting young families: implications for early childhood care and education. *Young Children, 42*(6), 34–40.

Hewlett, S.A. (1991). *When the bough breaks: the cost of neglecting our children.* New York: Harper Collins Publishers.

Hochschild, A. (1989). *The second shift: working parents and the revolution at home.* New York: Viking.

Leach, P. (1994). *Children first: what our society must do—and is not doing—for our children today.* New York: Alfred A. Knopf.

LeMasters, E.E., and DeFrain, J. (1983). *Parents in contemporary America: a sympathetic view.* 4th ed. Homewood, IL: The Dorsey Press.

Levitan, S.A., Belous, R.S., and Gallo, F. (1988). *What's happening to the American family? tensions, hopes, realities.* rev. ed. Baltimore: The Johns Hopkins University Press.

(1994). *Profiling Canada's families.* Ottawa, Ontario: The Vanier Institute of the Family.

Roberts, S. (1993). *Who we are: a portrait of America based on the latest U.S. census.* New York: Random House.

Rover, D., and Polifroni, F. (1985). *The "Leave It to Beaver" syndrome.* Presentation at NAEYC National Conference, New Orleans.

(1990, Winter). The twenty-first century family. *Newsweek Special Edition.*

Whitehead, B.D. (1993, April). "Dan Quayle was right. *The Atlantic Monthly, 271*(4), 47–84.

Chapter 2

Balaban, N. (1990, Mar.). Statement to the Montgomery County Council. *Young Children, 45*(3), 12–16.

Bettelheim, B. (1987). *A good enough parent: a book on child-rearing.* New York: Alfred A. Knopf.

Bigner, J.J. (1993). *Parent-child relations: an introduction to parenting.* 4th ed. New York: Macmillan Co.

Brazelton, T.B. Working parents. *Newsweek,* 66–70.

Bredekamp, S. (Ed.) (1987). *Developmentally appropriate practice in early childhood programs serving children from birth through age 8.* Washington, D.C.: NAEYC.

Bredekamp, S., and Shepard, L. (1989, March). How best to protect children from inappropriate school expectations, practices, and policies. *Young Children, 44*(3), 14–24.

Burr, W. (1970). Satisfaction with various aspects of marriage over the family life cycle. *Journal of Marriage and the Family, 32,* 29–37.

Charlesworth, R. (1989, March). "Behind" before they start? deciding how to deal with the risk of kindergarten failure. *Young Children, 44*(3), 5–13.

Elkind, D. (1970, April 5). Erik Erikson's eight ages of man. *New York Times Magazine,* 15-22

—. (1987). *Miseducation: preschoolers at risk.* New York: Alfred A. Knopf, Inc.

Galinsky, E. (1986). How do child care and maternal employment affect children? *Child Care Information Exchange, 48,* 19–23,

___. (1987). *The six stages of parenthood.* Reading, MA: Addison-Wesley Publishing Co. Inc.

Gonzalez-Mena, J. (1993). *The child in the family and the community.* New York: Macmillan Publishing Company.

Gottfried, A.E. and A.W. (Eds.). (1988). *Maternal employment and children's development.* New York: Plenum Press.

Harrison, B. (1986). *The shock of motherhood.* New York: Charles Scribner's Sons.

Hochschild, A. (1989). *The second shift: working parents and the revolution at home.* New York: Viking.

Hoffman, L.W. and M.L. (1973). The value of children to parents. In J.T. Fawcett (Ed.), *Psychological perspectives on population.* New York: Basic Books.

Kamerman, S.B. (1980). *Parenting in an unresponsive society: managing work and family life.* New York: The Free Press.

Karen, R. (1990, Feb.). Becoming attached. *The Atlantic Monthly,* 35–70.

LeMasters, E.E., and DeFrain, J. (1983). *Parents in contemporary America: a sympathetic view.* 4th ed. Homewood, IL: The Dorsey Press.

Loux, R. (1993). *Father love: what we need, what we seek, what we must create.* New York: Pocket Books.

Rollins, B., and Cannon, K. (1974). Marital satisfaction over the family life cycle: a reevaluation. *Journal of Marriage and the Family, 36,* 271–281.

Rossi, A. (1968). Transition to parenthood. *Journal of Marriage and the Family, 30,* 26–39.

Russell, C. (1974). Transition to parenthood: problems and gratifications. *Journal of Marriage and the Family, 36,* 294–302.

(1988). *Testing of young children: concerns and cautions.* Washington, D.C.: NAEYC.

Chapter 3

Burgess, R. (1993, March). African American children. *Child Care Information Exchange,* 35–38.

Gonzalez-Mena, J. (1992). *Multicultural issues in child care.* Mountain View, CA: Mayfield Publishing Co.

Chapter 4

(1983). *As the twig is bent: lasting effects of preschool programs.* The Consortium for Longitudinal Studies. Hillsdale, NJ: Lawrence Erlbaum Assoc. Publ.

Bronfenbrenner, U. (1976). *Is early intervention effective? A report on longitudinal evaluations of preschool programs.* (U.S. Dept. of Health, Education and Welfare, Office of Child Development.) Washington, D.C.: U.S. Govt. Printing Office.

(1991). *Caring communities: supporting young children and their families.* The Report of the National Task Force on School Readiness. Alexandria, VA: National Association of State Boards of Education.

Cicerelli, V., et al. (1969). *The impact of head start. An evaluation of the effects of Head Start on children's cognitive and affective development.* Westinghouse Learning Corporation and Ohio University. Washington, D.C.: Government Printing Office.

Collins, R.C., and Deloria, D. (1983). Head Start research: a new chapter. *Children Today, 12*(4), 15–20.

(1984). *Head Start policy manual.* Washington, D.C.: U.S. Dept. of HHS.

Hess, R.D. et al. (1971). Parent involvement. In E. Grotberg (Ed.), *Day care: resources for decisions.* Washington, D.C.: Day Care and Child Development Committee of America.

Lazar, and Darlington. (1979). Consortium for Longitudinal Studies. *Lasting effects after preschool: summary report.* Washington, D.C.: U.S. Dept. of Health, Education and Welfare.

Mann, A.J., Harrell, A.V., and Hunt, M.J. A review of Head Start research since 1969. *Found: long-term gains from early intervention.* Ed. B. Brown. Boulder, CO: Westview Press.

Midco. (1972). *Perspectives on parent participation in Head Start: an analysis and critique.* Washington, D.C.: Project Head Start.

NAEYC. (1984). *Accreditation criteria and procedures of the national academy of early childhood programs.* Washington, D.C.: NAEYC.

NAEYC. (1989). *Code of ethical conduct. Young Children, 45*(1), 25–29.

NASBE. (1988). *Right from the start: the report of the NASBE task force on early childhood education.* Alexandria, VA: NASBE.

Pettygrove, W.B., and Greenman, J.T. (1984). The adult world of day care. In J.T. Greenman and R.W. Fuqua (Eds.), *Making day care better: training, evaluation and the process of change.* New York: Teachers College Press.

Powell, D.R. (1989). *Families and early childhood programs.* Washington, D.C.: NAEYC.

Schweinhart, L.J., and Weikart, D.P. (1986). What do we know so far? A review of the Head Start synthesis project. *Young Children, 41*(2), 49–55.

___. (1993, Summer) Changed lives, significant benefits: the High/Scope Perry preschool project to date. *High/Scope Resource, 12*(30), 1, 10–14.

Chapter 5

Belsky, J., Steinberg, L., and Walker, A. (1982). The ecology of day care. In M.Lamb (Ed.), *Non-traditional families: parenting and child development.* Hillsdale, NJ: Lawrence Erlbaum Assoc. Pubs.

Galinsky, E., and Hooks, W. (1977). *The new extended family: day care that works.* Boston: Houghton Mifflin Co.

Honig, A.S. (1982). Parent involvement in early childhood education. In B. Spodek (Ed.), *Handbook of Research in Early Childhood Education.* New York: Free Press.

Hymes, J.L. (1975). *Effective home school relations.* rev. ed. Carmel, CA: Hacienda Press.

Powell, D.R. (1989). *Families and early childhood programs.* Washington, D.C.: NAEYC.

Preece, A., and Cowden, D. (1993). *Young writers in the making: sharing the process with parents.* Portsmouth, NH: Heinemann.

Chapter 6

Chilman, C.S. (1974). Some angles on parent-teacher learning. *Childhood Education, 51*(12), 119–125.

Galinsky, E. (1986). How do child care and maternal employment affect children? *Child Care Information Exchange, 48,* 19–23.

Hymes, J. (1974). *Effective home-school relations.* Sierra Madre: Southern California Assoc. for the Education of Young Children.

Katz, L. (1980). Mothering and teaching—some significant distinctions. In L. Katz (Ed.) *Current topics in early childhood education, 3.* Norwood, NJ: Ablex Publishing Corp.

Kontos, S., and Wells, W. (1986). Attitudes of caregivers and the day care experiences of families. *Early Childhood Research Quarterly, 1,* 47–67.

Lightfoot, S.L. (1978). *World apart: relationships between families and schools.* New York: Basic Books Inc.

Lombana, J.H. (1983). *Home-school partnerships: guidelines and strategies for educators.* New York: Greene and Stratton.

Platt, E.B. (1991). *Scenes from day care: how teachers teach and what children learn.* New York: Teachers College Press.

Swap, S. M. (1993). *Developing home-school partnerships: from concepts to practice.* New York: Teachers College Press.

Tizard, B., Mortimer, J., and Burchell, B. (1981). *Involving parents in nursery and infant schools.* Ypsilanti, MI: The High/Scope Press.

Yankelovich, Skelly, White, Inc. (1977). *Raising children in a changing society: the General Mills American family report.* Minneapolis, MN: General Mills.

Chapter 7

Canter, L. (1989, January). How to speak so parents will listen. *Teaching K-8,* 34–36.

Flake-Hobson, C. and Swick, K.J. (1979). Communication strategies for parents and teachers or how to say what you mean. *Dimensions, 7*(4), 112–115.

Fredericks, A.D. (1989, March). Step out to draw them in. *Teaching K-8,* 22–24.

Herin, L.R. and R.E. (1978). *Developing skills for human interaction.* 2nd. ed. Columbus, OH: Charles E. Merrill Publishing Co.

Jersild, A.T. (1955). *When teachers face themselves.* New York: Bureau of Publications, Teachers College, Columbia University.

Knapp, M.L. (1980). *Essentials of nonverbal communication.* New York: Holt, Rinehart and Winston.

McCroskey, J.C., Larson, C.E. and Knapp, M.L. (1971). *An introduction to interpersonal communication.* Englewood Cliffs, NJ: Prentice-Hall, Inc.

Mehrabian, A. (1981). *Silent messages: implicit communication of emotions and attitudes.* 2nd. ed. Belmont, CA: Wadsworth Publishing Co.

Meservey, L.D. (1989, June). Handle with care: strategies for retraining children in your program. *Child Care Information Exchange,* 21–24.

Chapter 8

Balaban, N. (1985). *Starting school: from separation to independence (a guide for early childhood teachers).* New York: Teachers College Press.

___. (1985). The name of the game is confidence: how to help kids recoup from separation anxiety. *Instructor, 95*(2), 108–112,

Hoyt, M. and Schoonmaker, M.E. (1991, Oct. 15). The day-care delusion: when parents accept the unacceptable. *Family Circle,* 81–87.

Jervis, K. (Ed.) (1987). *Separation: strategies for helping two to four year olds.* Washington, D.C.: NAEYC.

Johnston and Mermin, J. (1994, July). Easing children's entry to school: home visits help. *Young Children, 49*(5), 62–68.

Powell, D.R. (1989). *Families and early childhood programs.* Washington, D.C.: NAEYC.

Townsend-Butterworth, D. (1992). *Your child's first school: a handbook for parents.* New York: Walker and Co.

Chapter 9

Berger, E.H. (1991). *Parents as partners in education.* 3rd ed. St. Louis: C.V. Mosby Co.

Brock, D.R. and Dodd, E.L. (1994, March). A family lending library: promoting early literacy development. *Young Children, 49*(3), 16–21.

Doherty-Derkowski, G. (1995). *Quality Matters: excellence in early childhood programs.* Reading, MA: Addison-Wesley Publishers Limited.

Greenwood, D. (1995, Sept.). Home-school communication via video. *Young Children, 50*(6), 66.

Harms, T. and Cryer, D. (1978). Parent newsletters: a new format. *Young Children, 33*(5), 28–32.

Hymes, J. (n.d.) *Notes for parents.* Carmel, CA: Hacienda Press.

Jordan, S. (1995) Families are reading meaningful stories program, personal communication.

Manning, M., Manning, G., Morrison, G. (1995, Sept.). Letter-writing connections: a teacher, first-graders, and their parents. *Young Children, 50(6),* 34–38.

Powell, D.R. (1978). Personal relationship between parents and caregivers in day care settings. *American Journal of Orthopsychiatry, 48(4),* 680–689.

___. (1989). *Families and early childhood programs.* Washington, D.C.: NAEYC.

Parent and preschooler newsletter, from Preschool Publications, Inc., P.O. Box 1851, Garden City, NY 11530-0816.

Swap, S. (1987). *Enhancing parent involvement in schools.* New York: Teachers College Press.

Tizard, B., Mortimer, J., and Burchell, B. (1981). *Involving parents in nursery and infant schools.* Ypsilanti, MI: The High-Scope Press.

Transparent School (Registered Trademark) was developed by Dr. Jerold P. Bauch in 1987. For further information, contact Jerold P. Bauch, Director, The Betty Phillips Center for Parenthood Education, Box 81, Peabody College of Vanderbilt University, Nashville, TN 37203.

Chapter 10

Briggs, D.C. (1975). *Your child's self esteem.* Garden City, NY: Doubleday and Co.

Bjorklund, G. and Burger, C. (1987). Making conferences work for parents, teachers and children. *Young Children, 42(2),* 26–31.

Freeman, J. (1986). Customizing your parent conferences for better results. *Learning, 14(6),* 70–74.

Gordon, T. (1975). *Parent effectiveness training.* New York: Wyden.

Johns, N. and Harvey, C. (1987, Nov.). Engaging parents in solving problems: a strategy for enhancing self-esteem. *Child Care Information Exchange,* (58), 25–28.

Readdick, C.A.,Golbeck, S., Klein, E., and Cartwright, C. (1984). The child-parent-teacher conference. *Young Children, 39(5)* 67–73.

Southern Association on Children Under Six (SACUS). (1991). The portfolio and its use: developmentally appropriate assessment of young children. Little Rock, AR: SACUS.

Chapter 11

Bromberg, S. (1968). A beginning teacher works with parents. *Young Children, 24(2),* 75–80.

Fox-Barnett, M., and Meyer, T. (1992, July). The teacher's playing at my house this week! *Young Children, 47(5),* 45–50.

Gordon, J.J., and Breivogel, W.F. (Eds.) (1976). *Building effective home-school relationships.* Boston: Allyn and Bacon.

Gray, S.W. et al. (1983). The early training project 1962–80 in Consortium for Longitudinal Studies. *As the twig is bent: lasting effects of pre-school programs.* Hillsdale, NJ: Erlbaum.

Hillman, C. (1989) Teaching Four-Year-Olds. Bloomington, IN: Phi Delta Kappan.

Lambie, D.Z., Bond, J.T., and Weikart, D. (1980). *Home teaching with mothers and infants.* Ypsilanti, MI: High/Scope Educational Research Foundation.

Levenstein, P. (1971). The mother child home program. In M.C. Day and R. Parker (Eds.) *Preschool in action: explaining early childhood programs.* Boston: Allyn and Bacon.

Powell, D.R. (1990, Sept.) Home visiting in the early years: policy and program design decisions. *Young Children, 45(6),* 65–73.

Sheaver, D., et al. (1976). *Portage guide to early education.* Portage, WI: Cooperative Educational Service, Agency 12.

U.S. Dept. of Health, Education and Welfare. (Office of Child Development) (1974). *A guide for planning and operating home-based child development programs.* Washington, D.C.: U.S. Govt. Printing Office

U.S. Dept. of Health, Education and Welfare. (1976). *Home start and other programs for parents and children.* Washington, D.C.: U.S. Govt. Printing Office.

Chapter 12

Hopkins, P. (1977). Every father should be a nursery school mother at least once in his life. *Young Children, 32(3),* 14–16.

Horowitz, J., and Faggella, K. (1986). *Partners for learning.* Bridgeport, CT: First Teacher Press.

Knowler, K.A. (1988, Nov.) Orienting parents and volunteers to the classroom. *Young Children, 44(1),* 9.

Chapter 13

Auerbach, A.B. (1968). *Parents learn through discussion: principles and practices of parent group education.* New York: John Wiley and Sons, Inc.

Bauch, J.P. et al. (1973). Parent participation: what makes the difference? *Childhood Education, 50,* 47–53.

Dinkmeyer, D., and McKay, G. (1982). *The parents handbook: STEP.* Circle Pines, MN: American Guidance Service.

Florin, P.R., and Dokecki, P.R. (1983). Changing families through parent and family education. In I.E. Sigel and L.M. Laosa (Eds.), *Changing families.* New York: Plenum Books.

Gordon, I.J., and Breivogel, W. (Eds.) (1976). *Building effective home-school relationships.* Boston: Allyn and Bacon.

Gordon, T. (1975). *Parent effectiveness training.* New York: Wyden.

Luethy, G. (1991, May). An example of parent education at the work site. *Young Children, 46*(4), 62–63.

Powell, D.R. (1983). Individual differences in participation in a parent-child support program. In I.E. Sigel and L.M. Laosa (Eds.), *Changing families.* New York: Plenum Press.

___. (1986). Parent education and support programs. *Young Children, 41*(3), 47–52.

___. (1989). *Families and early childhood programs.* Washington, D.C.: NAEYC.

Rose, B. (1990, Winter). Early childhood family education. *Day Care and Early Education, 27–29.*

Sutherland, K. (1983). Parents beliefs about child socialization: a study of parenting models. In I.E. Sigel and L.M. Laosa (Eds.), *Changing families.* New York: Plenum Press.

Swick, K. (1985). Critical issues in parent education. *Dimensions, 14*(1), 4–7.

Tizard, B., Mortimer, J., and Burchell, B. (1981). *Involving parents in nursery and infant schools.* Ypsilanti, MI: The High/Scope Press.

Wilson, G.B. (1993). *Activities for parent groups.* Rev. Ed. Atlanta, GA: Humanics, Ltd.

Chapter 14

Blank, H. (1989, May). Child care and welfare reform: new opportunities for families. *Young Children, 44*(4), 28–30.

Coleman, J.S. (1987). Families and schools. *Educational Researcher, 16,* 32–38.

Dresden, J. and Myers, B.K. (1989, Jan.) Early childhood professionals: towards self-definition. *Young Children, 44*(2), 62–66.

Feeney, S., and Kipnis, K. (1989, Nov.) NAEYC code of ethical conduct and statement of commitment. *Young Children, 45*(1), 24–29.

Kagan, S.L. (1989, May). Dealing with our ambivalence about advocacy. *Child Care Information Exchange,* (61), 31–34.

Marx, E. and Granger, R.C. (1990, May). Analysis of salary enhancement efforts in New York. *Young Children, 45*(4), 53–59.

Taharally, L.C., and Smith, A.L. (1990, Winter). Building intergenerational bridges in early childhood. *Day Care and Early Education, 30–33.*

Washington, V., Johnson, V., and McCracken, J.B. (1995). *Grassroots success! Preparing schools and families for each other.* Washington, D.C.: NAEYC.

Chapter 15

Brislin, R.W. (1993). *Understanding culture's influence on behavior.* New York: Harcourt Brace College Publisher.

Brown, D.H. (1991). *Breaking the language barrier.* Yarmouth, ME: Intercultural Press.

Derman-Sparks, L. (1989). *Anti-bias curriculum: tools for empowering young children.* Washington, D.C.: NAEYC.

Dodd, C.H. (1991). *Dynamics of intercultural communication.* 3rd. ed. Dubuque, IA: Wm. C. Brown Publishers.

Gonzalez-Mena, J. (1992). *Multicultural issues in child care.* Mountain View, CA: Mayfield Publishing Co.

___. (1992, Jan.). Taking a culturally sensitive approach in infant-toddler programs. *Young Children, 47*(2), 4–9.

Jones, E., and Derman-Sparks, L. (1992, Jan.). Meeting the challenge of diversity. *Young Children, 47*(2), 12–18.

Neugebauer, B. (1990, August). Going one step further—no traditional holidays. *Child Care Information Exchange, 42.*

Phillips, C.B. (1988, Jan.). Nurturing diversity for today's children and tomorrow's leaders. *Young Children, 43*(2), 42–47.

Rosegrant, T. (1992). Reaching potentials in a multilingual classroom: opportunities and challenges. In *Reaching potentials: appropriate curriculum and assessment for young children, 1.* Washington, D.C.: NAEYC.

Samovar, L.A., and Porter, R.E. (Eds.) (1994). *Intercultural communication: a reader.* 7th ed. Belmont, CA: Wadsworth.

Wolfe, L. (1992). Reaching potentials through bilingual education. In *Reaching potentials: appropriate curriculum and assessment for young children, 1.* Washington, D.C.: NAEYC.

Chapter 16
On Divorce and Remarriage

Barney, J. (1990, Oct.). *Stepfamilies: second chance or second-rate? Phi Delta Kappan,* 144–147.

Camara, K. (1988). Family adaptation to divorce. In M.W. Yogman and T.B. Brazelton (Eds.), *Support of families.* Cambridge, MA: Harvard University Press.

Clarke-Stewart, A. (1989, Jan.). Single-parent families: how bad for the children? *NEA Today*, 60–64.

Coleman, M., Ganong, L.H., and Henry, J. (1984). What teachers should know about stepfamilies. *Childhood Education, 60*(5), 306–309.

Visher, E.B., and Visher, J.S. (1979). *Stepfamilies: a guide to working with stepparents and stepchildren.* New York: Banner/Mizel.

Wallerstein, J.S., and Blakeslee, S. (1989). *Second chances: men, women, and children: a decade after divorce.* New York: Ticknor and Fields.

On Parents of Children with Special Needs

Gallagher, J.J. (1989, Oct.). The impact of policies for handicapped children on future early education policy. *Phi Delta Kappan*, 121–124.

Gargiulo, R.M., and Graves, S.B. (1991, Spring). Parental feelings: the forgotten component when working with parents of handicapped preschool children. *Childhood Education*, 176–178.

Kupfer, F. (1984). Severely and/or multiply disabled children. *Equals in this partnership: parents of disabled and at-risk infants and toddlers speak to professionals.* Washington, D.C.: National Center for Clinical Infant Programs.

McGonigel, M.J., and Garland, C.W. (1990). The individualized family service plan and the early intervention team: team and family issues and recommended practices. In K.L. Freiberg (Ed.), *Educating exceptional children*, 5th ed. Guilford, CT: The Dushkin Publishing Group.

Working with Parents of Infants

Bowlby, J. (1988). *A secure base: parent-child attachment and healthy human development.* New York: Basic Books.

Brazelton, T. (1992). *On becoming a family: the growth of attachment before and after birth.* New York: Delacorte

Gonzalez-Mena, J. (1992). Taking a culturally sensitive approach in infant-toddler programs. *Young Children, 47*(2), 4–9.

Joffe, S., and Viertel, J. (1984). *Becoming parents: preparing for the emotional changes of first-time parenthood.* New York: Atheneum Books.

Karen, R. (1994). *Becoming attached: unfolding the mystery of the infant-mother bond and its impact on later life.* New York: Warner Books.

Meyerhoff, M. (1994, May). Of baseball and babies: are you unconsciously discouraging father involvement in infant care? *Young Children, 49*(4), 17–19.

Morris, S.L. (1995, Jan.). Supporting the breastfeeding relationship during child care: why is it important? *Young Children, 50*(2), 59–62.

Working with Abusive Parents

Barthel, J. (1991). *For children's sake. The promise of family preservation.* New York: The Edna McConnell Clark Foundation. 1991.

Caughey, C. (1991, May). Becoming the child's ally—observations in a classroom for children who have been abused. *Young Children, 46*(4), 22–28.

Helfer, R. (1975). *The diagnostic process and treatment programs.* U.S. Dept. of Health, Education and Welfare. Washington, D.C.: U.S. Govt. Printing Office.

Pimento, B., and Kernested, D. (1996). *Healthy foundations in child care.* Toronto, Ontario: Nelson Canada.

Tower, C. (1993). *Understanding child abuse and neglect.* 2nd ed. Boston, MA: Allyn and Bacon.

Working with Adoptive Families

Munsch, A.B. (1992, Nov.). Understanding and meeting the needs of adopted children and families. *Child Care Information Exchange*, 47–51.

Chapter 17

Boutte, G.S., Keepler, D.L., Tyler, V.S., and Terry, B.Z. (1992, March). Effective techniques for involving "difficult" parents. *Young Children, 47*(3), 19–22.

Cohen, A. (1993, March). Releasing a child to an adult "under the influence" or a non-custodial adult. *Child Care Information Exchange*, 15–16.

Freeman, E.B. (1990, May). Issues in kindergarten policy and practice. *Young Children, 45*(4), 29–34.

Gordon, T. (1975). *Parent effectiveness training.* New York: Hyden.

Jacobs, G. (1992, Nov.). The search for sick-child care. *Working Mother*, 80–85.

Losen, S.M., and Diament, B. (1978). *Parent conferences in the schools.* Boston: Allyn and Bacon.

Rundall, R.D., and Smith, S.L. (1982). Working with difficult parents. In Brigham Young University Press (Ed.), *How to involve parents in early childhood education.* Provo, UT: Brigham Young University Press.

Index